SAINT AUGUSTINE OF HIPPO

Essays dealing with his Life and Times and some features of his work

By
THE VERY REV.
FATHER HUGH POPE, O.P.
S.T.M., D.S.S.

LONDON
SANDS & CO.
(PUBLISHERS) LIMITED
15 KING ST., COVENT GARDEN, W.C.2

PRINTED IN GREAT BRITAIN
BY THE WHITEFRIARS PRESS LTD.
LONDON AND TONBRIDGE
FOR SANDS & CO. (PUBLISHERS) LTD.
15 KING ST., COVENT GARDEN
LONDON, W.C.2

FIRST PUBLISHED AUGUST, 1937

NIHIL OBSTAT : EDOUARDUS CAN. MAHONEY S.TH.D.
CENSOR DEPUTATUS

IMPRIMATUR : LEONELLUS CAN. EVANS
VIC. GEN.

WESTMONASTERII, DIE 11A MAII 1937

NIHIL OBSTAT : FR. BENEDICTUS O'DRISCOLL, O.P., S.T.L.
RICARDUS KEHOE, O.P., S.T.L., S.SC.LIC.

IMPRIMATUR : FR. BERNARDUS DELANY, B.LITT., O.P.
PRIOR PROVINCIALIS

'O vere sal terrae, quo praecordia nostra ne possint saeculi vanescere errore condiuntur! O lucerna digne supra candelabrum Ecclesiae posita, quae late Catholicis urbibus de septiformi lychno pastum oleo laetitiae lumen effundens, densas licet haereticorum caligines discutis, et lucem veritatis a confusione tenebrarum splendore clarifici sermonis enubilas!'

St. Paulinus to St. Augustine, *Ep.* xxv. i
inter Epp. S. Augustini.

PREFATORY NOTE

The origin of these Essays may serve to explain their somewhat disparate and, we fear, their uneven character. In September of 1930 a series of lectures was delivered in the Cathedral Hall, Westminster, in honour of the great Bishop of Hippo. These dealt with such subjects as St. Augustine's Commentaries on Genesis, by Dom Guiseppe Riciotti, C.R.L., with The Rule of St. Augustine, by Fr. Benedict Zimmerman, O.D.C., The Mystical Theology of St. Augustine, by Fr. Aidan Kenny, A.A., St. Augustine on Peace and War, by Fr. Vincent Scully, and, finally, on the De Civitate Dei, by Fr. Aldhelm Bowring, O.P. But it was felt that a series of more intimate addresses on the Saint's life and works would be appreciated by many who were hardly prepared for the subjects dealt with in the above more formal lectures.

These less formal addresses fell to the lot of the present writer and they are here presented in a less conversational and informal way than was possible under the circumstances of their original delivery.

The sketch maps will enable the reader to discover for himself most of the places mentioned and thus orientate himself when reading of life in Northern Africa.

The Essays have, with the exception of Nos. VII, VIII and IX, already appeared in the *Irish Ecclesiastical Record* and in the *Homiletic Review* published by the Dominican Fathers at Hawthorne, New Jersey, though they have since been considerably augmented. My thanks are due to the Editors of those Reviews for kindly giving me leave to republish them in book form.

FOREWORD

It is most gratifying that Fr. Hugh Pope has made available in book form the essays on St. Augustine which some of us were privileged to hear as lectures, or ' talks,' as he modestly called them, in 1930.

So well received were those addresses that an instant demand was made to have them in a permanent form. Not a few from amongst the audience candidly admitted that the Saint, of whom they thought they had some knowledge, had been revealed to them in a new light. That is not altogether surprising. The vast genius of St. Augustine, the wide range of his intellect, the gigantic force of his character, may well be calculated to convey a certain sense of remoteness as well as of grandeur. The estimate of the Saint as presented by the specialist student might often leave it unsuspected that Augustine can speak to-day as appealingly as he did in his sermons and letters, for example, 1500 years ago. That St. Augustine is revered as one of the noblest Doctors of God's Church, everyone knows. The *Confessions* are recognized as one of the world's great Classics. Most are acquainted with the general outline at least of the life of the son of St. Monica. But that Augustine is also an example for every soul seeking God is perhaps not so readily felt. The very richness and magnificence of the panegyrics of the Saint, the profound studies of him as Philosopher, Theologian and Doctor may at times seem to raise him to a plane beyond the reach of those less versed in higher studies.

Yet it is not perhaps too much to say that the noblest *rôle* to be attributed to him is that of spiritual guide in the common aim of every soul—to the knowledge and love of God. ' Why do I live ? ' he says in one of his sermons, ' unless it be that we may live together with Christ ? This is my desire, my honour, my glory ; this is my joy, this my riches. If I speak, although you do not listen, my own duty is done, but I do not wish to be saved without you.'

Happily there are many who do cherish the spirit of Augustine and train themselves to become, in his own words, 'spiritualis pulchritudinis amatores'—lovers of the Supreme Beauty which had so captivated him. A wider knowledge of our Saint will increase the numbers of those who will benefit by that spiritual guidance. Augustine's first biographer, Possidius, says that a knowledge of his life is even more edifying than the study of his writings: 'plus ex eo proficere potuisse qui . . . ejus praesertim inter homines conversationem non ignoraverunt.' The present work of Fr. Hugh Pope affords that valuable knowledge. St. Augustine here appears in his own surroundings of time and place and circumstances, in his wanderings spiritual and terrestrial, in the many aspects of his character, personality and spirituality. And withal we have here a useful guide and estimate of the work and writings of the Saint.

We may well note that Augustine lived and laboured in an age when the prevailing culture was threatened with ruin. In the year before his death the Vandals swarmed into Africa to destroy the work in which he had spent himself so devotedly. Rome had already fallen and Rome's civilization was breaking up in confusion and in waves of terrorism. Augustine foresaw it all and wept over the destruction, though he declared it was no great wonder that the works of man should perish when God, the end of all, was left out of count.

He had spent the best part of his life in learning and teaching in what consists the world's true and lasting hope, the nature of the things that alone endure and what is the goal of all human life.

Not unlike those times are our own days of confusion, crisis and unrest. Well would it be, could the teachings of Augustine be heeded towards the healing of the world's present sickness.

We hope that Fr. H. Pope's *St. Augustine of Hippo* may have a wide circulation and serve to stimulate many to zeal in the building up of the City of God.

ALOYSIUS SMITH, C.R.L.

CONTENTS

ABBREVIATIONS

Caill. A. B. Caillau et B. Saint-Yves, *Collectio selecta SS. Ecclesiae Patrum*, Tom. xxii–xxiv., 1829–1842, *cf. Miscellanea Agostiniana*, i. *S. Augustini Sermones post Maurinos reperti*, ed. Dom G. Morin, O.S.B., Rome, 1930, pp. 242–274.

Cass. *Bibliotheca Casinensis*, i–iii., 1783–1877, *Miscellanea Agostiniana*, i. pp. 399–419.

C.S.E.L. or *Corpus Scriptorum Ecclesiasticorum Latinorum*, Vindobonae (Vienna), by various Editors.

Den. Michael Denis, *S. Aurelii Augustini Hipponensis episcopi sermones inediti admixtis quibusdam dubiis*, Vienna, 1792: *cf. Miscell. l.c.* pp. 4–164.

Frangip. O. F. Frangipane, *S. Aurelii Augustini Hipponensis episcopi Sermones X ex codice Cassinen. nunc primum editi*, Rome, 1819. *Miscell. l.c.* i. 168–237.

Guelf. *Sermones Moriniani ex Collectione Guelferbitana*, 4096, ed. Morin, 1917: *cf. Miscell. l.c.* i., pp. 424–585.

J.T.S. *Journal of Theological Studies.*

Mai. *Nova Patrum Bibliotheca*, ed. Angelus Card. Mai, 1852; Card. Mai claimed to have given here no less than two hundred and two new Sermons by St. Augustine; but Dom Morin regards only twenty-six of these as genuine: *cf. Miscell. l.c.* i., pp. 277–386.

Miscellanea Agostiniana, see above, *s.v. Caill.*

Morin. *Sermones Moriniani, alii praeter Guelferbytanos, Miscell. l.c.* i., pp. 589–667.

P.L. *Patrologia Latina*, ed. Migne, 1845, vols. xxxii.–xlvii.

R.B. *Revue Biblique.*

In most printed editions of St. Augustine's works there is a double division, viz. into chapters (Roman figures) and sections (Arabic numerals); the latter are not, however, subdivisions of the former but form an independent series. Where this is the case we give references to the section only, *e.g.*, *Confess.* (Bk.) i. (section) 2. But in the case of the *De Civitate Dei*, for instance, a triple notation is requisite since the sections there are subdivisions of the chapters, hence *Civ. Dei*, XX. xx. 20.

INTRODUCTION

ALMOST from the time of his death St. Augustine dominated the thought of Christian Europe. Even now manuscripts from practically every century contain his works or portions of them. His authority was paramount when doctrinal points were in dispute and was only really called in question when the Reformation shook Europe. 'Augustinus cui contradicere impium est in iis quae tangunt fidem et mores,' St. Albert the Great, *Summa Theol.* II. *Tract.* xiv. *qu.* 184, *ad* qu. 3. The theological disputants of those days appealed to 'Augustine' whether they were Catholic or Protestant, and those who were unable to deny that he did teach the doctrines they were anxious to repudiate took refuge in a denial of his authority or at least in a perversion of his statements. This attitude of contempt for the great teacher was intensified when writers like Theodore de Bèze, Bayle, Leibnitz and Voltaire dealt with the problem of freedom of thought on religious questions. For all these men Augustine was the great example of intolerance and narrow-mindedness. Even to-day, though a milder tone prevails, writers such as Havet, Tanon, Creighton and Nickerson wholly fail to understand St. Augustine's attitude on the question of persecution. Nor has the virulent hatred for the very name of Augustine wholly died out yet; it would be hard to find grosser examples of misrepresentation than those which disfigure the pages of H. C. Lea.[1]

Yet side by side with this antipathy there has, during the last fifty years or so, been an ever-growing tendency to turn to the great Bishop of Hippo, and the recent celebrations of the fifteenth centenary of his death has brought a veritable flood of 'Augustinian' literature most of which is marked by an appreciation of his tremendous gifts and of the immense work he accomplished.

'Most of it'—alas, not all of it. For we have been told even

[1] See No. vi. pp. 299 ff. below.

so recently as 1911, that 'Augustine's influence extended for evil over practically the whole field of human activity, social and political, no less than religious.'[1]

If the pages which follow serve to kindle in the hearts of but a few a love for the 'Man of God' who was Augustine, Bishop of Hippo, for the wandering and wayward soul who sinned at Carthage and publicly repented at Carthage, for the speculative philosopher who laid aside speculations which fascinated him, so that he might better serve the 'pusillus grex' committed to his care, and who—again for the sake of all who applied to him—laboured unremittingly to express in limpid language the profoundest theological truths, these pages will have more than fulfilled their purpose. And if they do more, if they send some to Augustine himself, to those sermons and letters, even to those profound treatises which have made him immortal, then these pages will bring them to the feet of one who while 'absent, here in the body' yet most truly had 'his conversation in heaven,' whose abiding prayer was that of the Psalmist 'Unam petii a Domino, hanc requiram, ut inhabitem in domo Domini . . . ut VIDEAM voluptatem Domini, who could ever say, 'Ante Te omne desiderium meum,' whose life of unceasing toil was wholly governed by the prayer of the blind man: 'Lord, that I may SEE!' whose immense intellectual powers were ever subordinated to his faith, so that while St. Paulinus declared that Augustine '*saw* Divine Truth here on earth,' he himself was for ever insisting 'Nisi credideritis non intelligetis.'

This has been eloquently expressed by Abbot Butler:

Augustine [he says] is for me the Prince of Mystics, uniting in himself in a manner that I do not find in any other, the two elements of mystical experience, viz., the most penetrating intellectual vision into things divine, and a love of God that was a consuming passion. He shines as a sun in the firmament, shedding forth at once light and heat in the lustre of his intellect and the warmth of his religious emotion. . . . Who has been a greater intellectualist than Augustine, with his keen joy in philosophical speculation, and his ever-flowing output of intellectual writing, that to this day has influenced Western thought as none other since St. Paul?

[1] T. Allin, *The Augustinian Revolution in Theology*, 1911.

It is perhaps a realization of this aspect of St. Augustine's life and thought that has drawn so many to him in these days when—as a species of reaction against this mechanical age—men seem fascinated by the very words ' mystic ' and ' mysticism,' as though they felt that here perhaps lay an escape from an all-pervading but wholly unsatisfying materialism. The number of those who read his writings grows steadily. There are, of course, those Religious Communities which live by his ' Rule ' :

> Quam qui amant et sequuntur
> Viam tenent regiam

and such become by degrees impregnated with Augustine's spirit. But quite apart from those whose profession—so to speak—is a ' mystical ' one, a hidden life with God, there are numbers who have found in the *Confessions* something that satisfies their souls as no other spiritual book has ever been able to do. Nor are such people limited to the *Confessions*. In countries where the kinship between the Romance languages and Latin is closer than with us there is not perhaps the same need for translations from the Latin, but it is certainly true that no country has produced so many translations of Augustine's writings as has our own. No translation of course can do adequate justice to Augustine's wonderful prose-rhythm, to those cadenced sentences of a master of the art of rhetoric. But translations can give us the thought enshrined, and it is the thought rather than the words that we want.

Finally : though in these Essays we are concerned with the African Church, yet, lest we should have but a one-sided view even of Africa, we must not forget the great representatives of the Church in other parts of the Christian world during the last half of the fourth century. In Asia we have such giants as St. Basil, who died in 397, St. Gregory of Nyssa, *d.* 395, his namesake of Nazianzus, *d.* 390, while in 373 St. Athanasius had died at Alexandria. In Bethlehem St. Jerome is still living, ' sussurans in angulo,' and not to die till 420. St. Epiphanius had died in 403, but St. Paulinus of Nola in S. Italy is corresponding regularly with St. Augustine. At Rome a long line of illustrious Pontiffs had occupied the Chair of Peter :

Liberius, 352–366, Damasus, 366–384, Siricius, 384–398; these were followed by Anastasius, 398–402, Innocent I, 402–417, Zosimus, 417–418, Boniface, 418–423, Celestine, 423–432 and Sixtus, 432–440. Truly a galaxy of great names—and the greatest of all these is Augustine, Bishop of Hippo.

To all St. Augustine's children the Hymn *Magne Pater Augustine* is familiar, part of their inheritance as it were. But we give it here in full, for the composer has with amazing skill portrayed in its few stanzas the Father now 'securus' in heaven, the Guide of Religious, the Exponent of Holy Scripture, and the Religious Superior.

HUGH POPE, O.P.

Magne Pater Augustine
Preces nostras suscipe,
Et per eas Conditori
Nos placare satage,
Atque rege gregem tuum
Summum decus praesulum.

Amatorem paupertatis
Te collaudant pauperes ;
Assertorem veritatis
Amant veri judices ;
Frangis nobis favos mellis,
De Scripturis disserens.

Quae obscura prius erant
Nobis plana faciens,
Tu de verbis Salvatoris
Dulcem panis conficis,
Et propinas potum vitae
De Psalmorum nectare.

Tu de vita clericorum
Sanctam scribis regulam,
Quam qui amant et sequuntur
Viam tenent regiam,
Atque tuo sancto ductu
Redeunt ad Patriam.

Regi regum salus, vita,
Decus et imperium :
Trinitati laus et honor
Sit per omne saeculum :
Qui concives nos adscribat
Supernorum civium.
Amen.

SAINT AUGUSTINE OF HIPPO

I

ROMAN AFRICA

I. The Coming of the Romans — II. The Provinces — III. The Towns — IV. The Inhabitants — V. North Africa in St. Augustine's Day.

I—THE COMING OF THE ROMANS

It is quite impossible to understand the life, times and work of St. Augustine unless we have some idea of the Africa of his time. Geographically there is little or no difficulty, though the precise situation of many towns cannot now be determined; but the varying divisions between the Roman provinces and the relations subsisting between them and the ecclesiastical government are often a source of bewilderment. A very elementary sketch must suffice here; those anxious to obtain a fuller grasp of the problems can consult the standard works to which reference is made.

The very name 'Africa' is of uncertain origin: 'a satisfactory etymology has not yet been found for it.'[1] The portion of the vast continent with which alone we are concerned is the littoral stretching from Berenice to the Atlantic, and reaching back to the Atlas range which, at a distance varying from seventy to a hundred miles, runs parallel to the shore for a great portion of this stretch of some two thousand miles.

Africa has always been 'the Dark Continent,' the land of mystery. And though these terms apply nowadays only to Central Africa, indeed are rapidly ceasing to apply even there, yet comparatively few people have any idea of what North Africa was like in the fourth century of our era. An immense amount of work, however, has been done by the French who,

[1] Mommsen, *Provinces of the Roman Empire*, English trans., ii. 304 note.

owing to their occupation of Algeria, have, with amazing thoroughness, investigated Algeria and Tunisia and thus provided us with a wealth of material for the study of the country, the populace and their customs. Nor have they neglected the archæological side of the task ; for, quite apart from the *Corpus Inscriptionum Latinarum*, a mass of archæological detail, covering the Punic as well as the Roman occupation of North Africa, has been published.

The Romans came to a Phoenician Africa ; to them the rest of the populace, the displaced aborigines, meant nothing, though as a matter of fact they were naturally seething with discontent, and had, so far back as 395 B.C., laid siege to and stormed Carthage and Tunis, and the 'Afri' had rallied to Agathocles when he invaded Africa from Sicily.[1] As usual, however, the native population was disunited, and their disunion resulted in the gradual formation of the Roman provinces in Africa. For the only bond between the native populations was hatred of the oppressor, a bond which did not always suffice to hold them together, as we see in the second Punic War, when Gula allied himself with the Carthaginians, and Sifax, King of the Massessylians, aided the Romans.[2] The position was reversed before the close of the war, for Gula's famous son, Massinissa, revolted from the Carthaginians and joined the Romans, while Sifax went over to the other side. Scipio sent Massinissa to besiege Sifax's stronghold at Cirta, and the war ended with the battle of Zama. Massinissa had his reward, for he became the founder of the kingdom of Numidia,[3] while his son, Micipsa, made Cirta a centre of culture.[4]

II—THE FORMATION OF THE PROVINCES

In 146 B.C. the present Tunisia became the Province of Africa, and some twenty years later Gracchus established 6,000 Coloni in Numidia. Then came Jugurtha and his massacre

[1] See Mommsen, *History of Rome*, i. 418, 477–488.

[2] *Ibid.* ii. 217.

[3] Orosius, *Historia*, ix. xx. 36 ; Pelham, *Outlines of Roman History*, pp. 119–112 ; Gsell, *Histoire ancienne de l'Afrique*, vol. iii., ch. vii. ; *cf.* v. i. 3.

[4] Orosius, *Historia*, v. xi. 4 ; see E. Cat, *Petite histoire de la Maurétanie*, for an excellent summary of this period.

of the sons of Micipsa at Cirta where, however, he was finally crushed by Marius. Later on came the revolt of Pompey, who was joined by Juba, King of Numidia, but was finally defeated by Julius Caesar at Thapsus, with the result that the now subdued Numidia was added to the Province of Africa, as 'Africa Nova,' though there still remained the Republic of Cirta embracing such towns as Milevis, Chullu, and Rusicada.

With the advent of Caesar began the formal 'latinization' of Africa. From Caesar to the death of Tiberius, A.D. 37, the Province of Africa extended from Cyrene to the River Ampsaga, but from A.D. 37 the coast line from Cyrene to Thabraca was 'Proconsular Africa,' while the district westwards—including Cirta and the interior—was placed under a Praetor with the African Legion under him. Further west, Iol—afterwards Caesarea—was under King Bocchus, and Tingi or Tangiers under King Bogud, until the whole was united under Juba II and his son Ptolemy, 25 B.C.–A.D. 40, in which year the latter was put to death, and the two Provinces of Mauretania Caesariensis and Mauretania Tingitana came into existence. Thus ended the dynasty of Massinissa whose descendants had exchanged the throne of Numidia for that of Mauretania. It was not till A.D. 260 that a revolt on the part of the northern towns, Chullu, Rusucurru, Milevis, etc., was crushed by Maximian Hercules with the consequent suppression of the 'Coloniae Cirtenses' and the creation of the third Mauretanian Province, that of Mauretania Sitifensis so-called from its capital, Sitifis. Hence in the opening words of the Conference held in 411, Bishops are described as coming 'from all the Provinces of Africa, namely, from the Proconsular Province, from the Province of Byzacena, from Numidia, from Mauretania Sitifensis, Mauretania Caesariensis, and also from the Province of Tripolitania.'[1]

Finally, under Diocletian, these provinces were—with the exception of Mauretania Tingitana which formed part of the 'Diocese' of Spain—grouped under the 'Diocese' of Africa as follows: (*a*) *Tripolitania* from Cyrenaica to Lake Triton;

[1] *P.L.*, xi. 1250; *cf.* C. Toutain, *Les cités romaines de la Tunisie; Essai sur l'histoire de la colonisation romaine dans l'Afrique du Nord*, 1896, a particularly valuable work.

(*b*) *Byzacena* from Lake Triton to Horrea ; (*c*) *Africa Proper* from Horrea to Tabarka ; (*d*) *Numidia* from Tabarka to the River Ampsaga, with Lambesis as its capital ; (*e*) *Mauretania Sitifensis* from the River Ampsaga to Saldae on the coast ; (*f*) *Mauretania Caesariensis* from Saldae to the River Malva.[1]

In the mouth of a Roman, ' Africa ' would mean the country stretching from Cyrenaica to the River Ampsaga, thus embracing Tripolitania, Proconsular Africa and Numidia, though it might refer only to Proconsular Africa ; all that lay to the west of Numidia was known simply as Mauretania. Except for one journey to Caesarea, the capital of Mauretania Caesariensis, St. Augustine's life in Africa was spent in Numidia and Proconsular Africa, mainly in Hippo and Carthage, cities which lay some hundred and fifty miles apart, the one in Numidia, the other in Proconsular Africa. Destroyed by the Romans under Scipio, 146 B.C., rebuilt in part some twenty years later, it was not till the time of Caesar, 44 B.C., that the once famous city of Carthage recovered something of its former glory, but from that time till its capture by the Vandals under Genseric in A.D. 439 it again rivalled Rome, not now as a military power, but as the capital of Africa, as an educational centre.

III—THE TOWNS

Of some of the towns of Africa those, namely, which figure more particularly in the life of St. Augustine, we must give a

[1] For details on the varying arrangement of these Provinces see du Pin in *P.L.*, xi. 831–832 ; Mercier, *La Population de l'Afrique sous la domination romaine, vandale et byzantine*, 1897 ; Mommsen, *Provinces*, English trans., ii. 308–310 ; especially Willmanns, *Introduction to the Corpus Inscriptionum Latinarum*, viii. 1881 ; also Leclercq, *L'Afrique chrétienne*, i. 4–5 notes ; Jules Maurice, *Etude sur l'organisation de l'Afrique indigène sous la domination romaine*, 1896. Constantine, writing in A.D. 312, to Caecilian, Archbishop of Carthage, speaks of ' the Provinces of Africa, Numidia and Mauretania,' *cf.* Eusebius, *H.E.*, x. vi. 1 ; J. Marqardt, *De Provinciarum romanarum Conciliis et sacerdotibus*, 1872. F. G. de Pachterem, *Afrique Proconsulaire*, 1911 ; A. C. Pallu de Lessert, *Fastes des Provinces romaines de L'Afrique*, 2 vols., 1896 ; also *Les Assemblées provinciales et le culte provincial dans l'Afrique romaine*, 1884 ; *Etudes sur le droit public et l'organisation sociale de l'Afrique romaine ; Vicaires and Contes de l'Afrique*, 1872 ; *Fastes de la Numidie*, 1889 ; R. Poinsignon, *Essai sur le nombre et l'origine des provinces romaines*, 1846 ; S. Reinach, *Géographie de la Province Romaine*, 1884 ; Ch. Tissot, *Fastes de la province romaine de l'Afrique*, 1885, and especially his *Géographie comparée de la province romaine de l'Afrique*, 2 vols., 1884–1887.

somewhat detailed account. First of all will come TAGASTE, now Souk Arrhas, about fifty miles from Hippo. Here Augustine and his bosom friends, Severus,[1] Evodius and Alypius, were born. Situated in Proconsular Africa, on the River Medjerda, formerly the Bagradas, Tagaste became a municipality under Septimius Severus. The battle of Zama, which decided the second Punic war, was fought near by. There Augustine commenced his teaching life, with apparently some slight pecuniary support from the municipal authorities,[2] and when Alypius became its Bishop, A.D. 394, Augustine often visited him there. The people seem to have been most devout Christians, for Alypius triumphantly stated at the Conference of A.D. 411 that at Tagaste they had always enjoyed Catholic unity unimpaired,[3] while we owe to Augustine the curious story of how the populace there were so struck by the devotion of Pinianus, that they tried to force him to receive ordination and serve their Church.[4] Tagaste shared with Carthage, Cirta, Hippo, and some other churches the distinction of having the *Acta* of the Conference of A.D. 411 read during Lent.[5] Unquestionably the city owed much to the influence of Augustine and Alypius, but the Catholicism of the place had even deeper roots, for Augustine has recorded of one of its earlier Bishops, *Firmus nomine, firmior voluntate*, that he suffered dreadful tortures rather than lie.[6] Tagaste was perhaps the birthplace of yet another great African martyr, St. Crispina, who died for the faith at Theveste in the Diocletian persecution, for though in her *Acts* she is called ‘ Thagarensis ’ this is thought to be a misprint for ‘ Tagastensis.’[7]

HIPPO REGIUS, Augustine's episcopal see, was called in

[1] *Confess.* vi. 11, ix. 17, *Ep.* lxxxiv. 1, where Severus, Bishop of Milevis, is termed ‘ concivis meus ’; C. Toulotte, *Géographie de l'Afrique Chrétienne*, 1892–1894.

[2] *Confess.*, ii. 5.

[3] *Collatio*, i. 136.

[4] *Epp.* cxxiv.–cxxvi. Pinianus was the husband of the younger Melania, daughter of Publicola, the son of the elder Melania. On the sack of Rome in A.D. 410, they left that city with Rufinus who, however, died in Sicily; they then fled to Carthage and ultimately to Tagaste.

[5] St. Augustine, *De Gestis cum Emerito*, 4.

[6] St. Augustine, *De Mendacio*, 23.

[7] *De S. Virginitate*, 45 and notes in *P.L.* xl. 422-423, *cf. Sermon* cccliv. 5, and below, p. 57.

Punic Ubbone, whence the modern name Bona, turned by the Arabs into Annaba. The present Bona [1] lies about a mile and a quarter north-east of the older Hippo. In this ancient Phoenician foundation, of which the Romans made a 'Colonia,' [2] the Punic tongue was still spoken in Augustine's day.[3] The Donatists regarded Hippo as one of their strongholds [4] and there seem to have been so few Catholics there that the Donatist authorities were in a position to prevent bread being baked for them; Augustine reminded Petilian in A.D. 400 that

there are people still living here in Hippo where I live who well remember how your Faustinus, when he was in office and there were very few Catholics in the place, insisted that no one was to bake for them, so much so that a native of the place who owned a furnace and baked for one of our Deacons actually threw his landlord's bread out of his furnace before it was baked.[5]

That, of course, was, as Augustine says, long before his own time; but in the year 405 he felt bound to protest to the President Caecilian about the unrestrained violence of the Donatists 'in Hippo Regius and the neighbouring parts of Numidia.' [6] This disturbance arose out of the resentment felt by the Donatists at the *Decree of Union* promulgated, February 12, 405.

There seems, too, to have been a large and not particularly edifying Jewish population.

[1] Sallust, *Jugurtha*, 19.

[2] St. Augustine, *Ep.* xxxv. 3; *Contra Litt. Petiliani*, ii. 184; *De Civitate Dei*, XXII. viii. 11 and 20. There seems to be some doubt about this. The reference in *Corpus Inscriptionum Latinarum*, viii. 17403, may perhaps be a proper name, *Colonica*, see Souter in *J.T.S.* for January, 1931, p. 185 note, he would suggest that the Hippo referred to in *De Civitate Dei* is Hippo Diarrhytus. The fact, however, that St. Augustine twice speaks of Hippo Regius as 'Romana civitas,' also that he says 'strata nostra ab Imperatori munita est,' *Enarr.* ii. 10, on Ps. xxxii., would certainly suggest that Hippo was a Roman colony. It seems also to have been a military post, *Ep.* cxv.

[3] See *Epp.* lxvi. 2, cviii. 14, ccix. 3; *Sermons*, clxvii. 24, cclxxxviii. 3; *Inchoata Expos. in Ep. ad Romanos*, 13, *Haer.*, lxxxvii.

[4] *Epp.* xxiii., xxix. 11–12, xxxiii.–xxxv., xliii. 19, lxxxvi. and lxxxix., cxi. 1, cxxxix. 2, *Enarr.* ii. 19 *on* Ps. xxxvi.; *Tract.* vi. 25 *in Joann*, where we learn of the wealth of the Donatists in the palace; *Vita*, 7.

[5] *Contra Litt. Petiliani*, ii. 184.

[6] *Ep.* lxxxvi.

The Jew [says Augustine when preaching on Sabbath observance], would be better advised if he did something useful on his land (on the Sabbath) instead of quarrelling in the theatre ; while the Jewish women would do better if they spun wool on the Sabbath than spend the entire day in a frenzy of immodest dances.[1]

Indeed, the Jews seem to have been peculiarly hard to convert : ' The Jews, too, believe ; but only at the end of the world.' [2]

In a sermon on the Prodigal Son, Augustine dwells somewhat pathetically on their obstinacy ; his closing words on ' leaving them to God ' are singularly beautiful :

Just as the ' younger son ' grows daily in the person of the Pagans who become believers, so, too, the ' elder son ' returns, though rarely, from among the Jews. For they reflect upon the Church, they ask with wonderment what it is ; they see that while they have the Law, yet we too have it ; that they have the Prophecies, and we too ; that they have no longer any sacrifice, whereas we have the daily Sacrifice. . . . That ' elder son ' was angry and in his indignation refused to come in. Yet when his father spoke to him he did so, though he would not do so in reply to the mere servant. Indeed, Brethren, this is precisely what takes place. Often we convince Jews out of God's Bible, but because it is but a servant who is speaking to them, the ' elder son ' gets angry. How is that ? The sound of the music stirred thee, the dancing stirred thee, all the festivity in the house stirred thee, so, too, the banquet and the fatted calf that had been killed. No one keeps you out ! But so long as it is but a servant who speaks he goes away angry ; he will not come in. . . . But leave him to his own thoughts and then God begins to speak within him, that is, his Father goes out and speaks to His son : ' Come in and dine.' [3]

The Catholic population of Hippo was, as Augustine describes them, weak-kneed : ' The people of Hippo, whose

[1] *Sermon*, ix. 3, *cp.* cxxix. 3, cxcvi. 4 ; ' at the present time,' he remarks, ' no Jew is permitted to go to Palestine,' *Enarr.* ii. 10 *on* Ps. lxviii. ; *cf.* N. Slouschz, *Hebraeo-Phéniciens et Judéo-Berbères, Introduction à l'histoire des Juifs et du judaisme en Afrique*, 1908.

[2] ' Credunt et Judaei, sed in fine saeculi,' *Morin*, vii. 2.

[3] *Caillau*, II. xi. 8 and 10 ; *Miscell. Agost.* i. pp. 260–262.

servant the Lord has made me, are for the most part, in fact almost wholly, so weak that even a slight difficulty reduces them to a state of positive illness, and at the present moment they are so grievously afflicted that even were they not weak they could hardly survive it and save their souls.' [1] But they were devoted to their saintly Bishop and 'vehemently resented' [2] his occasional absences from their midst. It was the same with the people of Carthage to whom he could say: 'I know well the place I hold in your hearts.' [3] How far Augustine had succeeded in converting the inhabitants of Hippo by the time he came to die is uncertain, for when he said in a Christmas sermon of uncertain date: 'You are all Christians; through God's mercy the city is Christian'; [4] he may well be including the schismatic Donatists, for he is inveighing against certain superstitious practices connected with Baptism; he is not saying that 'all are Catholics.' One thing, however, he had succeeded in doing: he had changed the morals of the place; for when preaching at Bulla Regia against their excessive love of the theatre and certain horrible vices attached to it, he could say: 'In our Hippo, where such things have almost ceased to be, evil-living folk of that type have to be hired from here (Bulla).' [5]

In Augustine's day Hippo seems to have been far from healthy; the only shelter was from the north-west wind, not from the east wind: [6] 'Even this long letter I should not have been able to write unless I had been able after an illness to get away from Hippo where I was when your messenger came; even now I am racked with ill-health and fever.' [7] In harmony with this are his frequent allusions to the incomparable blessing of good health which, he naively remarks, 'is the patrimony of the poor.' [8] The rains, too, seem to have been a serious affair: Augustine speaks of the autumn rains as a grave matter, [9] to heavy rains

[1] *Ep.* cxxiv. 2, A.D. 411; *cf. Ep.* cxxii. 2.
[2] *Ep.* xxii. 9; *cf.* cxxii. 1, cxxiv. 2.
[3] *Enarr.* iii. 20 *on* Ps. xxxvi.
[4] *Sermon*, cxcvi. 4.
[5] *Sermon*, xvii. 2 (*Sermones inediti, P.L.* xlvi. 879).
[6] *Cf. Epp.* cxviii. 34, cxxvi. 4.
[7] *Ep.* cx., cxviii. 34; *cf. Epp.* x. 7, xxxviii. 1, lix. 1, cxxii. 1, ccxxx. 6, ccxxxi. 7, etc.
[8] *Enarr.* i. 2 *on* Ps. lxxvi.
[9] *Ep.* lv. 13.

at Carthage we owe his three wonderful sermons on Ps. xxxvi,[1] while in a sermon at Hippo he refers to 'these tremendous rains.'[2]

Always a purely provincial town, yet, as the port whence flowed the produce of fertile Numidia, Hippo had a peculiar importance. Covering some hundred and fifty acres, with perhaps 30,000 inhabitants in Augustine's time, it was linked up by a series of roads with such important places as Cirta or Constantina, about one hundred and eighty miles to the east, with Tagaste—Augustine's birthplace—about fifty-five miles south-east, with Madaura—where Augustine first went to school—twenty miles still further south, and with Theveste nearly one hundred and fifty miles almost due south. The Vandals laid siege to it, A.D. 430, and during that siege Augustine died; they captured it in 432; the Greeks rebuilt it towards the close of the fifth century, but it was finally destroyed by the Arabs, A.D. 697.

CALAMA, the modern Guelma, also figures largely in Augustine's life. It was probably a Phoenician town and certainly had a Punic populace.[3] Lying between Hippo and Cirta and geographically in Numidia,[4] it yet fell under the administration of Proconsular Africa;[5] in fact the ecclesiastical province of Numidia extended further east than did the civil province.[6] The Romans made Calama a 'Colonia' in A.D. 283.[7] In Augustine's day it was the scene of many disturbances, owing in part to riots by the pagan populace,[8] in part to the delinquencies of the notorious Crispinus, who occupied the Donatist See there in opposition to Possidius, the intimate friend and biographer of St. Augustine.[9] Genseric the Vandal took it in

[1] *Enarr.* ii. 1 *on* Ps. xxxvi.
[2] *Ep.* cxxiv. 1.
[3] Sallust, *Jugurtha*, 37–38, speaks of the local officials as Suffetes, and Neo-Punic inscriptions hail from there.
[4] *Contra Litt. Petiliani*, ii. 184, 228; *cf. De Civitate Dei*, XXII. viii. 12 and 20; *Ep.* xxxviii. 3.
[5] *Ep.* li. 1.
[6] *Ep.* liii. 6; *Contra Cresconium*, iii. 27, 30; *Vita*, 8; St. Optatus, *De Schismate Donatistarum*, i. 13; see Mansi, *Concilia*, iv. 433, 437.
[7] *Epp.* xci., ccxlv. 2; *De Civitate Dei*, XXII. viii. 13, 20.
[8] *Epp.* xxxviii. 3, xci. 8–10, A.D. 408; *Epp.* ciii.–civ.
[9] *Epp.* li. 1, lxvi. 1–2, cv. 4; *Contra Cresconium*, iii. 48–51; *Contra Litt. Petiliani*, ii. 184, 228.

A.D. 437; remains of huge Roman baths are to be seen there.[1]

CARTHAGE is, save for the schoolboy who has to learn something about the Punic wars, little more than a name to us nowadays. But in the time of St. Augustine the city was 'splendidissima Carthago,'[2] 'splendidissima Colonia Julia Aurelia Antoniana Karthago,'[3] 'alma et celsa Carthago,'[4] 'Africae caput et notissima civitas.'[5] Though we are apt to think of the city as purely a Phoenician foundation, the city of Dido, excavations have shown that the ubiquitous Egyptians preceded the 'Poeni,' though they have left but few traces behind them.[6]

But remains of the Phoenicians are abundant, sufficient to afford us some notion of the ancient glory of the city.[7] With the advent of the Romans, however, all was changed, and Augustine has left us a sad picture of the sorrows that descended

[1] See Gsell, *Atlas d'Algérie*.

[2] *E.g.*, in the *Acta Saturnini*, v. and vii., *P.L.*, viii., also at the Conference of A.D. 411, I. 5, *P.L.*, xi.

[3] The Proconsuls at first lived at Utica, but in 14–13 B.C. Saturninus removed to Carthage which then became known by the above official title.

[4] See Mansi, *Concilia*, iv. 51, 167, 181. The title *celsa Carthago* was applied to it by the African poet, Apuleius, *Metamorph*, vi. 4.

[5] *De Baptismo contra Donatistas*, ii. 16; *cf. Ep.* xliii. 7, cxviii. 9.

[6] See Mabel Moore, *Carthage and the Phoenicians*, 1905, where the very Egyptian character of the remains in the Necropolis of Douimes is pointed out.

[7] The first to attempt excavation at Carthage was Nathan Davis, see his *Carthage and Her Remains*, 1861, and a review in the *Dublin Review*, February, 1861. Most of his discoveries are in the British Museum on the stairway leading up to the Egyptian galleries, though no hint of their provenance is given, see A. W. Franks, *Papers Communicated by Davis on his Excavations*, Soc. of Antiquaries, London, 1860, vol. xxxviii. Since then the work of excavation has been almost wholly in the hands of the 'White Fathers' of Card. de Lavigerie, one of whom in particular, Père Delattre, has toiled unremittingly in unearthing the Punic remains. Of his innumerable publications, it will suffice to mention his *Nécropoles Puniques*, two vols., 1915, in conjunction with Gauckler; a summary account of P. Delattre's earlier work was given by M. le Marquis d'Anselme de Puisaye, *Etude sur les diverses publications du R. P. Delattre*, Paris, Leroux, 1895; *cf. Chronique archéologique africaine* in the *Revue Africaine*, 1893. See, too, Beulé, *Fouilles à Carthage*, 1861; also *Lettres de Carthage*, second ed. 1873. S. Reinach, *Les Fouilles à Carthage*, in the *Rev. Politique et littéraire*, third series, xi., 1886. More popular accounts will be found in R. Bosworth Smith, *Carthage and the Carthaginians*, 1894; Mabel Moore, *Carthage and the Phoenicians*, 1905; D. B. Sladen, *Carthage and Tunis*, two vols., 1906; Gsell, *Histoire ancienne de l'Afrique*, vols. ii.–iii. For detailed plans see Gsell, *Atlas archéologique;* C. Saumague, *Les recherches récentes sur la topographie de Carthage*, in *Journal des Savants*, April, 1931, pp. 145–147.

on the once prosperous and peaceful city when, through Rome's fear of her rival, the edict went forth *delenda est Carthago.*[1] Many years were to pass before Rome realized her mistake, but Gracchus repaired the error by making it a Roman Colonia, while Julius Caesar undertook the task of romanizing Carthage and the surrounding districts.[2] The Romans were, as always, thorough in their administrative and colonizing work, and Carthage could soon have claimed the title of a second Rome ; so that St. Prosper could say :

> An alium in finem posset procedere magna
> Carthago, cui dux Aurelius, ingeniumque Augustinus erat ?[3]

Even to this day the aqueducts built by the Romans still stand. The aqueduct outside Zaghouan is famous. It runs in a straight line for twelve leagues, and is calculated to convey 32,000,000 litres of water per diem. The Vandals destroyed it, as they did so much that was wonderful in Africa ; but after repeated destructions and restorations it was finally repaired by the Spanish authorities who made use of the services of Colin, a French engineer.[4] The Roman baths lie buried under modern buildings. Tissot gives views of Trajan's bridge at Simittu, now Chemtou.[5]

The real centre of life in Carthage must have been the harbour. This was double—an inner and an outer, the inner being formed of two ancient lagoons. Between these two harbours ran the triple town wall.[6] The sea seems to have gradually receded, so a great deal of dredging must have been done to keep the fairway clear.[7] The ' platea maritima ' or

[1] *De Civ. Dei*, I. xxx., II. xviii., III. xxi.

[2] See Audollent, *Carthage Romaine*, 1901, pp. 325–331.

[3] *Carmen de ingratis*, i. 90–92.

[4] *Cf.* Audollent, *l.c.*, p. 185 ; C. Saumagne, *Les recherches récentes sur la topographie de Carthage*, in the *Journal des Savants*, April, 1931, pp. 145–157 ; L. Bertrand, *Carthage romaine*, 1918 ; *Carthage*, 1930, useful for its account of the Roman officials ; *Villes d'or : Algerie et Tunisie romaines*, 1921.

[5] *La voie romaine de Carthage à Hippone par Bulla Regia*, 1884.

[6] See Baedeker, *Carthage in the Mediterranean.*

[7] Carton, *Questions Topographiques Carthaginoises*, 1919, where he shows in a series of sketches how the contours of the bay have changed owing to the way in which the sea has receded. This fact was noted by Guerin in 1862, *cf.* Audollent, *l.c.*, p. 199. See, too, C. Torr, ' Encore les Ports de Carthage,' in *Rev. Archéologique*, 1894 ; R. Lantier on Carthaginian topography in the *Mémoires de l'Académie des Inscriptions*, January-March, 1922 ; Dureau de la Malle, *Recherches sur la topographie de Carthage*, 1835.

'Promenade,' as we should call it, was a public meeting place; it was here that a Manichaean treatise assailing the *Law and the Prophets* was read out in the presence of a large and most attentive multitude.[1]

Along the same *Via maritima* were depicted in mosaic 'men with no neck, but their eyes in their shoulders'—a reminiscence, it would seem, of Polyphemus.[2] Somewhere near here, too, must have been set up the bones of the whale to which Augustine refers in answer to a correspondent who had asked his opinion on the possibility of any marine beast swallowing Jonas. Augustine's answer is remarkable:

> Leaving on one side the enormous bulk of certain marine animals of which naturalists tell us, how many men could have found room in the huge belly which must have lain behind those giant ribs so familiar to Carthaginians who gaze at them where they are set up in the open? What a yawning gulf that mouth presented! It looks like the mouth of a cave![3]

Père Delattre claims to have discovered that whale down on the shore, or at least where the shore once was, for the sea has receded now.[4]

The Romans covered the country with military roads, also with a series of forts situated at such places as Mascula,[5] Thamugadi where Trajan established a military depot, also at Lambesis where Hadrian established the army headquarters. From Lambesis, Thamugadi, Vegesilis, Theveste, Ammedaera, and the other forts, a chain of roads secured communication with Cirta, Calama, and Hippo. These forts lay along the slopes west of Mount Aures, and were meant to keep the inhabitants of Mauretania in check.[6]

THAMUGADI, the modern Timgad, was a very ancient town; its name is thought to be Berber. It took rank as a Colonia about A.D. 290, and Rome has left its stamp upon it in the ruins

[1] *Retract*, ii. 58.
[2] *De Civitate Dei*, XVI. viii. 1.
[3] *Ep*. cii. 31.
[4] *Cf*. Babelon, *Carthage*, p. 108; Berger, *Comptes rendus de l'Académie des Inscriptions et Belles Lettres*, 1893, p. 104; Delattre, *Notes Archéologiques*, 1892–1893, p. 3.
[5] Now Khemchela, *cf*. *Ep*. liii. 2–4; *Contra Cresconium*, iii. 30.
[6] See Mommsen, *Provinces*, English transl., ii. 319.

of the most magnificent system of baths in Africa ; fragments of the walls of this palatial building still stand to a height of twenty-three feet, the whole measuring some eighty-eight yards by seventy, and still showing remains of thirty-five chambers. It was notorious as a stronghold of the Donatists whom St. Augustine quotes as saying : ' And our Church, too, is a great one ! What do you think of Bagai and Thamugadi ? '[1] It was still a Donatist centre so late as A.D. 420, when Augustine wrote to the Tribune Dulcitius to deprecate his severe handling of the recalcitrant Donatists there ; for Dulcitius had felt compelled to tell them that unless they conformed they would be condemned to a well-deserved death.[2] Thirty years previously the town had become notorious through the enormities of its Donatist Bishop Optatus, ' under whom Africa groaned for ten years.'[3] He was succeeded by Gaudentius, one of the seven Donatist delegates at the Conference of A.D. 411, at which time Faustinianus was the Catholic Bishop of the place. There seems to have been a well-known library there in Roman times.[4] Timgad has become quite one of the ' sights ' for tourists to inspect.[5]

The great military centre was Lambesis, which was the scene of the martyrdom of St. Maximus, a Lector, and St. James, a Deacon, during the Valerian persecution. In A.D. 120 or thereabouts the Third Legion was removed thither from Tebessa to defend the passes of Mount Aures ; their camp, which became the headquarters of the army, lay about a mile to the west of the city.[6]

The famous old city of Cirta certainly goes back to Phoenician times ; its very name represents the Punic Kartha or ' city '

[1] *Enarr.* i. 26, *on* Ps. xxi.
[2] *Ep.* cciv. 3.
[3] *Contra Parmenianum*, ii. 4 ; *Epp.* xliii. 24, liii. 6, etc.
[4] Cagnat, ' Les Bibliothèques Municipales dans l'Empire Romain,' in the *Memoires de l'Académie des Inscriptions*, xxxviii. 1, 1906.
[5] See a very good account of it in Baedeker's *The Mediterranean.* For the scientific exploration carried out by the French see *Annuaire de la Société Archéologique de la Province de Constantine*, 1853–1862 ; *Journal Asiatique*, 1858–1859, ' Description de l'Afrique Septentrionale ', a translation from the Arabic of E. Bekri by McGurkin de Slane ; *Timgad, une cité Africaine sous l'Empire Romain*, Boeswillard, Cagnat et Ballu, Paris, 1891–1905.
[6] See Mommsen, *Provinces*, English trans., ii. p. 319 ; also Cagnat, *Guides en Algérie*, Paris, 1893 ; Mercier, *La Population*, *l.c.* 12–13.

seen in ' Carthage ' and the Biblical Kiriathiarim, Kiriath-Sepher, etc. It stands on a pinnacle of rock rising some thousand feet above sea-level and surrounded on three sides by the River Ampsaga ;[1] though seemingly impregnable, it was, as a matter of fact, stormed many times in its history. It is noteworthy that the bridge built so long ago as A.D. 335 only disappeared in 1857.[2] Cirta seems never to have been actually in the hands of the Phoenicians though it is stamped with their culture.[3] The Numidians under Siphax captured it, 203 B.C.,[4] and it became the residence of their kings until it was captured by Massinissa, the ally of Rome.[5] In the Jugurthan war Adherbal, successor to the throne of Massinissa, was overcome by Jugurtha, 112 B.C.,[6] who in his turn was overthrown by Marius in a battle near the city, 107 B.C.[7] It ranked as a ' Colonia ' from 64 B.C. till A.D. 304, when the Numidian Alexander revolted, only, however, to be routed by Maxentius in 311. Two years later the Romans restored the ruined city and gave it the name of Constantina which it retains to this day. According to Strabo the place was remarkable for its wealth under the Numidian kings.[8]

Many outstanding men added lustre to Cirta either by the fact that they were born there or lived there ; many, too, were in the Roman Senate, for example M. Cornelius Fronto, the tutor of Marcus Aurelius. The poet Apuleius, called of Cirta, was born at Madaura *c.* A.D. 125 ; we have also such names as Sulpicius Apollinaris of Carthage and Aulus Gellius the historian.[9]

The part played by the city in Christian times was an unfortunate one. There was a Catholic bishop there, of course,

[1] C. Vars, *Cirta, ses monuments, son administration, ses magistrats, d'après les fouilles et les inscriptions*, 1895 ; Gsell, *Atlas de l'Algérie*, where a plan of Cirta is given, Pl. xvii. See Bouchier, *Life and Letters in Roman Africa*, 1913, p. 23 ; see, too, an account of the site in Sallust, *Jugurtha*, 21–23.

[2] Bouchier, *l.c.*

[3] See Gsell, *Recueil des mémoires publié à l'occasion du quatorzième Congrés des Orientalistes*, p. 369.

[4] Livy, xxx. 12, 44.

[5] Strabo, XVIII. iii. 13.

[6] Sallust, *Jugurtha*, 21–23.

[7] *Ibid.*, 88.

[8] Strabo, XVII. iii. 13.

[9] See Fronto, *ad Amicos*, ii. 10 ; Minucius Felix, *Octavius*, viii. 6, xxxi. 2.

from very early times, and one, Crescens, was at the Council held at Carthage A.D. 256.[1] But when the city next figures in ecclesiastical history it is the scene of the notorious council held there in 305 when Silvanus of unhappy memory was simoniacally appointed to the see,[2] and the seeds of the Donatist schism were laid.

IV—OF THE INHABITANTS

The Roman conquerors of Africa came, as we have seen, to a Phoenician Africa, and it was with these Phoenician colonizers that they were mainly concerned. They knew, of course, that these latter were themselves invaders, and that behind them lay a body of aborigines of whom they spoke indifferently as Mauri, Getuli, Barbari, Lybii, etc.;[3] it was only in the Numidian wars that they began to realize that these aborigines could not be despised, but had to be reckoned with. Had you asked a Roman during the last century before Christ what he understood by the 'Afri' or Africans, he would have replied that this was a generic term embracing all the heterogeneous peoples of North Africa. He would have told you that the Mauri dwelt in the west, in the territory known to him as Mauretania; that the Libyans were in the east, in what he called Tripolitania; the Numidians he would have placed in the north between the foregoing; the Getuli he would have explained as wild folk dwelling in the higher plateaus and deserts further south. Probably, too, he would have classed all these peoples together under the heading 'Barbari.'

The traveller to-day, however, would never hear any of these terms applied to the indigenous peoples of North Africa,

[1] *De Baptismo contra Donatistas*, vi. 24.

[2] *Ep.* liii. 4, etc.

[3] The many problems connected with the various aboriginal races will be found discussed in Duprat, *Essai historique sur les races anciennes et modernes de l'Afrique septentrionale*, 1845; H. Fournel, *Les Berbers*, 1875; Fougères et Contenau, *Les Premières Civilisations*, 1927; L. Halphen, *Les Barbares*, 1926; Hondas, *Ethnographie de l'Algérie*, 1886; E. Mercier, 'La Population de l'Afrique' in the *Recueils de la Société Archéologique*, vol. xxx., 1897; P. Monceaux, *Les Africains*, 1894; V. Piquet, *Les Civilisations de l'Afrique du Nord*, 1917; W. B. Squire, *A Description of the Tribes of Tunisia*, 1916; F. R. Rodd, *People of the Veil, being an account . . . of the wandering Touareg Tribes . . . in the Central Sahara*, 1926. Tertullian, *Adv. Judaeos*, 7, *P.L.* ii. 650, speaks of the Getuli as already converted in his day.

though he would recognize the Roman *barbari* in the name 'Berber.' The modern ethnologist knows all these peoples as Kabyles, Touaregs, Arabs and Berbers. It seems now generally agreed that there were in the main two streams of indigenous peoples; the Ethiopians or black peoples in the Sudan or south; and the Libyans or whites in the north.[1] But it is difficult to account for the presence of these whites or comparatively fair-skinned peoples. For while it seems clear that a migratory movement can be traced from the Sahara desert to the north-west coast, also that there was a movement from Southern Europe to the North African coast,[2] yet ethnologists are not agreed in saying that the white element is due to this European invasion, nor will they allow that it is due to the fifth-century Vandal invasion; for these blonde people form the large majority of the Moroccan district or the Mauretanias.[3]

Whatever the explanation, the fact remains that the people whom we now term 'Berbers' consist of both browns and blondes, the latter, with their fair skins, brown hair and blue eyes, predominating; thus while the Mauri, Getuli and Numidians are all dark, the Libyans are fair; yet all are comprised under the modern terms 'Touareg' and 'Kabyles,' or more broadly still 'Berbers.'[4] There is no need to suppose that by St. Augustine's time the Phoenicians had been exterminated. For Augustine has various references to them and their language;[5] and since he goes out of his way to secure the

[1] Tissot, *Géographie de la province romaine de l'Afrique*, i. pp. 385 ff.

[2] *Ibid.*, p. 390.

[3] Tissot, *l.c.*, would suggest that these blonde peoples were of Aryan origin, and points out that in the monuments of the Nineteenth Egyptian Dynasty the 'Libou' or Libyans are portrayed as blue-eyed and fair-haired; he regards them, therefore, as Indo-Europeans who passed into Africa from Spain, *l.c.*, p. 414.

[4] Tissot, *l.c.*, p. 390 ff. See Mommsen, *The Provinces of the Roman Empire*, Engl. tr. ii., ch. xiii., *The African Provinces*, where he says that the aborigines who were on the spot when the Phœnicians founded Carthage were known as Maxyas, and later—under the Romans—as Mazices; that these correspond to the Amazigh of the Riff and the Imoshagh of the Sahara; that these are not the blacks of the Sudan, nor are they Egyptians, but are known, according to the district in which they appear, as Libyans in the east, Mauri in the west, Getuli in the south and Berbers in the north; we to-day embrace them all in the comprehensive term 'Berbers,' and the majority of them are fair, p. 303.

[5] *Epp.* lxvi. 2, cviii. 14, ccix. 3; *Sermo*, clxvii. 4, clxxxviii. 3; *Haer.* lxxxvii.

services of a Punic-speaking priest for one of his districts,[1] the Puni must have still been a factor to be reckoned with.

Some, it is true, hold that the Phoenician element was a negligible one, and that the language spoken of as ' Punic ' by Sallust and St. Augustine was really Libyan or Berber.[2] But Augustine does not use terms carelessly, and that he himself had more than a nodding acquaintance with Punic is not only antecedently probable but seems borne out by his use of it. Thus he translates a Punic proverb into Latin on the ground that ' you do not all know Punic ' ;[3] he points out that the Punic for ' three ' is the same as the Latin *salus* ;[4] he knows the meaning of Punic proper names ;[5] he tells us that Macrobius, the Donatist Bishop of Hippo, had provided a Punic interpreter for the rude bands of Circumcellions who apparently could not understand Latin.[6] Even in Hippo itself Punic must have been the prevailing language, for Augustine found it hard to secure Latin-speaking clergy.[7] He says that the Hebrew word *Messias* ' is kin to the Punic, as indeed are many if not all Hebrew words.'[8] All this accords with other testimonies : Apuleius says of his own son : ' He speaks nothing but Punic although he has learned a certain amount of Greek from his mother ; Latin he neither can nor will speak ' ;[9] St. Jerome, too, tells us that Punic was used officially till the close of the first century A.D.,[10] while from many African towns we have Punic inscriptions dating from the first and second centuries.[11] It is

[1] At Fussala, *Ep*. ccix. 3.
[2] Mercier, *La Population d'Afrique*, 1897, p. 15.
[3] *Sermo*, clxvii. 4.
[4] *Inchoata Expositio in Ep. ad Romanos*, 13 ; *P.L.* xxxv. 2096.
[5] *Quaestiones in Heptateuchum*, vii. xvi. ; see *Epp*. xvii. 2, ccix. 2–3 ; *Sermo*, clxvii. 4 ; *Inchoata Expositio in Ep. ad Romanos*, 13 and *cp*. St. Jerome on Gal. iii. 10, *P. L.* xxvi. 358 ; St. Augustine, *Contra Litt. Petiliani*, ii. 238–239 ; *De Peccatorum Remissione*, i. 34 ; *Haer*. lxxxvii., etc.
[6] *Ep*. cviii. 14.
[7] *Ep*. lxxxiv. 2.
[8] *Contra Litt. Petiliani*, ii. 239 ; *cf*. Tract. xiv. 7, xv. 27 *in Joann.*
[9] *Apologia*, quoted by Toutain, *Les cités romaines de la Tunisie*, 1896, p. 201. Apuleius in his *Apologia* also quotes a letter in Greek written by his wife, who was born at Oea or Tripoli ; similarly it is said of Septimius Severus, who was born at Leptis, that he was *Graecis litteris eruditissimus ;* at the same time a knowledge of Greek seems to have been confined to the towns on the coast ; Toutain, *l.c.*, p. 197.
[10] *Ep*. xcvii., and this in the very towns just mentioned as being more or less hellenized, namely Leptis and Oea.
[11] *E.g.* Mactaris, whence comes a votive stele to Baal Hermon with an

true, of course, that Punic is not found in any public document later than the time of Tiberius;[1] but it was the language of culture in its own sphere, while absent from coins where, naturally enough, the language of the ruling Latins found place.[2] As late as the time of the Antonines the Punic towns on the coasts were ruled by their Suffetes, though these were soon replaced by *duoviri et decuriones*.[3] As for the Berber and Libyan languages, the former was popular in the Sahara district,[4] while in the purple-producing island of Girba, where there were two episcopal sees,[5] Libyan was spoken, as Berber indeed is to this day.[6]

It might seem idle to insist on such points. But unless we grasp the fact that great numbers, more especially among the Donatists, belonged to races that had no affinity with Rome though living under Roman dominion, which spoke languages unknown to the conquerors and had a civilization of their own, we shall not do justice to many of the problems that had to be faced in the North Africa of the fourth century A.D.

V—NORTH AFRICA IN ST. AUGUSTINE'S DAY

In endeavouring, then, to form a picture of the North African population in St. Augustine's day we should probably not have to eliminate many nationalities now present there. We should have to place in the foreground the dominating Romans, the governing class with its crowds of soldiers and

inscription in Neo-Punic; similarly at Thucca, Simittu and Mididis; Toutain, *l.c.*, p. 201.

[1] See Mommsen, *Provinces*, ii. 326 ff.

[2] Mommsen, *ibid*. This, of course, was only true where the Romans really held sway; Punic inscriptions on coins hail from such towns as Leptis Magna, Oea, Sabrata, Thenae and Thusdrus during the reigns of Augustus and Tiberius, Toutain, *l.c.*, p. 197. Some of the very early *Acts* of the Martyrs from Carthage, Oea and Leptis Magna are in Latin, showing that even in the latter unimportant towns the local courts insisted on the official language.

[3] Mommsen says that Phoenician was in use along the coast from Leptis to Tingi or the present Tangiers, especially round Carthage, and no less in Numidia and Mauretania, *Provinces*, ii. 326 ff.

[4] Mommsen, *l.c.*; Gsell, *Histoire ancienne de l'Afrique*, vol. i. v.

[5] *Collatio*, A.D. 411, i.

[6] Mommsen, *l.c.*, 328.

officials.[1] Perhaps next to them in importance would come the *coloni*, or retired men of war, established on the land as small proprietors and privileged people.[2] Then would come the merchant class made up for the most part of Hellenes who, in addition to their business-like tendencies, were still, despite the ascendency of the Romans, a very considerable element in the cultured life of the country.[3] The Jews, too, would be there, perhaps even more numerous than they are to-day, and with no less keen an interest in the financial aspect of affairs.[4]

The Arabs, too, would be there, though not known by that name, nor welded, as they were afterwards to be by Mohammed, into a homogeneous body of fanatics. Only the modern Europeans would have to disappear from the picture, and even these might be said to represent the Roman conquering class of those earlier times. But behind all these would come the immense mass of the displaced peoples. These it is who interest the student of the North Africa of Augustine's day; for they are the people amongst whom he lived as a much loved Bishop, to whom he preached his wonderful sermons, for the salvation of whose souls he fought against the degrading Manichaean heresy, against the disruptive forces of the Donatist schism, and against the Pelagian heresy which made such appeal

[1] The *Comitatus* or court of the Roman Vicar of Africa was enormous, *cf.* Audollent, *Le Carthage*, pp. 343 ff.; Pallu de Lessert, *Les assemblées et le culte provincial dans l'Afrique romaine*, 1891; Fournier, *Les Officialités au Moyen Age*, 1880. In fact the number had to be legislated for, and Valentinian I. enacted in A.D. 365 that they were not to exceed three hundred, *Codex Theodosianus*, I. xv. 5, ed. Mommsen, I. 52, an enactment that had to be repeated in A.D. 386, *ibid.*, i. xv. 12. The Conference of A.D. 411 was an imposing spectacle, not merely because of the immense number of Bishops who met there, five hundred and sixty-five, but also because of the concourse of Roman officials present. With many of these Augustine was on very familiar terms, see, for example, his correspondence with Marcellinus, *e.g.*, *Epp.* cxxxiii., cxxxviii., cxliii., cli., etc.; with Macedonius, *Epp.* clii.–cliii., and with Count Boniface, *Epp.* ccxx., clxxxv., see, too, the spurious correspondence given in *P.L.* xxxiii., Appendix.

[2] For these *coloni* see Ward, *Roman Provincial Administration*, 177 ff. The number of small towns was very great, Strabo, xvii. iii. 15, speaks of three hundred in Carthaginian territory alone, *cf.* Pliny, *Nat. History*, v. iv. 38; see Mommsen, *Provinces*, ii. 332, for towns in which the Augustan veterans were established.

[3] Mommsen, *ibid.*, 333 ff.

[4] See above, p. 7 and notice St. Augustine's frequent references to them, *De Civ. Dei*, XXII. viii. 21; *Sermo*, v. 5, xvii. 9; *Epp.* xliv. 6, cxxvi.; *Tract. versus Judaeos*, *P.L.* xlii. 51–64, 1131; *cf.* P. Bérard, *S. Augustin et les Juifs*, 1913.

to the *intelligentsia* of that day. Who, then, were these peoples who flocked to hear him, who applauded so enthusiastically when he preached, who were torn in two by the Donatist schism which was proving the bane and curse of Africa ?

The extent of the Roman domination in Augustine's day may be gauged from Pliny who speaks[1] of five hundred and sixteen communities in Africa ; six of these—though perhaps we ought to double the number—he calls *coloniae*, two he terms 'Latin towns,' fifteen were communities of Roman burgesses. These facts speak eloquently for the thoroughness of the Roman occupation, and it is necessary to bear them in mind if we would form any adequate notion of the surroundings in which Augustine lived. In addition to the above there were also, as we have seen, remains of the once dominant Phoenicians and of the aboriginal races, so that it will be evident that the North Africa of St. Augustine's day was a welter of nations with a corresponding welter of languages and, of course, of morals. A century and a half before Augustine St. Cyprian had drawn a terrible picture of the lax morals of the Christians themselves,[2] and had foretold the disasters which actually came to pass during the Aurelian and Decian persecutions when the enervated Christians flocked to commit public apostasy.[3]

For the *Pax Romana* had brought luxury in its train, and while the towns may have been small, yet we find everywhere traces of baths, theatres, splendid tombs and luxury of all sorts,[4] while even during the Vandal invasion the beauty of the houses was noteworthy.[5] Bribery and corruption seem to have been the order of the day ;[6] there was much oppression, too, of the

[1] *Nat. Historia*, v. iv. 28.

[2] St. Cyprian, *De Lapsis*, 5–6 ; *cf. Ep.* vii. (xi.) 1–2, 5 ; *Testimonia*, iii. xv. 47 ; P. Monceaux, *Les Africains*, 1894.

[3] St. Cyprian, *De Lapsis*, 9.

[4] See Mommsen, *Provinces*, ii. 339.

[5] Victor of Vita, *De Persecutione Vandalica*, i. 3. St. Augustine repeatedly warns his flock not to pervert the idea of Lent by indulging in strange delicacies while ostentatiously abstaining from forbidden foods, *Sermo*, ccvii. 2, ccviii. 1, ccx. 10. For the great establishments kept up by some of the wealthy people see *Enarr*. i. 8 *on* Ps. lxiv.

[6] St. Cyprian, *Ep*. i. 10, also Nos. 6 and 12, for the prevailing contrast between the rich and the poor, and for the immense amount of crime of which everybody was cognizant in Africa at the time, *cf*. St. Augustine, *Sermo*, xvii. 4 ; *Enarr*. i. 9 *on* Ps. lxiv.

poor,[1] while the Africans were a bye-word for their immorality[2] and drunken habits. The latter vice seems to have been extraordinarily prevalent. Men laughed at it, and looked upon it as a mere nothing ; [3] they even ate salt food so as to provoke a thirst,[4] so that Augustine was driven to thunder against drunkenness in sermon after sermon.[5]

The Donatists were notorious drunkards ; St. Augustine insinuates that they spent the whole of Ascension Day drinking ;[6] even their nuns were addicted to this vice.[7] The Decian persecution in which St. Cyprian suffered martyrdom seems to have purified the Christian body which had become exceedingly remiss, but the terrible Vandal persecution does not seem to have had any such effect on African morals, for Salvian, writing towards the close of the fifth century, loudly proclaims that ' we Christians are worse than the " Barbari," '[8] and he proceeds to draw a dreadful picture of the prevailing bribery and corruption, adding a terrible story of a rich man and the fate he suffered for refusing assistance when a poor man asked him for it.[9]

Yet there was another side to the picture. For whereas the literary output of Rome during the first four centuries of the Christian era was meagre in the extreme, we have a series of African writers who won for themselves a high place in Latin literature. Among the pagan writers were such famous authors as Terence and Apuleius of Madaura, A.D. 114–184. The latter was the author of *The Golden Ass.*[10] Africa was very proud of him, and at Oea or Tripoli, where he had taught, a statue was erected to him ; [11] ' Apuleius qui nobis Afris Afer est

[1] *Sermo*, xiv. on Dives and Lazarus.
[2] *Sermo*, cccxcii. 1–3.
[3] *Sermo*, xvii. 3 ; *De Baptismo contra Donatistas*, iv. 27.
[4] *Confess*. viii. 3.
[5] *Sermo*, xvii. 2–3, cli. 4, ccxxv. 4, cclii. 4, *cp. Epp*. xxii. 6, xxix. 5 and 11.
[6] *Ep*. xxix. 8 ; they are drunken usurers, *Sermo*, xlvii. 17.
[7] *Epp*. lv. 35, xciii. 48–49 ; *Contra Epistolam Parmeniani*, ii. 19, iii. 18 ; *Contra Litt. Petiliani*, i. 26, ii. 93–94, 174, 195, 239.
[8] *De Providentia*, iii.–iv.
[9] *Ibid*., iv.
[10] See *The Golden Ass of Lucius Apuleius*, translated by William Adlington, 1566, reprinted many times since, and re-edited by Whibley, 1893, Seccombe, 1913, and Gaselee, 1915 ; *cf*. Augustine, *De Civitate Dei*, xviii. 1.
[11] Augustine, *Ep*. cxxxviii. 19.

notior,'[1] says Augustine. The pagans even claimed that Apuleius worked miracles as great as those performed by the Christian teachers.[2] Terence was, of course, the idol of Africa. When his famous line in the *Heautontimoroumenos*, i. 1, 25, 'Homo sum, humani nil a me alienum puto,'[3] was mouthed in the theatre, 'the entire assembly,' says Augustine, 'was roused; learned and unlearned alike stood up and applauded.'[4]

Augustine himself quotes Terence's plays largely, more especially the *Andria*;[5] even the aged Donatist Bishop of Caesarea in Mauretania, Emeritus, quoted it at the Conference of A.D. 411.[6] Yet Augustine complains bitterly of the harm done by Terence's lascivious plays.[7] Of other pagans, such as Fronto of Cirta and Apollinaris of Carthage, little is known.

Nor were the Christians behind their pagan compatriots in their literary output. We need mention only Arnobius of Sicca. Born about A.D. 260, he was at first a violent opponent of Christianity, but was converted and wrote his *Apologia adversus Nationes*. He died *c.* 327. Then there was Lactantius, Arnobius' pupil at Sicca; when about forty years of age he went to Asia Minor where he occupied the chair of rhetoric at Nicomedia. He became a Christian about the year 300, but continued to occupy his chair till in 306 Galerius closed the school at Nicomedia. Later on he became tutor to Crispus, son of Constantine. He wrote his *De Opificio*, *c.* 305, the *Instituta* between 307 and 311, also an *Epitome* of the last named, *De Ira Dei*, 310–311, and his most famous work, *De Mortibus Persecutorum*, about 314. Minucius Felix was a contemporary of St. Cyprian, and wrote some fifty years

[1] *Ibid.*, 19.

[2] So Marcellinus complained to Augustine, *Epp.* cxxxvi. 1, cxxxviii. 18, *cf.* cii. 22. See P. Monceaux, *Apulée, roman et magie*, also A. Kretschmann, *De Latinitate L. Apulei Madaurensis*, 1865.

[3] *Cf. Contra Julianum*, iv. 83, where it is somewhat differently given.

[4] *Ep.* clv. 14.

[5] *Ep.* ccl. viii. 5; *De Civitate Dei*, XIV. viii. 2; xxv. 1; XIX. v., etc.

[6] Mansi, *Concilia*, iv. 127.

[7] *Confess.* i. 16, iii. 2; *Enarr.* i. 11 and 23, *on* Ps. lxxx. i. 8, *on* Ps. cxlvii.; *De Tempore Barbarico*, 4; *De Catechiz. rudibus*, 25; *Ep.* xci. 4–5; *De Civitate Dei*, I. xxxii.; the Council of Arles, can. 5, inflicted excommunication on the frequenters of the theatre. Terence himself was taken prisoner to Rome after the second Punic war, Orosius, *Historia*, IV. xix. 6, 20.

before the two last named his very beautiful dialogue called *Octavius*.[1]

We need do no more than name such famous masters of true eloquence as Tertullian and St. Cyprian; the latter always spoke of Tertullian as his 'master,' though their temperaments were so very different. Half a century later came C. Marius Victorinus, born in Proconsular Africa about A.D. 300; he became a famous professor of rhetoric at Rome, but was converted to Christianity through reading the Bible. Augustine has preserved a beautiful account of his courage in making public profession of his faith;[2] in 362 he had to resign the chair of rhetoric owing to Julian the Apostate. His commentaries on *Galatians*, *Philippians* and *Ephesians* still exist.

St. Optatus may not be remarkable for his style, but we owe him a debt as the author of the *De Schismate Donatistarum*, *c.* 366, a work which struck the first blow at this long dominant schism. Lastly we have St. Augustine himself and his disciple Orosius. The truth is that the Africans of those days had a craze for education, and, what is perhaps more remarkable, for Latin culture.[3] It was this that won for St. Augustine the remarkable place he occupied even amongst those who had no sympathy with his Christianity. For in their eyes he exemplified in a marked degree that culture which the Africans admired; in him they had one who had carried off the prize for rhetoric at Rome itself, and had thereby added lustre to the African name.[4] Hence they flocked to hear him preach, his letters were read and copied in remote districts, and even his polemical works were devoured.[5] Hence the phenomenon of young men like Julian of Eclanum[6] and Vincentius Victor of Mauretania[7] who were so anxious to break a lance with the champion of

[1] See Monceaux, *Histoire de la littérature Latine Chrétienne*, 1924, p. 59; also his *Histoire littéraire de l'Afrique du nord*, seven volumes, 1901–1923.

[2] *Confess.* viii. ii.

[3] Augustine mentions a certain Simplicius who could repeat passages of Cicero and Virgil backwards, *De Anima et ejus origine*, iv. 9.

[4] *Confess.* vi. 6; *Vita*, 1; *Contra litt. Petiliani*, iii. 25.

[5] *Vita*, 18; *De Anima et ejus origine*, ii. 18; *Epp.* xc. 8, cii.; *cf. De Praedestin. Sanctorum*, 9; *Ep.* cxix. 6, clxix. 12, cxciii. 10; *De Gestis Pelagii*, 19; St. Fulgentius, *Ep.* xiv. 14.

[6] See *Contra Julianum*, vi. 40.

[7] Victor was so pleased with his work that he read it aloud to a big gathering, *De Anima et ejus origine*, iv. 4 and 39.

orthodoxy ; even defeat secured them a species of immortality ! This partly explains, too, the ferocity of the attacks levelled against him by the Donatists ; they were jealous of his reputation and feared his dialectical skill.

While it is difficult, then, at this distance of time to recapture any adequate impression of what life in Carthage must have been in St. Augustine's day, there was certainly a wealthy class there, men who had grown rich in commerce ;[1] also a large body of officials,[2] representatives of the imperial court ; the military, too, were there, as well as many landed proprietors.[3] There must also have been an immense number of workpeople—unsung in history, and—since Carthage was a most important seaport—there must have been a considerable nautical element in the town.[4] The population has been estimated at some half million ;[5] not an improbable figure, for the capital city drew to itself, not only from the interior, but also from the sea, since communication 'over-seas' was extraordinarily frequent,[6] and Carthage became—next to Rome—the greatest mart on the Mediterranean seaboard. This immense crowd of peoples of divers nationalities, divers tongues and creeds, had to be fed and entertained, and all alike had to have some form of religion. The circus and the theatre catered for their amusements ; the markets for their food ; the churches and the heathen temples for their religion.

[1] See St. Augustine's frequent sermons on the danger of riches, *e.g.*, *Enarr.* i. 10, *on* Ps. xxxvi. ; note his remark, 'non potest negotium esse sine fraude,' *Enarr.* ii. 14, *on* Ps. xxxiii.

[2] With these Augustine was in close relations, sometimes, indeed, as in the case of Marcellinus, they were his most intimate friends, note amongst others Macedonius, Vicar of Africa, *Vita*, 25 ; *Epp.* clii.-clv. ; Olympius, *Magister Officiorum* in succession to Stilicho, *Epp.* xcvi.-xcvii. ; Largus, Procurator of Africa, A.D. 415, 418–449, *Ep.* cciii. 6 ; *cf. Cod. Theod.* X. x. 27–28. *See Les Progrés de la vie urbaine de l'Afrique du Nord sous la domination romaine*, J. Toutain in *Mélanges Cagnat*, 1912.

[3] *Ep.* lviii.

[4] *Ep.* ccxvi. 6.

[5] Babelon, *Carthage*, p. 107.

[6] *Ep.* xliii. 20.

Note :

In addition to strictly scientific works published in *Comptes rendus* and in Geographical or Archæological Journals the following will be found useful :—

G. Boissier, *L'Afrique Romaine*, 4th ed., 1909, also an English translation, *Roman Africa*, trans. by Arabella Ward, 1899.
Bouché-Leclercq, *Manuel des Institutions romaines*, 1886.
E. S. Bouchier, *Life and Times in Roman Africa*, 1913.
R. Cagnat, *L'Armée romaine d'Afrique*, 1892 and 1912.
R. Cagnat et A. Merlin, *Inscriptions latines d'Afrique*, 1923.
G. Gsell, *Histoire ancienne de l'Afrique du nord*, 1913–1927 ; also *Les Monuments Historiques de l'Algérie ; Atlas de l'Algérie*, 1902–1911.

II

CHRISTIAN AFRICA

I. The Coming of Christianity to Africa and the Decay of Paganism—II. The African Episcopate and its Councils—III. Sinners and Saints—IV. Of the Liturgy in General: Public Prayer; The Feasts; The Catechumens—V. The Sacrifice of the Mass—VI. Church Buildings in Africa.

I—THE COMING OF CHRISTIANITY TO AFRICA

We have seen something of the people who dwelt in the African cities in St. Augustine's time. Of greater interest, however, is the character of the Christianity in this romanized part of the world. How it first came to be planted there we simply do not know. Various statements by Popes Innocent I, Gregory the Great, Leo IX seem to take for granted that Africa was evangelized from Rome,[1] but these may be little more than oratorical expressions. Indeed St. Augustine may seem to negative an apostolic origin for the African Church when he says, 'some barbarian peoples came to the faith later than Africa.'[2] Two passages in Tertullian are sometimes quoted in favour of the view that the African Church was founded by Apostles. Yet when Tertullian says, *Communicamus cum Ecclesiis Apostolicis*, he is making little more than a purely general statement, not asserting the apostolic origin of the African Church;[3] so, too, when, endeavouring to overthrow the African custom of not veiling virgins, he appeals to the custom of those Churches 'quas et ipsi Apostoli vel Apostolici viri condiderunt,' he seems rather to imply thereby that the African Church was not of apostolic origin.[4]

[1] Innocent I, *Ep.* xxv. 2; St. Gregory, *Epp.* lib. i. 77, viii. 33; Leo IX, *Ep.* lxxxiii.; *cf.* Leclercq, *Dict. d'Archéologie, s.v., Carthage,* also his *L'Afrique Chrétienne*, ii. 218.

[2] *De Unitate Ecclesiae*, 37.

[3] *De Praescriptionibus*, 21; *P.L.* ii. 38.

[4] *De Virginibus velandis*, 2; *P.L.* ii. 939.

We first hear of the African Church in the case of the Martyrs of Scillium and Madaura,[1] about A.D. 180, and shortly after that date we have the famous *Acts* of SS. Perpetua and Felicitas which show us that there already existed a Church highly organized and possessing an established hierarchy, including deacons and even catechists. It is hard to discover how numerous the Christians were at this time, though one writer estimates their number in North Africa at that period as about 100,000, but it is not clear how he arrives at this estimate.[2]

Christianity would naturally appeal to the simple folk and to the oppressed, of whom there were very many. For wonderful as the Roman rule was, there can be no doubt that it involved an enormous amount of oppression. Taxes were a heavy burden, conscription a worse one. The rise of tyrant after tyrant, with resulting wars and miseries, made peace and happiness ideals hardly ever capable of being realized. Moreover the Romans, by adopting the Phoenician and Getulian deities, as well as by their system of planting out their veteran soldiers as *Coloni*, had gradually produced what we may term a *Creole* race, mixed in blood, religion and morals.[3] This appears in the absence of indigenous names in the surviving inscriptions; men's very names had become latinized and nationality was fast disappearing.[4] Since, then, Christianity at least offered an equality which appealed to what was highest and best among these subject denationalized peoples, it is not surprising that even in the remoter country districts it met with a warm welcome.

[1] See *L'Eglise d'Afrique et ses premières épreuves sous le règne Septime-Sévère*, in the *Revue historique*, 1879, vol. xi. 244. Scilla or Scillis was in Proconsular Africa. The Feast of these martyrs was kept on July 17 when their *Acts* were read. Their relics are in the Basilica of SS. Giovanni e Paolo at Rome; *cf. Sermon*, clv., also *Sermon*, xvi., *P.L.* xlvi. 869.

[2] Munter, *Primordia Ecclesiae Africanae*, 1829, p. 24, quoted by Leclercq, *Dict. d'Archéologie*, *s.v. Afrique*.

[3] Mercier, *La Population de l'Afrique*, 1897, p. 20.

[4] *Ibid.*, p. 21. Yet that the native population persisted is evidenced by such recurrent expressions as: 'Gens Suburburum, Civitas Nattabutum, Gens Numidarum at Tubursicum, Gentes foederatae,' to the N.W. of Sitifis; *cp.* Boissier, *La Littérature africaine*, ch. vii.; E. Buonaiuti, *Il Cristianismo nell' Africa romana*, 1928; P. J. Mesnages, *L'Afrique Chrétienne*, 1912; *Le Christianisme en Afrique*, 3 vols. 1914–1915; E. Mercier, *Histoire de l'Afrique septentrionale*, 3 vols. 1888–1891.

At the same time the mixed character of those who gave their adherence to Christianity proved a source of weakness; the widely divergent nations dwelling in Mauretania, Numidia and Proconsular Africa might sink their racial differences in Christianity for a time, but it would be unreasonable to expect that their religion should consistently hold in check a conglomeration of peoples always conscious of the foreign yoke under which they had to live, and at times only too ready to throw it off. We have an instance of this in Firmus, who in A.D. 372 rebelled and destroyed Iol or Caesarea, the capital of Mauretania Caesariensis; and Firmus was but one of many such rebels. The same restlessness infected the African Christians; and while their characteristic hot-headedness produced, when sublimated by religion, a veritable army of martyrs, it also provided the material for all sorts of schisms and heresies.

Carthage, which has been described as a vast Punic cemetery, also as a huge museum of colonial Rome, has with even greater truth been termed 'an immense Christian reliquary.'[1] For just as the inhabitants had readily absorbed Roman civilization, so did they drink in Christianity. Churches sprang up everywhere; even the heathen temples were converted into 'Basilicas' as the Africans called them. And with the churches came the saints. It is enough to mention Tertullian—though he did go wrong afterwards, St. Cyprian, St. Optatus and St. Augustine; to these should be added the mighty host of martyrs who proved the 'seed of the Church' in North Africa.

The roll of the Martyrs in Africa was the glory of the Church there. Mons. L. Bertrand twice[2] quotes, as though from St. Augustine, the words: 'Africa sanctorum martyrum corporibus plenum est,' while Cardinal Lavigerie drew up a Litany of Martyrs for every day of the year,[3] indeed, St. Augustine himself says: 'There is hardly a day in the year on which some Martyr has not won his crown.'[4] No one can read the

[1] Babelon, *Le Carthage*, p. 92.

[2] *L'Eglise d'Afrique*, a discourse in the amphitheatre at Carthage, May 19, 1930, and *Villes d'Or*, p. 134; but he gives no reference neither can I find any such passage in St. Augustine's works.

[3] L. Bertrand, *Carthage*, p. 52; *cf.* E. Buonaiuti, *Il Cristianismo nell' Africa romana*, 1928.

[4] *Denis*, xiii. 1, *P.L.* xlvi. 855.

account given by Victor of Vita of the triumphant combats of the Martyrs during the Vandal persecution without a thrill: some of them positively 'danced to martyrdom.'[1]

'Even to-day in Numidia,' says Augustine, 'it is the custom for God's servants to salute one another with "If you overcome." Even here in Carthage and in all Proconsular Africa, in Byzacena too and even in Tripoli the servants of God are wont to adjure one another "By your crown" . . . "My joy and my crown," said the Apostle, "stand fast in the Lord."'[2] This adjuration seems to have been common to the Donatists as well as Catholics: 'Your people,' writes Augustine to Proculeianus the Donatist Bishop of Hippo, 'salute ours "by our crown," and our people salute yours "by your crown."'[3] Such salutes seem to have been a serious matter: 'A person says: "Oh! If only I were well off! Lord, make me well to do! So and so is better off than I am; I salute him, but he does not return my salute; I salute him again and still he does not return it! Lord, make me well off too!" But,' asks Augustine, 'if you find him so unpleasant, why want to be like him?'[4]

How strong numerically the Catholic body must have been in Hippo in St. Augustine's day we can gather from one of the saint's sermons on the Feast of St. Laurence:

One thing I do know, and you know it as well as I do, and that is that in this city there are many houses in which there is not even a single pagan; nor a single house in which there is not a Christian. Indeed if you look more closely you will not find a house in which there are not more Christians than pagans.[5]

Indeed, Faustus complained that there were almost more nuns in the Catholic Church than women who were not nuns![6]

St. Augustine draws the practical moral: 'You realize, then, the inevitable conclusion: there would be no wrongs in the city if the Christians decided there should not be;

[1] Of Victorianus of Hadrumetum he says: 'Tripudians in Domino feliciterque consummans, martyrialem coronam accepit,' *De Persecutione Vandalica*, v. 4.
[2] *Caillau*, II. vi. 2.
[3] *Ep.* xxxiii. 5.
[4] *Mai*, cxxvi. 11.
[5] *Sermo*, cccii. 19.
[6] *Contra Faustum*, xxx. 4.

hidden wrongs, perhaps ; public, no, if only the Christians forbade them.'[1] And on another occasion : 'For long Christians did not dare answer a Pagan ; now, thanks be to God, it is a crime to remain a Pagan !'[2] Yet it is not always easy to estimate aright the position or the attitude of the Pagans towards Christianity. That very many became Christians is certain : 'What !' you say with amazement, 'So and so has become a Christian ! That man become a believer !'[3] So, too, when preaching on the wholly unlooked for conversion of Faustinus :[4]

What has just taken place, before your very eyes, is not my doing but God's. I never dreamed of it. Your expectations, and mine, too, for that matter, were very different. You are well aware of the recent insistent demand which has been voiced here : 'The officials[5] of this city must not be Pagans ; Pagans must not lord it over Christians.' That alone was meant. But that the very man we were crying out against should himself become a Christian was never dreamed of by any Christian, though Christ Himself was bringing it about. We have heard him say aloud and with true piety : 'I have no wish for office, I want to be a Christian.' . . . Pagans and sinners are through a variety of causes waxing old so that even they seem in a sense to be keeping to-day's feast :[6] badly, wickedly, miserably, it is true, yet your eyes have seen how many are being delivered from paganism. . . . So the Pagans wax old, they are diminishing in number ; they will come to an end, either through coming to the faith or by dying out.[7]

Over against this, however, we have to set the riots caused by the Pagans at Calama,[8] Augustine's frequent references to the baneful effect on Catholics of their Pagan surroundings and to the human respect which at times made them ashamed to

[1] *Ibid.*
[2] *Enarr.* ii. 12 *on* Ps. lxxxviii, *cf. De Divinatione Daemonum*, 14, *De Consensu Evangelistarum*, i. 27, *Sermons*, lxii. 17, lxv. 10.
[3] *Morin*, i. 1.
[4] This perhaps took place A.D. 401 ; *cf. Morin, Miscellanea*, i. p. 593.
[5] 'Majores.'
[6] That of St. John the Baptist.
[7] *Morin*, i. 1–4 ; *cf. Frangipane*, viii. 5.
[8] *Epp.* xci. 8, xciii. 10, ciii. ; *cf.* pp. 126–27.

practise their religion.[1] There undoubtedly existed, too, in Africa a body of cultured and influential Pagans who held aloof altogether from Christianity though they corresponded with Augustine, *e.g.*, Longinianus,[2] Maximus of Madaura,[3] others, too, who were frankly dismayed at the spectacle afforded by the then state of the world.[4] Pagan feasts, too, were at times celebrated with extravagant and irritating solemnity,[5] though the Christians were able to lodge a successful protest against this.[6]

Indeed, since the time of Constantine [7] a succession of Edicts against Paganism had been promulgated by Constantius,[8] A.D. 341, 342, 354, when their temples were closed; by Gratian, Valentinus and Theodosius, 381, 382, 385, 391 in February and June; [9] by Theodosius, Arcadius and Honorius, 392; [10] by Arcadius in 395, 396, and four times in 399; [11] again, in great detail, by Arcadius, Honorius and Theodosius, 407–8, when it was enacted that idols were to be removed if people worshipped them, the temples were to be applied to public uses, the Bishops were to report if the edict was not observed, while judges who neglected to enforce it were liable to a fine of £20 in gold.[12] Honorius and Theodosius published a similar Edict in 415 'not merely for Africa but for all countries.'[13]

Hence Augustine could say: 'Nowadays no one remembers the time when we were put to confusion; days when it was a disgrace to be a Christian. No one remembers them; all have forgotten them.' [14] Catholics could go to and fro wearing their

[1] *Epp.* cxcix., cccxxx. 4; *Sermon*, lxii. 9; *Enarr.* i. 16 *on* Ps. xxxix., i. 12 *on* Ps. lxviii.

[2] *Epp.* ccxxxiii.–ccxxxv.; *cf. Ep.* cii. and *Retract.* ii. 31.

[3] *Epp.* xv.–xvi.; *cf. Ep.* L, *Sermon*, ccxxxii. 17; *Enarr.* i. 6 *on* Ps. xxiv., i. 8 *on* Ps. cxxxvi.

[4] *Sermon*, lxxxi. 7–9.

[5] *Ep.* xciii. 10; *Contra Epistolam Parmeniani*, i. 15; *Contra Gaudentium*, i. 51.

[6] *Ep.* ciii. 13; *Sermon*, xxiv. 6.

[7] December 17, 320, *Cod. Theodosianus*, XVI. x. 1; Mansi, *Concilia*, i. 897.

[8] *Ibid.*, x. 2–4.

[9] *Ibid.*, x. 7–11.

[10] *Ibid.*, x. 12; Mansi, i. 900.

[11] *Ibid.*, x. 13–18, the last one being for Africa.

[12] *Ibid.*, x. 19; Mansi, i. 902; *Ep.* xci. 8.

[13] *Ibid.*, x. 20; Mansi, i. 903; *cf.* G. Boissier, *La Fin du Paganisme: étude sur les derniers luttes religieuses en occident au quatrième siècle*, 1891.

[14] *Enarr.* i. 8 *on* Ps. liv., i. 9 *on* Ps. lix.

distinctive dress without molestation, and the pagan theatre crowd would only say pityingly that such poor folk had missed a great deal :

Sometimes [says Augustine] when the theatre or the amphitheatre is over, when their doors vomit forth that crowd of lost folk, with their minds full of the hollow shows they have seen, of people who find their nourishment in things not merely useless but dangerous, who think with glee of things pleasant but deadly, they often see God's servants passing by—and they recognize them by their gait or their dress or their headgear, or they know them by sight—and then they say to themselves or to one another 'Oh, those unhappy people! What they *have* missed!'[1]

It is clear, then, that in Augustine's day the Christians were free to practise their religion, whether they were Donatists or Catholics. But Paganism was far from being dead.

It is incontestable [says M. Toutain] that many of the heathen cults dating from pre-Roman times survived in Africa under the domination of Carthage and when the Numidias and the Mauretanias were independent. Some of these cults were Punic, others Berber or Libyan, that is to say more peculiarly indigenous in character, though it seems certain that during Roman Imperial times the worship of Baal, of Baliddir, of Hathor Miskar, and more especially of Saturn and Coelestis, rather than the cults deriving from the more ancient Libyan populations, constituted the religion of Carthage.[2] The same authority maintains that 'the evidence of the far greater portion of the documents now known to us goes to show that both in sanctuaries far removed from the towns and comparatively inaccessible, as well as in the city temples and in chapels belonging to rural districts, popular devotion to the native deities was exhibited at all or any season of the year as best suited popular convenience and opportunities for assembling.'[3]

[1] *Enarr.* i. 8 *on* Ps. cxlvii.
[2] *Cultes paiennes*, iii. pp. 44–45.
[3] *Ibid.*, p. 61.

Still there was a large Catholic population, and, as Augustine reminds them, it was easy for them to have good Catholic friends if they chose.[1] But just as there were many good Catholics so there were many bad ones [2] who by their disedifying lives incurred a grave responsibility, so that Augustine has often to lament the fact that pagans were deterred from becoming Catholics by the bad example of many Catholics who were such in little more than name.[3]

II—THE AFRICAN EPISCOPATE AND ITS COUNCILS [4]

The first Bishop we hear of is Agrippinus of Carthage.[5] He appears to have succeeded to that see about A.D. 197. But when we meet him he is already presiding over a Council held in that city and comprising seventy Bishops. This was somewhere between A.D. 218 and 222, and is the first Council known to us of the long series held in Africa.[6]

Only a few years later we find St. Cyprian presiding over three Councils in 255 and 256. In the last of these no less than eighty-seven Bishops took part, and they hailed from Numidia, Proconsular Africa and remote Mauretania. It was the same even after the Decian and Diocletian persecutions had decimated the Church; for when the famous Conference between the Catholics and the Donatists was held at Carthage in A.D. 411, no less than 279 Donatist Bishops were confronted by 286 Catholic Bishops, and it was acknowledged that many were absent on either side through illness or distance, and that many sees were at the moment unoccupied.[7] Some fifty years later

[1] Multos enim inventurus es, si et tu talis esse coeperis, *De Catechiz. Rudibus*, 49.

[2] *Quaest. xvii in Matth.*, qu. xi. 3–4.

[3] *Enarr.* ii. 6 *on* Ps. xxx.; *Sermo*, xlvii. 28.

[4] Du Pin, *P.L.* xi. 823–875, gives a geographical list of episcopal Sees and their occupants; *cf.* Duchesne, *Les Eglises séparées*, 1896, p. 286; Ferrère, *La Situation religieuse de l'Afrique Romaine*, 1897; Hefele-Leclercq, *Histoire des Conciles*, ii. 85 note; Leclercq, *L'Afrique chrétienne*, i. 171–172.

[5] For Agrippinus see St. Cyprian, *Epp.* lxx. 4, lxxiii. 3; St. Augustine, *De Baptismo contra Donatistas*, ii. 13–14, iii. 17; *De Unico Baptismo*, 22. See, too, Leclercq, *L'Afrique Chrétienne*, i. 32, note.

[6] Their names are unfortunately lost, see Morcelli, *Africa Christiana*, ii. 46.

[7] *Collatio*, i. 209–215; *Breviculus Collationis*, i. 14; see below, pp. 117–120

the Vandal persecutor, Hunneric, sent 464 Bishops into exile,[1] while at the Council of Carthage held in 525, no less than 180 episcopal sees are enumerated in Proconsular Africa alone though but forty-eight Bishops were actually present.[2] The Archbishop of Carthage was Primate over the entire African Church,[3] but the provinces had their Primates as well, for as early as A.D. 314 we hear of Primates of Tripolitania and Mauretania,[4] while at the Council held in 347–8 under Gratus, Archbishop of Carthage, the Province of Byzacena, too, had its Primate; [5] even so early as 305, towards the close of the Diocletian persecution, Secundus of Tigisi seems to have been Primate of Numidia.[6]

That lists of the Bishops of various dioceses were kept is evidenced by Tertullian; [7] this was especially the case with the Bishops of Rome.[8] From these lists the names of departed Bishops were recited during Mass: 'We should not, if we thought him a criminal,' says St. Augustine, 'repeat the name of Caecilian at the altar among the other Bishops whom we believe to have been faithful and innocent in life.' [9] Bishops were held in great honour as successors of the Apostolic body.[10] They were judges in the Church,[11] and it was part of their duty before God to intercede for criminals.[12] But human nature

[1] Victor of Vita, *Hist. Persecutionis Vandalicae*, i. vii. 23, ix. 29.
[2] Leclercq, *Dict. d'Archéologie Chrétienne*, *s.v. Afrique*.
[3] See Mansi, *Concilia*, iii. 719, 734, 782; *Codex canonum Ecclesiae Africanae*, canons 17, 39, 85; St. Augustine, *Ep.* lix., *P.L.* xi. 827, the Appendix; Pope Felix, *Ep.* ii. in Mansi, *Concilia*, iii. 412; F. D. Moorrees, *De Organisatie van de Christellke Kerk von Noord-Afrika in het licht van de brieven van Augustinus*, 1927; R. Massigli, *Primat de Carthage et Metropolitain de Byzacène. Un conflit dans l'Eglise Africaine au VIe siècle*, in *Melanges Cagnat*, 1912; De Mas-Latrie, *L'Episcopus Gumnitanus et la primauté de l'évêque de Carthage*, in the *Bibliothèque de l'Ecole de Chartes*, 1883, p. 72; Schelstraate, *Ecclesia Africana sub primatu Carthaginiensi*, 1679.
[4] See Constantine's letter to Anulinus, Hefele-Leclercq, ii. 85, note.
[5] Hefele-Leclercq, *ibid.*
[6] *Ibid.*
[7] *De Praescriptionibus*, 32.
[8] St. Irenaeus, *Adv. haer.* iii. 3; St. Optatus, *De Schismate Donatistarum*, ii. 3, etc.
[9] St. Augustine, *Sermo*, ccclix. 6.
[10] Pope Innocent I, *Ep.* iii. ad Basilium; *cp.* St. Jerome, *Adv. Luciferanios*, 9, 11, 23; *P.L.* xxiii. 173–174, 184, also St. Cyprian, *Epp.* xlv. 2, li. 12, 24, lvii. 3, lxviii. 5, lxxi. 3, lxxii. 26.
[11] Optatus, *l.c.*, vii. 7.
[12] St. Augustine, *Epp.* clii.-iii.

would not be what it is if such a position did not rouse ambitious notions ; and that such ambitions did tarnish the fame of the African Church is clear from the decrees of the Council held at Carthage in A.D. 347–8.[1]

Nothing better serves to bring home to us the immense number of these Bishops than the fact that at the Council of Hippo in A.D. 393 it was seriously proposed that for the consecration of a Bishop twelve Bishops should be required ; but the prudent Aurelius, Archbishop of Carthage, deprecated any change from the ancient custom,[2] a decision which the Council of Carthage endorsed by entering it in the *Breviarium Canonum*.[3] The suggestion, however, was no innovation, for the Donatists seem to have been in the habit of employing twelve consecrators ; at any rate the dissenting Maximianists did so, as we learn from the decree fulminated against the twelve consecrators of Maximianus by the main Donatist body in 394 at the Donatist Council held at Bagai.[4]

Conversely, nothing better serves to show the desolation due to the Vandal invasion, followed as it was by the Arab hordes, than the fact that when Gregory VII wanted to consecrate a Bishop in Africa he could not find even three consecrating Bishops ![5]

The African Church was remarkable, too, for its numerous Councils. We referred above to the first known Council, held under Agrippinus, A.D. 218–222. We then have seven held by St. Cyprian[6] who in some years held two Councils. The next we learn of was held in 347–8 by Gratus.[7] Then come two Councils between 386 and 389. Of the first we know practically nothing, the second, held by Genethlius, has left us thirteen canons.[8]

[1] See capp. x. and xii., Labbe, *Concilia*, ii. 717 ; *cf*. Morcelli, *Africa Christiana*, ii. 246 ; Pope Zosimus, *Ep*. ix. 3.

[2] *Codex canonum Ecclesiae Africanae*, can. 49 ; Labbe, *Concilia*, ii. 107.

[3] *Breviarium Canonum*, *Ibid*., can. 39.

[4] *Contra Cresconium*, iii. 59.

[5] *Epp*. iii. 19–21, du Pin, *P.L*. xi. 835. For the three consecrating Bishops see Eusebius, *H.E*. vi. xliii.

[6] See Hefele-Leclercq, i. ; they will also be found in Routh, *Reliquiae Sacrae*, iii. 93–131.

[7] This is sometimes called Carthage I, see Labbe, *Concilia*, ii. 719 ; Hefele-Leclercq, ii. 76, note.

[8] Hefele-Leclercq, ii. 76 ; Mansi, *Concilia*, iii. 691.

With his successor, Aurelius, who is too little appreciated, overshadowed as he was by the giant figure of his devoted disciple, Augustine, the African Church took on a new lease of life. Succeeding to the See of Carthage, A.D. 391,[1] he presided over at least twenty Councils till his death in 429–30.[2] The first of these was the famous Council of Hippo, October 8, 393. We do not know how many Bishops were present, but they were sufficiently numerous for Possidius to describe the Council as *plenarium totius Africae Concilium*.[3] Augustine was then only a priest of two years' standing, yet such was the impression he had already made on the episcopal body in Africa that at their demand he preached before them the treatise preserved for us under the title of *De Fide et Symbolo*.[4]

This Council decided that a Council of all the Provinces of Africa should be held each year.[5] This does not seem to have been done, though there was one held in the next year, 394, which is generally known as the First Council of Carthage,[6] presumably because it was the first held there by Aurelius, justly regarded as the Father of the African Church of that time. Such was the importance of the decisions arrived at in the Council of Hippo, that the Bishops of the Province of Byzacena made a summary of them and insisted on its insertion into the *Acta* of the second of the two Councils held in 397,[7] Carthage II and III.[8] We need not dwell further on these Councils of Carthage. Though not held yearly so far as we know, yet in several years, notably A.D. 401 and 408, two Councils were held. It would be a mistake to regard these meetings as merely Provincial Synods; they were far more than that, not solely by reason of the great numbers of Bishops who attended them, but also because of the very serious matters dealt with. The burden imposed on the Bishops by such

[1] Hefele-Leclercq, ii. 82.
[2] *Ibid.*, 97. For Aurelius see especially pp. 322 ff. below.
[3] *Vita S. Augustini*, 7.
[4] *Ibid.*
[5] *Codex canonum Ecclesiae Africanae*, can. 9; Hefele-Leclercq, ii. 86.
[6] Hefele-Leclercq, ii. 97.
[7] This Council was really held in two parts, on June 26 and August 27, when forty-three Bishops were present, Hefele-Leclercq, ii. 98–100; Labbe, *Concilia*, ii. 1165.
[8] Hefele-Leclercq, ii. 98.

frequent attendance proved, however, too great,[1] and the Eleventh Council of Carthage decided, June 13, 407, that in future these great meetings should only be convened when the needs of the entire African Church demanded it.[2]

Much the same thing was done by the Council held at Carthage A.D. 418, when, to save the Bishops—at least two hundred in number—from being too long absent from their dioceses it was decided that three should be chosen from each Province to represent, under Aurelius the Archbishop, the whole Episcopal body; Vincent of Culusis, Fortunatianus of Sicca and Clarus being chosen to represent the Province of Carthage, and Alypius, Augustine and Restitutus that of Numidia.[3]

III—SINNERS AND SAINTS

Amid a people such as Augustine had to deal with there must naturally have been a good deal of superstition.

What particularly vexes me [he wrote] is that while many things laid down in Holy Scripture as most salutary are but little regarded, yet an immense number of baseless notions are current, so that a person would be more severely reproved for setting his bare foot on the ground while keeping some ‘ octave ’ than if he were to drown himself in drink. I think that all such things should, when not based on the authority of Holy Scripture, nor on the pronouncements of Episcopal Councils, nor established by any custom of the Universal Church—admitting too of innumerable variations due to differing local practices, and this to such an extent that it is practically impossible to discover why men, whenever the opportunity offered, adopted them—all these excrescences should, I think, be unhesitatingly lopped off. For while it may safely be argued that there is nothing contrary to faith in these practices, yet the fact remains that they encumber religion itself with all sorts of observances; whereas God meant religion to be a thing of freedom unencumbered by a multitude of abstruse rites. The

[1] See the statements by Alypius and others, *Codex canonum Ecclesiae Africanae*, can. 90; Labbe, *Concilia*, ii. 1105.

[2] Can. 1, Hefele-Leclercq, ii. 157; so, too, Council of Milevis II, A.D. 416, can. 9; Labbe, *Concilia*, ii. 1540; *Codex canonum Ecclesiae Africanae*, can. 95, *ibid.*, 1113.

[3] Can. 19, or can. 127 in the *Codex canonum Ecclesiae Africanae*, *cf.* Hefele-Leclercq, ii. p. 195.

condition of the Jews of old might almost seem, in comparison, to have been more endurable.[1]

Other superstitious practices were curiously modern, such as turning over the pages of the Bible to get guidance from a chance text :

Some there are who draw lots from the pages of the Gospel, and though this is preferable to consulting devils, yet I dislike the practice since it means converting God's oracles, meant to tell us of the next world, into a means for getting hints about the affairs of this world and the vanities of this life.[2]

Again, Africa had been the scene of many glorious martyrdoms ; perhaps, then, it was only to be expected that a misguided cult of those who had shed their blood for Christ should develop. The Donatist schism arose, at least in part, from the unregulated and fantastic piety of a foolish woman who took offence when the Archdeacon Caecilian reproved her for it.[3] And though it seems to have been the practice to keep these shrines hidden from the knowledge of the pagans—' the faithful know,' says Augustine, ' the places where the martyrs are commemorated '[4]—yet it became necessary to legislate against the number of such shrines, especially against such as apparently did not actually contain any relics at all.[5]

And it must be confessed that if the laity were guilty of many gross failings, there were undoubtedly grave faults on the part of the clergy too. At Sardica, Hosius complained of the way in which some Bishops were always on the look-out for more important sees : ' No Bishop,' he said, ' has ever yet been found trying to secure translation from a large city to a smaller one.'[6] He also found reason to complain of the way in which the Bishops succeeded in getting to the Imperial court ;[7] this, he said, was a vice ' especially affecting the African Bishops '

[1] *Ep.* lv. 35.
[2] *Ibid.*, 37.
[3] St. Optatus, *De Schismate Donatistarum*, i. 16 ; *cf.* St. Augustine, *Breviculus*, iii. 26 ; *Ep.* xliii. 17 ; *Contra Epistolam Parmeniani*, i. 5 ; *Contra Cresconium*, iii. 33 ; *De Unitate*, 6 and 73, etc.
[4] *De Virginitate*, 46.
[5] *Codex canonum Ecclesiae Africanae*, can. 83 ; Labbe, *Concilia*, ii. 1097.
[6] Cap. i. ; Labbe, *Concilia*, ii. 627.
[7] *Ibid.*, cap. ix.

who disregarded the enactments of their Archbishop Gratus and who hung about the court simply 'to seek for worldly honours.'[1] Hence the repeated legislation against clerics who moved about from church to church in search of more lucrative employment,[2] also against Bishops who wrangled over questions of precedence,[3] or who insisted on appointing their own successors.[4] Not that Africa stood alone in this respect. We know how strongly St. Jerome spoke about the haughtiness of the Bishops in his day:[5] 'let them seek the toil, not the dignity of the episcopate.'[6] Hence the legislation prohibiting them from holding ordinations outside their own dioceses;[7] hence, too, the scandals attaching to some episcopal elections.[8]

The truth, of course, was that in too many cases these African Bishops were in reality little more than parish priests, and their sees villages rather than towns. This was emphatically true of the Donatists, as Alypius of Tagaste pointed out at the Conference of A.D. 411:[9] 'Let it be entered in the *Acta* that all the above Bishops were consecrated for villages or farms, not for cities'; Pope Zosimus said the same.[10] This practice had long been forbidden by the Councils of Laodicea and of Sardica: 'Leave should not be given for the consecration of a Bishop for any mere village or small town where one priest is enough: it is not necessary to have a Bishop there; to do so only cheapens the episcopal title and authority.'[11] It can be no matter for surprise, then, to find that these African Bishops were not always edifying in their lives.

The Donatists seem to have been particularly bad. Such men as Optatus, Bishop of Thamugadi, under whom 'Africa

[1] *Ibid.*, cap. viii.
[2] Pope Siricius, *Ep.* x. 16; St. Jerome, *Ep.* lxxxiii, *ad Oceanum*, etc.
[3] *Codex canonum Ecclesiae Africanae*, can. 86; Labbe, *Concilia*, ii. 1100.
[4] Council of Antioch, A.D. 341, can. 23; Labbe, *Concilia*, ii. 671.
[5] See St. Jerome on Matthew xii., also on Gal. iv. 12.
[6] St. Jerome on Sophon, iii. 1–7, *P.L.* xxv. 1443; *cp.* Tertullian, *De Baptismo*, 17.
[7] Pope Celestine, *Ep.* iv. 6; Council of Carthage, A.D. 348, can. 10 Pope Siricius, *Ep.* x. 18.
[8] *Epp.* ccxiii. 1 and 4.
[9] *Collatio*, i. 181, *P.L.* xi. 1326, *cf.* du Pin, *ibid.*, 832, and below, p. 140.
[10] *Ep.* ix. 3.
[11] The Council of Sardica, can. 6; Labbe, *Concilia*, ii. 631, du Pin, *P.L.* xi. 832.

groaned for ten years,'[1] brought disgrace on their rank; and Optatus did not stand alone. Drunkenness was rife among the Donatists of all ranks,[2] even among the nuns,[3] while the most disgraceful immoralities were brought home to some of their Bishops during the investigations made in the course of the Conference of A.D. 411.[4] Among the Catholic Bishops, too, there were very grave scandals. We have only to recall what St. Augustine himself suffered from the irregular life of his own nominee, Antony of Fussala, whose conduct was so disgraceful that St. Augustine actually proposed to the Pope that he (Augustine) should resign his bishopric since he had been guilty of consecrating so unworthy a member of the episcopal bench; but in the same year, 423, Antony was deposed by the Council of Numidia.[5] Augustine suffered much, too, from Paul of Cataqua,[6] from Bishops Boniface and Spes,[7] also from Honorius and Splendonius [8] at Cirta, in the church of which city their condemnation had to be read out by Fortunatus.

The ambition which seems to have been one of the prevalent failings appears to have been accentuated by the curious system whereby primatial rights—except in the case of the see of Carthage—went by antiquity in consecration;[9] St. Augustine himself had to deal with the case of Xantippus, whose primatial rights were apparently being disregarded.[10]

[1] *Contra Epistolam Parmeniani*, ii. 4; *Ep.* xliii. 24; *Contra Litt. Petiliani*, i. 120.

[2] 'Voragines,' St. Augustine terms them, *Contra Litt. Petiliani*, ii. 233, *cf.* 174, 195; their drunken habits were *omnibus notum atque quotidie*, *ibid.*, 78, 93. Note Augustine's illuminating remark: 'One never sees a person drunk at table; when he does get drunk it is at night, not during the daytime "which the Lord hath made",' *Guelf.* viii. 1.

[3] *Contra Epistolam Parmeniani*, ii. 19.

[4] *Collatio*, i. 130, 187–188, 207, *cf. Contra Litt. Petiliani*, ii. 61, 195; iii. 37, 40, 43.

[5] *Ep.* ccix. 2–3, 10.

[6] *Ep.* lxxxv. 1.

[7] *Epp.* lxxvii. and lxxviii.; *cf. Ep.* ccviii. 2.

[8] *Contra Litt. Petiliani*, iii. 44.

[9] Council of Milevis, August 27, 402; Labbe, *Concilia*, ii. 1323. Hence perhaps the declaration by the Council of Hippo, 393, can. 29, that Bishops were not to be styled *summus sacerdos* nor *princeps sacerdotum*, Hefele-Leclercq, ii. 88; 'Praesumus, sed si prosumus,' Augustine reminds them, *Guelf.* xxxii. 3, and 'nomen quaerat Episcopus, non rem,' *ibid.*, 6; he points out further that 'Christus est Episcopus episcoporum,' *ibid.*, 8.

[10] *Ep.* lix. 1–2, lxv. 1. For the primatial rights of Carthage see Leclercq, *L'Afrique chrétienne*, i. 76–83.

But there is another side to this picture of the African Church. After giving a glowing account of the lives led by many solitaries, by many monks and nuns in Africa,[1] Augustine continues :

How many Bishops have I known who were most excellent and holy men, how many priests, deacons and ministers of the Sacraments, men whose virtue appears to me all the more admirable and praiseworthy in that it is so difficult to lead such a life when surrounded by all kinds of men and in our present turbulent times ? [2]

He then passes to the laity :

There are in the Catholic Church [he says] innumerable members of the faithful who use not this world, there are those, too, who ' use it as though they use it not.' . . . How many rich men, how many householders in the country districts, how many merchants, soldiers, governors of cities, senators, people of either sex, who have made the sacrifice of all empty and transient things ? [3]

There are, of course, many who fall away :

You have only to look round and see for yourself how few are the churches, whether in town or country, in which there are not some who have been found out in their sin, some even who have been degraded from their clerical state.[4]

Some parents, too, had no wish to see their children enter the religious life :

Someone says to you : ' Let me dip into your purse,' and you promptly shut it up. But supposing someone asked you for your son ? You who are so slow with your purse ; what would you do if asked for your son ? I am going to say something which I can only say with grief and shame. There are many women who have a great desire to serve God, and if they have the courage they say to their parents : ' Let me go ; I want to be God's handmaiden.' But what answer do they get ? No, you shall not have your way ; you shall not do what you want but what I want.' [5]

[1] *De Moribus Ecclesiae Catholicae et Manichaeorum*, i. 65–67.
[2] *Ibid.*, 69.
[3] *Ibid.*, 77.
[4] *Contra Litt. Petiliani*, iii. 35, 36.
[5] *Denis*, xx. 12.

There must have been profiteers in Africa in those days :

> How many people aim at rising in the world through the failure of others ! How many want others to have to sell so that they themselves may be able to buy ! How people oppress one another, even devour one another if they can ! And when one big fish has gone and eaten another smaller than itself he himself is promptly swallowed by a yet bigger one ! [1]

As for the character of the episcopate as a body, it is sufficient to point out with St. Augustine that there were many who had resigned their episcopal office because conscious of very light faults,[2] for, as he insists more than once : 'We are not Bishops for our own sakes, but for the sake of those to whom we administer the Lord's Sacraments,' [3] or, as he wrote to an unworthy Bishop : 'It is not for a Bishop to see how best he can lead a deceitful life,' [4] and again : 'A Bishop's duty is *non praeesse sed prodesse.*' [5] But the supreme proof of the sanctity of the episcopal body in Augustine's day was the fact that as a preliminary to the Conference with the Donatists in A.D. 411 all the Catholic Bishops agreed to surrender their sees to the Donatists if the latter won their case. The story is best told in Augustine's own words :

> When, previous to the Conference, some of us were discussing the matter amongst ourselves, and insisting that Bishops ought to be for the peace of Christ or not to be at all, I must acknowledge that as I looked round upon them I found it hard to imagine them ready to make, through humility, such a sacrifice to the Lord. I said to myself as one does : 'So and so can do it, so and so cannot ; such an one will agree, such another will not hear of it' ; for I was talking in accordance with my own ideas—we cannot see into the hearts of men ! But when we came to discuss the matter openly in a Council of all the Bishops, nearly three hundred in number, all were in such absolute agreement, all were so on fire, that they were ready to lay aside their episcopal dignity for the unity of Christ —not indeed that this would mean loss of their dignity, for by

[1] *Enarr.* i. 9 *on* Ps. lxiv.
[2] *Contra Cresconium*, ii. 13 ; *cf. Ep.* lxix. 1.
[3] *Contra Cresconium*, ii. 13 ; *cf. Ep.* cxxviii. 3 ; *De Gestis cum Emerito*, 7.
[4] *Ep.* lxxxv. 2.
[5] *De Civitate Dei*, XIX. xix.

so doing they would but be commending it to God's keeping. There were only two there who did not agree ; one was a man advanced in years, who boldly declared that he did not agree, the other merely showed his disagreement by his silence. But when the others upbraided the old man who had spoken out so boldly he changed his mind and the other his countenance.[1]

IV—THE LITURGY IN GENERAL

Considering the large part played by the African Church in the Christian life of the Universal Church, considering the number of saints, martyrs, bishops and doctors it produced, considering, too, the position occupied by the liturgical services in the daily life of Christians in Africa as elsewhere, it is certainly matter for surprise that not a vestige of the liturgical works there used has been preserved for us. Africa stands alone in that respect, and we can only attribute the wholesale destruction of such treasures to the Vandal persecution and the subsequent Mohammedan invasion.[2]

The *Acts* of the early martyrs, those of Scillium and Abitina, for instance, as well as the *Acts* of SS. Perpetua and Felicitas and of St. Maximus [3] do, however, enshrine scraps of information, mostly fragments of prayers, which are all the more precious in that they are so scanty. In the *Acts* of the Scillitan martyrs, for instance, we note such expressions as ' the Lord our God Who is in heaven ' ; ' Deo gratias ' ; ' to whom be honour and glory for ever and ever, Amen '—a fragment of the Doxology ; ' we have renounced the devil and follow in the footsteps of Christ,' evidently an allusion to the rite of baptism ; while the

[1] *De Gestis cum Emerito*, 6, *cp. Ep.* cxxviii. 3 ; *Breviculus*, i. 5 ; *Sermo*, x. 8.

[2] See E. G. Atchley, *Ordo Romanus Primus*, p. ix. ' The rule is general that no contemporary record was made, public or private, marking the chief steps in the evolution (of the liturgy).' Edmund Bishop, *Liturgica Historica*, 39, *cf.* the *Dublin Review*, October, 1894. That a certain amount of confusion owing to variations in practice should have arisen was only to be expected, see *Codex canonum Ecclesiae Africanae*, can. 103 ; Labbe, *Concilia*, ii. 1117 ; Innocent I, *Ep.* i., *Prologue*, Labbe, *l.c.*, ii. 1245 ; Dom Cabrol, *The Prayer of the Early Christians*, trans. by Dom E. Graf, 1930 ; Augustine Krazer, O.P., *De Antiquis Ecclesiae Occidentalis Liturgiis, illarum origine, progressu et Ordine*, 1786 ; W. Roetzer, O.S.B., *Des Hlg. Augustinus Schriften als liturgiegeschichtliche Quelle*, 1930.

[3] These fragments are collected together in Cabrol and Leclercq, *Reliquiae Liturgiae Vetustissimae*, I, *Ab Aevo Apostolico ad Pacem Ecclesiae*, 1900-1902.

reference to 'the Books of the Gospels and the Epistles of the Holy Apostle' is peculiarly valuable. In her vision St. Perpetua sees the Divine Shepherd; He gives her a draught of milk which she receives 'with joined hands' and then says 'Amen'; she refers to the baptismal rite when she says: 'the Spirit told me that there was nothing to be asked for in the water but patience in (the sufferings of) the flesh'; her prayers for her brother, Dinocrates, who is described as suffering in Purgatory, are well known. The martyrs of Abitene make patent reference to the Mass and Holy Communion: 'in Collecta fui, et Dominicum celebravi quia Christianus sum,' says St. Saturninus; and again: 'the priest Saturninus replied by the suggestion of the Spirit of the Lord: "In all tranquillity (*securi*) we celebrated the *Dominicum*"'; 'Why?' asked the Proconsul, 'because' came the reply, 'the *Dominicum* cannot be omitted'; and once more 'Collectam gloriosissimam celebravimus, ad Scripturas dominicas legendas in Dominicum convenimus semper.'[1]

That there was a great deal of intercessory prayer is evidenced by the large use made of litanies, and the frequent reference to the official prayers of the Church for various classes of people: 'You hear the priest of God at the altar exhorting God's people to pray for unbelievers . . . or for catechumens . . . or for the faithful';[2] also for heretics.[3] 'To-day, yesterday and the day before we prayed for rain';[4] so, too, for enemies,[5] and for the king.[6]

The liturgical character of this prayer is clear: 'When the brethren are gathered together in church, is not that a time for singing holy things, save only when the lessons are read, or there is a discussion, or the Bishop offers up prayer aloud, or the deacon's voice indicates the moment for prayer in

[1] Cabrol and Leclercq, *l.c.*, p. 132. The *Collecta* denotes the 'assembly' of Christians, the term has passed on to denote the prayers or *Collects* which presumably they said together with the priest: the *Dominicum* for which they were 'collected' is the *Corpus Dominicum* or the *Coena Dominica*, *cf.* 1 Cor. xi. 20.

[2] *Ep.* ccxvii. 2 and *cp. ibid.*, 26; *cf. De Praedest. Sanctorum*, 15; *De Dono Perseverantiae*, 15 and 63.

[3] *Ep.* clxxxv. 2.

[4] *Sermo*, lvii. 3.

[5] *Contra Julianum, Opus imperf.* vi. 41; *De Civitate Dei*, XXI. xxiv. 1.

[6] *De Civitate Dei*, XIX. xxvi.; *Ep.* clxix. 17.

common ? '[1] The last expression may contain an allusion to the *Flectamus genua*. When St. Augustine says that after Easter and until Pentecost ' we pray standing as a sign of the Resurrection, whence the same custom is observed at the altar on all Sundays and the *Alleluia* is sung as a reminder that one day our sole occupation will be to praise God,' [2] he is clearly speaking of the Sundays throughout the year, only excepting those in Lent and Advent. Apropos of the solemn chanting of the *Alleluia*, Victor of Vita tells a beautiful story :—

When on a certain Easter Sunday the faithful were assembled in church and the doors were closed through fear of the Arians, the latter mounted on the roof and shot arrows through the windows ; and then, while the people were singing heartily to God, a lector mounted into the pulpit and chanted the *Alleluia*. But as he sang, an arrow pierced his throat, the book fell from his hand and he, too, fell down after it.[3]

St. Augustine frequently points out that these official prayers of the Church were in no sense perfunctory.[4] He insists that they have a value independent of the moral character of the minister, for they are heard : ' non pro perversitate praepositorum sed pro devotione populorum ' ; [5] this teaching hit, of course, at the very foundations of Donatism which was based on the gratuitous supposition that only a morally good minister could confer a valid Sacrament. According to Leclercq the African Christians would appear to have had no prayers addressed to the Holy Spirit alone ;[6] certainly the Council of Carthage, 397, can. 23, enacted that all prayers said at the altar must be addressed *ad Patrem*.[7]

Lent was observed with great strictness.[8] It is always spoken of as ' the forty days of Lent,' [9] though, since they did not

[1] *Ep*. lv. 34 ; *cp*. *Ep*. clxix. 12–17.
[2] *Ep*. lv. 28.
[3] *De Persecutione Vandalica*, i. xiii.
[4] *De Dono Perseverantiae*, 63.
[5] *Contra Epistolam Parmeniani*, ii. 15 and 17.
[6] *La Vie Chrétienne primitive*, 1928, p. 49.
[7] Labbe, *Concilia*, ii. 1170.
[8] *Ep*. lv. 28, 32.
[9] *Sermo*, cxxv. 1 ; ccix. 1 ; ccx. 8. Thus Father Thurston says that the fast began on Monday of the sixth week before Easter, *Lent and Holy Week*, 1904, p. 18 ; in other words it lasted for six times six days or thirty-

fast on the Sundays,[1] and there is nowhere any hint that the days from Ash Wednesday to the first Sunday of Lent were added to make up the deficiency, the actual fast can only have lasted for thirty-six days. The practice of observing these forty days is spoken of as a feature of the Universal Church or that of the *Orbis terrarum*.[2]

That the Feasts of the great Martyrs, *e.g.* St. John the Baptist, St. Laurence, St. Vincent of Saragossa, the Martyrs of Abitene and of Scillium, were kept with great solemnity, is evidenced by the annual sermons preached on their 'Dies natales.' But in Africa the Feasts of SS. Perpetua and Felicitas, and especially of St. Cyprian, were the great solemnities. The latter Saint's day was prepared for by a fast of three days. When preaching at Carthage St. Augustine concluded a sermon by saying :—

I am unable to withstand the petitions of my own flock [at Hippo] for my return ; but since your request that I should not leave you before the Feast of St. Cyprian has been endorsed by the holy old man [Archbishop Aurelius] I will end my sermon with this : the Feast of St. Cyprian is indeed upon us ; you have made up your minds to do violence to my feelings by keeping me here for that Feast ; let us, then, who are so keen on sermons, also be keen upon fasting.[3]

Yet at the same time, at least when Augustine first came on the scene, certain Christian feasts were marked by disgraceful orgies, even in the churches themselves, and he has left us a vivid account of the strong measures he felt compelled to take in order to secure the cessation of such practices.[4] The first day before the Kalends of January was celebrated by the pagans with an orgy, and as an offset to this the day was kept as a

six in all ; in accordance with this, *Aelfric* in his *Homilies*, ed. Thorpe, i. p. 178, given by Thurston, *l.c.*, p. 20 note, speaks of Lent as the tithe of 365 days or—with Sundays of Lent omitted—as 36 days.

[1] *Ep*. xxxvi. 28, this was expressly forbidden by the Council of Sarragossa, cap. ii., A.D. 381 ; Labbe, *Concilia*, ii. 1009.

[2] *Sermo*, ccx. 8.

[3] *Frangipane*, v. 6 where see Dom Morin's note (*Miscell. Agost.* i. p. 219) on the same custom prevailing in Spain, *cf. P.L.* lxxxv. 850–856 ; lxxxvi. 708–724. 'You say "to-day it is a Martyr's feast ; I shall walk in the procession and wear my best cloak perhaps." Far better wear your best conscience,' Augustine drily remarks. *Frangipane*, iii. 6.

[4] *Ep*. xxii. 2 ; xxix. 2–3 ; *Sermo*, cccli. 11 ; *Sermo*, xiii. 2 ; *P.L.* xlvi. 857 ; *De Civitate Dei*, VIII. xxvii. 1–2.

fast by the Catholics.[1] On these fast days and, of course, during Lent, the first meal was not taken till the ninth hour or at three o'clock in the afternoon.[2]

We do not know what the African practice was for Palm Sunday, but the pilgrim Egeria, who went from Spain to Palestine about A.D. 380, has left us a vivid account of the scenes in Jerusalem on that day.[3] In Africa Holy Thursday was a busy day, for the Lenten fast seems to have meant abstinence from washing as well as from food, whence the notion that, on that day at least, people could receive Holy Communion without fasting.[4]

The washing of the feet, or the 'Maundy,' does not appear to have been an African custom; indeed some seem to have associated it with baptism.[5] The Triduum of Holy Week, 'crucifixi, sepulti, suscitati sacratissimum triduum,'[6] is mentioned by St. Augustine but he gives no details as to the mode of observing it.

On Good Friday alone was the Passion read, and then only from St. Matthew's Gospel: 'I did at one time wish to have the Passion read every year according to each of the Evangelists; in fact I did so once, but when people found they were listening to something to which they were not accustomed they were disturbed in mind.'[7] Augustine may have been trying to make up for this when on one Good Friday, after referring to the solemn reading of the Passion, he read out and commented on the Passion according to St. John xix. 17–42.[8]

Holy Saturday began, of course, with the evening of Good Friday[9] when people assembled in crowds for the night watch.[10] During this vigil they occupied themselves with the lessons read to them and with prayers. Several of St. Augustine's sermons were preached during time of waiting for the coming of Him of whom 'as you have just said when declaring your

[1] *Sermo*, cxcviii. 1–3.
[2] *Ep*. xxiv. 9.
[3] Given by Father Thurston, *Lent and Holy Week*, 192–193.
[4] *Ep*. liv. 9–10.
[5] *Ep*. lv. 33.
[6] *Ibid*., 24.
[7] *Sermo*, ccxxxii. 1.
[8] *Sermo*, ccxviii.
[9] *Sermo*, ccxxi.
[10] *Sermo*, ccxviii. 1.

faith by reciting the Creed, " He will come to judge the living and the dead " ';[1] he is referring, of course, to the Catechumens then standing round in their white baptismal garments ; and who had that day come out of the font and had solemnly made their profession of faith by reciting the Creed.[2]

To these neophytes the Bishop was particularly devoted and many of his sermons are addressed to them :—

When [he says to them] according to to-day's solemn custom you pass out from those ' cancelli ' in which you have during your spiritual infancy been kept apart from the rest and take your place amidst God's people, take care to keep company with those who are good.[3] I am not suggesting that you will not find people leading good Christian lives. God forbid I should ever think such thoughts of God's threshing-floor ! Were that so, why should I toil as I do ? No, look for good people and imitate them ; be good yourselves and you will find them. . . . Believe me, you will find plenty of good Christians : good married men who are faithful to their wives, good married women who, too, are faithful to their husbands ; people who refuse to lend out their money at usury, people who prefer to suffer loss rather than commit a fraud. Only be what they are and you will speedily find them. They may be few, but that is only in comparison with the crowd.[4]

The ceremonies of the Easter ' Vigilia '—which was the vigil *par excellence*—were heightened by the entrance of their

[1] *Sermo*, ccxxiii. 2.

[2] *Sermo*, ccxxiii. 1, 2.

[3] *Mai*, xciv. 7. When the Donatists actually rebaptized a matricidal deacon they stood him ' within the " cancelli " high up and conspicuous for all to see,' *Ep*. xxxiv. 2. These ' cancelli '—a term retained in our ' chancel '—played an important part in early church services ; a diminutive form of ' cancer ' or ' lattice,' the ' cancelli ' stood for the balustrades or low wall marking off the sanctuary, whence the Latin ' adytum ' for a sanctuary as an unapproachable spot. Generally of pierced or open stonework, they were often highly decorated and sometimes to be assigned a place there was a mark of distinction (see the illustration from the Arch of Constantine, *Fig*. 2,000 in the *Dict. d'archéologie*, *s.v.*, *Cancelli*). At other times those who stood at the ' cancelli ' were the onlookers, not the actors ; thus St. Augustine invited Felix the Manichean to ' select anyone of the brethren standing at the " cancellum " ' as a guarantor for his good faith, *De Actis cum Felice Manichaeo*, xx., *P.L.* xlii. 534. Cicero, *In Verrem*, speaks of the ' cancelli ' as—in modern parlance—' the bar of the house.' Two famous examples of ' cancelli ' occur in the Basilicas of San Clemente and San Lorenzo, Rome.

[4] *Guelf.*, xviii. 2.

Bishop who came in after the vigil had begun: 'Precisely then, as I who have now just come to you, find you "watching" in His Name, so may the Lord Himself, in whose honour we have these celebrations, find His Church "watching" with the light of their minds when He comes.'[1]

But many of these Catechumens shrank from taking the final plunge and being baptized. It was but natural. Indeed it was—though for different reasons—what Augustine himself had done, and he could sympathize with their fears:—

Let each Christian among you set about—if he is still a catechumen—having his sins forgiven. For he already bears Christ's sign on his forehead, he already has the entry to the church, he already invokes Christ's great Name; but he is still bearing the burden of his sins, for they are not yet remitted, since such remission is only granted in holy Baptism. No catechumen should say to himself: I am afraid of becoming one of the faithful lest I should sin again afterwards. For not to sin again afterwards is in his power; whereas it is in no man's power not to have sinned. He has the means of not sinning; what can he do so as not to have sinned? For what is done is done; what is past you cannot make as though it had not been, but you cannot do what is future. Why, then, be misled by the devil's perverted suggestions? Such a man is afraid of future sins which he has not yet committed; he is not afraid for past sins which he has committed and of which he bears the burden. The former you have not committed; the latter are a burden on you. Perhaps you will not commit the future ones; indeed if you make up your mind not to, you will not commit them, just as, if you make up your mind to it, you can blot out past sins. 'No, but I cannot do that!' you say: then take refuge in Him who can blot them out.[2]

But when Catechumens did make up their minds they were most carefully instructed, first of all in their faith, and, therefore, the *Creed* was taught to them; then in their Christian life, and for this purpose they were taken through the *Lord's Prayer* clause by clause.

The *Lord's Prayer* [the Bishop tells them] is given to the

[1] *Wilmart*, iv. 3.
[2] *Casin.*, II. cxiv. 3.

newly-baptized, so that since we cannot here live without sin, we may say every day, 'Forgive us our trespasses.'[1] But 'since the due order is that you should first believe, and, as a result, call upon God, to-day you receive the Creed wherein you express your faith; after eight days you will be given the Lord's Prayer wherewith you call upon God.'[2] And again: 'After eight days you will have to give an account[3] of what you have to-day received (the Creed). Meanwhile your god-parents[4] will have to teach you so that you may be found well prepared, they will also teach you how to keep watch at break of day in the prayers which you here offer. The Creed is now given you for the first time for you to learn it with all diligence. No need for any of you to be afraid or to refuse to learn it through fear. Be quite at your ease, for we are your father and do not carry a ferula nor a schoolmaster's rod. If you make some verbal mistake that does not mean that you are wrong in the faith.'[5]

V—THE SACRIFICE OF THE MASS

Mass was said daily: 'Is not Christ daily immolated?[6] In harmony with this are the repeated allusions to daily Communion, a point on which Augustine always insists in his sermons on the Lord's Prayer when arriving at the petition: 'Give us this day our daily bread'; 'in that petition we can,' he says, 'ask for our daily temporal needs or for the Daily Bread of the altar';[7] elsewhere he says that the 'daily bread' may be the lessons read out in the church, or the hymns they have been singing,[8] but he always brings in the daily reception of the Holy Eucharist. When, then, we find it stated that the liturgical offices were not at first celebrated daily during Lent,

[1] *Guelf.* ix. 3.
[2] *Guelf.* i. 1; *cf. Sermons*, lvi. and lvii. 1.
[3] Redditurі estis.
[4] Parentes qui vos suscipiunt.
[5] *Guelf.* i. 11. In this sermon to those preparing for Baptism St. Augustine analyses the whole *Creed*, Article by Article, *Miscellanea Agostiniana*, i. pp. 441-450.
[6] *Enarr.* i. 15 *on* Ps. lxxv.; *cf. Ep.* xcviii. 9.
[7] *Ep.* liv. 2, xcviii.; *Sermo*, liv. 10, lvii. 7, lviii. 12, lix. 6, cccli. 6; *Enarr.* i. 15 *on* Ps. lxxv.; *Confess.* v. 9, ix. 13, etc. See, too, St. Chromatius, *Tract.* xiv. 5 on *St. Matthew*, *P.L.* xx. 276, 277.
[8] *Sermo*, lviii. 12.

and this on the ground that in ancient liturgies the *Tract* only appears for Mondays, Wednesdays and Fridays,[1] or when Duchesne says that Mass was only said on Sundays,[2] such statements must be taken as referring solely to the solemn and public services presided over by the Bishop.[3]

The Mass, of course, fell into two parts ; the Mass of the Catechumens and the actual Mass. First of all were read the *Acts* of the Martyrs whose *Memoria* was being celebrated.[4] The clergy then entered and the *Introit* was sung during the entry, much as the *Ecce Sacerdos Magnus* is now sung as the Bishop enters the church. The lessons were then read, and sonorously : *Lector ascendit*,[5] *sonante lectore*.[6] These were read daily,[7] and sometimes there were a great number of them : ' Out of all the lessons which we have just heard read, notice the first one, taken from the Prophet Isaias—for though we cannot remember or repeat them all, yet I fancy the last one read may still linger in your memories ' (Isaias lvii.). After this came the lesson from the Apostle (2 Cor. vii.).[8] The Lessons on Holy Saturday were, as we should expect, very numerous.[9] It is often possible to discover from a sermon

[1] Thurston, *Lent and Holy Week*, p. 187.

[2] *Christian Worship*, p. 230, quoted by Thurston,. *l.c.*, p. 152.

[3] For such ' private ' Masses note the words of can. 9 of the Council of Carthage held under Genethlius either A.D. 387 or 390 : ' If a priest celebrates privately without leave of the Bishop he must be deprived of his dignity ' ; here the expression ' agenda voluerit celebrare ' finds its parallel in St. Augustine's ' Quae aguntur in precibus sanctis . . . ut accedente verbo fiat Corpus et Sanguis Christi,' *Denis*, vi. 3, see pp. 54 and 56 below, also Batiffol in *J.T.S.*, July, 1915, p. 539, Hefele-Leclercq, II. i. 78.

[4] *Codex canonum Ecclesiae Africanae*, can. 46 ; Labbe, *Concilia*, ii. 1072 ; *Frangipane*, vi. 1.

[5] *Sermo*, xvii. 1. Note St. Chrysostom : after quoting Isaias xvii. he asks : ' Do you know where that is to be found ? Hardly any of you, I fear. Yet, week by week and two or three times a week, the Lessons are read to you. When the lector mounts the pulpit he first says whose book it is, this or that Prophet or Apostle or Evangelist. Then he reads out the passage for you to note it and to take it to heart, so that you may know not only what is there given but why it is written and by whom. Yet all in vain and to no purpose ; for your whole preoccupation is with the things of this world ; the things of the spirit do not interest you.' *Hom*. viii. on the *Epistle to the Hebrews*.

[6] *Ibid*., 2.

[7] ' In Ecclesiae lectiones quotidie auditis,' *Sermo*, lvii. and, as Augustine reminds Petilian, who had said that the Catholics were not allowed to read the Bible—' even when there is no sermon, lessons from Holy Scripture are read,' *Contra Litt. Petiliani*, ii. 210–211.

[8] *Sermo*, xlv. 1 and 3.

[9] *Sermo*, ii. ; *P.L.* xlvi. 821.

what Epistle or Lesson or Gospel was read. For example when preaching on Rom. vii. 24 a portion of *Tobias* was read ;[1] so, too, when preaching on a Saturday on the infirm man at the Probatica the virtue of almsgiving was illustrated by a Lesson from *Tobias* ;[2] in one sermon on *Dives and Lazarus* the Lesson was from 1 Peter i.[3] On a Wednesday in Easter week ' Lectiones evangelicae de domini nostri Jesu Christi resurrectione sollemniter ex ordine recitantur,'[4] where the expression ' ex ordine ' hardly seems to mean that all the Resurrection narratives were read, for the sermon deals solely with Luke xxiv. From Easter the *Acts of the Apostles* were always read, as Augustine repeatedly mentions.[5] In the East and in Africa John xvii. was read during Easter week, elsewhere on any Saturday before Palm Sunday.[6] The sermon, which followed on the reading of the Gospel, was based either on the *Introit* Psalm,[7] or on one of the lessons,[8] or on the psalm sung at the *Gradual*,[9] or on the Gospel itself. The lessons and the Gospel are always said to be ' read ' or ' recited '[10] whereas the psalms were sung : ' Audivimus, concorditerque respondimus, et Deo Nostro consona voce cantavimus.'[11]

On the occasion there referred to the sermon was on Psalm xciii. 12, though, if we are to judge by Augustine's *Enarrationes in Psalmos*, the entire psalm was sung both at the *Introit* and at the *Gradual*. These combined recitations and chantings were spoken of as ' the Apostle, the Psalms, and the Gospel,'[12] and

[1] *Mai*, clviii. 2–3.
[2] *Mai*, cxxviii. 4.
[3] *Mai*, xiii.
[4] *Mai*, lxxxvi, 1.
[5] *Mai*, lxxxvi. 3 ; *Sermon*, ccxxvii. ; *P.L.* xxxviii. 1100 ; *Sermon*, cccxv. 1 ; *De Praedest. Sanctorum*, 4.
[6] *Morin*, iii., see his *Praefatio* to the sermon, *Miscellanea*, i. 595–596.
[7] *Sermo*, xviii. 1.
[8] *E.g.*, *Sermo*, vii. 1, on Exod. xx. 3 ; xlvi. on Ezech. xxxiv ; xlviii.–xlix. on Mich. vi. ; xli. 1 on Ecclus. xii. where Augustine confined himself to preaching on verse 28 : ' for I cannot comment on it all,' etc.
[9] *E.g.*, *Sermo*, xix. on the *Miserere* ; *cp. Sermo*, cliii., clxv., etc.
[10] *E.g.*, *Sermo*, lii. 1, liii. 1, lv. 1, ci. 1, cii. 1, etc.
[11] *Frequenter cum Psalmista cantavimus* (Ps. xxvi. 14). *Sermo*, xl. 1 ; *cf.* xlvii. 1, cliii. 1, where the *Psalmista* is not ' the Psalmist ' or David, but the official cantor, see Council of Carthage, 398 (?), can. 10 ; Labbe, *Concilia*, ii. 1200.
[12] *Sermo*, clxv. 1, clxxvi. 1, where instead of the *Propheta* we have the *Apostolicon*, *cf. Sermo*, clxxx., etc.

on one occasion at least we can gather from the sermon which were the Psalms, Lessons and Gospel for that particular day, for the sermon in question dealt with the lesson from 1 Timothy i. 15, 16, *Fidelis sermo*, the *Gradual*, Psalm xciv.: *Venite adoremus*, and the Gospel was that of the Ten Lepers, Luke xvii. 12–19.[1]

The custom of singing the Psalms, 'whether before the Oblation or whilst what had been offered was distributed to the people,' was bitterly resented by a Catholic layman, Hilarus, who objected to this practice, then recently introduced at Carthage.[2] The reference is, of course, to the chant at the Offertory and at the *Communio*. Augustine's reply to Hilarus is unfortunately lost.[3]

But, *pace* Hilarus, the solemn, harmonious and devout singing of the Psalms was very dear to Augustine. He felt that it really made his people pray, provided they understood what they were singing. Hence his *Enarrationes in Psalmos* which are not, nor were meant to be, a commentary, but simply a series of devout meditations. The choral or alternating singing had been introduced at Milan by St. Ambrose who took it over from the Eastern Church,[4] and Augustine has told us how the psalmody affected him after his conversion,[5] also how he lamented that in some African churches people were remiss in singing Psalms.[6] From his own people he demanded an intelligent use of the Psalms[7] such as must, he felt, have characterized the Psalmody of the Jewish Temple;[8] they have, he insists to be sung 'cum laetitia . . . in sonum jubilationis';[9]

Every human soul [he says] that sings with attention the Psalms of God must needs then reflect on his own peculiar difficulties, he must experience a certain interior emotion when he realizes that he, too, is suffering from some trial, whether from within or from without, and then he will refer the words

1 *Sermo*, clxxvi.
2 *Retract*. ii. 11.
3 *Ibid*.
4 *Confess*. ix. 15.
5 *Ibid*., ix. 8–12.
6 *Ep*. lv. 34.
7 *Enarr*. i. 9 *on* Ps. xlvi.
8 *Enarr*. i. 1 *on* Ps. lxviii.
9 *Enarr*. i. 8 *on* Ps. xxxii.

he is singing to his own particular trial. . . . You see your neighbour singing, and singing with real feeling, you see how his very look accords with the Psalmist's words, you see how sometimes his face is even wet with tears, how he sighs as he repeats the words.[1]

When the sermon was over the words, *fit missa Catechumenorum*,[2] were pronounced, in other words, 'let the catechumens depart.' Then followed the real Mass, beginning with the Offertory.[3] So distinct was this Mass from the preliminaries, namely, the *Introit*, Epistle, *Gradual*, Gospel and sermon, that it might even be celebrated in another church: 'Let this suffice for you by way of a sermon in this holy place,' says Augustine, after a brief sermon on the Twenty Martyrs, 'for the days are short (*pauci*), and there still remains much for us and your charity to do in the Basilica Major.'[4]

More than one sermon shows how carefully St. Augustine took his neophytes, the newly baptized, through the Mass.

I promised you who have just been baptized that I would expound to you the Sacrament of the Lord's Table which you now see and of which you partook last night. You ought to know what you have received, what you are going to receive, and what you should receive every day. The bread, then, which you see on the altar is, when sanctified by the Word of God, the Body of Christ. That chalice there, or rather what that chalice contains, is, when sanctified by the Word of God, the Blood of Christ.

After explaining to them that this is the Sacrament of unity he repeats the words *Sursum corda* and *Gratias agamus* as preparatory to the 'sanctification of the Sacrifice of God,' 'after which we say the Lord's Prayer'; then comes the kiss of peace and the neophytes communicate. Augustine warns them against irreverent reception: 'What you see passes away: but the invisible Thing thereby signified does not pass away but abides.'[5] In another sermon to the neophytes:

[1] *Mai*, xv. 1.
[2] *Sermo*, xlix. 8: 'Ecce post sermonem fit missa catechumenorum, manebunt fideles, venietur ad locum orationis.'
[3] *Sermo*, xlix. 8; *Enarr.* i. 7 *on* Ps. cxxix.; *Ep.* cxlix. 16.
[4] *Sermo*, cccxxv. 2.
[5] *Sermo*, ccxxvii.; *cp. Ep.* cxlix. 16.

'The Sacrifice of our times is the Body and Blood of the Priest Himself. . . . Recognize then in the Bread what hung upon the tree; in the chalice what flowed from His side.'[1] The 'discipline of the secret' is constantly referred to by St. Augustine. With such a motley crowd drawn from all classes it was impossible to speak plainly on the mysteries of the faith save to the initiated: 'Cast not your pearls before swine,' the Master had said. Over and over again we meet with the expression *Quod norunt fideles*—'What the faithful understand.'[2] The catechumens, of course, understood that there was a 'mystery,' and presumably must have had more than an inkling of what was meant when Augustine said to them: 'In this our Daily Bread—if you understand what the faithful receive and what you yourselves will receive when you are baptized. . . .'[3] For the Bishop did not hesitate at times to address himself very plainly 'to both classes'—the baptized and the catechumens or *Audientes* :—

As we heard when the holy Gospel was read out, our Lord Jesus Christ exhorted us to eat His Flesh and drink His Blood, promising us eternal life if we did so. But you who have listened to this have not yet all understood. Those among you who are baptized, the faithful, know what He meant. But those of you who are still called 'catechumens' or 'hearers' could indeed be called 'hearers' as the Gospel was read out, but could you be described as 'understanders'? We will speak then to both classes.

He begins by reminding the faithful of the obligation of realizing what It is they receive, and then he turns to the others :—

But you who do not yet eat nor drink, hasten, now that you are invited, to this great banquet. During these days the magistrates[4] feed you; but it is Christ Who feeds you every day; that is His table set there in the middle. Why then is it,

[1] *Sermo*, iii. 1–2; *P.L.* xlvi. 827–828.
[2] *Sermo*, iv. 31, v. 7, lviii. 5; *Enarr.* ii. 28 *on* Ps. xxi., *Tract.* xxii. 5, 13 *in Joann.*
[3] *Sermo*, lvi. 10.
[4] Reading 'magistratus,' the reference being presumably to a time of scarcity when the municipality provided meals.

you 'hearers,' that while you see His table set you do not approach to the banquet ? Perhaps when the Gospel was read just now you were saying within yourselves : 'What can He mean when He says : " My flesh is meat indeed and My blood is drink indeed " ? How can the Lord's flesh be eaten or His blood drunk ? ' . . . The truth is veiled, but it will, if you wish it, be unveiled. Come forward and make profession of your faith, and you will find your question answered.[1]

Once more to the newly-baptized :—

You who are now re-born to a new life, and who are for that reason called 'infants,' you especially who now see this, listen attentively so that you may, as I promised you, realize what this means. And do you, too, you members of the faithful who are already accustomed to it, do you, too, listen ; for reminders are useful, lest we forget. What you see on the Lord's table is, so far as external appearances go, the same as what you are wont to see on your table at home. For the sight of a thing is one thing, its real meaning another.[2] For you yourselves are the same people as you were ; you are not bringing new faces here ! And yet you are 'new' ; old in bodily appearance, new by sanctifying grace, just as This, too, is new. Up to the present it is, as you see, bread and wine. But the sanctifying words reach it and that bread will then be the Body of Christ and the wine will be His Blood. The Name of Christ, the grace of Christ, does this ; with the result that what you see remains the same to the sight, but its power and efficacy are quite other than they were. Had you eaten of it before those words were said it would have filled your stomach ; if you eat of It now It will nourish your mind.[3]

On another occasion, speaking of those who crucified Christ but afterwards became Christians, he says : 'the Blood they had previously shed they afterwards drank.' [4] Once more, *ad Infantes :* after reminding them that they are like the Israelites coming out of Egypt, crossing the Red Sea and then eating manna in the desert : 'Your manna you receive by participating

[1] *Sermon*, cxxxii. 1.
[2] 'Ipse est visus, sed non ipsa virtus.'
[3] *Guelf.* vii. 1, *cf.* 'accedit verbum ad elementum et fit Sacramentum,' *Tract*, lxxx. 3 *in Joann.* ; *De Cataclysmo*, 3 ; *P.L.* xl. 694 ; *cf. De Trin.* iii. 10 ; *Sermon*, ccxxvii., etc.
[4] *Mai*, xxvi. 2, lxxxvi. 3.

in food from this altar' 'de sancti altaris participatione,'[1] surely a reminiscence of the words of the Canon of the Mass 'quotquot ex hac altaris participatione.' Once more, on John vi. :—

Eat Christ, then; though eaten He yet lives, for when slain He rose from the dead. Nor do we divide Him into parts when we eat Him: though indeed this is done in the Sacrament, as the faithful well know when they eat the Flesh of Christ, for each receives his part, hence are those 'parts' called 'graces.' Yet though thus eaten 'in parts' He remains whole and entire; eaten 'in parts' in the Sacrament, He remains whole and entire in heaven.[2]

Yet again: 'Dearly beloved, persevering meditation on all these things (the Resurrection of Christ) should be our daily celebration of Easter. We must not celebrate Easter to the exclusion of the thought of Christ's Passion and Resurrection, for His Body and Blood are our daily food.'[3]

At other times, however, we find him saying: 'Only the faithful understand—hence we cannot discuss it now,'[4] or: 'If we ask a catechumen: "Do you eat the flesh of the Son of Man and drink His Blood?" he does not understand what we are saying.'[5] This secrecy extended to the administration of the other Sacraments, too: 'Who would baptize in the presence of the profane?' asks Augustine.[6]

But when not hampered by the 'discipline of the secret' the plainness with which Augustine speaks about the Sacrifice of the Mass and of the Real Presence of Christ in the resulting Holy Eucharist is remarkable. In a sermon preached at the *Memoria* of St. Cyprian, or on the spot hallowed by his martyrdom, he says :—

Out of hatred of Christ the crowd there shed Cyprian's blood, but to-day a reverential multitude gathers to drink the

[1] *Mai*, lxxxix. 1.

[2] *Mai*, cxxix. 1; *cf. Sermon*, cxxxi. and *cp.* the many phrases in St. Thomas' *Lauda Sion: e.g.*, 'Manet tamen Christus totus sub utraque specie . . . nec sumptus consumitur . . . integer accipitur . . . non confractus, non divisus, etc.'

[3] *Wilmart*, ix. 2.

[4] *Enarr.* ii. 28 *on* Ps. xxi.; i. 12 *on* Ps. xxxix.

[5] *Tract*, xi. 3 *in Joann.*

[6] *De Unico Baptismo*, 2.

Blood of Christ . . . for Cyprian by his immolation here prepared this altar whereon neither does he feed nor is he given to us as our food, but whereon a Sacrifice is offered to God to whom Cyprian himself was offered.[1]

He even identifies Christ with the altar on which He is offered : 'He shows you His own altar, in other words Himself.'[2] What could be more emphatic than : 'When He commended to us His own Body, saying, "This is My Body," he bore His own Body in His very hands.'[3] Or again : 'He took into His hands what the faithful understand ; He in some sort bore Himself when He said : "This is My Body."'[4] After emphasizing the horror of the Jews who thought they were meant to eat 'the very flesh they saw and drink the very blood they saw,'[5] he goes on to speak with amazing openness of the way in which we eat Christ's very Body and drink His very Blood.[6] 'The very first heresy,' he says, 'was formulated when men said : "this saying is hard and who can bear it ?"'[7] And again : 'There was, then, a certain High Priest sent by the Lord God and He took from us what He would offer to the Lord. . . . Thou art the Priest, Thou the Victim, Thou the Offerer, Thou the Offering.'[8] 'Felix Victima, vera Victima, hostia immaculata !'[9]

Take, then, and eat the Body of Christ [he says to the Catechumens now receiving their final instructions] ; you, too, who, in the Body of Christ, are already members of Christ, do you take and drink the Blood of Christ. . . . For just precisely as It is changed into you when you eat It and drink It, so are you changed into the Body of Christ when you lead devout and obedient lives. [Augustine then read the words of Consecration or Institution] : You have read that, or at least heard it read, in the Gospels, but you were unaware that the Son of

[1] *Sermo*, cccx. 2 ; *cf. De Civitate Dei*, VIII. xxvii. 1.
[2] *Sermo*, cccxxxii. 2 ; *cf. Contra Faustum*, xx. 21.
[3] *Enarr*. i. 10 *on* Ps. xxxiii.
[4] *Ibid*., ii. 2.
[5] *Enarr*. i. 8.
[6] *Ibid*., ii. 10, ii. 25 ; *Sermo*, xc. 5, cxii. 4, cxxxii. 1, cccli. 1.
[7] *Enarr*. i. 23 *on* Ps. liv. See *Le sacrifice eucharistique dans la tradition Africaine*, G. Philips in the *Rev. Eccles. de Liége*, 1930–1931.
[8] *Enarr*. i. 6 *on* Ps. lxiv.
[9] *Enarr*. i. 6 *on* Ps. cxlix. 6.

God was that Eucharist. Now, however, with your hearts sprinkled and with a pure conscience, washed, too, with pure water, Accedite ed Eum et illuminamini, et vultus vestri non erubescent.[1]

This Sacrifice of the Mass was essentially a sacrifice for sin.[2] It was offered, too, for the living and the dead,[3] though only for those who have been baptized.[4] Evodius, Bishop of Uzala, when describing the holy death of a young man, says : ' We gave him honourable burial, such as befitted so great a soul ; for three days we sang hymns in praise of the Lord round his tomb, and on the third day we offered the Sacraments of our Redemption ' ;[5] while Augustine says to Apringius, the Proconsul and brother of the martyred Marcellinus, ' in the Holy Mysteries we pray for you.'[6]

When discussing in a letter to St. Paulinus the precise meaning attaching to St. Paul's ' obsecrationes, orationes, interpellationes, gratiarum actiones ' (Timothy ii. 1)[7] ' supplications, prayers, intercessions and thanksgivings ' in the Rheims and in the Revised versions, St. Augustine says :—

I prefer to understand by these terms what the entire—or very nearly the entire—Church observes, and I therefore take ' supplications ' as referring to those prayers which we offer in celebrating the Sacraments before we begin the blessing of that which lies on the Lord's table : ' prayers ' will refer to those which are said when It is blessed, sanctified and broken up for distribution ; practically the entire Church closes this whole petition with the Lord's Prayer.

The Greek word προσευχάς, here rendered *orationes*, had been taken by some as meaning ' adoration ' owing to the preposition. This Augustine will not allow ; he prefers to take it as meaning *ad votum*. Though his etymological notions need not concern us, his next words are of great interest :—

[1] *Denis*, iii. 3.
[2] *Contra duas Epistolas Pelagii*, iii. 16 ; *cp. De Civitate Dei*, X. xxxi.
[3] *De Anima et ejus origine*, i. 13.
[4] *Ibid.*, i. 10, 13, 14 ; ii. 15 ; iii. 18.
[5] *Ep.* clviii. 2.
[6] *Ep.* cxxxiv. 1.
[7] *Ep.* cxlix. 16.

Now all those things which we offer to God are said to be 'vowed,' more particularly the oblation at the altar, for in this Sacrament we express the supreme desire we have to dedicate ourselves to Christ, and so abide for ever with Him, compacted into the Body of Christ. The outward sign of this goal (*cujus rei Sacramentum*) is that 'we being many are one bread, one body.' Consequently I think that in the preparation of this sanctification the Apostle desired that *προσευχάς*, that is 'prayers,' should fittingly be made.

In full accordance with this he says, after the dismissal of the catechumens, *venietur ad locum orationis*,[1] and he continues: 'interpellations, or, as your (St. Paulinus') texts have it, "postulations," are used when the blessing is pronounced on the people; for at that moment the Bishops, as "advocates," offer to the merciful power of God those on whom they have laid their hands. When this is over and all have received the Sacrament, "thanksgiving" concludes the whole.'[2] Here we have some striking details: all prayers up to the Offertory at Mass are treated as 'supplications'; those down to and including the Communion of the faithful as 'prayers'; the last blessing is a 'postulation' or 'interpellation,' while the final 'thanksgiving' is appropriately so called.

Presumably the 'thanksgiving' is represented by our Post-communion prayer, and that seems to have been preceded by the blessing. The only portions of the Preface which had been preserved for us until the publication by Dom Morin of the *Sermones inediti*, see *Miscellanea Agostiniana*, vol. i, were the 'Sursum corda' with its response[3] and the 'Gratias agamus' with its response. But in one of those Sermons we have a detailed account of the opening words of the Preface:—

To-day you will hear what indeed you heard yesterday. But to-day you will have an explanation of what you heard and of the Response you made, though probably you yourselves were silent when the Response was made in spite of the fact that yesterday you were taught what the Response was. After

[1] *Sermo*, xlix. 8.
[2] *Ep*. cxlix. 16.
[3] *Sermo*, xxv. 2, ccxxvii.

the salutation with which you are already familiar, namely 'Dominus vobiscum,'[1] you heard the words 'Sursum cor,'[2] which are a compendium of the true Christian life. . . . That is why you make the Response 'Habemus ad Dominum.' . . . The priest then continues: 'Domino Deo nostro gratias agamus.'[3] . . . There then come the things done in the holy prayers which you will hear, for by the application of the Word is made the Body and Blood of Christ. Take away the word and it is but bread and wine, add the word and you have the Sacrament. And to those words you say 'Amen.'[4] . . . Then comes the *Lord's Prayer* which you have already received and learned. Why do we say it before receiving the Body and Blood of Christ? Because of our human weaknesses. For we may perchance have entertained unbecoming thoughts or spoken unfitting words, seen what it is better not to have looked on, listened with some pleasure to words which it would have been better not to have heard: then, if, by reason of this world's allurements and our human weakness, we have contracted any such stain it is washed away by the *Lord's Prayer* wherein we say: 'Forgive us our trespasses,' that so we may come forward in all security, with no fear lest what we receive we should be eating and drinking unto condemnation to ourselves. Then is said 'Pax vobiscum': a great mystery[5] that kiss of peace![6]

The triple *Sanctus* may be referred to by Tertullian:[7] 'Cui illa Angelorum circumstantia non cessat dicere "Sanctus, Sanctus, Sanctus"'; similarly in the *Acts* of SS. Perpetua and Felicitas: 'Et introivimus et audivimus vocem unitam dicentem "Agios, Agios, Agios"'; its general use was imposed

[1] 'The words "Dominus vobiscum" which you hear at the Lord's Table we are also wont to use when we salute (the people) from the apse, in fact whenever we pray we say those words,' *Guelf.* vii. 3.

[2] Elsewhere Augustine has 'corda' *e.g.*, *Sermon*, xxv. 2, ccxxvii, *De Dono Perseverantiæ*, 43; *Frangipane*, iii. 5; but *cp. Guelf.* vii. 3.

[3] The order is peculiar; elsewhere as we have it now: 'Norunt fideles ubi et quando dicatur "Gratias agamus Domino Deo nostro,"' *Sermon*, lxviii. 5; *Guelf.* vii. 3.

[4] Clearly, then, the words of Consecration were said out loud for all to hear and to make answer. The first allusion to the words being said in secret occurs in the *Ordo Romanus*, ii. ed. G. C. Atchley, 1905.

[5] 'Mysterium,' perhaps better 'Sacrament.'

[6] *Denis*, vi. 3; *P.L.* xlvi. 835.

[7] See Tertullian, *De Oratione*, iii., where he may imply that it was then the custom to recite the *Sanctus*.

by Pope Sixtus: 'Hic constituit ut intra actionem sacerdos incipiens populo hymnum decantaret "Sanctus, Sanctus, Sanctus, Dominus Deus Sabaoth."'[1] At what point the 'commemoration of the living' was made we do not know, but St. Cyprian refers to it as to a well-known custom.[2]

Nowhere do we find any allusion to the actual words of consecration,[3] though St. Augustine constantly refers to the fact: 'We receive for our soul's salvation what is duly consecrated by mystic prayer in memory of the Lord's Passion for us;[4] that Sacrifice,' he says, 'is the Body of Christ.'[5] We seem to have at least an echo of the *Unde et memores* in St. Cyprian,[6] also in St. Fulgentius of Ruspe, *c.* A.D. 530: 'cum tempore Sacrificii commemorationem mortis Ejus faciamus.'[7] The commemoration of the departed is mentioned explicitly:—

> The entire Church observes the tradition delivered to us by the Fathers, namely, that for those who have died in the fellowship of the Body and Blood of Christ, prayer should be offered when they are commemorated at the actual Sacrifice in its proper place, and that we should call to mind that for them, too, that Sacrifice is offered.[8]

In fact prayer for the dead was a marked feature of Christian life and practice in Africa:—

> We do not pray for the martyrs, but we do pray for the other dead of whom commemoration is made.[9] Nor are the souls of the faithful departed cut off from the Church, which even now is the Kingdom of Christ. Were it so, we should not make commemoration of them at the altar of God when we receive

[1] *Liber Pontificalis*, ed. Duchesne, i. 128, quoted by Dom Cagin, *L'Euchologis*, ii. 98.
[2] *Ep.* lxii. (lix.) 4; *Contra Epistolam Parmeniani*, iii. 29; *cf.* W. C. Bishop, *J.T.S.*, January, 1912, p. 272.
[3] But see *Denis*, iii. 3 quoted above, p. 59, and Batiffol in *J.T.S.*, July, 1915, 539.
[4] *De Trinitate*, iii. 10.
[5] *De Civitate Dei*, XXII. x.
[6] *Ep.* lxii. (lxiii.) 2 and 10.
[7] *Ad Fabianum*.
[8] *Sermo*, clxxii. 2, clxxiii. 1; *De Cura pro mortuis*, 6, *De Anima et ejus Origine*, ii. 21.
[9] *Sermo*, clix. 1; *cf.* cclxxxiv. 5, cclxxxv. 5, ccxcvii. 3.

the Body of Christ. Nor again, would it be of any avail to hasten to baptize a person who is in danger lest he should depart this life without it; nor would we make haste to reconcile a person who is perchance cut off from the body of the Church by being in a state of penance or having a guilty conscience. For we only do these things because the faithful, even those who have departed this life, are members of that body.[1]

The passages in the *Confessions* [2] and in the *Enchiridion* [3] are too well known to be repeated here. But note the following beautiful description of the natural grief caused by the death of some well-beloved one :—

Who would not feel sad when he looks at a body which had lived by the soul, but is now lifeless on that soul's departure? He who once walked now lies still; he who once talked is now dumb; his closed eyes no longer see the light; his ears are deaf to the sound of our voice; his bodily members have ceased to function; for there is no one there to set those feet in motion, no one there to move those hands, to stir the organs of sense to their due perceptions. Yet surely this is a house which some invisible indweller used once to adorn? Yes, but he has gone whom none ever saw; that alone remains which we cannot look on without grief! [4]

The vivid faith of an African mother appears in an inscription from Cartenna :—

MI . FILI . MATER . ROGAT . UT . ME .
AD . TE . RECIPIAS . [5]

A similar one hails from Narbonne or perhaps Autun :—

LAGGE . FILI .
BENE . QUIESCAS .
MATER . TUA . ROGAT . TE .
UT . ME . AD . (TE) RECIPIAS .
VALE.[6]

[1] *De Civitate Dei*, XX. ix. 2; *cf.* XXI. xxiv.; XXII. viii. throughout.
[2] *Confess.* ix. 12.
[3] *Enchiridion*, 100 and 110.
[4] *Sermo*, clxxiii. 3.
[5] Cabrol and Leclercq, *Monumenta Liturgiae*, i. 15.
[6] *Ibid.*, p. 16.

Fasting Communion was unquestionably the rule. When Augustine says in the course of a sermon : ' We have plenty of time ; we have begun early ; the breakfast hour is not near,' [1] he is taking the question of fasting reception for granted. Similarly when meeting the argument that Christ instituted the Holy Eucharist after the Last Supper, when neither He nor the Apostles were fasting, he says :—

> Surely there is no ground for repudiating the custom of the Universal Church in accordance with which people always receive fasting ? It was the will of the Holy Spirit that out of reverence for such a Sacrament the Body of the Lord should enter the mouth of a Christian previous to any other food.[2]

At the same time he is willing to make an exception for those who wish to receive on Holy Thursday during the Church Offices. His words are worth noting :—

> A probable argument appeals to some people in favour of offering and receiving the Body and Blood of the Lord after they have partaken of food, on one particular day in the year, the day, namely, when He instituted the Supper ; this they urge on the ground that they desire especially to commemorate that day. But I think it more fitting to offer (the Sacrifice) at an hour when a person who is fasting can, previous to the meal [3] at the ninth hour, come to the Offering. We compel no one, then, to take a meal before the Lord's Supper, nor, on the other hand, do we oppose those who hold another view. As a matter of fact, I do not think this practice is due to anything more than that on that day, in nearly every district, practically everybody bathes. And since some also keep the fast, the Sacrifice is offered early for the sake of those who would take a meal—since fasting and bathing are incompatible—but It is offered in the evening for the sake of those who are not fasting.[4]

The Council of Hippo—at which Augustine was present

[1] *Sermo*, cxxviii. 6.
[2] *Ep*. liv. 8.
[3] Reading ' ante ' with seven MSS. ; if we read ' post ' with the rest of the MSS., it will be question of people coming for the Sacrifice only and not for Communion.
[4] *Ep*. liv. 10 ; see *Codex canonum Africanae Ecclesiae*, 41 ; Labbe, *Concilia*, ii. 1069.

as the preacher but not as a bishop, for he was not yet consecrated—enacted that Communion was to be received fasting 'except on the anniversary of the day on which the Lord's Supper is celebrated.'[1]

The martyrs were solemnly commemorated, and their *Memoriae* as well as those of holy nuns were 'known to the faithful,' 'fidelibus notum est quo loco martyres et quo defunctae sanctae moniales ad altaris sacramenta recitentur.'[2] This commemoration may presumably be identified with our *Nobis quoque peccatoribus.* The recitation of the *Pater noster* followed.[3] It is said to be recited daily 'at the altar';[4] the petition 'Give us this day our daily bread' may be offered either with reference to our daily needs or to the daily Bread of the Holy Eucharist;[5] the people are exhorted to strike their breasts at the words 'Forgive us our trespasses.'[6]

The kiss of peace or the *Pax* followed, and the people responded *Et cum spiritu tuo.*[7] The 'breaking of the Bread' was a very solemn function, and is spoken of as falling under the 'discipline of the secret,' *norunt fideles.*[8] The Holy Eucharist was received by each into his hands which he 'cupped,' *conjunctis manibus*;[9] after receiving he said 'Amen.'[10] During the distribution a Psalm was sung.[11] Then came the 'thanks-

[1] Can. 28 of the Council of Carthage, 397, which took over the decisions of Hippo; Labbe, *Concilia*, ii. 1171.

[2] *De Sancta Virginitate*, 46; *cf. De Civitate Dei*, XXI. x.

[3] *Ep.* cxlix. 16, and p. 61 above.

[4] *Sermo*, lviii. 12; *cf. Sermo*, ccxxvii.; *De Dono Perseverantiae*, 63.

[5] *Sermo*, lix. 6; *cf. Sermo*, liv. 10; lvii. 7; lviii. 5.

[6] *Sermo*, cccli. 6.

[7] *Sermo*, ccxxvii.; *Enarr.* i. 13 *on* Ps. cxxi. i. 10, *on* Ps. cxxiv.; *cf.* Tertullian, *De Oratione*, 14.

[8] *Sermo*, ccxxxiv. 2; *cf. La 'Fraccion del Pan' en los primos tempos de Cristianismo*, R. Ejarque, 1916; G. Lecordier, *La doctrine de l'Eucharistie chez S. Augustin*, 1930; J. Wilpert, *Fractio Panis : la plus ancienne représentation du sacrifice eucharistique*, 1896.

[9] *Contra Epistolam Parmeniani*, ii. 13; *cf. Contra Litt. Petiliani*, ii. 53; St. Cyprian, *De lapsis*, 15; St. Pacian, *De Poenitentia*, 2. Pope Cornelius narrates how Novatus compelled people while they were holding the Blessed Sacrament to swear that they would not desert his faction; *Ep.* ii. 7; Eusebius, *Hist. Eccles.* vi. 43, 44; vii. 9. See above, pp. 27, 43, 46, etc., for the case of St. Perpetua.

[10] Eusebius, *l.c.*, vii. 9. See an inscription in the chapel of Bishop Alexander at Tipasa in Numidia:—

OMNIS . SACRA . CANENS .
SACRAMENTO . MANUS .
PORRIGERE . GAUDENS .

[11] *Retract.* ii. 11; *cf.* perhaps *Ep.* cxlix. 16.

giving' or our Post-Communion prayer.[1] Finally, the Bishop gave his blessing ; St. Augustine may be paraphrasing the form of blessing when he says : ' we pronounce the blessing over the people, desiring for them and begging from the Lord that He may make them abound in mutual charity with one another and towards all men, and be, according to the riches of His grace, strengthened with might in His spirit.'[2]

VI—CHURCH BUILDINGS IN AFRICA

In early Christian days in Africa, as elsewhere, the faithful met in private houses, and later on, in times of persecution, the same was necessarily the case, notably during the Diocletian persecution.[3] With the gradual decay of Paganism the heathen temples were, as was to be expected, converted into Christian churches ; of this we have examples at Cirta, Tebessa, Lambesis, Tigzirt, Tipasa, and elsewhere ;[4] but, so far, archæological research has failed to find vestiges of any churches anterior to the Diocletian persecution A.D. 303–305.[5]

Christians, especially in Africa, spoke of their churches as ' Basilicas,' ' in ecclesiis basilicisque,' says Victor of Vita,[6] for, as Dom Cabrol points out, ' Ecclesia, Basilica or Basilica Dominicum are convertible terms.'[7] The same term was used in Italy, though less exclusively ; Paulinus, the biographer of St. Ambrose, speaks of the ' Basilica Ambrosiana quae dicitur,'[8] though really it was the ' Basilica SS. Naboris et Felicis MM ' ; he also mentions the Basilica Portiana,[9] as well as the Basilica SS. Apostolorum.[10]

The ruins of these basilicas are scattered all over Africa ; at Tipasa, for instance, are remains of two basilicas, of two

[1] *Ep.* cxlix. 16.
[2] *Ep.* clxxiv. 4 ; *cf.* 1 Thess. iii. 12, and Ephes. 16.
[3] St. Optatus, *De Schismate Donatistarum*, 14.
[4] *Cf.* St. Augustine *Sermo*, clxiii. 2 ; *Ep.* ccxxxii. 3.
[5] Leclercq, *Dict. d'Archéologie, s.v., Afrique*, col. 659.
[6] *De Persecutione Vandalica*, i.
[7] *Dictionnaire d'Archéologie*, i. 626.
[8] *Vita Sti. Ambrosii*, 13.
[9] *Ibid.*, 18.
[10] *Ibid.*, 33.

minor churches and of two cemetery-chapels.[1] The Basilica of St. Salsa in that town apparently dates from before the end of the fourth century A.D., and the ruins indicate a length of some hundred feet with a breadth of forty-eight feet.[2] At Timgad are remains of two basilicas, of one chapel and of one cemetery-chapel;[3] one of the basilicas was known as the 'Basilica Gregorii' after its founder, Flavianus Gregorius; it perhaps dates from the time of Constantine. Another church there, measuring 198 feet by 54 feet, formed part of an immense monastery covering over 20,000 square yards.[4] At Tigzirt, the ancient Rusuccuru, there seem to have been four basilicas which were divided between the Catholics and the Donatists.[5] At Matifou or Raguniae are vestiges of a church which was destroyed by the Vandals and the ruins of which were only unearthed in 1899–1900;[6] at Utica was a 'Basilica Massae Candidae'[7] in memory of an immense crowd of Martyrs 'more in number than the hundred-and-fifty-three fishes,' says St. Augustine,[8] who also seems to imply—'moneat te Massa redditi debiti mei'[9]—that they were so named from the mass of whitening bones; at Lemellae the basilica was seized by the Donatists when Julian the Apostate was acting as their patron;[10] at Tebessa are still to be seen the ruins of a magnificent fourth-century church of which the columns, the apse, the presbyterium and the baptistery are even now standing;[11] here St. Crispina suffered martyrdom under Anulinus.[12] 'She was a wealthy and delicate woman.'[13] 'What joy filled that holy

[1] Leclercq, *Dictionnaire d'Archéologie*, i. 659; S. Gsell, *De Tipasa urbe*, 1894.
[2] *Ibid.*, 688–689.
[3] *Ibid.*, 659; Babelon, *Carthage romain*, p. 108.
[4] Ballu, *Guide illustré de Timgad*, 1897.
[5] See Duprat, *Monographie de la Basilique de Tebessa* (*Theveste*), 1895–1896.
[6] See L. Bertrand, *Villes d'or*.
[7] *Sermon*, cccvi. 2, cccxi. 10.
[8] *Enarr.* i. 9 *on* Ps. xlix., 'martyrum atque multorum,' *Morin*, xiv. 1; they died on August 18, A.D. 259; *cf. Sermon*, cccvi. and perhaps *Sermon*, cccxxx.; Possidius, *Indiculus*, ix.
[9] *Enarr.* i. 17 *on* Ps. cxliv.
[10] St. Optatus, *De Schismate Donatistarum*, ii. 17.
[11] See Ch. Duprat, *Monographie de la Basilique de Tebessa* (*Theveste*), 1895-1896.
[12] *De S. Virginitate*, 43.
[13] *Enarr.* i. 13 *on* Ps. cxx.

woman Crispina whose Feast we are keeping to-day! She rejoiced when they arrested her, when they led her to judgement, when they cast her into prison, when they brought her out in chains, when they threw her on the rack, when her case was tried, when they condemned her; in all these things she rejoiced, while unhappy people even deemed her unhappy who was then rejoicing before the Angels!'[1] Similar remains appear at Thelepte[2] where the African Council of A.D. 418 would seem to have been held,[3] where also St. Fulgentius of Ruspe was born; the ruins are some three and a half miles in circumference. Similar ruined basilicas are found at Ammedaera[4] and at Sicca Venerea—so-called owing to a temple of Astarte there, and officially known as 'Colonia Julia venerea Cirta Nova Siga,' otherwise 'New Cirta,'[5] but now called Kef; the present Mohammedan mosque there occupies the site of the old Christian church.[6]

These African basilicas differed much in form from those at Rome,[7] for they were rectangular[8] in shape and generally had three, sometimes five,[9] and, in the case of the famous Damous el Kharita, nine naves.[10] The semicircular apse was used for meetings;[11] this apse was square on the outside, the angles

[1] *Enarr.* i. 3 *on* Ps. cxxxvii.

[2] S. Gsell, *Edifices chrétiens de Ammadera et de Thelepte*, 1902.

[3] Labbe, *Concilia*, i. 1577; Hefele-Leclercq, *Histoire de Conciles*, ii. 73.

[4] See Gsell, *l.c.*, and L. Bertrand, *Villes d'or.*

[5] S. Gsell, *Atlas archéologique*; *cf.* Labriolle, *Latin Christianity*, p. 189 m.; St. Augustine, *Ep.* ccxxix. 1; Mommsen, *Provinces*, ii. 332.

[6] Monceaux et Gauckler, *Basiliques chrétiennes de Tunisie*, Plates v.–vii.

[7] Where, according to St. Optatus, *De Schismate Donatistarum*, ii. 4, *cf.* i. 13, there were no fewer than forty Basilicas. These African Basilicas were more Syrian and Egyptian than Roman in form, Leclercq, *L'Afrique chrétienne*, ii. 27. See views of the churches recently laid bare at Jerash (Gerasa) in Palestine, *Quarterly Statement of the Palestine Exploration Fund*, October, 1929, January, 1930; also *Art and Archaeology*, March, 1925.

[8] 'From the number of the columns we may be able to gauge the shape of the Tabernacle, whether it was square or round or a square-sided oblong with longer and shorter sides, as is the case with many Basilicas,' St. Augustine, *In Heptateuchum*, II. clxxvii. 5.

[9] As at Dermech and Feriana, *cf.* Gauckler, *Basiliques chrétiennes.*

[10] This was discovered in 1878, see Delattre, *Notes Archéologiques . . . de la Basilique de Damous-El-Karita*, also Leclercq, *Dict. d' Archéologie*, *s.v.*, *Carthage*, col. 694; it measured some 200 by 135 ft.; it is difficult to identify it with any Basilica of St. Augustine's time.

[11] When describing the scene when the populace at Hippo were so stirred by the devotion and piety of Pinianus, the husband of the younger Melania, that they made determined efforts to have him ordained priest, though he was already married, Augustine says that 'those of higher rank and dignity

being occupied by sacristies. The west end, with its façade, often had three doors, and the upper walls were pierced for windows.[1] Very rarely does there seem to have been any portico or square atrium as at Rome.[2] The choir stood in front of the Presbyterium and access to it and the altar was by the 'cancelli' or grills and up two little stairways.[3] At Tipasa, Tebessa or Theveste, and at other places, remains of galleries with staircases on the outside have been found. The floors were covered with mosaics and the capitals, lintels and cornices seem to have been lavishly decorated.[4] At Dermech in Carthage the five naves are separated by columns which carry the window-pierced walls.[5]

That these African churches must have been very large is evidenced by the number of naves some of them had. St. Augustine more than once refers to the great and imposing size of a church; he speaks, for instance, of 'this mighty and spacious church'[6] and thanks God 'Who has consecrated this spacious church by the presence here of St. Cyprian's holy body.'[7] The church referred to was that of the 'Mappalitia,' a term thought to refer to rustic huts;[8] here St. Cyprian's body lay, whereas the basilica at Carthage[9] stood on the spot where he was martyred. The numerous excavations carried out by the French archæologists have corroborated the above statements about the size of the basilicas. At Haidra, for instance, the ruins show that the church there measured some 188 feet in length and 45 in breadth,[10] while the church at Feriana seems

came up to him in the apse,' *Ep.* cxxvi. 1. After the birth of their two children Pinianus and Melania made vows of perpetual chastity, Pinianus becoming a monk in a monastery on Mt. Olivet and his wife becoming Abbess of a convent hard by, see Holweck, *Saints*, *s.v.*, *Pinianus*.

[1] Victor of Vita, *Persecutio Vandalica*, i. 13.

[2] Leclercq, *Dict. d'Archéologie*, i. 669.

[3] *Sermon*, cccxxii.; *Ep.* xxxiv. 2; Paulinus, *Vita S. Ambrosii*, 14.

[4] *Sermon*, xv. 1.

[5] Dermeche church, discovered by Gauckler in 1899, was built on the corner of what the discoverer describes as 'a vast cemetery which began at Dermeche on the sands and spread right up the slopes to the very gates of Carthage,' *Nécropoles Puniques*, 1915, ii. 252.

[6] *Sermon*, ccclxii. 7.

[7] *Sermon*, cccxii. 6.

[8] See St. Jerome, *Prologue* to his *Commentary on Amos*.

[9] *Sermons*, i. 5 and ii. 9 *on* Ps. xxxii.

[10] Monceaux et Gauckler, *Basiliques chrétiennes de Tunisie*, p. 16.

to have been as much as 206 feet long and 73 feet broad.[1] Nor did these churches stand isolated and alone ; they were often surrounded by huge dependent buildings, including large Baptisteries which were sometimes cruciform, at other times hexagonal or octagonal in shape.[2] These various buildings, including side-chapels, were added by degrees to the original church until the whole mass covered an immense area ; at Timgad, for example, the church buildings, including a huge monastery, covered some 20,000 square metres.[3] When the Donatists, owing to the anti-Catholic policy of Julian the Apostate, returned in triumph in A.D. 361 from exile, they at once seized on these wealthy churches with their immense appanages, and there can be little doubt but that the schism would have ended far earlier than it did had not their leaders dreaded more than anything the consequent disestablishment.[4]

The sites of many of these historic basilicas have experienced great vicissitudes. Sometimes, as at Maktar, an old pagan temple was converted into a Christian church and could boast of a crypt, so, too, at Henchir Krima a Roman temple was thus transformed. But at Sicca and Sufes, the modern Sbiba, the converse has taken place, for the present mosque stands on the site of what was once a Christian church.[5]

In Carthage itself there seem to have been at least twenty churches.[6] To mention but a few : we know of the Basilica of St. Agesilaus,[7] also of the 'Basilica Novarum' in the 'Area nova' where, as St. Augustine informs us, Mensurius the Archbishop, when asked to surrender copies of the Bible during the Diocletian persecution, hid in the 'Basilica Novorum'—the spelling is uncertain—copies of certain heretical works which the ignorant searchers took for Bibles.[8] There was also

[1] *Ibid.*
[2] *Ibid.*
[3] Ballu, *Guide illustré de Timgad.*
[4] 'Vos qui pro cathedris vestris sic contenditis injuste !' *Psalmus contra partem Donati*, line 244 ; *cf. Contra Litteras Petiliani*, ii. 134, 203, 224 ; *Contra Gaudentium*, i. 50 ; *Ep.* xciii. 15 and 50 ; see, too, Labbe, *Concilia*, i. 1524.
[5] Monceaux et Gauckler, *l.c.*
[6] Babelon, *Le Carthage Romain*, p. 108 ; Dureau de la Malle, *Topographie de Carthage*, p. 214.
[7] *Vita S. Fulgentii*, 56.
[8] *Breviculus Collationis*, iii. 25, *cf. Sermon*, xiv. ; for the spelling see Victor of Vita, *l.c.*, i. 3.

the 'Basilica Celerina'[1]—so-called from Celerina, mother of the Martyrs Laurence and Ignatius[2]—this basilica is perhaps to be identified with that erected in honour of the Scillitan Martyrs,[3] though the Maurist editors of St. Augustine seem to distinguish them when they assign Sermon clv. to the 'Basilica Scillitanorum' and Sermon clxxiv. to the 'Basilica Celerina.' Then there was the 'Basilica Coelestis,' formerly, as its name shows, the temple of the goddess Coelestis, the African counterpart of Astarte. According to St. Prosper her temple was immense,[4] and her cult was very popular in heathen Africa; St. Augustine frequently refers to her and to the veneration in which the Africans held her.[5] St. Cyprian was, of course, held in the highest veneration by the Africans:—

Is there any part of the world where Cyprian's eloquent words are not read, his doctrine praised, his charity appreciated, his life held up as a model, his death venerated, his martyrdom celebrated? . . . Many people in all sorts of places possess copies of his voluminous writings; but we here must needs be more thankful than most for we are allowed to have amongst us his holy body and limbs; so let us pour out before his tomb our heartfelt prayers to the Lord to whom he was well pleasing and by whose grace he was what he was.[6]

Victor of Vita speaks of 'the two beautiful and spacious churches of the holy Martyr Cyprian, one where he shed his blood, the other where his body lies buried, a spot known as the Mappalitia.'[7] In the former, known as the 'Memoria,' Augustine preached Sermons xiii., xlix., cxiv., cxxxi., cliv., cccv., cccix.–cccx.; in the 'Mappalitia' Sermons xxxiv., cccxi.–cccxiii., cccxxv., while various *Enarrationes* on the Psalms were delivered in one or other of these churches, *e.g.*

[1] *Sermons*, xlviii. and clxxiv.; Victor of Vita, *De Persecutione Vandalica*, I. viii. 25.

[2] See Leclercq, *L'Afrique Chrétienne*, i. 136.

[3] Victor of Vita, *l.c.*, i. 3.

[4] *De Praedestinatione*, iii. 38, *cf.* Mommsen, *Provinces*, ii. 331.

[5] *De Civitate Dei*, II. ii.; *Sermon*, cv. 12; *Enarr.* i. 7 *on* Ps. lxii. m., i. 14 *on* Ps. xcviii.

[6] *Guelf.* xxvi. 2; *cp. Sermon*, cccx. 1, *P.L.* xxxviii. 1412–1413, and *Denis*, xv. 2.

[7] Victor of Vita, *l.c.*; St. Augustine, *Sermon*, lxi. 17; Monceaux, *Le tombeau et les basiliques de S. Cyprien* in *Rev. Archéologique*, xxxix. 1906, p. 189; see above, p. 69, and below, p. 84.

Sermons i–ii. on Ps. xxxii.—*cf.* i. 5, ii. 9; Sermon i. on Ps. xxxviii. i. 23, on Ps. lxxx.—*cf.* i. 23, perhaps, too, on Ps. lxxxv. In 1899 there were laid bare the ruins of a hitherto unknown basilica which had been erected on the site of an ancient Punic cemetery at Dermech on the Carthaginian seashore. All its columns had been taken from other places and the area covered some 130 yards in length and 68 in breadth; it is supposed to date from the time of Justinian, after the Vandal domination was over; but the Arabs destroyed it in A.D. 698.[1]

In addition to the above there was the 'Basilica Fausti,' so-called from its builder, Faustus; here the XVIth. Council of Carthage was held on May 1, 418.[2] St. Augustine often preached in it,[3] and it was so large that Bishop Deogratias was able to use it as an asylum for the refugees from Rome when that city was sacked by Genseric in A.D. 455.[4] Then there were the Basilicas of Gratian,[5] of Honorius,[6] of St. Peter 'in regione tertia,'[7] of St. Paul 'regionis sextae,'[8] as well as the 'Basilica secundae regionis' in which several of the great African Councils were held, notably those of A.D. 404, 407, 409 and 410;[9] in this basilica, too, Stilicho published his decree against the Donatists in A.D. 407. But the most famous of all these great Carthaginian churches was that known as the 'Restituta,' so-called perhaps from Restitutus, Archbishop of Carthage, but more probably it was so termed as having been 'restituta' by the usurping Donatist occupants. This was certainly the case at Uzala where Evodius, the Bishop of that See, says that a miracle was wrought 'in a basilica which had been usurped by the Donatist party, but afterwards "restituta" to Catholic

[1] See Monceaux et Gauckler, *Basiliques chrétiennes de Tunisie*, 1913, p. 16; Delattre, *La Basilique de Dour-es-Schott à Carthage*, Académie des Inscriptions, July, 1922.

[2] See note on *Sermon*, ccclix. *in P.L.* xxxviii.

[3] *Sermon*, xxiii., *cf. Sermo*, cxi. 2, where Augustine asks his hearers to come on the morrow to the 'Basilica Fausti' there to celebrate the anniversary of the consecration 'of the old man Aurelius' their Archbishop; see, too, *Sermon*, cclxi.

[4] Victor of Vita, *l.c.*, I. viii., II. vi., IV. 9.

[5] *Sermon*, clvi.

[6] *Sermon*, clxiii.

[7] *Sermon*, xv.

[8] *Sermon*, cxix, *cf. Miscell. Agost.* i. 665.

[9] See Mansi, *Concilia*, iii. 794, 798, 799; v. 496, 498, 500, 503; Hefele-Leclercq, ii. 157; *P.L.* xliii. 811–812.

Unity, as it is to-day. From this fact it derives its name, and is rightly called "Ecclesia restituta."'[1] The 'Restituta' at Carthage was also known as the 'Basilica Major,'[2] a title which may have been given to it as being what we should call the Cathedral Church, for Victor of Vita says that the 'Bishops always resided there.'[3] It had a third title—even a more glorious one—for in it reposed the bodies of SS. Perpetua and Felicitas who were regarded as its patrons.[4] St. Augustine often preached there and the African Councils of A.D. 390 and of September, 401, were held there.[5]

Nor does this list complete the tale of Carthaginian churches. St. Augustine tells us of a basilica which had once belonged to a sect known as the 'Tertullianists' who had, however, practically died out in his day and whose church had in consequence been handed over to the 'Catholica.'[6] Another church, the 'Theoprepia,' was famous not only because it had been taken over from the Donatists, but also because it was on its walls that Augustine caused the *Acta* of the great Conference

[1] *De Mirabilibus S. Stephani*, i. 7; *P.L.* xli. 839; *cf. De Gestis Pelagii*, 26; *P.L.* xliii. 808.

[2] See Delattre, *Basilica Majorum ou Une Area Chrétienne à Carthage*, Académie des Inscriptions, December, 1924, an account—with an album of views—of ruins which he had excavated some twenty years previously. There is some doubt about the spelling 'Major*em*' or 'Major*um* (*P.L.* xxxviii. 1194 note); if the latter spelling is correct, then the meaning is obscure. See, too, his *La Basilica Majorum, Tombeau des Saintes Perpétue et Felicité*, Académie des Inscriptions, 1906–1907. Delattre denies the identification of the 'Restituta' with the 'Basilica Majorum,' *cf.* Leclercq, *Dict. d'Archéologie, s.v., Carthage*, col. 2251. But the reading 'Major*um*' seems commonly accepted; in which case this Basilica is not to be confounded with the Basilica Major which Dom Morin suggests may have been the same as the Basilica Leontiana, *Miscell.* i. 666, on the ground that *Sermon*, cxlviii. on the Twenty Martyrs was followed on the same day by *Sermon*, cclx. at the Mass and 'in the Basilica Leontiana,' while in the case of two similar sets of two sermons on the same Feast of the Twenty Martyrs the first in one case was in the 'Memoria' of the Martyrs, *Sermon*, cccxxv. 2, 'adhuc nobis in majore basilica restant quae agamus cum Charitate vestra,' *Sermon*, cccxxvi., while in the latter instance *Sermon*, cclvii. was also at the 'Memoria' and followed by *Sermon*, cclviii., 'ad Basilicam Majorem, eadem die,' see notes on these *Sermons* in *P.L.* xxxviii., cols. 132, 1193–1194.

[3] Victor of Vita, *l.c.*, I. v. 15.

[4] In the *Acts* of the 2nd Council of Carthage the two titles are combined: 'Basilica Perpetua(e) Restituta,' *cf. Sermo*, cccxlv.

[5] *E.g.*, *Sermones*, xix., xxix., xxxiv., xc., cxii., clxv., cclviii., cclxxvii., cclxxx., ccxciv., cccxli. and *Enarr.* i. *on* Ps. lvii., *cf. Miscell.* i. 665–666, *Denis*, xiii., *P.L.* xlvi. 855.

[6] *Ep.* cxxxix. 1; *Retract.* ii. 27.

between the Catholics and the Donatists in A.D. 411 to be affixed.[1] Yet another was the 'Basilica Tricliarum' or 'Tricillarum'; Augustine tells his hearers at the close of a sermon that the next sermon will be in the church so named.[2] It is not quite certain whether the 'Basilica Florentia' was in Carthage or in Hippo Diarrhytus. For when preaching in an unnamed city for the dedication of the church, Augustine said: 'You have honoured your Bishop in calling this church "Florentia,"'[3] and though it has been suggested that this was the 'Basilica Florentia' in Carthage, and built by the famous Archbishop Aurelius whose other name was Floreas,[4] it seems far more probable that the reference was to the well-known Florentius, Bishop of Hippo Diarrhytus and a great personal friend of Augustine's.[5] He was one of the chosen Counsellors at the Conference of 411,[6] where he was made the subject of a violent attack by Victor, the Donatist Bishop of Hippo Diarrhytus.[7] He was twice chosen to represent at the Imperial court the case of the Catholics against the Donatists, once by the African Council of October 13, 408, when he, with Praesidius and Benenatus, was commissioned to state their case to the Emperor,[8] and again by the Council held in June, 410, when Possidius, Augustine's life-long friend and afterwards his biographer, was added to their number.[9] Florentius and three other Bishops combined with Aurelius the Archbishop and with St. Augustine to write to the Bishops of Gaul on the erroneous views of a monk, Leporius, on the Incarnation.[10]

We know of at least two other basilicas in Hippo Diarrhytus, those of St. Quadratus and the 'Margarita.' In the former

[1] *Sermo*, ii. 29 *on* Ps. xxxii., whence it would seem that both the following sermons were preached there; *cf. Sermo*, liii. See, too, *Gesta Collationis* (A.D. 411).

[2] *Enarr.* iii. 29 *on* Ps. xxxii.; see J. Vauitrin, *Les basiliques chrétiennes de Carthage*, 1933.

[3] *Sermon*, ccclix. 9. This may now be regarded as certain, *cf. Sermon*, cccxcvi. and Dom Morin, *Miscell. Agost.* i. 666.

[4] See the note in *P.L.* xxxix. col. 1599.

[5] 'Sanctus frater et coepiscopus meus, Florentius,' *Ep.* cxliii. 4.

[6] *Collatio*, i. 55; *P.L.* xi.

[7] *Ibid.*, Nos. 139 and 142.

[8] Labbe, iii. 810; Hefele-Leclercq, ii. 158.

[9] Hefele-Leclercq, ii. 159; Morcelli, *Africa Christiana*, iii. 43.

[10] *Ep.* ccxix, A.D. 426.

St. Augustine certainly preached one sermon,[1] perhaps two.[2] Quadratus was Bishop of Utica and one of the Twenty Martyrs who were especially venerated all over Africa, and were known as the ' Massa candida.'[3] In the Basilica Margarita, he preached a sermon in aid of the Bishop there who, finding his basilica too small, was pulling it down and building a bigger one. There seems to have been some grumbling about this on the part of some of the faithful who had long worshipped there, and presumably the good Bishop hoped to pacify the discontented ones by getting Augustine to preach. The latter took the bull by the horns :—

If you saw someone pulling down his house you might blame him ; yet if you knew his reason for doing so you would not do so. Now here we are in this basilica and it is cramped, there is something small about it ; consequently the master of the house wants to build another, with the result that this one has to come down. Perhaps some of you when you saw the work of demolition begin said : ' Isn't this the spot where we used to pray ? Did we not call on the Name of God here ? What are people about, pulling it down ? ' You were disgusted at what they were doing because ignorant of their reason for so doing. Augustine then applied the same idea to God who does things that seem strange to us simply because we do not know why He does them, whereas He Himself knows full well what He is doing and why.[4]

He further illustrates his point by an exceedingly happy allusion to the amphitheatre in the town which had recently fallen down ; there had been no need for any one to pull it down, as they had done with the basilica.[5]

At Hippo Regius, ' Hippo nostra ' as St. Augustine calls it, were many basilicas, for example that of St. Leontius ;[6] not

[1] *Denis*, xxiv. ; *P.L.* xlvi. 921 ff., preached on Sunday, September 26—after A.D. 410 ; *cf. Miscell. Agostin.* i. 141.

[2] The fact that *Denis*, xviii. is a sermon on St. Quadratus is no proof that it was preached in the basilica dedicated to that Martyr at Hippo Diarrhytus, for *Morin*, xv., on the same Saint, was preached in St. Cyprian's church at Carthage.

[3] See p. 76 for the question of their identity.

[4] *Denis*, xxi. 8.

[5] *Ibid.*, 13.

[6] *Sermons*, cclx. and cclxii. ; but *cf.* pp. 75–76.

only was it dedicated to him but, as Bishop of the See, he apparently built the church ; at any rate St. Augustine, when preaching there on the Ascension, said : 'This church celebrates to-day its own peculiar feast, for to-day is the deposition (or anniversary of the death) of its builder, St. Leontius.'[1] Two Feasts in honour of the Saint were kept, one in February, the other, just referred to, at Ascensiontide.[2] Another famous basilica was that of The Twenty Martyrs.[3] It is not certain who these were ; Baronius identified them with Twenty Martyrs of Tarsus; but since they were held in special veneration in Africa it is more probable that they suffered there.[4] Augustine has preserved for us the names of three of them : Victoria, Valeriana and a Bishop, Fidentius.[5] These Martyrs were much appealed to by people in need, and Augustine has preserved a quaint story of a tailor named Florentius who

lost his cloak and had not enough money to buy himself another. So he appealed to the Twenty Martyrs whose 'Memoria' is very well known here, and in a loud voice he prayed for a new cloak. But some boys standing by heard him and jeered at him ; they taunted him all the way back, shouting out that he had asked the Martyrs for 500 folles[6] wherewith to buy himself clothes ! The tailor, however, held his peace. But as he walked along he found a huge fish washed up on the shore and just about dead. The boys, who were somewhat repentant by this time, helped him to get hold of it, and he sold it for 300 folles for pickling to a cook named Catosus, a good Christian man, to whom he told the whole story. The tailor meant, of course, to purchase some wool with the money so that his wife might at her convenience make him the necessary clothing. But when the cook came to cut up the fish he found a gold ring in its stomach ! Filled with compassion for the tailor, and also with a feeling of awe, he at once gave him the ring, adding as he did so : 'See how the Twenty Martyrs have clothed you !'[7]

[1] *Sermon*, cclxii. 2 ; *cf.* 'In die natalis S. Leontii' ; *Ep.* xxix. 1.

[2] *Ep.* xxix. 8 and *Sermon*, cclxii. 2.

[3] Augustine preached several sermons here, *e.g.*, *Sermon*, cxlviii. and perhaps ccxxvi.

[4] See note in *P.L.* xxxviii. col. 1449, on *Sermon* cccxxv.

[5] *Ibid.*

[6] The 'follis' was a small copper coin.

[7] *Civitate Dei*, XXII. viii. 9.

Other basilicas in Hippo Regius were the 'Basilica Pacis,' where the historic Council of Hippo, A.D. 393, was held, and at which Augustine preached—though not yet a Bishop, and without a seat in the Council; in the same basilica thirty-three years later he was to explain to his beloved flock his reasons for asking them to accept Eraclius as his successor.[1] There was also a 'Basilica Regionis secundae,'[2] a 'Basilica S. Stephani'—or rather a 'Memoria' to him[3] where, as Augustine says with calm conviction, the most amazing miracles were wrought:—

Let me first of all remind you of what I know, indeed of what we all know to be a fact, one which cannot be disputed, one which meets the eyes even of those who have no wish to see it: that miracles of healing are every day being worked at the 'memoria' of the glorious and blessed Martyr (St. Stephen) here reposing in our midst. Yet equally certainly many who ask for cures are not heard. Now such people should not imagine they are being left in the lurch; their first duty is to examine their own hearts and see if they are asking aright.[4]

There was also one dedicated to St. Theognis.[5] The Donatists, too, had, as everywhere, their basilica where Proculeianus sat and where 'in their drunken orgies they stimulate themselves by singing Psalms of purely human composition and sneer at us for our restrained singing of the Prophets' Divine Canticles.'[6]

[1] *Ep.* ccxiii. 1, A.D. 426.
[2] Can. 90 inter *Canones Ecclesiae Africanae*, *cf.* Labbe, iii. 787, 794, 798.
[3] *Civitate Dei*, XXII. viii. 13, 15, 20; *Sermons*, ccxvii. and cccxviii.; see, too, *De Mirabilibus S. Stephani* by Evodius, *P.L.* xli. Appendix.
[4] *Wilmart*, xii. 5; *cp. Sermon*, cccxxiii. 3.
[5] *Sermon*, cclxxiii. 7. Theognis was Bishop of Hippo and was present at the Council held by St. Cyprian, A.D. 256, *De Baptismo contra Donatistas*, vi.
[6] *Ep.* lv. 34.

III

A BRIEF SKETCH OF THE LIFE OF ST. AUGUSTINE OF HIPPO[1]

I. The Early Years—II. At Cassiciacum—III. His Life as a Bishop—IV. His Companions and Disciples—V. Personal Details.

O Pater amplissime Augustine, qui non solum vitae sanctitate, sed etiem miro sapientiae tuae fulgore, Christi Ecclesiam luce propria, luce plena, luce fixa irradiasti ! Si enim sapientia lux est, quis in Ecclesia Dei ita lucet ut Augustinus ? A sole omnia lucent, ab Augustino omnes qui post ipsum fuerunt doctores sapientiae lumen accipiunt, ipse vero propria luce lucet, quam a nullo hominum, sed a Deo solo accepit, nullo enim tradente, nullo magistro cunctas didicit disciplinas.—St. Thomas of Villanova, *Concioni de S. Augustino.*

I—THE EARLY YEARS : AFRICA, ROME AND MILAN

The future Bishop of Hippo and Doctor of the Church was born in A.D. 354, probably in November, at Tagaste in

[1] Of the various 'Lives' of St. Augustine we can only mention a few : *St. Augustine, Bishop of Hippo*, Anonymous, by a Vincentian Father, 2nd ed. 1888 ; Gill, Dublin ; popular but useful. L. Bertrand, *Vie de S. Augustin*, 15th ed. 1913 ; *Autour de S. Augustin*, 5th ed. 1921. C. Boyer, S.J., *S. Augustin*, in the series *Les Moralistes Chrétiens*, 1932. Ad. Hatzfeld, *S. Augustin*, 4th ed. in the *Saints* series, translated into English by E. Holt, 1898. G. Lapeyre, *S. Augustin et Carthage*, in *Miscellanea Agostiniana*, Rome, ii. G. Papini, *Sant' Agostino*, 1929 ; translated as *St. Augustine*, by M. P. Agnetti, 1930. Portalié, S.J., *S. Augustin*, in the *Dictionnaire de Théologie*, Vacant et Mangenot, 2268–2472, Paris, 1901 ; a very detailed study of the Saint's writings. For Possidius' *Vita Augustini* see below, pp. 125–6. Poujoulat, *Histoire de S. Augustin ; sa vie, etc.*, 1845–1846 ; 1847, 1852. P. Schaff, *Der hlg. Augustinus*, translated as *The Life and Labours of St. Augustine, a historical sketch*, 1854. A. Shirley, *St. Augustine of Hippo*, 1925.—More General Studies : E. Gilson, *Introduction à l'étude de S. Augustin*, 1929, 2nd ed., 1931. E. Jolivet, *Etudes sur S. Augustin*, 1930. G. Kruger, *Augustin, Der Mann und sein Werke*, 1930. Eleanor MacDougall, *St. Augustine. A Study in his personal religion*, 1930. W. Montgomery, *St. Augustine : Aspects of his Life and Thought*, 1914. *A Monument to St. Augustine, Essays written in Commemoration of his XVth Centenary*, 1930. B. J. Warfield, *Studies in Tertullian and Augustine*, 1930. *Etudes sur S. Augustin* (A.D. 430–1930), par R. Jolivet, *cf.* Boyer et autres, 1930 (*Archives de Philosophie*, Vol. vii.). *Mélanges augustiniens à l'occasion du xve. centenaire*, Paris, 1931. O. Noordmans, *Augustinus*, 1932.

Proconsular Africa,[1] where, too, his bosom friend Alypius, afterwards its Bishop, also first saw the light. Augustine's parents were people of moderate circumstances; Possidius, the saint's disciple, friend, and biographer, calls them *Curiales*,[2] a term which suggests that the family held some official position in the municipality. They had to make considerable sacrifices to secure for the boy the education for which his undoubted talents fitted him,[3] though as a matter of fact the expenses were mainly borne by one of the principal citizens of Tagaste, Romanianus,[4] who to the end maintained a warm affection for Augustine and committed his son Licentius to his care. This boy was devotedly attached to Augustine, and, endowed with a really philosophical mind,[5] took a vivacious if somewhat boyish part in the discussions at Cassiciacum.[6] He had a poetical bent, too,[7] and penned in honour of Augustine a poem which the latter criticized somewhat scathingly.[8] Unfortunately Licentius' proclivities harmonized only too well with his name, and though thoroughly converted to Christianity he at one time gave Augustine much anxiety.[9]

Augustine's father, Patritius, was a pagan, and Augustine, in one of his eulogies on his mother, tells us of his father's savage outbreaks of temper, despite his usually kindly disposition.[10] But such was Monica's patience that, unlike some 'milder-mannered' husbands in the town who left conspicuous marks of their brutality on the faces of their spouses, he never seems to have laid hands on her, much to the astonishment of other sadly battered wives who scanned Monica's features for

[1] Strictly speaking, in Numidia Proconsularis.

[2] *Vita*, i.; *cf.* *Confess.* ii. 5, ix. 19, 22; *Sermo*, ccclvi. 13, Pope Innocent I, *Ep.* ii. 14, iii. 9. 'Strictly speaking, "curiae" are those sections (curiae) which we find established in every city, whence the terms "curiales" or "decurions," for people, that is, who are in a "curia" or "decuria," and you are well aware that every city has such "curiae" . . . a single city may have many such, at Rome, for instance, there are thirty,' *Enarr.* i. 7 *on* Ps. cxxi, etc. *De Cura Mortuorum*, 15.

[3] *Confess.* i. 19, iv. 28–31.

[4] *Contra Academicos*, ii. 3.

[5] *Ibid.*, i. 4 and 29.

[6] *De Ordine*, i. 21; *Beata Vita*, 6, etc.; *Retract.*, 6.

[7] *Contra Academicos*, i. 4 and 29.

[8] *Ep.* xxvi. 3.

[9] *Ep.* xxvi. 3, xxvii. 6, xxxii. 3.

[10] *Confess.* ix. 19: 'Sicut benevolentia praecipuus ita ira fervidus.'

what, knowing Patrick's disposition, they expected—perhaps even hoped—to find there. Monica, however, would contrive to turn such criticisms by a laughing remark that matrimony was but a school for maids.[1] Her patience with her husband had its reward : ' Finally, at the close of his life here on earth, she gained even her husband for Thee,' [2] for Patritius became a catechumen when Augustine was sixteen and died a year later.[3] Augustine's brother, Navigius, apparently became a Christian at the same time as Augustine ; he was presumably the *frater meus quiddam* who was present at the deathbed of St. Monica.[4] He, too, took part in the discussions at Cassiciacum,[5] in the course of one of these he naively acknowledged that he had foolishly yielded to the blandishments of the boy Licentius, and eaten some sweets ' despite the state of my health.'[6] Whether there were other sons we do not know, though the expression *frater meus quiddam* and Augustine's remark that Monica *nutrierat filios* [7] might suggest that she had several sons.[8]

To Augustine's sister, whose name is unknown to us, but who was for a long time superior of his monastery of nuns at Hippo, we are indebted for the Rule of St. Augustine. For it was owing to difficulties that arose in the community when, on her death in A.D. 424, a new superior succeeded her that the Bishop drew up this letter of practical guidance in the religious life.[9]

For Augustine's early years we have the testimony of his own *Confessions*. He was sent to school at the pagan town of Madaura,[10] which lay some twenty miles south of Tagaste and

[1] *Ibid.*, 21.
[2] *Ibid.*
[3] *Ibid.*, ii. 6, iii. 7 ; *Contra Academicos*, ii. 3.
[4] *Confess.* ix. 27.
[5] *De Ordine*, i. 5.
[6] *De Beata Vita*, 19.
[7] *Confess.* ix. 22.
[8] Augustine names ' my nephew, Patrick, the sub-deacon,' immediately after ' the deacons and subdeacons ' of his monastery ; and classes him among those ' whom I have found to be all that I could wish,' *Sermon*, ccclvi. 5.
[9] *Ep.* ccxi. 4
[10] *Confess.* ii. 5. Madaura is the present Madaourouch, a spelling which confirms the reading Madauros of the early texts. For its pagan character see *Epp.*, xvii. 4, ccxxii. and ccxxxii. See S. Gsell, *Atlas archéologique. Fouilles à Souk-Arhas*, p. 33. For Apuleius see above, p. 21, *Epp.* xvi., xvii. and cii. 32, also *De Civitate Dei*, VIII., xvi.

was famous as the birthplace of the African poet Apuleius. In this as in all African schools flogging was the rule : 'When I was a child,' Augustine pathetically says, 'I besought Thee with no little earnestness that I might not be flogged at school, but Thou didst not hear me.'[1] When at Madaura he began to suffer painfully in his stomach, so much so that his parents removed him for a year.[2] Already a catechumen, he went in his sufferings to his mother and begged, though unavailingly, for baptism, for he thought he was going to die.[3] After the year's rest at Tagaste his parents sent him to Carthage where he devoted himself to the study of literature. Here, in his sixteenth year, he fell into vicious habits.[4] A son, Adeodatus, was born to him when he was about eighteen, and it was not till years after, when he was at Milan, that he broke off his irregular life ; the mother of Adeodatus returning to Africa and there vowing herself to a life of chastity.[5]

Adeodatus seems to have died almost immediately after Monica : 'Speedily Thou didst snatch him from this world, and I recall his memory with all the more "security" [Augustine's favourite word] in that I have no reason to feel anxious about his boyhood or his youth.'[6] The boy's early development astonished his father : 'When hardly fifteen he surpassed many learned and serious-minded men in his intellectual equipment, . . . in him there was naught of me save my sin.'[7] He, Adeodatus, also took his part in some of the discussions at Cassiciacum : 'With us,' says his father, 'was one who, though the youngest of us all, yet possessed a mind which—unless I am prejudiced by my love of him—gives great promise for the future.'[8] In the discussion *De Beata Vita*, held during three days to celebrate Augustine's thirty-third birthday, Adeodatus, in answer to the question : 'Who possesses God ?' gave in the simplicity of his heart a reply which Monica

[1] *Confess.* i. 14, *cf. Contra Julianum, Opus Imperfectum*, iii. 154, vi. 13.
[2] *Ibid.*, ii. 5.
[3] *Ibid.*, i. 17.
[4] *Ibid.*, ii. 2.
[5] *Ibid.*, vi. 25.
[6] *Confess.* ix. 14.
[7] *Ibid.*
[8] *De Beata Vita*, 6.

applauded, but which must have caused his father a twinge: 'He whose soul is unspotted.'[1]

It was presumably during his sojourn at Carthage that Augustine contracted the habit of swearing which he had such difficulty in breaking off later on.

I myself used to swear regularly, for I had contracted that baneful and deadly habit. But, dearly beloved, I assure you that from the time I began to serve God and realized how harmful a thing was this habit of swearing I got terrified, and through fear I put a bridle on what had become a rooted habit.[2]

Apropos of the danger of swearing or of getting unreliable people to take their oath upon things, Augustine tells a story which, he says, he had never told to his flock before, of a certain well-known inhabitant of Hippo 'a simple, innocent-minded man, with whom many of you, indeed all you people of Hippo, were familiar, and whose name was Tutuslymeni'—a proper name which, curiously enough, Augustine declines, calling him 'Tutumlymeni' in the accusative. His story, which he himself told to the Bishop, was to the effect that he had had occasion to make a neighbour take his oath on some matter, and the latter had sworn falsely. That night Tutuslymeni dreamed that he was brought before the Supreme Judge who asked him why he had made a man take an oath when he knew perfectly well that he was not to be trusted. When Tutuslymeni replied that the man in question had denied that he had some property of his; 'Would it not have been better to have gone without your property than to endanger the loss of that false swearer's soul?' asked the Judge. Whereupon he was so severely flogged that when he awoke he found his back covered with weals. Tutuslymeni, concludes Augustine, 'committed a grave sin and he was punished for it; but any of you who after this sermon and such a warning as that go and do the same thing will commit a far graver sin!'[3]

It was at Carthage, too, that he got entangled in the Manichaean heresy,[4] though he never became more than an 'auditor'

[1] *Ibid.*, 12.
[2] *Sermo*, clxxx. 10; *cf.* cccvii. 5; and *Vita*, by Possidius, 25.
[3] *Sermon*, cccviii. 5.
[4] *Confess.* v. 14.

amongst them,[1] certainly never a 'priest' of the sect.[2] Still his connexion with them lasted for nine years, or from his nineteenth to his twenty-eighth year, that is from A.D. 373–382.[3] But he gradually grew disgusted with them,[4] for he realized the hollowness of their pretensions. 'When once I had worked out and analysed the point which disturbed me most and on which Manichaeanism more especially insisted, I realized that it would be difficult to discover a more inept—or to put it more mildly—a more incautious and baseless statement than theirs, namely that the Sacred Scriptures had been corrupted!'[5] With his customary thoroughness Augustine set to work and subjected the claims and the writings of the sect to a most minute and laborious examination. The results appeared in the marvellous series of treatises against them which covered the period between his ordination and his consecration as a Bishop, and even later:[6] 'How could I,' he writes to Cresconius, 'have ever passed a judgment on Manichaeanism, that most pestilential and empty-headed teaching which every Christian must needs anathematize, if I had been content merely to talk about it and could not appeal to the many and various treatises I had compiled against it, and so left no loophole for your calumnies against me?'[7]

[1] *Contra Fortunatum* 3; *Contra Litt. Petiliani*, iii. 24; *De Utilitate Credendi*, 2.

[2] *Contra Litt. Petiliani*, iii. 20.

[3] *Confess.* iii. 11–15, iv. 1, v. 10.

[4] *De Moribus Manichaeorum*, 68–72; *Contra Epistolam Fundamentalem*, xi.

[5] *De Utilitate Credendi*, 7; *cf. De Beata Vita* 4.

[6] The principal anti-Manichaean treatises will be found in *P.L.* xlii.; *De Utilitate credendi*, *c.* A.D. 391; *De duabus animabus contra Manichaeos*, *c.* 391; *Disputatio contra Fortunatum Manichaeum*, *c.* 392; *Contra Adimantum Manichaei discipulum*, *c.* 394; *Contra Epistolam Manichaei quam vocant Fundamenti*, *c.* 397; *Contra Faustum Manichaeum*, *c.* 400, *cf. Retract.* II. vii. 1; *Acta cum Felice Manichaeo*, December 7 and 12, 404; *De Natura Boni*, *c.* 405; *Contra Secundinum Manichaeum*, *c.* 405; *Contra Adversarium Legis et Prophetarum*, *c.* 420. Incidentally Augustine deals with the Manichaeans in many places, *e.g.*, *De Vera Religione*, *Epp.* lxxix. and ccxxxvi.; *Sermons*, i., ii., xii., l., cliii., clxxxii., cclxxxvii.; *Enarr. on* Ps. cxl. See, too, *De Genesi contra Manichaeos* and *De Moribus Manichaeorum*.

[7] *Contra Cresconium*, iii. 91. See Stoop, *Essai sur la diffusion du manichéisme dans l'empire Romain*, 1909; J. Rickaby, S.J., *The Manichees as St. Augustine saw them*, 1925; M. de Beausobre, *Histoire critique de Manichée et du manichéisme*, 1734; A. Dufourcq, *De Manichaeismo apud Latinos quinto sextoque saeculo*, 1900; P. Alfaric, *Ecritures mani-*

Astrology long exercised a fascination for him,[1] though he set his face against the practice of divination[2] to which so many Christians were addicted in his day.[3] Disgusted, too, with the unruly manners of the students who attended the lectures he was now himself giving at Carthage,[4] Augustine made up his mind to go to Rome and teach there.[5] But on this point he had to reckon with Monica, who was most anxious he should not go. 'I deceived her,' he laments, 'when she clung to me and tried to make me come back home or at least to let her come with me; I pretended that I was anxious not to leave a friend of mine until the wind allowed him to sail.'[6] All are familiar with the picture depicting Augustine in the stern of the vessel while Monica kneels on the shore in an agony of soul. The little chapel in the background of that picture is the memorial chapel of St. Cyprian, where Monica spent the night in prayer for her wayward son.[7] In Rome he promptly fell ill; 'but though in such danger I did not then want to be baptized; alas, how much better I was when I was ill as a boy, for then I begged for baptism.'[8] His state of soul during those first months was truly pitiable; for long it was uncertain which way he would turn. He might so easily have become another Julian the apostate, but the grace of God was to make him Augustine of Hippo.

It was Monica, with her prayers and her daily attendance at Mass,[9] who saved him, as he acknowledges with touching simplicity. For she, of course, followed him to Milan despite the tempestuous seas which frightened the sailors but which

chéennes, 1918; F. Cumont, *Recherches sur le manichéisme*, 1908; on the Manichaean documents discovered in the Fayoum in 1931, see *Syria*, xxxiii., p. 403, *J.T.S.* July, 1933, p. 266 and especially April, 1934, where F. C. Burkitt shows that St. Augustine's views of the Manichees and their doctrines were justified, p. 184. A. V. W. Jackson, *Researches in Manichaeism, with special reference to the Turfan fragments*, 1932. *Writings in connection with the Manichaean Heresy*, in the translation edited by M. Dods, Vol. v.

[1] *Ep.* lxv. 6–15.

[2] *Confess.* iv. 5.

[3] *De Catechizandis rudibus*, 11; see his *De Divinatione Daemonum*, *P.L.* xl. 581 ff., and edited separately by Haar, 1931.

[4] *Confess.* v. 14.

[5] *Ibid.*

[6] *Ibid.*, 15.

[7] *Ibid.*

[8] *Ibid.*, 16.

[9] *Ibid.*, 17.

had no terrors for her, ' for in a vision Thou hadst promised her safety.'[1]

Let us take a glance at the future Saint, Bishop and Doctor, now that he is on the threshold of conversion. Not very tall, dark, spare, a typical African, hot-blooded, with a zest for life and what it will bring him, already an acknowledged master of what was then known as ' rhetoric,'[2] but which really stood for what we should call a liberal education, an African with the Roman world at his feet, a man with a great gift for friendship which never left him, one who was apparently seldom allowed to be alone but always had friends and disciples round about him—yet a man always ill at ease. The Manichees have failed him, and he feels tempted to coquet with the Academicians who maintained that there really was nothing knowable.[3]

Certainly his was a mixed character. A slave to baser passions, yet always yearning for the truth. A mystery to himself and to his friends. At one time praying intensely for the gift of chastity : ' Give me chastity and continence ; yet not now ! '—truly the prayer of a boy, as he himself says : ' At the threshold of my adolescence.'[4] At another time proclaiming that chastity is impossible ; now striving after the truth ; now despairing of finding it.[5] Yet he tells us himself that in the midst of all this mental turmoil, when in the depths of a degradation which he felt so piteously, the love of the Holy Name of Jesus never left him,[6] and throughout all that time of doubt he seems to have gone to church, though perhaps not quite regularly.[7] Again and again do his thoughts turn to the Catholic faith—his mother's faith, indeed his own faith, for he had been a catechumen.[8] Yet he is haunted by the conviction

[1] *Confess*. vi. 1.

[2] Even after his conversion he concedes that three things could disturb his peace of soul : ' fear of losing those whom I love, fear of pain and fear of death,' *Soliloquium*, i. 16 ; *cp*. *Ep*. xxxi. 1–3 to St. Paulinus.

[3] *Confess*. v. 19, 25 ; *De Beata Vita*, 4 ; *De Utilitate Credendi*, 20 ; *De Civitate Dei*, XIX. i. 1–3. Later on the Donatists scoffed at him as an ' Academicus,' *Contra Litt. Petiliani*, iii. 24.

[4] *Confess*. viii. 17.

[5] *Ibid*., vi. 1.

[6] *Ibid*., iii. 8.

[7] *Ibid*., iii. 5.

[8] *Confess*. i. 17, yet *cp*. v. 25.

that that faith could never be maintained in face of the arguments of the Manichees.[1]

But all the time it was God he wanted, though he was not aware of it.[2] As we read *The Confessions*, penned thirteen years after his conversion, we feel that from his childhood Augustine had been a theologian, that he had really never had any interest save in the things of the spirit and therefore of God. The poignant words of the opening chapters are full of this cry for God, for understanding of Him, possession of Him; and though at the time he penned these undying phrases he had come into that inheritance, we feel that he is looking back on the years of strife and fixing once and for all in deathless words the thoughts and yearnings that had haunted him first in the old days at Madaura, then at Carthage and Rome, and finally at Milan. This may explain, in part at least, how it was that from the instant of his conversion Augustine seems to enter into the very fullness of his Catholic inheritance.

At one stride he appears as the finished theologian; he never wavers; he grows in knowledge, of course; he even changes his mind on the workings of grace,[3] and on the interpretations to be put on such passages as Romans vii.;[4] but all the time he *knows*.[5] St. Paulinus must have felt this when he wrote—extravagantly as we might think—' I consult you, you who see as it were through God.'[6] Severus, the Bishop of Milevis, felt the same when he hailed Augustine as ' God's truly busy bee, building up for us combs full of heavenly nectar,'[7] words

[1] *Ibid.*, v. 25.
[2] *Ibid.*, ii. 8, 10.
[3] *De Praedestinatione Sanctorum*, 7, as against his teaching in *Quarundam Propositionum in Ep. Sti. Pauli ad Romanos*; *cf. Retract.* 1, xxii. 3, 4.
[4] *Contra Julianum*, vi. 70.
[5] His wonderful discussions on the difference between wisdom and knowledge in *De Trinitate*, xii. 22, for example, find as complete expression in his very early *Ad Simplicianum*, ii. 2, *P.L.* xl. 140. Indeed, it is to this very work that Augustine makes appeal when insisting that on the question of grace and predestination he has always held the doctrine which he defended against Pelagius: ' This doctrine,' he says, ' I began to understand more clearly in that examination of the question which I wrote to Simplicianus of blessed memory, the Bishop of Milan, in the very outset of my Episcopate; then I recognized that the very beginning itself of faith was God's gift, and I asserted that doctrine,' *De Dono Perseverantiae*, 52 and 55, *P.L.* xlv. 1026–1027, and *De Praedestinatione Sanctorum*, 8, where he repeats these assertions, *P.L.* xliv. 966.
[6] *Ep.* cxxi. 14.
[7] *Ibid.*, cix. 1.

afterwards to find their echo in the well-known lines of the great hymn :—

> Magne Pater Augustine
> Frangis nobis favos mellis
> De Scripturis disserens.

Count Darius, too, uses expressions in writing to Augustine which would shock modern ears :—

> Thrice—nay four times, nay as someone, I have forgotten who, says—a thousand times happy should I be were it possible for me to meet you and gaze on your bright features with their starry look, if I could but hear your divine voice and listen to you singing the praises of God ! Then I should almost fancy I was standing in heaven's courts, listening to God's voice, not from a distance as when in church, but actually standing close to His tribunal ! [1]

Augustine's stay at Rome was not a lengthy one. First of all he discovered that if the students at Carthage had been rowdy, those at Rome, though perhaps more civilized, had a bad habit of not paying their fees.[2] How unruly the students of Rome were and how much strict supervision was needed appears from an imperial enactment of March 12, 370, some fifteen years previous to Augustine's arrival in Rome as professor of rhetoric.[3] We learn thence that students had to have

[1] *Ep.* ccxxx. 1 ; *cp. Ep.* ccxxxiv.

[2] *Confess.* v. 22.

[3] 'De Studiis Liberalibus Urbis Romae et Const(antino) P(olitanae) Imppp. Val(entini)anus, Valens et Gr(ati)anus AAA ad Olybrium P(raefectum) U(rbi).

'Quicunque ad Urbem discendi cupiditate veniunt, primitus ad magistrum census provincialium judicum, a quibus copia est veniendi, ejusmodi litteras perferant, ut oppida hominum et natales et merita expressa teneantur : deinde ut in primo statim profiteantur introitu, quibus potissimum studiis operam navare proponant ; tertio et hospitio eorum sollicite censualium norit officium, quo ei rei impertiant curam, quam se adseruerint expedire. Idem immineant censuales ut singuli eorum tales se in conventibus praebeant, quales esse debent, qui turpem inhonestamque famam et consociationes, quas proximas putamus esse criminibus, aestiment fugendas neve spectacula frequentius adeant aut adpetent vulgo intempestiva convivia. Quin etiam tribuimus potestatem, ut, si quis de his non ita in urbe se gesserit, quemadmodum liberalium rerum dignitas poscat, publice verberibus adfectus, statimque navigio superpositus abicietur urbe domumque redeat. His sane qui sedulo operam professionibus navant, usque ad vigesimum suae aetatis annum Romae liceat commorari. Post id vero temporis qui

official leave to come from the provinces for the purpose of study; that inquiry was made concerning their homes, their family and qualifications; that their lodgings were under control, and that their behaviour while in Rome was well looked after. They were warned about the company they kept, about frequenting the theatre and about dining out. If proved unruly they were liable to a public flogging and might then be shipped home at once. A yearly report, too, on the progress of such as really did work, was demanded.

Augustine began to feel, too, that the profession of rhetoric was becoming debased, and that in consequence he might be morally responsible for the bad use to which his pupils would almost certainly put the training he was giving them.[1] Moreover, he had developed such serious chest trouble that it seemed probable that he 'would not be capable of the labour involved in that profession.'[2]

All these factors combined to make him regard as a remarkable intervention of Providence[3] a piece of news which now reached him. At that time the Prefect of Rome was Symmachus, that illustrious pagan whose defence of Paganism, the *Relatio Symmachi*, has come down to us, and who is perhaps to be identified with the '*potentissimus* Senator' who befriended Alypius.[4] Augustine, then, heard that the Prefect had received from the Milanese a notification that they wanted a professor of rhetoric from Rome, and that they would put a public conveyance at the disposition of any candidate.[5] Augustine took up the challenge, went to Milan, delivered his oration and carried off the prize. Afterwards he was ashamed of what he

neglexerit sponte remeare, sollicitudine praefecturae etiam impurius ad patriam revertatur. Verum ne haec perfunctorie fortasse curentur, praecelsa sinceritas tua officium censuale commoneat, ut per singulos menses, qui vel unde veniant quive sint pro ratione temporis ad Africam vel ad ceteras provincias remittendi, brevibus comprehendat, his dumtaxat exceptis, qui corporatorum sunt oneribus adjuncti. Similes autem breves ad scrinia mansuetudinis nostrae annis singulis dirigentur, quo meritis singulorum institutionibusque compertis utrum quandoque nobis sit necessarii, indicemus. Dat. III. id. Mart. Trev(iris) Valentiniano et Valente III AA. Conss.'—*Codex Theodosianus*, XLV., ix. 1, ed. Mommsen.

[1] *Ibid.*, ix. 2.

[2] *De Beata Vita*, 4.

[3] *Confess.* v. 23.

[4] *Ibid.*, vi. 15, 16.

[5] *Confess.* v. 23; *cf. Vita*, i. *Contra Litt. Petiliani*, iii. 30.

felt had been but a piece of lying rhetoric, yet ' So it was that I came to Milan and to Ambrose the Bishop . . . all unknowing I was led by Thee to him, that through him I might be brought, well knowing it, to Thee.' [1] He speedily fell under the charm of Ambrose's personality, perhaps even more impressed by an eloquence and learning which surpassed that of Faustus the Manichee, ' though Ambrose,' he says, ' was not so cheery nor so attractive in manner as was Faustus.' [2] Augustine frankly confesses that his object in attending the Bishop's sermons ' may not have been a correct one,' for it was his eloquence and learning rather than the soundness of his doctrine that attracted him ; still the fact remains that he and Monica used to go regularly, albeit from different motives, to hear Ambrose.[3]

What a picture he has left us of the saintly Bishop :—

I could not, he says, ask him what I wanted as I would have liked to have done, for crowds of busy people in whose needs he was interested kept me from him. And when not occupied with them he devoted the scanty time left him to refreshing his body with needful food or his mind with reading. And ever as he read his eyes followed the page and his mind pondered what it imbibed, but his tongue was silent. Often when we came—for none were forbidden to enter, nor was it customary to announce visitors—we would find him thus reading in silence. So we, too, would sit for long and watch him in silence—for who would have dared disturb a man so engaged ? Then would we steal away, for we realized that during that brief space thus won for the refreshment of his mind he was taking holiday from preoccupation with other men's affairs, and had no desire to be called away to other things . . . perhaps, too, it was with a view to saving his voice—which in his case easily got weak—that he thus very wisely read in silence.[4]

Augustine's state of mind at this time was one with which in these days many are familiar—he found himself driven to face the claims of Catholicism. He, therefore, who up to now had been wont to sneer at the prophets and the Sacred Scrip-

[1] *Confess.* v. 23.
[2] *Ibid.*
[3] *Ibid.*
[4] *Ibid.*, vi. 3.

tures,[1] began seriously to study St. Paul's Epistles.[2] Still, as he tells us, he had not yet reached the stage of being ashamed that he was not a Catholic ; he was only ashamed that he had had such ridiculous ideas about what Catholics believed,[3] and it was a relief to him to find now that they did not really hold the 'childish trifles' he had attributed to them.[4]

He began to go regularly to church,[5] but thought he would remain a catechumen until he was certain :[6] 'for I wanted to be as certain of the things that I did not see as I was certain that seven and three make ten.'[7] How terrible this intellectual struggle was the saint has revealed to us in words which will never die. But we are so familiar with and so impressed by his poignant account of his struggle to overcome the weakness of the flesh,[8] that, almost unconsciously, we think of Augustine's conversion as a turning away from sin. There is truth in this—terrible truth : 'the allurements of wife and reputation did, I confess, prevent me from making speedy advance in philosophy,'[9] but the intellectual struggle was a far graver one : 'It was perhaps twelve years,' he says with regret, 'since the reading of Cicero's *Hortensius* in my twenty-first year had aroused in me a love of wisdom.'[10] In his mental agony he sought advice from one of those hidden souls who so often control the destinies of great men. This was that Simplicianus who, according to Baronius, had been sent to Milan as guide and instructor to St. Ambrose by Pope Damasus the moment the Pontiff heard of Ambrose's elevation to the See of Milan.[11] Though already advanced in years he was destined to succeed

[1] *Confess.* iii. 9 and 18.

[2] In the spring of A.D. 386, *Contra Academicos*, ii. 5, 6. Towards the close of his life he speaks somewhat disparagingly of those early writings which he composed before he became really familiar with the Bible, *Contra Julianum*, vi. 39. Yet his *De Sermone Domini in monte*, written A.D. 394, before he became a Bishop, shows his profound knowledge of Holy Scripture.

[3] *Confess.* vi. 4.

[4] *Ibid.*, vi. 5.

[5] *Ibid.*, viii. 13.

[6] *Ibid.*, v. 25.

[7] *Ibid.*, vi. 6.

[8] *Ibid.*, viii. 19.

[9] *De Beata Vita*, 4.

[10] *Confess.* iii. 7–9, viii. 17 ; *De Beata Vita*, 4, 10, 22 ; *Soliloquium*, i. 17.

[11] *Annales ad ann.*, 375, 385. It is hard to discover on what Baronius based this statement.

St. Ambrose as Bishop of Milan when the latter died in A.D. 397. We possess two letters from St. Ambrose to Simplicianus in answer to questions the old man had put to him on the sacrifices of the Levitical law.[1]

To this same Simplicianus Victorinus the rhetorician had gone on the eve of his own great renunciation.[2] It was, too, 'the holy old man Simplicianus, who later presided as Bishop over the church at Milan, who used to tell us that a certain Platonist was in the habit of saying that the beginning of the *Gospel according to John* ought to be written in letters of gold and set up in a conspicuous position in every church.'[3] A signal proof of the veneration in which Simplicianus was held appears in Canon xlviii. of the Council of Carthage, A.D. 397, which declared that as for the decision the Conciliar Fathers had arrived at with regard to the Donatists: 'placuit ut consulamus fratres et consacerdotes nostros Siricium (the Pope) and Simplicianum.'[4]

Simplicianus received Augustine kindly, but, with supreme tact, instead of discussing his intellectual difficulties, he told him the story of the wonderful conversion of another famous professor of rhetoric at Rome, Victorinus, who had died in the faith after making courageous public profession of it.[5]

Of Simplicianus, who in reality played so large a part in dissipating his doubts, we hear no more till some ten years later when, in 397, we find him writing to Augustine, then a Bishop of little more than a year's standing, humbly to ask his advice. The latter's reply, *De Diversis, ad Simplicianum*, was apparently his first work as a Bishop, and he refers to it more than once.[6]

But the end was not yet come for Augustine. His intellect was convinced but his will still vacillated, still 'bound fast by the chains of the flesh and long-continued habits.'[7] Here the

[1] *Epp. Sti. Ambrosii*, lxv. and lxvii.; *P.L.* 1222, 1227.
[2] *Confess.* viii. 4.
[3] *De Civitate Dei*, X. xxix. 2.
[4] Mansi, *Concilia*, iii. 891.
[5] *Confess* viii. 3–5.
[6] *Retract.* ii. 1; *De Octo Quaestionibus Dulcitii*, vi. 2; *De Praedestinatione Sanctorum*, 8. Simplicianus died in the early part of June, 400, see Mansi, *Concilia*, iii. 946.
[7] *Confess.* viii. 10; see K. Adam, *St. Augustine, the Odyssey of his soul*, translated by Fr. J. McCann, O.S.B., 1932.

intellect had no place; nor could Simplicianus help him. It needed the moving story of the life of St. Antony, so artlessly set forth by a fellow-African, Pontitianus, then holding high position in the Milanese court, to break Augustine's bonds.[1] The story of that last scene in the garden is too well known, too sacred almost, to be repeated here; it has to be read in the heart-broken words of Augustine himself.[2] At length, however, in the September of A.D. 386, he, with Alypius and Adeodatus, was enrolled among the *Competentes* or people actually preparing for baptism.[3]

Certain popularisers, with but a superficial acquaintance with Augustine's life and work, and still less familiarity with the Romano-African world of those days, pretend to be disgusted not so much by the irregularities of Augustine's early life—irregularities which no one deplored more bitterly than he[4]—as by the fact that he did not at once marry his mistress on his conversion.[5] We have yet to learn that it is the custom even in these days for 'converts' to take such a step; we fancy many of to-day's moralists would hold up their hands in dismay at the idea of a marriage where there was no love, and would excuse a man's leaving his mistress in the lurch simply on the ground that now at length he really has fallen in love, and with an eligible person. Nowhere does Augustine anywhere suggest that he was in love with his mistress, though he does say that he was always faithful to her. But he does tell us that he had fallen in love with Some One else. In his *Soliloquy* between himself and *Reason* he makes *Reason* ask:—

'Do you love anything save knowledge of yourself and of God?' To which he answers: 'I might reply that so far as my present feelings go I do love nothing else; but it would be safer to reply: "I do not know." For it often happens that just when I fancy that nothing else (save God) has power to stir my affections, something occurs to my mind which

[1] *Confess.* viii. 13–30.
[2] *Ibid.*, viii. 28; *cf.* *Contra Julianum*, vi. 56, where Augustine seems to be depicting the struggle he himself went through.
[3] *Confess.* ix. 14; *De Fide et Operibus*, 9; *De Utilitate Credendi*, 2.
[4] *Enarr.* iii. 19 *on* Ps. xxxvi.
[5] Rebecca West, *St. Augustine*, 1933; see a scathing, but fully justified review by G. C. Heseltine in *G.K.'s Weekly*, February 3, 1933.

affects me far otherwise than I had hoped would be the case.' *Reason* then suggests that he might like to take a wife, and asks whether he is able to withstand the temptations natural to our fallen state. But to this Augustine replies: 'I shrink from all that with horror and I can only recall such things as those with loathing. No! The greater my hope of one day seeing That Exceeding Beauty for which I so earnestly yearn, the more intensely do my love and desire turn towards It.'[1]

There you have the true 'conversion' of Augustine. It was not merely 'aversio a peccato' but that 'conversio ad Deum,' without which all turning away from sin is hollow and meaningless.

While differing widely in tone from Miss West's volume we cannot but regret that M. Louis Bertrand should have published his *La femme qui était retournée en Afrique*, 1920. The mother of Adeodatus, be it remembered, 'returned to Africa, making a vow to Thee, my God, that she would never know another man.'[2] Yet M. Bertrand, than whom no one has a deeper knowledge of St. Augustine,[3] disregarding Augustine's positive statements, presents us with a purely fanciful picture according to which Lucius, Bishop of Theveste, had asked Augustine, not yet a priest, to preach to the catechumens there. He journeys thither on horseback, while Adeodatus, who is in a dying state, travels in a litter. One of the said catechumens is Januarius, a friend of Adeodatus and son of that unnamed friend of Augustine's whose loss at Carthage he had so bitterly deplored.[4] But at Theveste was Adeodatus' mother, now styled 'Modesta' by M. Bertrand, and said to be the daughter of the custodian of the Basilica of St. Cyprian at Carthage. She is represented as having left Augustine at Milan after a dispute. The dying Adeodatus demands to be allowed to see his mother and over his deathbed Augustine and 'Modesta' kiss. The story of Augustine and Monica, of Adeodatus and his mother, is one of the world's greatest romances. Was it worth while erecting on this undying story so feeble and so baseless a fabrication?

[1] *Soliloquium*, i. 16–17.
[2] *Confess*. vi. 25.
[3] See *Bibliography*, p. 78.
[4] *Confess*. vi. 7–12.

But, as he wrote long after, 'conversion spells trouble.'[1] First there came appalling toothache :—

I was in agony with it [he says], so much so that I could not even speak. But I bethought me to ask my companions to pray for me to Thee, O God of all health. So I wrote my request on wax and handed it to them to read. No sooner had we got on our knees than the pain fled. But what an agony it was ! And whither did it go ? Indeed, O Lord my God, I was terrified, for never in all my life had I experienced such pain.[2]

BIBILOGRAPHY

Prosper Alfaric, *L'Evolution intellectuelle de S. Augustin : du Manichéisme au Néoplatonisme*, 1918.
H. Becker, *Augustin : Studien zur seiner geistigen Entwicklung*, 1908.
B. Lagewie, *S. Augustinus, Eine Psychographie*, 1925.
J. Martin, *S. Augustin*, in the series *Les grands philosophes*, 2nd ed., 1907.
E. MacDougall, *St. Augustine : A Study of his Personal Religion*, 1930.
H. A. Naville, *St. Augustine, Etude sur le développement de sa pensée jusqu'à l'epoque de son ordination*, Geneva, 1872.
A. Pincherle, *Il decennio de preparazione di Sant' Agostino*, A.D. 386–396, in *Ric. Relig.* 1930–1932, *Sant 'Agostino d'Ippona, Vescovo e Teologo*, Bari, 1930.
Hugh Pope, O.P., *The Teaching of St. Augustine on Prayer and the Contemplative Life*, 1935.

II—AT CASSICIACUM

On deciding to become a Christian Augustine had withdrawn to a villa immortalized under the name of Cassiciacum, which had been lent to him and his companions by a certain Verecundus of Milan.[3] Though he had decided to give up the profession of rhetoric, he had as yet formed no other plans.[4] Here at Cassiciacum he, with Monica, Alypius, Adeodatus, Navigius his brother, Licentius, son of his old patron Romanianus, Trygetius of Tagaste, Rusticius and Lastidianus, Augustine's cousins, also Evodius of Tagaste who had been baptized some little time before,[5] held those disputations which

[1] *Enarr.* i. 1 *on* Ps. lxxxiii.
[2] *Confess.* ix. 12 ; *cf. Soliloquium*, i. 21.
[3] *Confess.* ix. 5 ; *De Beata Vita*, 6 and 31. See F. Meda, *La controversia sul* '*Rus Cassiciacum*,' in *Miscellanea Agostiniana*, Rome, ii. pp. 49–59.
[4] *Confess.* ix. 2 and 7.
[5] *Ibid.*, xvii. ; see, too, *De Beata Vita*, 6 ; De Ordine, i. 5 ; for Alypius and Evodius see below, pp. 113–120.

show that if Augustine had not become a bishop he would have devoted himself to the study of philosophy.[1]

A perusal of the *Dialogues*[2] held during these quiet days spent at Cassiciacum shows us the patient Monica in her element. All her earthly desires have been accomplished. The ' difficult ' Patritius had long before been won for God and had died in the bosom of the Church ;[3] and now the wayward Augustine had followed in his father's footsteps ; for the first time she sees him really at peace. Here now at Cassiciacum she has a family after her own heart. She sees all these young men, Alypius, whose career she has followed so long at Tagaste and at Carthage and who was afterwards to become Bishop of their native town, her other son Navigius, her nephews, too, Rusticius and Lastidianus, Trygetius—also from Tagaste, and Licentius, son of that Romanianus who had befriended her family so steadfastly, all these she sees gathered round the beloved Augustine and hanging on his words. They seem to have talked and discussed almost all day long ; but Monica looked after their bodily welfare and kept an eye on Augustine's health[4] as she had done when he was a small boy with a stomach-ache, as she had done later on, too, when she found him in Rome prostrate with sickness.

She had always been proud of him and his intellectual gifts, though dismayed at his moral aberrations. But these latter are now a thing of the past, and the prevision she had always clung to—that he would one day be as she herself was—has come true. At Rome she had found him half converted, for he had told her he was weary of the Manichees ; but even then she had shown no exuberant feeling, had merely replied that she was convinced he would not stop half-way, but would in the end come into the fullness of his Christian inheritance.[5] But here now, in their retired villa, the words of that unknown Bishop—himself a converted Manichaen[6]—who had dried her

[1] See *Ep.* ci. 3.
[2] D. Ohlmann, *De Sancti Augustini dialogis in Cassisiaco scriptis*, 1897 ; E. Fischer, *De Augustini disciplinarum Libro qui est ' De Dialectica,'* Jena, 1912.
[3] *Confess.* ix. 22.
[4] *De Ordine*, i. 23.
[5] *Confess.* vi. 1.
[6] *Ibid.*, iii. 21.

tears with his consoling promise, have been fulfilled, and this, the son of her tears and prayers, is safe.

In this atmosphere of peace and happiness Monica appears in a new light. One day, when her son and his disciples were busy discussing and the notaries were looking dismayed because their note-books were full, Monica, says Augustine, stepped in

and asked what progress we had made, for she knew what was the subject under discussion. I bade the notaries write down, as was our custom, the fact that she had come in, also the question she had put. But she exclaimed : 'Why, what are you doing ? I have never learned from any of the books you read that women were allowed a part in such discussions !' 'Mother,' I answered, 'you know the meaning of the Greek term "philosophy," in Latin, "love of wisdom." Now those Sacred Scriptures which you have taken so deeply to heart tell us not to despise or jeer at philosophers, but only at the philosophers of this world. . . . Since, then, you love that true philosophy much more than you love me—and well do I know how much you love me ; since, too, you have made such progress in that true philosophy that you have no longer any dread of fortune's mischances, not even of death itself, though those are things which fill with dismay even the most learned men, since, too, all will acknowledge that therein lies the supreme goal of philosophy, why then should I not gladly call myself your disciple ?' [1] To this she sweetly and humbly replied that she had never before known me tell such an untruth, and as I realized that we had already poured out such a flood of words that the note-books were crammed and there were no more tablets left, we agreed to postpone the discussion and have pity on my digestion.[2]

But when the discussion was resumed and Augustine had closed it with a beautiful prayer that they might all attain eternal happiness with God, he turned to Monica and said :

That these our desires may be most truly fulfilled is a task, mother, which we impose on you in all earnestness. For I unhesitatingly affirm that it was in answer to your prayers that God gave me my present determination to prefer nothing to

[1] *De Ordine*, i. 31, 32.
[2] *Ibid.*, i. 33.

the search for truth, to desire nothing else, to think of nothing else, to love nothing else. Nor shall I ever cease to believe that through your prayers we shall win that immense good for which, through your merits, we have learned to yearn.[1]

On Augustine's birthday Monica provided a dinner, and during three days they held the discussion *De Beata Vita*. When in the course of it Licentius was asked why we ate food, and had promptly replied : 'For the body's sake,'[2] and when the further question was put : 'What, then, does the soul feed on ?' it was Monica who replied : 'I believe the soul feeds on nothing else save knowledge and understanding.' Trygetius seems to have demurred to this, but Monica retorted that he himself had given the best possible proof of it,

For when dinner was only half way through you admitted that you had not noticed what cups we were using, and you explained that you were thinking of something else ; yet that did not prevent your hands and mouth from being busy during the rest of the meal. . . . Your mind, then, was occupied with your thoughts and fancies.[3]

At a further stage in the discussion Monica answered the question : whether a man is happy if he has what he wants, by saying : 'Yes, provided it is good.' 'I,' says Augustine, 'laughed with glee and said : "Now, mother, you there touched the very heights of philosophy !"' He added that had she been familiar with Cicero's *Hortensius* she would have quoted it, as he himself proceeded to do.[4] Meanwhile the boy Licentius seems to have been examining the food supply and found it inadequate, so he ejaculated : 'I think he must be happy who has *not* got what he wants !' this with a peevish smile. They all laughed and bade him eat up the small bit he had. But Augustine adds : 'I, their host, was dismayed at the insufficiency and unsuitableness of the provisions before us, and looked with a smile at my mother. But she with a woman's

[1] *De Ordine*, ii .52.
[2] *De Beata Vita*, 7.
[3] *Confess.* viii.
[4] *Confess.* x.

tact said : " Now please tell us all about the Academicians and their opinions." '[1]

When at the conclusion of this discussion Augustine had expatiated at length on the supreme vision of God, the eternal Truth, and insisted that that was the only thing that could ever satisfy the human soul,

My mother suddenly called to mind some words which she dearly loved to remember, and, as though awakening to the real meaning of her faith, she sang with joy the words of our priest (St. Ambrose) : *Fove precantes Trinitas*,[2] ' there,' she added, ' you have, beyond all question, the happy life ; for it is the perfect life to which we can, in well-grounded faith, eager hope and burning charity, trust that we who are hastening on the way thither may finally be brought.'[3]

Augustine's conversion is assigned with all probability to the September of A.D. 386, when he was finishing his thirty-second year ; while his baptism took place at Easter in the following year, 387.[4] His own account of what he then experienced is well known, yet the familiar words will bear quoting once more :—

We were baptized, and all anxiety about our past life slipped away from us. In those days I could never be sated with the indescribable sweetness that overwhelmed me when I recalled the profundity of Thy counsels wherewith Thou didst secure the salvation of the human race. How I wept as I listened with deep emotion to the hymns and canticles so sweetly sung in Thy Church ! As the sound of them rang in my ears truth shone so

[1] *Ibid.*, xv., xvi.
[2] St. Ambrose, hymn *Deus Creator omnium.*
[3] *De Beata Vita*, 35.
[4] *Confess.* ix. 28 ; *Soliloquium*, i. 17 ; *Contra Academicos*, iii. 43 ; St. Prosper, however, in his *Chronicon* assigns Augustine's baptism to A.D. 385. See F. Magani, *La data e il luogo del battesimo di S. Agostino*, Pavia, 1887 ; *Oeuvre de Hippone, Quinzième centenaire de la conversion de S. Augustin*, 1886 ; L. Gourdon, *Essai sur la conversion de S. Augustin*, 1900 ; W. J. Sparrow Simpson, *St. Augustine's conversion. An outline of his development to the time of his ordination*, 1930 ; A. D. Knock, *Conversion : The old and the new in religion from Alexander the Great to Augustine of Hippo*, 1933 ; Theodore Bret, *La Conversion de S. Augustin*, 1900 ; U. Mannucci, *La conversione di S. Augustine e la critica recente*, in *Miscellanea Agostiniana*, Rome, ii. pp. 22–47 ; G. Boissier, *La conversion de S. Augustin*, in *Rev. de deux mondes*, January, 1888 ; W. B. Thomas, *The Psychology of Conversion, with especial reference to St. Augustine*, 1935.

clearly in my heart and devoutest feelings so flooded my soul that tears ran down my cheeks and all was well with me.[1]

His solemn baptism must have made an immense impression in Milan, and people must have felt much as they did at Rome when the rhetorician Victorinus was baptized. Simplicianus, we remember, had told Augustine the story of that unforgettable scene, and as we ponder it we have only to read ' Augustine ' for ' Victorinus ' to picture what took place when Ambrose and Augustine went down into the font together, and when the neophyte came out and solemnly read aloud his new-found creed :—

When the time came for him (Victorinus) to make his profession of faith—a profession drawn up in clear and definite words and committed to memory, and which it was the practice at Rome for those coming to Thy grace to read out loud from an elevated position in the sight of all the faithful, the clergy—so we are told—suggested to Victorinus that he might do this in private, a concession often made to people who were nervous about doing it publicly. But he preferred to make profession of his salvation in the presence of the whole people. For, he said, it was now no question merely of that kind of salvation he had taught in his rhetoric classes, yet that salvation he had at that time taught publicly. . . . When, then, he went up to read out his profession of faith, everybody—for all had known him—shouted out his name, so that as he appeared there rang out from the surging and excited crowd a cry of ' Victorinus ! Victorinus ! ' But silence came on them as they listened intently and eagerly. Then so courageously did he read out in clear tones his profession of the true faith that all wanted to take him to their hearts.[2]

Of the ceremony of his own baptism Augustine tells us nothing, though he frequently refers to the fact that it was St. Ambrose who actually baptized him.[3] Truly ' the child of those tears had not been allowed to perish.'[4] What those two great

[1] *Confess*. ix. 8–12, 14 ; *cf. Contra Acad*. i. 3 ; *De Beata Vita*, 7 ; *De Ordine*, i. 5.
[2] *Confess*. viii. 5 ; see the *Vita* prefixed to the Maurist edition of the works of St. Augustine, II. xi. 4, *P.L*. xxxii. 142.
[3] *De Nuptiis et Concupiscentiis*, i. 40 ; *Ep*. xxxvi. 2 ; *Contra Julianum*, i. 10, also i. 21, where he speaks of St. Ambrose as *Doctorem meum*.
[4] *Confess*. iii. 21.

Doctors of the Church must have felt during that solemn baptism we are left to imagine. Christian feeling has not unnaturally seen in the *Te Deum* the expression of their emotions, though there is no actual foundation for the notion that it was then composed ; it is not improbable, however, that St. Ambrose's treatise, *De Mysteriis*, penned almost certainly in that same year, 387, was written for the occasion. Shortly after their baptism the little party decided to return to Africa, and it was while waiting for the boat at Ostia that Monica died.[1]

The deathless story of the death of Monica the *pacifica !* [2] Who can read it and not sense its exquisite beauty ? The colloquy at the window in Ostia on the vision of the Eternal Truth, when the past with its vicissitudes seemed to have slipped away from them and the invisible world wrapped them round ; [3] the trance into which she fell, and her waking cry : ' Where was I ? ' followed by the immediate declaration that so far as her body was concerned they might lay it there, in a land that was not hers, but that for her soul they were to be mindful at the altar of God wherever they might be ; [4] the quaint assurance she offered to those who protested that she ought to be buried in her native land : ' Nothing is far from God ; no reason to fear He will find it difficult at the end of the world to know whence to raise me ' ; [5] the passionate grief of Adeodatus ; [6] the way Evodius—to relieve their pent-up feelings—intoned the hundredth Psalm ; [7] all these form a picture full of pathos. As Augustine, thirteen years later, pens his description of that unforgettable scene, we feel that he is living it over again, that he is standing once more at the tomb ' where the price of our redemption was offered for her hard by where her body lay ere we committed it to the grave.' [8]

But his grief stunned him, and he found that the fountains of his tears had dried up :—

[1] *Ibid.*, ix. 17 ; November 17, 387.
[2] *Ibid.*, 21.
[3] *Confess.* ix. 23.
[4] *Ibid.*, 27. See Ch. Boyer, *La contemplation d'Ostie*, 1930.
[5] *Ibid.*, 28.
[6] *Confess.* ix. 29.
[7] *Ibid.*, 31.
[8] *Ibid.*, 32.

Though I went and bathed yet I found myself the same as I was before ; the bitterness of my grief had not been sweated out of my heart. But I went to sleep and when I awoke there came into my mind those truth-compelling verses penned by Thy servant Ambrose :—

Deus, Creator omnium,
Polique Rector vestiens
Diem decoro lumine,
Noctem sopora gratia :

Artus solutos ut quies
Reddat laboris usui,
Mentesque fessas allevet,
Luctusque solvat anxios.[1]

Peace then flooded his soul and he prayed :—

May she then rest in peace with her husband ! And inspire, O Lord my God, my brethren, Thy servants, Thy children, my masters whom I serve by voice, heart and pen, so that whoso-ever my read these lines may remember at the altar Monica Thy servant, with Patritius, once her husband, through whom Thou didst bring me, I know not how, into this life. May they remember with devout affection my parents in the passing light of this world, as also my brethren in our Mother the Catholic Church, under Thee, our Father, for they, too, are my fellow-citizens in the eternal Jerusalem for which Thy people here in exile yearn from the day of their going out from Thee till their return to Thee.[2]

' So, on the ninth day of her illness, then in the six-and-fiftieth year of her age, and in my own three-and-thirtieth year, her devout and holy soul was freed from her body.'[3] When he saw her die Adeodatus ' burst into tears,'[4] but Navigius and the bystanders silenced him for they felt that tears were out of place, as Augustine declares : ' Hers was no unhappy death, indeed she was not wholly dead as are the reprobate when they die.'[5] Over and over again does Augustine return to the subject of his mother's virtues and of the debt he owed to her

[1] *Confess.* ix. 32.
[2] *Ibid.*, 37.
[3] *Confess.* ix. 28.
[4] *Ibid.*, 27.
[5] *Confess.* ix. 29.

life, her example and her prayers.[1] He could never forget how cruelly he had once misinterpreted a dream in which she had seen a presage that he would be as she was, namely, a Catholic, but which he had ungenerously interpreted as meaning that she would become a Manichaean like himself.[2] Nor could he forget that her hatred of his heresy had been such that she had seriously thought of not allowing him to sit at table with her.[3]

The death of Monica seems to have changed the plans of the little company, for though Augustine says nothing of it in his *Confessions*—which is, of course, not a biography, nor presents events in strict chronological order—yet in his *Retractations* he carefully distinguishes between (*a*) what he wrote in retreat near Milan, *i.e.*, at Cassiciacum, namely, *Contra Academicos*, *De Beata Vita*, *De Ordine* and the *Soliloquium*,[4] (*b*) what he wrote at Milan itself on his return from the country preparatory to his baptism, namely, *De Immortalitate Animae* and *De Musica*, though he only finished this and five connected treatises (which latter never consisted of more than rough notes) on his return to Africa,[5] and (*c*) what he wrote 'after being baptized when I was at Rome,' namely, *De Moribus Ecclesiae Catholicae* and *De Moribus Manichaeorum*, *De Quantitate Animae*, and finally *De Libero Arbitrio*, the last two books of which treatise he finished in Africa after his ordination.[6] This means that he returned to Rome after the death of Monica.

No one can read these *Dialogues* nor the earlier letters, those to Nebridius in particular, without feeling that in Augustine the Bishop and Pastor of souls the world lost a great philosopher. His reading had been wide ; he had studied much of Aristotle, more perhaps of Plato ; his mind was essentially that of the investigator and the thinker. Much has been written, more especially of late, on his philosophical position. But we fancy Augustine himself would have insisted that he followed no particular school, that he was a pragmatist in the best sense of

[1] See, for example, *Confess.* ii. 7, iii. 19, v. 16, ix. 22 ; *Le Ordine*, i. 31, 32.
[2] *Confess.* iii. 30.
[3] *Ibid.*, iii. 19. See Abbé Bougaud, *Histoire de Sainte Monique*, 2nd ed., 1866.
[4] *Retract.* i. 1–4.
[5] *Ibid.*, 5–6.
[6] *Retract.* 7–9.

the word, for he wanted a philosophy that would 'work' in his hands, or rather through his pen and his voice, for the salvation of men's souls.

Of the immense bibliography on the subject we can but mention the following. But it is almost a case of "Quot homines, tot sententiae,' for so many writers seem to find it hard not to read their own minds into Augustine and to discover in him just precisely what they themselves want to find.

The Philosophical Teaching of St. Augustine

A. In General

A. Casamassa, O.E.S.A., *Le fonti della filosofia di S. Agostino*, in the *Acta hebdomadae augustinianae thomisticae*, 1931, pp. 88–96.
W. Cunningham, *St. Austin, and His Place in the History of Christian Thought*, 1886; the Hulsean Lectures for 1885.
F. Lasbax, *La Philosophie dans l'Afrique du Nord et l'histoire de l'esprit africain*, 1922.
C. Boyer, S. J., *Philosophie et théologie chez S. Augustin*; *Essais sur la doctrine de S. Augustin*, 1933.

B. Psychology

J. Morgan, *The Psychological Teaching of St. Augustine*, 1932.
M. Ferraz, *Psychologie de S. Augustin*, 1862 and 1869.

C. Illuminationism

M. Horoy, *De la Parole Interieure d'après S. Augustin*, 1862.
L. M. Card. Parocchi, *Del lume dell' intelletto secondo la dottrina de' SS. dottori, Agostino, etc.*, 1881.
R. Jolivet, *La Doctrine de l'Illumination chez S. Augustin*, in *Rev. Philosophique*, 1930, pp. 382 ff.; *Dieu, soleil des esprits, ou la doctrine augustinienne de l'illumination*, 1934.

D. Neoplatonism

C. Boyer, *Christianisme et néoplatonisme dans la formation de S. Augustin*, 1920.
L. Grandgeorge, *S. Augustin et le Néo-Platonisme*, 1896.
R. Jolivet, *S. Augustin et le néo-platonisme chrétien*, 1932.
T. J. Parry, *Augustine's Psychology during his first period of literary activity, with special reference to his relations to Platonism*, 1913.
A. Sanvert, *S. Augustin. Etude d'âme*, 1906.

E. Special Questions

R. Jolivet, *Essai sur les rapports entre la pensée grecque et la pensée chrétienne . . . de Plotin et S. Augustin, ou le problème du mal*, 1931.
J. Guitton, *Le Temps et l'Eternité chez Plotin et S. Augustin*, 1933.
J. Barrion, *Plotin und Augustinus*, 1935.
C. Boyer, S.J., *L'Ideé de verité dans la philosophie de S. Augustin*, Paris, 1921; *La théorie Augustinienne des raisons séminales*, in *Miscellanea Agostiniana*, Rome, ii., pp. 795–819; *La Philosophie augustinienne, ignore-t-elle l'abstraction?* 1930.
Marion Le R. Burton, *The Problem of Evil: a criticism of the Augustinian point of view*, 1909.
I. Sestili, *Augustini Philosophia pro existentia Dei*, in *Miscellanea Agostiniana, Rome*, ii. pp. 765–793.
W. P. Tolley, *The Idea of God in the Philosophy of St. Augustine*, 1930.

III—HIS LIFE AS A BISHOP

We can touch but briefly on the remaining facts of Augustine's life. He returned to Africa ' on the death of the tyrant Maximinus '[1] towards the close of A.D. 388. He then settled at Tagaste where he founded a monastery and led a life of retirement and study until, in 391–2, he was most unexpectedly ordained priest at Hippo.[2] The Primate of Numidia at that time was Megalius, the Bishop of Calama. He seems to have listened to some report unfavourable to Augustine, and in consequence wrote a letter in which he spoke disparagingly about him. This fell into the hands of the Donatists who made capital out of it;[3] but Augustine points out that they omitted to say that ' when called upon in a meeting of the Bishops to prove what he had urged against me, Megalius spontaneously withdrew the charge and apologized.'[4] Megalius died A.D. 397, having consecrated Augustine as Coadjutor Bishop to Valerius, the aged Bishop of Hippo, two years previously.[5]

' How intimately my cares are bound up with those of the Church you can gather from the fact our blessed Father, Valerius, is not content with my being simply one of his priests, but is determined to lay on me the still greater burden of the Episcopate,' Augustine to St. Paulinus, A.D. 396.[6]

The Council of Nicaea, canon 8, had forbidden the co-existence of two bishops in a see.[7] It was only later on that Augustine became conscious of this irregularity, and it was probably owing to him that the third canon of the Council of Carthage, A.D. 397, laid down that Bishops were to remind those whom they were consecrating of the decrees of the Councils, ' lest they should find that they had done something contrary to them.'[8]

Augustine has left us a touchingly simple account of his elevation to the priesthood and the episcopate.

[1] *Contra Litt. Petiliani*, iii. 30.
[2] *Sermo*, cccl v. 2; *Vita*, 3–4; *Ep.* cxxvi. 7.
[3] *Contra Litt. Petiliani*, iii. 19; *Contra Cresconium*, iii. 92.
[4] *Ibid.*, iv. 79.
[5] *Sermo*, ccclv. 2; June-July, 395.
[6] *Ep.* xxxi. 4.
[7] Labbe, *Concilia*, ii. 14.
[8] Mansi, *Concilia*, iv. 1167.

So much did I dread being made a Bishop [he said] that when I found that God's servants were talking seriously about the reputation I had made I was careful not to go to places where I knew there was no Bishop. . . . But I came to this city (Hippo) to see a friend whom I thought I could win over to God's service and who might perhaps enter our monastery. I felt quite safe since a Bishop was in occupation of the see. But I was caught and made a priest, and once that step had been taken I was made a Bishop.[1]

He himself tells us of the tears he shed when made priest[2] in his forty-first year, about Christmas of A.D. 395;[3] and we can appreciate the feeling way in which he speaks of the responsibilities of that office which weighed so heavily upon him.[4] Possidius, who wrote Augustine's life after living in closest intimacy with him for forty years,[5] remarks that with the advent of Augustine 'the Catholic Church in Africa began to lift up its head.'[6] For in very truth, from the day of his consecration, if not of his ordination, Augustine's whole outlook on life underwent a radical change. Henceforth he simply lived for the spiritual needs of his flock[7]—a flock which in time became almost co-extensive with Northern Africa. He had been in the habit of reading half a book of Virgil a day,[8] but he now gave up his reading of the classics,[9] though to the end of his days he quoted them freely.[10] Henceforward all his studies were, as he wrote to St. Jerome, devoted to furthering the needs of his strangely mixed flock: 'If I have any knowledge of Holy Scripture I must perforce expend it on the people of God; but my ecclesiastical preoccupations wholly preclude me from

[1] *Sermo*, ccclv. 2.
[2] *Ep.* xxi. 2.
[3] *Sermo*, cccxxxix. 1.
[4] *Sermo*, cccxxxix. and cccxl.
[5] *Vita*, *Praefatio*.
[6] *Vita*, 7.
[7] See *Epp.* lxxv. 6; lxxii. 23; cx. 6; ccxiii. 5-6. When writing to his flock he speaks of himself as *congregalis vester vel certe canis vester*; *Contra Litt. Petiliani*, iii. 11.
[8] *De Ordine*, i. 26; see G. Combès, *S. Augustin et la culture classique*, 1937.
[9] *Ep.* ci. 3; cxviii. 2 and 9.
[10] See for instance, *Ep.* cxviii. 3 where he quotes Persius, also *Contra Julianum*, iv. 67, etc.

devoting myself to any other study than such as is necessary for the instruction of my flock.'[1]

How touching his words to them :—

> If we who feed you fear and tremble, fearing, as we do for our flock, how much more should the sheep themselves stand in fear ? The care of you must be our affair ; but your part is obedience ; ours is the shepherd's anxiety, yours the flock's humility. And although we may indeed seem to you to speak from an elevated position, yet also are we prostrate under your feet in fear ; for well we know the strict account we shall have to give of that same lofty position.[2]

And again : ' May the Lord grant me so intense a love of you that I may be able even to die for you, if not in effect yet at least in desire.'[3]

He wrote—or rather he dictated—copiously : ' For I have made up my mind that, God willing, any leisure time I may have over from those occupations which the needs of the Church whose servant I am, demand, must be wholly devoted to ecclesiastical studies ; indeed I think that in that sphere I may, by God's mercy, be of some use even to posterity.'[4] This latter feeling was indeed more than a feeling, it was a profound conviction.[5] And it was justified by events, for even in his own lifetime his writings were known so far west as Mauretania Caesariensis[6] and even outside Africa.[7]

But his rapidly growing fame alarmed him. His humility took fright. Hence the *Confessions*, from which we have quoted so freely. This—the best known of all Augustine's writings—saw the light about A.D. 400,[8] and he penned its

[1] *Ep.* lxxiii. 5.

[2] *Sermon*, cxlvi. 1 ; *cf. Enarr.* i. 1–2 *on* Ps. cxv. where on the words : ' Credidi, propter quod locutus sum ' he explains why and how a Christian minister should preach.

[3] *Casin*, I. cxxxiii. 5, ' aut effectu aut affectu.'

[4] *Ep.* cli. 13.

[5] See, for example, *Epp.* xciii. 53, cxlvii. 5 ; *De Spiritu et Littera*, 61.

[6] *De Anima et ejus origine*, ii. 18.

[7] *Ep.* xciv. 1 ; cii. ; cxliii. 4 ; cxlix. 12 ; ccxi. 5 ; *Vita*, 18 ; *Retract.* ii. 56 ; *De Praedestinatione Sanctorum*, 9 ; see, too, St. Fulgentius, *Ep.* xiv. ; Victor of Vita, *Historia Persecutionis Vandalicae*, i. 3.

[8] Between A.D. 397 and 398 according to F. di Capua, *Miscellanea Agostiniana*, ii. p. 678 note.

self-revealing story lest men should think too highly of him.[1] When, towards the close of his life, he sent a copy to Count Darius who had asked for it, he says :—

Herein you have a portrait of me which will prevent you from praising me beyond my deserts ; therein you have to believe me—not other people—about myself ; in that mirror you can see me, you can see what I was and through my own fault. If you find therein anything that pleases you, then in company with me praise Him whose praises for His work in me I would have men sing ; but do not praise me. ' He made us, not we ourselves ' ; rather had we made shipwreck of ourselves, had not He who made us, re-made us. And when you discover me in that volume, then pray for me that I fail not but may be brought to perfection. Pray, my son, pray ; for I know well what I am saying, I know what I am asking for. Think it not something unfitting, something beyond your merits. You will be robbing me of a very great help if you do not do so.[2]

See, too, an exquisite Sermon *De Ordinatione Episcopi*, wherein he draws a picture of what a true Bishop ought to be, and then says of himself :—

May God grant, then, that I may, with the help of your prayers, be what you would have me be—you who wish me well—may be, too, what He would have me be who called me and bade me assume this office. At the same time, whatever I may be, your hope must not be in me. I must speak disparagingly of myself, for I must now speak as your Bishop : I want to rejoice in you, not to be inflated by your praise.[3]

The volume of the *Confessions* was widely read, as indeed he hoped it would be.[4] Some disliked it, though Augustine says :

[1] *Confess*. x. 3–4, 60. Indeed Augustine had need of all the humility possible ; for the eulogies men passed upon him were sufficient to intoxicate one less solidly rooted in God than Augustine of Hippo, *cf*. for what to us seems extravagant praise, *Epp*. xxiv. 2, xxv. 1–2, cix. 1, cxix. 6, cliv. 1, ccxvi. 1, ccxxx. 1, ccxxxiv. 1, etc.

[2] *Ep*. ccxxxi. 6.

[3] *Guelf*. xxxii. 9. When this Sermon was first published by Dom Morin in the *Rev. Bénédictine*, 1913, pp. 398–408, people 'marvelled that so glorious an example of Augustine's eloquence, " vere aureus sermo," should so long have been unknown,' Morin, *Praef*. in *Guelferbitanus, Sermo*, xxxii., *Miscellanea Agostiniana*, i. p. 563.

[4] *De Perseverantia*, 53 ; *Confess*., *l.c*.

'I know that many of my brethren enjoyed it and still do so.'[1] Others openly sneered at these 'confessions.' They made capital out of them and treated them as a joke, Augustine's great adversary, Petilian, the Donatist Bishop of Cirta, being a great sinner in this respect, and speaking contemptuously of the Bishop of Hippo's 'past.'[2] But it called for an even more depraved character than Petilian to make vile jokes about St. Monica, and that was Julian of Eclanum, the Pelagian, the son of Augustine's old friend, Bishop Memor. For St. Augustine had in his *Confessions* told[3] with all simplicity the story of how Monica had in her early youth developed a childish liking for wine; her habit of taking surreptitious sips might have grown into a vice had it not been for a wise old nurse who nicknamed her *meribibula*. This story Julian referred to with sneers, even insinuating that this fact perhaps explained Augustine's teaching on the transmission of original sin.[4]

Secundinus, the Manichee, while praising Augustine's 'former life and studies, yet felt constrained to ask in wonderment, who could have brought about this sudden change.'[5] But all such insinuations Augustine calmly faced; he was content to ask his opponents to imitate him only in his repentance. What must have been the feelings of his audience at Carthage when he preached there his three famous sermons on Psalm xxxvi., and in the course of the third said :—

Here in this very city I led an evil life, I confess it. And just as I rejoice over God's grace in me, so for my evil past I—what? Shall I say 'grieve'? Certainly I would were I now as I then was. Shall I say 'rejoice'? No, that I cannot say, for would that I had never been such! For I suffer torture in my thoughts; I have to struggle against evil suggestions; my conflict with the enemy who tempts me is a daily one, well-nigh an unceasing one.[6]

[1] *Retract.* ii. 6.
[2] *Contra Litt. Petiliani*, iii. 11.
[3] *Confess.* ix. 18.
[4] *Contra Julianum, Opus Imperfectum*, i. 68.
[5] *Contra Secundinum Manichaeum*, xxiv.
[6] *Enarr.* iii. 19, *on* Ps. xxxvi. See, too, Augustine's autobiographical sermon, *Sermo*, ccclv. 3; also *Contra Litt. Petiliani*, iii, 11; *Epp.* cxliii. 2–3; cxliv. 1–2.

St. Fulgentius himself tells us that the first of these three sermons led to his conversion.[1] But the more Augustine belittled himself the more overwhelming became the torrent of praise, even of adulation, that was poured out on him. It was perhaps natural for St. Paulinus to hail him, as we have seen, as 'the man of God, the Doctor of Israel in the Church,'[2] to speak of his writings as 'divinely inspired,' as those of one who 'saw God';[3] but then the pagans said the same or similar things.[4] Even Augustine's bitterest enemies, the Donatist leaders, did all in their power to prevent their people from reading what he wrote against them, so clear was his style, so cogent his arguments and, above all, so persuasive his charity.[5] They dubbed him 'a mere dialectician'[6] and a Manichaean;[7] they called up every scrap of gossip about him they could discover, even about his ordination.[8] But all in vain.

From the highest to the lowest, men realized that in the Bishop of Hippo Africa possessed a man of absolute integrity, of consummate sanctity and profound learning. When he appealed to Macedonius, the Vicar of Africa, in favour of a condemned man,[9] the Vicar, after some correspondence, yielded to his request, 'for,' he said, 'your letter is so full of acute insight, knowledge and holiness that nothing can surpass it; moreover, all this is combined with such modesty that unless I do what you ask I am afraid the fault will be on my side.'[10] Small wonder that the saint's humility took fright, and that he made use of every occasion that offered for demeaning himself. Nowhere does this appear more strikingly than in his correspondence with St. Jerome, who was certainly very trying. The latter had, in a somewhat testy answer to Augustine, compared himself to a worn-out ox, and therefore begged to be excused from discussing questions with the younger man;

[1] St. Fulgentius, *Vita*, iii. 19.
[2] *Ep.* xciv. 3; cxxi. 2.
[3] *Ep.* cxxi. 14,; *cp. Ep.* xxv. 1–2.
[4] See the letter from Longinianus, *Ep.* ccxxxiv. 1, and *cf. Ep.* xc.
[5] *Contra Cresconium*, i. 40; ii. 11.
[6] *Contra Litt. Petiliani*, iii. 19.
[7] *Ibid.*, 20.
[8] *Contra Cresconium*, iii. 92, iv. 78.
[9] *Epp.* cli.–clv.
[10] *Ep.* cliv. 1.

Augustine was quick to seize the occasion : 'An ox can kick,' he said, 'and you may be worn out in body but not in vigour of mind ; so I present myself—if I have done anything wrong please kick hard.'[1]

His life from the day of his consecration was one of unremitting toil, as we shall see when we come to treat of Augustine the preacher. As the years go by we find him tired and worn,[2] complaining of weakness,[3] finding it difficult to sleep,[4] suffering from the heat,[5] also from the extreme cold.[6] Indeed he seems always to have been delicate. Early in his episcopal life he began to suffer from a distressing complaint,[7] and had—perhaps in addition—some malady of which his friends were cognisant,[8] and apropos of which he remarks : 'I can only do what I wish when I cease to wish to do what I cannot.'[9] So early as A.D. 401 he has to excuse himself from attendance at a Council on the ground of ill-health.[10]

It was the same when, in 410, he apologized to the people of Hippo for his continued absence, and pointed out that nothing but ill-health saved him from having, like his brethren in the episcopate, to go overseas on the affairs of the Church.[11] At times, too, he was absent from Hippo, recuperating.[12] Towards the close of his life, in 428, we find his devoted friend Count Darius sending medicine[13] which Augustine gratefully acknowledges while most earnestly begging for prayers : 'for my danger,' he writes, 'is greater than yours since the shepherd has to render an account of his flock.'[14] How tired he felt appears in his reference to old age so early as A.D. 402, when he

[1] *Ep*. cliv. 1.
[2] *Ep*. lxxiii. 4 ; *cf*. cxlviii., also on the subject of Orosius, *Ep*. clxvi. 2, also *Contra Julianum*, v. 17.
[3] *Sermo*, lxxvi. 1 (perhaps spurious, *cf*. ed. Caillau, xxiv., p. 52) ; *Wilmart*, xii. 1 and 5.
[4] *Ep*. ccxx. 8.
[5] *Ep*. xxxviii. 1 ; cxxxi. 1.
[6] *Ep*. cxxiv. 1, A.D. 411 ; *Sermo*, ccciii. 1.
[7] *Ep*. cclxix.
[8] *Ep*. xxxviii. 1.
[9] *Ep*. x. 1 and cli. 13.
[10] *Ep*. x. 1, 'Non valo quod volo nisi omnino desinam plus velle quam valeo.'
[11] *Ep*. lix. 1.
[12] *Ep*. cxxii. 1.
[13] *Ep*. cxviii. 34.
[14] *Ep*. ccxxx. 6.

speaks of himself as *aetate pene jam senex*,[1] also in 408, when he looks back on his youth as something long past;[2] it is not astonishing, then, that in 414 he should say: 'old age is now creeping on,'[3] though he still had sixteen more years before him.

IV—AUGUSTINE'S COMPANIONS AND DISCIPLES

When Augustine founded his monastery at Tagaste and his later one at Hippo, he presumably never dreamed that these houses would prove to be nurseries for bishops.

Yet Possidius tells us that 'Augustine, when petitioned for them, provided various important churches with nearly ten men (as bishops) whom I personally knew, men of holy, mature, virtuous and learned character.'[4] St. Paulinus seems to have had a glimpse of what would ensue when, so early as A.D. 396–7, he speaks of 'Aurelius, Alypius, Augustine, Profuturus and Severus, all of them already Bishops.'[5] AURELIUS of course was the saintly Archbishop of Carthage, which See he governed from A.D. 391 to 429, presiding over no less than twenty Councils during that time.[6] One of Augustine's earliest letters, when he had been ordained but a year, was to his Archbishop, asking his advice and lamenting some of the scandals he had found at Hippo. Yet he had already won the affections of his flock; for he adds that they are 'vehemently protesting against my lengthy absence and refusing to believe that it was for the purpose of seeing some property which you have bestowed on the brethren.'[7] It was Aurelius who urged Augustine to write his immortal volumes on the Holy Trinity, or at least to finish them. 'Juvenis inchoavi, senex edidi,' he writes; the delay was partly due to the immense difficulty of the subject,[8] partly to the fact that the earlier books or

[1] *Ep*. ccxxxi. 7.
[2] *Contra Litt. Petiliani*, iii. 31.
[3] *Ep*. xciii. 1; cli. 13; we do not know the date of *Sermo*, cxxviii. 11, when he says: *nos qui senuimus*.
[4] *Vita*, 11.
[5] *Ep*. xxxii. 1.
[6] Hefele, *Histoire des Conciles*, ed. Leclercq, 1908, ii. 97.
[7] *Ep*. xxii. 9.
[8] Augustine repeatedly refers to the fact that he was unable to finish his *De Trinitate*: in or about A.D. 410 he wrote to that effect to Consentius,

chapters had somehow got into circulation contrary to his intention, and had already appeared in a corrupt form ; but now, A.D. 416, ' owing to the insistent demands of my brethren and especially because of your bidding, I publish them ; they are not corrected as I could have wished, but as I best could, for I did not wish them to appear to differ too much from the portions already circulating surreptitiously.'[1] Another work due to the demands of Aurelius was *De Opere Monachorum*, which appeared about A.D. 400.[2] It is probable that the letters addressed by Aurelius to the Tribune Marcellinus apropos of the Donatist demands at the Conference of A.D. 411,[3] as well as the letter to the defeated and embittered Donatists after that Conference,[4] perhaps, too, the letter of the African Bishops to Pope Innocent I on the Pelagian question,[5] were actually from Augustine's pen. One last work was dedicated by Augustine to Aurelius, namely, his *De Gestis Pelagii*, A.D. 418. This was but fitting, for quite apart from the fact that Aurelius was the Archbishop, he had proved himself a tower of strength throughout that trying period, and owing to him the African Episcopate had presented a united front to the adversary.[6]

A domestic little touch appears when, at the close of a very brief sermon, St. Augustine said : ' The anniversary of the consecration of our aged Lord Aurelius is to-morrow ; he bids you through me to deign to come and celebrate it devoutly in the Basilica of Faustus.'[7] Indeed such was the veneration and esteem in which Aurelius was held by the entire episcopate of Africa that they allowed him who ' had to bear the burden of all the Churches and of all the *Ordinandi*,' to act at his own discretion in ordaining priests or consecrating Bishops, and to do so without applying to the neighbouring Bishops.[8] The Council held in September, 401, gave him leave to dictate and

Ep. cxx. 13, also in 412 to Marcellinus, *Ep.* cxliii. 4, and twice over in A.D. 415 (?) does he say the same to Evodius, *Epp.* clxii. 2 and clxix. 1.

[1] *Ep.* clxxiv., A.D. 416.

[2] *Retract.* ii. 21.

[3] *Ep.* cxxix.

[4] *Ep.* cxli.

[5] *Ep.* clxxv.

[6] *De Gratia Christi et de Peccato Originali*, 2–4, gives quotations from the proceedings against Coelestius held at Carthage by Aurelius.

[7] *Sermon*, cxi. 2.

[8] Mansi, *Concilia*, ii. 1080 ; *Codex canonum*, 55

to sign all Conciliar documents.[1] The relief afforded by the former decision must have been very great, for, as Aurelius himself said : ' In this very church where we are gathered I have frequently, practically every Sunday, to hold an ordination ' ; he must have meant by this the consecration of a Bishop, for episcopal consecrations formed the subject of the discussion, the term *ordinare* being used both for making priests and Bishops.

As for the Bishops whom Augustine himself trained, it would not be too much to say that his work in North Africa would have been impossible without them. Though he himself was a giant among them and overshadowed them all, yet, while they looked up to him and revered him, they lived on terms of intimate and familiar friendship with him. He corresponded regularly with them, visited them whenever opportunity offered, and was always intensely interested in their work.

Possidius does not name those ' nearly ten whom I personally knew,' but as we turn over the pages of Augustine's correspondence, sermons and treatises, the names of certain Bishops recur again and again. First and foremost of these is ALYPIUS, immortalized in Augustine's *Confessions*. Born at Tagaste, like Augustine, though younger than he and apparently of somewhat better birth,[2] he was always ' frater cordis mei,'[3] a friendship which Julian disgracefully represented.[4] There was at one time some misunderstanding between Augustine and Alypius' father, and it is not clear whether this had anything to do with Alypius' passing infatuation with the theatre and the games[5] or with his tragi-comic arrest as a thief.[6] Like Augustine he was slow to accept Catholicism, but for different reasons. For he was convinced of thc Apollinarist views on the Incarnation and held that in Christ there was no human

[1] See *Vita S. Fulgentii*, 41 ; Morcelli, *Africa Christiana*, iii. 10.
[2] *Confess.* vi. 11, 'exodem quo ego ortus erat municipio, parentibus primatibus municipalibus, me minor natu.'
[3] *Ibid.*, ix. 7.
[4] *Contra Julianum, Opus imperfectum*, i. 7, ' vernula peccatorum ejus Alypius.'
[5] *Confess.* vi. 11–13.
[6] *Ibid.*, 14–15.

soul.[1] But he came to Augustine at Milan, travelling barefoot,[2] was baptized with him and Adeodatus, and took part in the Dialogues held at Cassiciacum.[3] He returned to Africa with Augustine, and some six years later, A.D. 394,[4] was consecrated Bishop of his native city, Tagaste. Later on he became Primate of Numidia.

Augustine himself was, as we have seen, precluded by delicate health from travelling overseas on the business of the Church, but Alypius seems to have undertaken much of this for him. Certainly he was a great traveller. We find him in Palestine where he sees St. Jerome and fascinates Augustine by his description of that venerable hermit;[5] he was with Augustine at Tubursicum where they had a discussion with Fortunius the Donatist Bishop there.[6] The two friends were then on their way to Cirta—a Donatist stronghold where Petilian, who had been stolen by the Donatists from his Catholic parents and was, later on, after he had practised at the bar, ordained and consecrated, ruled in stormy hatred of the Catholics and more particularly of Augustine.[7] At Cirta they consecrated Fortunatus as successor to Profuturus who had died not long after his own consecration as Bishop of the same See.[8] Presumably it was the Pelagian controversy that took Alypius to Rome in A.D. 418;[9] when there Count Valerius showed him Julian the Pelagian's latest attack on St. Augustine's *De Nuptiis*. In the same year Alypius was at Hippo,[10] and, again in the same year, travelled as far west as Caesarea of Mauretania with Augustine,

[1] *Ibid.*, vii. 25.

[2] *Ibid.*, ix. 14: 'Placuit et Alypio renasci in Te mecum . . . fortissimo domitori corporis, usque ad Italicum solum glaciale nudo pede obterendum insolito ausu.'

[3] *Ibid.*, ix. 6; *De Beata Vita*, 6 and 31.

[4] Morcelli, *Africa Christiana*, ii. 317, is certainly wrong in assigning this to a decade earlier or A.D. 384. Alypius subsequently became Primate of Numidia, *Ep.* ccxxvii.

[5] *Ep.* xxviii. 1, A.D. 394–395.

[6] *Epp.* xliii.–xliv.

[7] 'Versutior fuit causidicus, et forensium cautionum atque cavillationum peritior, quam causa postularet,' Baldwin, *Historia Donatistarum*, given in *P.L.* xi. 1441. Augustine himself styles him 'maledicus conviciator,' *De Unico Baptismo*, 27. For his hatred of Augustine see *De Unitate*, 24, *Contra Litt. Petiliani*, ii. 38, iii. 11, 17, 19, 20, 30, *Retract.* ii. 25, etc.

[8] *Ep.* xliv. 1 and 13.

[9] *De Nuptiis et Concupiscentiis*, ii. 1.

[10] *Ep.* clxxxviii.

and there they had a tragic meeting with their old, embittered and irreconcilable enemy Emeritus, the now disregarded Donatist Bishop of that city.[1] Alypius is commemorated in the Roman Martyrology for August 15, and his death is assigned to the year 430. If that date is correct then he died about a fortnight before his lifelong friend, master and fellow-bishop. In a letter written to him, A.D. 428–9 Augustine addresses it to 'Alypio seni.'

Augustine and Alypius wrote many letters in conjunction. An early one, shortly after Augustine had been made Bishop, in A.D. 395, and two years after Alypius' elevation to the Episcopate, was written to the Archbishop Aurelius to express their delight at the then unprecedented step the latter had taken in making his young priests preach in his presence.[2] Two letters at least they addressed to St. Paulinus and his wife Theresia, the first in A.D. 398, asking for copies of the former's treatise against the pagans,[3] and the other in the midst of the Pelagian controversy, about A.D. 417.[4] St. Paulinus and Theresia often wrote to the two Bishops and opened with the words 'Paulinus et Theresia peccatores,' though they omit that when writing to a layman like Romanianus, the father of Licentius.[5] Augustine had had good reason to feel anxious about the last-named who promised to be somewhat of a scamp.[6] He was—or fancied himself—a bit of a poet[7] and it is significant that in many MSS. of Augustine's *De Musica* it is asserted that that Dialogue was held with Licentius.[8] Some of the conjoint letters of Augustine and Alypius deal with the Donatist controversy; one tells a correspondent, Generosus, how to deal with a Donatist who insists that he has had a vision of Angels—so his Church must be the true one;[9] another is to a doctor recently converted from Arianism,[10] while two were written in conjunction with

[1] *De Gestis cum Emerito*, 5.
[2] *Ep.* xli.
[3] *Ep.* xlv.
[4] *Ep.* clxxxvi.
[5] *Ep.* xxxii. 1.
[6] *Ep.* xxvi., xxvii. 6, xxxii. 5; *De Ordine*, i. 21, ii. 29; *Contra Academicos*, iii. 7.
[7] *Ep.* xxvi.
[8] See *Admonitio*, *P.L.* xxxii. col. 1080.
[9] *Ep.* liii., *c.* A.D. 400, *cf. Ep.* lxx.
[10] *Epp.* clxx and clxxi., *c.* A.D. 415.

Samsucius of Sabana to Severus, Bishop of Milevis, and deal with the case of a young Sub-deacon at Sabana who has misbehaved himself.[1] One of the most interesting of these joint epistles was to urge Castorius to accept the See of Bagai[2] where his brother Maximianus had recently died owing to his brutal treatment at the hands of the Donatists[3] who also seized his church,[4] with the result that very severe 'novae leges' were enacted against them by the Emperor Honorius.[5] Maximianus is commemorated in the Roman Martyrology on October 1.

The friendship between Augustine and Alypius lasted all their lives and the former found in the Bishop of Tagaste his greatest support in his many trials. Even before either of them was consecrated Augustine begs the Archbishop to let Alypius be with him as he is in difficulties, and he writes a touching letter of thanks for the permission accorded.[6] When commending Romanianus to St. Paulinus, Augustine urged that he was 'kin to the venerable and verily blessed Alypius the Bishop; him you will, I am sure, take warmly to your heart; and rightly so, for whosoever thinks kindly of Alypius must need think of the great mercy of God and His wondrous gifts. Unhesitatingly, then, will I leave Alypius wholly to your care.'[7] It was to the same Romanianus that St. Paulinus wrote congratulating the African Church on the possession of 'Aurelius, Alypius, Augustine, Profuturus and Severus, now all of them Bishops.'[8]

The picture of Alypius as we see him in the pages of Augustine's *Confessions* is of a bright and earnest person who is tremendously loyal to his friends. But to appreciate a wholly different aspect of his character we must give some account of the great Conference held in A.D. 411 between the Catholics and the Donatists.[9] Its true history yet remains to be written.

[1] *Epp.* lxii.–lxiii.
[2] *Ep.* lxix, *cf. Contra Cresconium*, iii. 47.
[3] *Ep.* lxxxviii. 7.
[4] *Ep.* clxxxv. 26.
[5] *Contra Cresconium*, iii. 47.
[6] *Ep.* xxii. 1.
[7] *Ep.* xxvii. 5, *cf. Ep.* xxviii. 1 to St. Jerome.
[8] *Ep.* xxxii. 1.
[9] The *Acta*, or as they were called, the *Gesta* of this Conference, are for some reason or other not included in the *Opera* of St. Augustine, but they are given in *P.L.* xi., *Opera Sancti Optati*, also in Mansi,

But, briefly, this Conference marked the culmination of the efforts of Augustine and his fellow-Bishops against Donatism; it also sounded the death-knell of that century-old schism—it had begun precisely one hundred years before, in A.D. 311.[1] For years the Catholic Bishops had tried to get the Donatist Bishops to meet them in a public discussion on the nature, origin, rights and wrongs of the schism. But nothing would induce the Donatist authorities to agree to any such round-table conference.[2] At length, however, the Emperor Honorius was induced to insist that the opposing parties should meet under the presidency of Marcellinus the Tribune. In obedience to the Edict no less a number than 279 Donatist Bishops and 285 Catholic Bishops came to Carthage. It had been arranged that seven delegates chosen by each side should alone conduct the discussion. But the Donatists—determined to render the proceedings nugatory—disregarded this and, to the dismay of the seven Catholic delegates, all 279 Donatists marched into the appointed meeting. This meant that all the 285 Catholics had to come in as well, and during the whole of one stormy day—not 'sitting' for though repeatedly asked by the president to be seated, the Donatist Bishops refused to sit 'in the seat of pestilence' (Ps. xxv. 4–5), *i.e.*, amid the Catholics[3]—they wrangled over the claims of individual Bishops to be present, and made the most outspoken comments on one another. This occupied the whole day, and it was agreed to meet next day when only the seven delegates with their assessor Bishops and notaries came together.[4] But the whole of the

Concilia, iv. We owe them in their present state to Marcellus the Memorialist, *cf. P.L.* xi. 1231. Marcellus prefixed 224 *Capitula* summing up the proceedings on the first day, 73 for the second day and 587 for the third day; but of these latter we have only the *Gesta* corresponding to Marcellus' *Capitula*, 1–281; indeed the whole is in a bad way 'propter veterem per notas scribendi rationem'—or shorthand, Baluze, *P.L.* xi. 1226. The missing portions, however, can be supplemented from Augustine's *Breviculus Collationis* or his own abbreviated account of the proceedings, *P.L.* xliii. 613–650, also from his *Ad Donatistas post Collationem*, *ibid.*, 651–690. For a brief account of the Conference see G. Lapeyre, in *Miscellanea Agostiniana*, Rome, ii., pp. 111–122.

[1] See St. Optatus, *De Schismate Donatistarum*.

[2] *Epp*. xxiii. 6–7, xxxiii. 2, xxxv. 2, 4, etc.

[3] *Collatio*, i. 144, ii. 4–7; *Ad Donatistas post Collationem*, 7, *Breviculus Collationis*, ii. 1.

[4] *Collatio*, ii. 2; Mansi, *Concilia*, iv. 168.

second day, June 2, was spent in futile wrangling over the official *Acta* which had not yet been written out in full, but only in shorthand. This, so the Donatists contended, was quite insufficient and they demanded and secured a further delay of six days so that they could have the fully written account. The final meeting was on June 8 when, after the most unseemly wrangling, the Donatists had reluctantly to allow a full discussion of the only point that mattered : Which was the True Church ? Here they failed lamentably and Marcellinus pronounced his decision in favour of the Catholics.[1] This was followed by an Imperial Edict against the Donatists, January 30, 412 ;[2] Marcellinus was slain on September 13 of the same year, when Marinus threw him and his brother Apringius into prison on the plea that they had been adherents of the rebel Heraclianus, and his enemies, the defeated Donatists, secured his judicial murder.[3] Marcellinus is commemorated in the Roman Martyrology, April 6. Honorius in indignation published a truly terrible Edict against the Donatists on June 23, 414, whereupon they appealed for help to Count Boniface.[4]

During this conference Alypius appears in a new light. He is now some fifty-six years of age, but he is unchanged. Loyal as ever to Augustine, we see him now vehement in his denunciation of the Donatists, ever the enemies of Augustine and of the Church. During all these years they have been triumphing, lording it over the little Catholic flock ; but now they are pinned down. For the long-wished-for public debate between the Catholics, so long ousted, and the church of the Donatists, so long ' established,' is at length staged and there is no escape. But though they must have known that the Donatists, fighting for very life as they were, would prove difficult to handle,

[1] Mansi, *Concilia*, iv. 263 ff.

[2] *Codex Thedos*. I. xvi. 11 ; also in *P.L.* xi., Appendix.

[3] *Ep.* cli. 11 ; St. Jerome, *Dial. cum Pelagianis*, iii. 19 ; Orosius, *Historia*, vii. 42.

[4] ' Magnum jurisprudentiae decus,' Baldwin styles him, *P.L.* xi. 1441. For his saintly character, *cf.* St. Augustine, *Epp.* cxxxvi., cxxxviii., cxl. 1, cli. 8–9 ; Augustine commends the ' paterna diligentia ' he had shown during the Conference, *Ep.* cxxxii. 2, also his amazing patience throughout those wearisome three days, *De Gestis Pelagii*, 25. To Marcellinus he wrote *De Origine Animae*, and to him he dedicated his *De Spiritu et littera* and *De Peccatorum Remissione et Meritis*.

neither Alypius nor any of the Catholic Bishops can ever have dreamed that the schismatics would prove themselves such past masters in the art of obstruction as they did. As the scene unfolds before us we see how every possible effort was made to render the discussion futile and to stave off any endeavour to deal with the one essential point : Which is the true Church ? We can see Alypius and others, too—save Augustine who only once betrayed a most justifiable irritation—getting more and more angry. Over and over again does Alypius complain of the deliberate delays and of the appalling length of the resulting *Acta*.[1] You Donatists will persist in discussing individual characters in the story of the schism, he says, and you refuse to face the real issue.[2] 'Many falsehoods were bandied about the day before yesterday. To save the populace from deception it must be positively stated that it is they who are asking for a postponement.'[3] He caught them out in presenting signatures of Bishops who were not present ;[4] he showed that Petilian's cavils tended to throw discredit either on the trustworthiness of the President's court or on the chosen custodians of the records of the meeting ;[5] he exclaimed, and justifiably, that many of the Donatist Bishops only had villages for their Sees.[6] When there was a most unpleasant scene owing to a personal attack on Augustine, and a hubbub ensued, Alypius insisted that this 'row' should be put on record.[7] When the name of Felicianus of Musti, who had notoriously started a sub-schism of his own and had revolted from the jurisdiction of Primianus the Donatist Archbishop of Carthage, was raised, Alypius somewhat maliciously asked whether Felicianus was in communion with Primianus ; but he could get no answer to that inopportune question.[8] When Petilian complained that though the Emperor wished to frighten him into submission he had no wish to see him persecuted, Alypius blurted out : 'And you are not even frightened,' and when Petilian took that as a compliment

[1] *Collatio*, ii. 40, iii. 12, 18, 88, 206.
[2] *Ibid.*, iii. 68, 119.
[3] *Ibid.*, ii. 71.
[4] *Ibid.*, i. 174.
[5] *Ibid.*, ii. 21.
[6] *Ibid.*, i. 181.
[7] *Ibid.*, iii. 240.
[8] *Collatio*, i. 222–224.

Alypius rejoined : ' No, you are not frightened, you have never even been afraid ! '[1] When it had been proved that one of the Donatists signatures was that of a Bishop who died en route and who therefore could not have signed a document drawn up in Carthage which he never reached, Petilian, in vexation at the awkward predicament in which they found themselves, ejaculated : ' After all, it is but human to die ! ', back came Alypius' riposte : ' Human to die ; inhuman to lie ! '[2]

The confrontation of the opposing parties, with the resulting spectacle of two Bishops in most of the Sees and full of undisguised hostility towards one another, had at least served to bring into open day the hopelessly divided state of Africa ; it was not without a certain sense of satisfaction, then, that when his turn came to answer to his name Alypius said : ' Would that every other city could rejoice in the same old-time unity as does my Tagaste ! '[3]

EVODIUS was one of Augustine's earliest companions in religious life, and, like him, was born at Tagaste. He began life as a soldier, but was converted to Catholicism before Augustine, and immediately devoted himself to the service of God ; ' simul eramus,' says Augustine, ' simul habitaturi placito sancto.'[4] He speedily joined the little company at Cassiciacum and was present at St. Monica's deathbed when Adeodatus burst into tears which Evodius checked by ' taking up his psaltery and intoning Ps. c. : *Misericordiam et judicium cantabo Tibi*, *Domine*, which they all took up together.[5] He returned to Africa with Augustine[6] and became a member of his community. When we next hear of him he has been having an interview with Proculeianus, the Donatist Bishop of Hippo, who, as he reported to Augustine, seemed well disposed and ready to hear what the Catholics had to say for themselves.[7] He seems to have been consecrated about a year after Augustine but before Possidius, A.D. 396.[8] His See, Uzala, was near

[1] *Ibid.*, iii. 26–28.
[2] *Ibid.*, i. 208.
[3] *Ibid.*, i. 136.
[4] *Confess*. ix. 17.
[5] *Ibid.*, ix. 31.
[6] *Ibid.*, ix. 17.
[7] *Ep*. xxxiii. 2, A.D. 395–396, before Evodius' consecration.
[8] *Ep*. clxxxiii., where note the order in which Pope Innocent addresses

Utica, and there Evodius had erected a shrine or 'Memoria' in honour of St. Stephen 'long before we had done so at Hippo.'[1] For Evodius had a very great devotion to the Proto-martyr who worked amazing miracles there and elsewhere in Africa.[2] He it was who had the treatise *De Miraculis S. Stephani* drawn up.[3]

Evodius seems to have been favoured with many visions of the dead, though he speaks of them as dreams.[4] Apropos of the death of a holy young man whom he had known intimately, Evodius furnishes us with an interesting piece of liturgical information: 'We gave him a fitting funeral, such as became a soul like his; for during the space of three days we sang hymns of praise to the Lord round his tomb, and on the third day we offered up the Sacrifice of our redemption.'[5] His devotion to Augustine is touching. He writes him long letters on doctrinal subjects and Augustine takes it for granted that he has copies of his works such as the *De Vera Religione*, *De Quantitate Animae*, *De Libero Arbitrio*, etc.[6] In fact in the two last-named Evodius was one of the disputants, as Augustine reminds him: 'You ask a lot of questions of a very busy man, and what is worse, you seem to think the answers to such questions can be dictated off-hand, though the problems presented are so difficult that even when carefully dictated or written the answers can hardly be brought within the grasp of even such a mind as yours. . . . But if you will but recall points that you know well, or at least, unless I am mistaken, did once know well, though you may possibly have forgotten the discussions we had together and which I committed to writing, whether *De Quantitate Animae* or *De Libero Arbitrio*, you will find there the answer to your questions.'[7] Only with

the Bishops: Augustine, Alypius, Evodius, Possidius, though, contrary to the general rule, Augustine is named before Alypius who had not only been consecrated before him but was Primate of Numidia. For the meticulous care taken about placing Bishops according to the date of their consecration see *Ep*. lix.

[1] *De Civitate Dei*, XXII. viii. 21.

[2] *Sermon*, cccxxiii. 3.

[3] *P.L.* xli. 833–854.

[4] *Epp*. clviii.–clxiii., clxix., A.D. 414–415.

[5] *Ep*. clviii. 2.

[6] *Ep*. clxii. 2, A.D. 415.

[7] *Ep*. clxii. 2, *c*., A.D. 415.

an intimate friend could Augustine have indulged in the above ironical remark about Evodius' intellectual capacity ; only to one knit to him in the closest friendship could he have said : 'See what (a long letter) a busy man like me has contrived to write to a lazy man like you ! '[1]

Evodius was certainly not dull-witted. For when troubles arose in a certain monastery owing to the failure of the monks to understand Augustine's teaching on grace and predestination, the Abbot, Valentinus, wrote to Evodius for counsel. The Bishop replied : 'While praising your zeal we trust it will not prove contentious ; for contention only causes disturbance of mind, whereas zeal demands real piety. I say then that the first man created, namely Adam, had the fullest possible possession of free will ; but when his free will was wounded, then was it weakened. Hence though even in man at present there is free will, yet is it a wounded free will. . . . The servants of God should, then, read what the Fathers have written ; for these latter are replete with devout feelings touching the Divine gift. But when the servants of God fail to understand what they read they should not straightway blame the writers but should pray for understanding '[2]—a truly Augustinian remark ! The treatise *De Fide contra Manichaeos*, long falsely attributed to St. Augustine, is assigned in one MS. to Evodius.[3] Like so many in those days, Evodius was a great copyist and we find him copying out Eusebius' *Chronicle* for St. Augustine.[4] He also had the privilege of a quasi martyrdom ; for the Council held at Carthage on June 26, 404, sent him and Theasius to Rome to state the Catholic case against the enormities perpetrated by the Donatists,[5] and a later Council sent them again on the same errand.[6] Petilian inveighed against these ambassadors 'quos praecursores ac navigatores semper habent, furiaeque suae legatos, qui expetant sanguinem,

[1] *Ep.* clxix. 12.
[2] *Ep.* ccxvi. 3 and notes in *P.L.* xxxiii. 776.
[3] *P.L.* xlii. 1140.
[4] St. Paulinus, *Ep.* xxiv. 3, *cf.* xxv. 5 (*inter Epp. S. Augustini*).
[5] *Codex canonum Ecclesiae Africanae*, 93, *P.L.* xi. 1202, xliii. 811 ; Hefele-Leclercq, ii. 155–156. We learn from *Ep.* lxxx. 1 that they were to see St. Paulinus on their way, and that at the time that letter was written, March, 405, they had not yet returned.
[6] *Collatio*, 411, iii. 141 ; *cf. Ep.* xcvii. 4, and for the effects of their mission, *Ep.* clxxxv. 29.

expetant proscriptiones, incutiant metus, pericula ingerant, homines per provincias diversas occidant'; [1] but he was careful not to say that his fellow-Donatists had scourged and grievously wounded them both on their return from their embassy in A.D. 408.[2]

Of all Augustine's companions and fellow-Bishops, SEVERUS, Bishop of Milevis, was perhaps the one most loved. Born at Tagaste [3] and of about the same age as Augustine, Severus idolized his fellow-citizen, whom he addresses in what to our ears are almost fulsome terms: 'I read your works extensively . . . indeed all time would not suffice me for reading your letters,' and he speaks of Augustine's 'elegantem famulatum, succinctam munditiam, fidelem ac castum simplexque ministerium.' [4] But we can pardon him all his exaggerated expressions for having penned the golden words: 'O vere artificiosa apis Dei, construens favos divini nectaris plenos, manantes misericordiam et veritatem, per quos discurrens deliciatur anima mea.' [5] These two friends addressed one another in terms of the deepest affection: for Severus Augustine is 'Venerabilis, desiderabilis, toto sinu charitatis amplectendus,' [6] while the latter calls Severus 'beatissimus, venerabiliter charissimus et sincerissimus,'[7] 'germanissimus et familiarissimus animae meae.'[8]

Severus seems to have been consecrated before Augustine if we are to judge by St. Paulinus' words,[9] but it is remarkable that Augustine, who is so meticulously careful about giving people their full and correct titles, should, so late as A.D. 401, address him as 'consacerdos' only and not as 'coepiscopus.' [10] It was a great grief to these intimate friends that 'the needs of Mother Church, which have—for the sake of the next world—to be preferred to the needs of this present world, compel us

[1] *Collatio*, iii. 141.
[2] *Codex canonum Ecclesiae Africanae*, cvi., *P.L.* xliii. 814.
[3] *Ep.* lxxxiv. 1, 'dulcissimus concivis meus.'
[4] *Ep.* cix. 1.
[5] *Ibid.*
[6] *Ibid.*
[7] *Ep.* lxii. 1, *cf.* lxiii. 1.
[8] *Ep.* cx. 4, *cf. Ep.* cclxx.
[9] *Ep.* xxxii. 1.
[10] *Ep.* lxxii. 1, where it is evident from the context that Severus is the Bishop of the place.

to live so far apart,' and Augustine complains to Novatus that 'my most dear friend and fellow-citizen Severus hardly ever writes to me now, and when he does do so it is only on scraps of paper, and most of those are filled with news of other people's cares and troubles.'[1] But on one occasion at least Severus paid a visit to Augustine at Hippo. The latter opened his sermon that day by saying: 'Our brother Severus still deprives us of the joy we should feel at hearing from him the sermon he owes us! Yet he agrees that he does owe us one. In every church he visits the Lord gladdens the hearts of the people through his mouth; much more, then, has this church a claim to the same happiness since from it the Lord sent him out to spread the faith in other places. Still I suppose we must give in to him. We must let him put off his sermon, not wholly deprive us of it. Make him realize that he is your debtor; do not let him off till he has paid his debt!'[2]

Severus died A.D. 426. He had already designated his successor; but Augustine went to Milevis to preside over the election and Severus' choice was ratified by the people.[3] One scene in the lives of these two Saints we should have liked to have witnessed, and that was when they sat and watched experiments with a magnet and were 'stupefacti'![4]

Profuturus, of whom Augustine says: 'Mihi es alter ego,'[5] had before his elevation to the episcopate been a monk in Augustine's monastery. He was the bearer of the ill-fated letter which Augustine wrote to Jerome but which through a series of mischances went to Rome instead.[6] For just as he was sailing 'he had to accept the burden of the episcopate, and shortly afterwards died.'[7] After his death he, as well as Privatus and Servilius, 'whom I well remember as men of holy lives who came from our monastery,[8] appear to me in dreams and tell me things which afterwards come to pass as they had

[1] *Ep.* lxxxiv. 1.
[2] *Enarr.* i. 1 *on* Ps. xcvi.; *cp. Enarr.* i. 1 *on* Ps. cxxxi.
[3] *Ep.* ccxiii. 1.
[4] *De Civitate Dei*, XXI. iv. 4, the whole account should be read.
[5] *Ep.* xxxviii.
[6] *Ep.* xxviii.; see below, pp. 211, ff.
[7] *Ep.* lxxi. 2.
[8] Reading 'processisse' with the Vatican MS., others have 'praecessisse.'

said.'[1] Profuturus' See was that of Cirta in which he was succeeded in A.D. 394–5 by Fortunatus.[2]

To POSSIDIUS we are indebted for that invaluable marvel of compression the *Vita Sancti Aurelii Augustini Hipponensis Episcopi*,[3] which he had made up his mind to write even when a layman,[4] an account of 'what I myself have seen in him or heard from his lips,'[5] for, as he says when completing his self-imposed task: 'I feel that those were able to glean far more fruit from Augustine who had the privilege of actually looking on him and hearing him speaking before them in the church.'[6] To Possidius we also owe the *Indiculus Librorum, Tractatuum et Epistolarum Sancti Augustini Hipponensis Episcopi* which, while it shows how marvellously the Saint's works have, on the whole, been preserved, yet betrays certain lamentable gaps in our present editions.[7]

Possidius succeeded Megalius, who had consecrated Augustine,[8] in the See of Calama, A.D. 397,[9] and as he survived to write the *Life* of the latter he must himself have been a Bishop for close on forty years. Megalius had been Primate of Numidia[10] and in that position Crescentianus succeeded him,[11] and after

[1] *Ep.* clviii. 9; *cf. Epp.* xcii. 1, clix. 5, clxix. 11 for Augustine's mind on this subject.

[2] *De Unico Baptismo*, 29, *Contra Litt. Petiliani*, ii. 99.

[3] *P.L.* xxxii. 33–66; *cf.* Harnack, *Possidius: Augustinus Leben eingeleitet und übersetzt*, 1930; also for his *Indiculus librorum, tractatuum et epistolarum S. Augustini, P.L.* xlvi. 5–22; *cf.* A. Wilmart, *Operum S. Augustini Elenchus a Possidio ejusdem discipulo Calamensi episcopo digestus, Miscellanea Agostiniana*, Rome, ii. pp. 149–233; Donatien De Bruyne, *Une énigme dans la liste des écrits d'Augustin rédigée par Possidius, ibid.*, pp. 317–320.

[4] *Vita*, 1.

[5] *Ibid.*

[6] *Ibid.*, 31.

[7] For example, of the thirteen letters addressed by Augustine to various Donatists only *Ep.* xxxiii. to Proculeianus, *Ep.* lxxxvii. to Emeritus, and *Epp.* li. and lvi. have come down to us.

[8] Megalius had, for reasons unknown to us, written an angry letter to Augustine as yet only a priest. This was in circulation among the Donatists who made great capital out of it. But as Augustine points out, when called upon in a Council to prove his allegations against Augustine and discovering that he had been misled, Megalius publicly apologised, *cf. Ep.* xxxviii. 2, *Vita* 8, *Contra Cresconium*, iii. 92, iv. 79; *Breviculus Collationis*, iii. 9.

[9] *Ep.* xxxviii. and *Praefatio* Maurorum, *P.L.* xxxii. col. 21.

[10] *Ep.* xxxviii.

[11] Crescentianus wrote to Aurelius at the Council of Carthage, 397, announcing the fact.

him Alypius of Tagaste became Primate.[1] 'In my brother and colleague Possidius,' says Augustine to Memorius the Bishop, who was, by the way, the father of the unhappy Julian of Eclanum, 'you will discover in effect my double.'[2] The Catholic Bishop of Calama had to face great opposition from the Donatists in that city where they were led by their notorious Bishop, Crispinus, just as Augustine had to suffer from an equally unscrupulous Donatist Bishop of Hippo, the truculent Proculeianus.[3] The Donatist fanatics had made at least one—fortunately unsuccessful—attempt on Augustine's life;[4] but they were more successful in their attack on Possidius who, on taking possession of his See, had denounced the Donatists; they stole his beasts of burden and his equipage and wounded him severely. Forced in self-defence to take action against Crispinus who had instigated the affair, Possidius claimed that as a technical 'heretic' the Donatist Bishop was liable to a fine of £10 in gold. When Crispinus indignantly maintained in the Proconsular court that though a schismatic he was no heretic, Possidius felt that the matter could not rest there, so a public disputation between the rival Bishops was held, with Augustine in the chair: 'while an immense multitude of Christians both in Carthage and throughout all Africa anxiously awaited the result, which was that Crispinus was, by a written sentence of the Proconsular court, declared a heretic.'[5] Mulcted to the tune of £10 in gold he—despite the fact that Augustine immediately secured him exemption from paying the fine—appealed to the Emperor, but the latter ratified the sentence and reimposed the fine which, however, was never paid.[6]

The pagans in Calama were also a source of trouble. An Imperial Edict forbidding heathen celebrations had been published in June, 407. Despite this a huge concourse of pagans at Calama held public festival and danced in procession

[1] See p. 114.
[2] *Ep.* ci. 1: 'In quo nostram non parvam praesentiam reperies.'
[3] He declined to restrain the excesses of the Donatists and he refused to enter into any discussion with Augustine on the merits of their respective claims, *cf. Epp.* xxxiii., xxxv., lxxxvi. and cv. 3.
[4] *Vita*, 12.
[5] *Vita*, 12; *Sermon*, xix. 8, *P.L.* xlvi. 892.
[6] *Ibid.*

before the doors of the Catholic Church which they proceeded on three separate occasions to pelt with stones, and to which they finally set fire, with the result that one man was killed, while the mob sought everywhere for Possidius whom they had determined to slay. All this was done with the connivance of the magistrates who, as events showed, could easily have repressed the outbreak.[1]

In February, 405, the Emperor had published the famous *Edict of Union* whereby the Donatists were to be compelled to conform. This was withdrawn in A.D. 409 with disastrous results, and the African Bishops felt compelled to send an embassy to the Imperial court to protest. This embassy consisted of Florentius, Bishop of Hippo Diarrhytus, Praesidius, Benenatus, and Possidius, Bishop of Calama.[2]

FORTUNATIANUS, Bishop of Sicca, was one of Augustine's most trusted companions, and was sent by the Council held at Carthage on June 16, 408, on an embassy to Honorius the Emperor to state the Catholic case against the Donatists. He was also one of the seven delegates chosen to represent the Catholic Bishops at the Conference of A.D. 411. Augustine entrusted him with the delicate mission of pacifying a Bishop, unnamed, who seems to have taken offence at something Augustine had written to him.[3] Fortunatianus apparently died A.D. 413, and seems to have been succeeded immediately by Urbanus who was certainly the occupant of the See of Sicca during the Council of Carthage, A.D. 419, and to whose elevation to the episcopate Augustine refers when writing to St. Paulinus, *c.* A.D. 414.[4] Fortunatianus played a very important part in the Conference of A.D. 411, where he was one of the chosen seven delegates for the Catholic episcopate.[5] Apart from repeated insistence on the obstructionist tactics of the Donatists,[6] he was mainly instrumental in securing that the one question at issue : Explain how and why you come to be in schism, was really faced. Fortunatianus of Sicca must be carefully

[1] *Ep.* xci.
[2] At the Council held at Carthage, June, 410.
[3] *Ep.* cxlviii. 1 and 18.
[4] *Ep.* xclix. 34.
[5] *Collatio*, i. 55, Mansi, *Concilia*, iv. col. 80.
[6] *Ibid.*, i. 50, 66, 68, 168–172 ; ii. 17, 26.

distinguished from Fortunatianus Neapolitanus who was present at the Councils of Carthage, A.D. 418 and 419.[1]

FORTUNATUS of Cirta became Bishop of that distracted See A.D. 394–5, for it is practically certain that it was when on his way with Alypius to consecrate Fortunatus that Augustine passed through Tubursicum and had his curious discussion with Fortunius, the Donatist Bishop there.[2] Some three years later we find Fortunatus at Cirta with Serenus and Victor.[3] Again three years later, Augustine, Alypius and Fortunatus addressed a joint letter to the Donatists at Cirta where difficulties seem to have been so great as to call for the help of a coadjutor Bishop, Delphinus.[4] At the Conference of A.D. 411 Petilian bitterly complained of having to face two Catholic Bishops in his district.[5] These difficulties no doubt arose in part from the fact that Cirta was a Donatist stronghold, but they were also due to the scandalous life of a deacon who went over to the Donatists, was rebaptized by them and even raised to the priesthood by Petilian, though when the latter discovered the unhappy man's iniquities he expelled him. His crimes seem to have been committed in Gaul, for the Gallic Bishops informed the African Church of his misdeeds and Fortunatus publicly read out their condemnation of him in his church at Cirta.[6] Fortunatus was one of the seven Catholic delegates in 411 where he, like the others, tried in vain to keep the Donatists to the one essential point: Which is the True Church, 'for,' he added, 'it is a crime that the people should be driven into error by being kept in suspense.'[7] The names of Fortunatus and Fortunatianus were read out one after the other in the roll-call of the Catholic Bishops, and it was like Petilian to suggest that they were one and the same person and that the Catholics were trying to swell their numbers by multiplying Bishops.[8] Perhaps, however, he was having his revenge on Fortunatianus who a moment before had declared that he only knew Petilian—

[1] See *P.L.* xlvii. 278; Hefele-Leclercq, ii. 195.
[2] *Ep.* xliii. and xliv. 1 and 6.
[3] *Ep.* liii., *c.* A.D. 400.
[4] *Ep.* cxxxix. 4, *Contra Litt. Petiliani*, ii. 228.
[5] *Collatio*, i. 65.
[6] *Contra Litt. Petiliani*, iii. 44.
[7] *Collatio*, iii. 14.
[8] *Ibid.*, i. 140–141.

the greatest of all the Donatist Bishops—by name, whereas he did know that the Church at Sicca—his own See—was undivided.[1] It must have been exceedingly gratifying to Augustine to hear from a number of people at Cirta that as a result of that wearisome and apparently fruitless meeting many of them had embraced the Catholic faith. They somewhat naively tell him that their case is like that of Polemon who in the course of a discussion with Xenocrates on the virtue of temperance was converted from his drunken ways though he was actually drunk at the moment ! [2]

URBANUS, a disciple of St. Augustine, was only a priest when he brought to Augustine in 412 Marcellinus' letter asking Augustine about original sin,[3] but two years later, in A.D. 414, Augustine ended a long letter to St. Paulinus with the remark that ' Peregrinus, who accompanied our brother Urbanus when the latter went to assume the burden of the episcopate (at Sicca), has not returned to Hippo.' [4] Later on Urbanus appears to have encountered at Rome people infected with Pelagian views ; for Augustine says in a sermon : ' I was horrified when I heard such views. Not that I heard them with my own ears, but my fellow-Bishop Urbanus, who formerly was a priest here, and is now Bishop of Sicca, told me on his return from Rome ' of a discussion he had had with such people.[5] Whether Urbanus' attitude on this subject offended Pope Zosimus we do not know, but when Urbanus felt bound to depose and excommunicate Apiarius, a priest of Sicca,[6] the latter appealed to the Pope, who demanded his restoration and threatened Urbanus with the same penalty unless he yielded ; [7] a threat repeated by the Legates whom Zosimus sent to formulate various points on which he insisted when a provincial African Council was held at Carthage towards the close of A.D. 418.[8]

[1] *Ibid.*, i. 139.
[2] *Ep.* cxliv. 2, *c.* A.D. 412.
[3] *Ep.* cxliii. 2.
[4] *Ep.* cxlix. 34, *cf. Vita* xi. where Possidius enumerates Urbanus amongst the Bishops trained by Augustine.
[5] A fragment of a sermon preserved by Eugippius, *P.L.* xxxix. 1719.
[6] Hefele-Leclercq, ii. 196, *cf. ibid.*, i. 504–505, 764 notes, Mansi, *Concilia*, iv. 401–440.
[7] *Ibid.*, ii. 196.
[8] *Ibid.*, ii. 197.

But by that time Apiarius had repented and been restored to his position by Urbanus though the Council felt it advisable to remove him from Sicca.[1] The last time we hear of Urbanus is about A.D. 429, when Augustine writes to Count Darius saying that he has heard of him from Urbanus and Novatus.[2]

Whether VINCENT of Culusis was a disciple of St. Augustine does not appear; his name does not, so far as we are aware, occur in any of the latter's letters. But he must have been a man of great weight for he, with Fortunatianus of Sicca, was sent as ambassador to the Emperor with full powers to ask for the appointment of ecclesiastical lawyers and to arrange certain fiscal matters.[3] At the Conference of A.D. 411 Vincent was one of the seven delegates,[4] and it is significant that when answering his name at the preliminary investigation, he could say of his diocese 'Catholica est,' and that the irrepressible Donatist Deacon Habetdeus could only retort that 'there had been a Donatist representative there (whether Bishop or priest he does not say) but that he had recently gone over to them (the Catholics).'[5]

At the Council of Telepte or Zelle,[6] A.D. 418, as also at the Council of Carthage in 419, when 207 Bishops were present, Vincent and Fortunatus are especially named after 'the Legates of the African Provinces.'[7]

Of PEREGRINUS we know little. As a deacon he accompanied Boniface of Cataqua when the latter went, apparently from place to place, trying to secure that the facts of the Conference held between the Catholic and Donatist Bishops in A.D. 411 should be widely circulated and read.[8] Two years later he became Bishop though his See is not mentioned: 'My fellow-deacon Peregrinus,' writes Augustine in A.D. 414, 'from the time he left me, when he went with Urban our brother to shoulder the burden of the Episcopate, has not yet returned to

[1] *Ibid.*, ii. 209.
[2] *Ep.* ccxxix. 1.
[3] Hefele-Leclercq, ii. 157; can. 3.
[4] Mansi, *Concilia*, iv.; *Gesta Collationis*, i. 2.
[5] *Collatio*, i. 138.
[6] 'More correctly "Zelle",' Hefele-Leclercq, ii. 196, but *cf.* Mansi, *l.c.*, iv. 381 note.
[7] Mansi, *l.c.*, iv. 402–408.
[8] *Ep.* cxxxix. 2, May, 412.

Hippo.'[1] To him Augustine and Alypius addressed a conjoint letter in A.D. 415.[2]

Of SERVILIUS, who also appeared after death to Evodius,[3] we know nothing save that he was one of the signatories of the letter addressed by the African Episcopate to Pope Innocent I on the condemnation of Pelagianism they had pronounced in 416.[4] On one of the occasions—for there would seem to have been more than one—when he appeared to Evodius, the latter says: 'After his death I saw brother Servilius in a dream whilst I was still living in the monastery, and he remarked to me that whereas we here on earth strive to arrive at an understanding of things by our reason, there (in heaven) he and such as he rest tranquil in the joys of contemplation.'

Of BONIFACE, Bishop of Cataqua, we know little beyond the fact that he was a close friend of the Bishop of Hippo who stayed with him at Cataqua on at least one occasion.[5] Boniface succeeded to the See of Cataqua about A.D. 408 under difficult circumstances; for his predecessor Paul, a convert of St. Augustine's, and one who had himself made many converts, had by some financial transactions disgraced, as Augustine tells him, not only his own See but the whole Church of Hippo.[6] Boniface was present at the Conference of A.D. 411, and seems to have been one of those Bishops who took care that the *Gesta* or detailed account of the proceedings on that occasion should be read in his church.[7]

Nor must we forget those other less-known helpers, the monks of Augustine's monastery whose names figure now and and again in his letters, and always in terms of affectionate remembrance: 'Lucillus, my deacon,'[8] 'Brother Barbarus, for so long at Hippo, ever a fervent and eager hearer of the word of God,'[9] 'my fellow-deacon Timothy.'[10] Then, amongst

[1] *Ep.* cxlix. 34.
[2] *Ep.* clxxi.
[3] *Ep.* clviii. 9.
[4] *Ep.* clxxv. 1, *cf.* Innocent's reply, *Ep.* clxxxi.
[5] *Ep.* cxlix. 2, A.D. 414.
[6] *Ep.* lxxxv. 1, *c.* A.D. 405; *cf.* *Epp.* xcvi. 2, xcvii. 3, xcviii., all written *c.* A.D. 408.
[7] *Ep.* cxxxix. 1–2.
[8] *Ep.* lxxxiv. 1.
[9] *Ep.* clix. 1.
[10] *Ep.* cx.

many unnamed, the Deacons Valens and Faustinus, the latter of whom had once been a soldier, was then converted, baptized, and ultimately 'ordained a Deacon';[1] next comes a touching remembrance of 'Severus the Deacon whose affliction under God you all know of; yet (though he has lost the sight of his eyes) he has not lost that of his mind!' and the Bishop goes on to tell how Severus had succeeded in securing a house and property for his mother and sister through certain kind friends;[2] Hipponensis, another Deacon at Hippo, has just freed his slaves,[3] while Eraclius—whom Augustine was then suggesting as his successor in the See of Hippo—'stands there before you, and his good deeds, too, shine before your eyes,' for, amongst other things, Eraclius had built a shrine, apparently in honour of St. Stephen.[4] Then comes Leporius the priest, a man of considerable substance 'yet he left all, and I, says Augustine, took him in his poverty; not so much because he was poor but because he had put into effect what the words just read to you[5] taught him'; last of all Barnabas who, as the Bishop proceeds to tell, had been cruelly maligned but whose character he now vindicates before them all.[6]

By these monks, then, and by these great Bishops, whom he had formed for the most part in his monastery where they had looked forward to nothing but a life of prayer and study, but whom God had destined to play a wonderful part in the African Church, was Augustine's work and his influence made permanent. Even though the Vandal persecution seemed to sweep away the edifice he had so laboriously built up, yet in the heroism shown by the African Bishops in that fearful ordeal, we can surely trace the effect of Augustine's example and training.[7]

* * * * * *

[1] *Sermon*, ccclvi. 3–4. In this sermon Augustine, 'now grey-haired' (*ibid.*, 13), might almost be said to 'call the roll' of the members of that monastery at Hippo which he had so loved; as a matter of fact he names but a few, and those in the main because they had been the subject of ungenerous cavillings.

[2] *Ibid.*, 5.

[3] *Ibid.*, 6.

[4] *Ibid.*, 7.

[5] *Ibid.*, 10; Acts, iv. 31–35.

[6] *Ibid.*, 15.

[7] L. R. Holme, *The Extinction of the Christian Church in N. Africa*, 1898.

V—PERSONAL DETAILS

Personal details of Augustine's life are comparatively rare, though Possidius has preserved a certain number for us. He dined at eleven o'clock in the morning, the usual hour as it would seem.[1] His table was generously supplied,[2] but he was strict in many ways, for instance, the number of cups of wine was limited, and anybody who swore was fined by losing one cup.[3] At meals he allowed of no uncharitable talk, and in order to prevent it he had written over the table the lines :

> Quisquis amat dictis absentem rodere vitam,
> Hanc mensam indignam noverit esse sibi.

When on one occasion some of his fellow Bishops forgot themselves on this point he rose from the table and said : 'Either that inscription must be erased or I must leave the room ! '[4]

Sobriety was not an African virtue, and Augustine himself seems to have found it hard to observe the complete moderation he would have desired in eating and drinking, for he mentions the subject frequently. In his *Confessions* he had said : ' Drunkenness is far from me ; have mercy on me lest it take hold of me ! But *crapula* has at times got hold of Thy servant.'[5] By *crapula* he seems to mean a satiety due to food rather than drink, for, writing against Julian, he says : ' Drunkenness does not justify the condemnation of wine nor *crapula* of food.'[6]

> When [he writes] we have to make use of the pleasure necessarily attaching to the refreshment of our bodies, who can express in words how that same pleasure prevents us from realizing where necessity ceases and the limits demanded for the preservation of health have been reached ? When we have agreeable things to eat that pleasure plays hide and seek with us and makes us overpass those limits. We think that enough

[1] *Sermo*, cccxlv. 5, except on fast days when the first meal was at 3.0. *Ep*. liv. 9.
[2] *Vita*, 22.
[3] *Vita*, 25.
[4] *Ibid*., 22.
[5] *Confess*. x. 45 ; yet *cp*. *Sermo*, ccvii. 2.
[6] *Contra Julianum*, iv. 73.

is not enough and we gladly yield to pleasure's importunities, persuading ourselves that after all we are only looking after our health, when all the time we are seeking satiety. When that satiety fills us with regrets then we see how wrong we have been, and, through dread of such late repentance, we then eat less than suffices to stay our hunger—*ita nescit cupiditas ubi finitur necessitas*.[1] What sober-minded man [he exclaims] would not prefer that we should be able, were it possible, to take dry or liquid foods without any carnal pleasure in feasting—just as we take in the air ![2]

'There are many men who surpass any four-footed animal in greediness . . . though it would be hard to find anything more greedy than a goose.'[3]

We are afforded a hint about his own ways at table when he says :—

I have called the pleasure attached to eating 'bearable,' because it is not so intense as to be able to break off or distract our thoughts from the things of wisdom if our minds are occupied with them. For during meals not only do we frequently occupy our minds with lofty matters but we hold discussions on them, and between mouthfuls and while drinking we talk together and listen without distraction to what one another says, and if there is something we want to know or to remember we can readily do so, more especially if we are being read to.[4]

His personal poverty was remarkable. On settling down at Tagaste he surrendered his patrimony *paucis agellulis paternis contemptis*.[5] This poverty he says, *vehementer adamavi*, and he urged it on his clerics, though compelling none to follow his example.[6] Hence his determination to accept no legacies.[7] Possidius tells us, too, that in times of stress among the people the Bishop melted down the church plate,[8] as so many other pastors of the Church have done. How few could boldly

[1] *Ibid.*, 70.
[2] *Ibid.*, 68.
[3] *Contra Epistolam Manichaei*, 35.
[4] *Contra Julianum*, iv. 71.
[5] *Ep.* cxxvi. 7, *cf. ibid.*, 9–10.
[6] *Ep.* clvii. 39 ; *cf. Vita*, 23–24 ; *Sermo*, ccclv. 2, 4–5 ; ccclvi. 1, 6, 13–14.
[7] *Vita*, 24 ; *cf. Sermo*, ccclv. 4–5.
[8] *Vita*, 24.

challenge their opponents and say that their life was well known, and that they could call eminent witnesses to attest to its unblemished character? Yet Augustine was not afraid to challenge investigation into his life when Petilian and other Donatist leaders endeavoured to besmirch his reputation: 'Were it necessary to prove all this to people who are sceptical and call it in question, I could call many reputable men who would prove redoubtable witnesses to the whole course of my life.'[1]

He was severe on the subject of the personal poverty of his monks, nor did he ever allow them to dine out.[2] He wore linen next his skin—if, that is, he is talking of his own personal habits—and wool over that.[3] Probably the Latin-speaking Africans adhered to Roman fashions in dress. According to the sumptuary laws laid down by the Emperors in A.D. 382, officials were bound to wear a mantle (*paenula*), also an inner garment fastened with a girdle, 'but in such wise that by covering the chest with cloaks of varying colour they may afford recognizable indications of their position in society.'[4] Augustine seems to have worn shoes, not sandals,[5] though the sumptuary laws of A.D. 397 forbade the use of *tzangas*, a species of soft Persian shoe, also of *braccae* or breeches; such articles of clothing, it is declared, *intra urbem venerabilem nemini liceat usurpare.*[6]

Possidius tells us that his tablespoons were of silver,[7] also that he wore no ring,[8] though as a matter of fact when signing a certain letter he does say: 'I have sealed this letter with a ring showing the face of a man looking to one side.'[9] These seemingly trifling details could be multiplied; but, trifling though they are, they serve to show us something of the man who was Augustine, Bishop of Hippo, a man so acceptable in the sight

[1] *Contra Litt. Petiliani*, iii. 30.
[2] *Sermo*, cclvi. 13.
[3] *Ibid.*, where he speaks of the *byrrhus* and the *linea tunica*. The former is supposed to have been a shaggy outer garment; a little further on he talks of a *byrrhus pretiosus*.
[4] *Codex Theodosianus*, XIV., x. 1.
[5] *Sermo*, ci. 7.
[6] *Codex Theodosianus*, XIV., x. 2–3.
[7] *Vita*, 22.
[8] *Ibid.*, 24.
[9] *Ep.* lix. 2.

of God that a miracle long asked for at the intercession of St. Stephen, sought for in Caesarea of Cappadocia, begged for at the intercession of St. Laurence at Ravenna, again at the shrine of St. Stephen at Ancona, and lastly at Uzala in Africa, was finally granted at Hippo owing to the merits of Augustine. For, says the narrator : 'three months ago your Holiness appeared to my sister in a vision with the very same features as those on which we are now looking, whence we understood that we had to come here. And I, too, often afterwards saw your beatitude as we passed through other cities on our journey hither, and I saw you then precisely as I see you now.'[1]

It can have fallen to few to have fought so many battles and have seen them triumphantly won as did Augustine. He had routed the Manichees, he had seen the Donatist schism broken ; he had spent his last eighteen years striving against the most insidious of all heresies, that of Pelagius, and, in spite of an opposition that at one time seemed near to crushing him, he saw it defeated. When in A.D. 416 the Emperors Honorius and Theodosius wrote to Aurelius, the Primate of all Africa, informing him officially of the steps he was to take for the final suppression of this pestilence, it is significant that at the same time they wrote to the same effect to Augustine, though he was no Primate. Fourteen years later, A.D. 430, Honorius wrote to St. Augustine inviting him to attend the Council of Ephesus to be held in the following year. But the 'Doctor gratiae' was already dead.[2]

* * * * * *

Sanctus Praesul Augustinus
Assumptus est cum Angelis
Ubi gaudet cum Prophetis
Laetatur cum Apostolis
Quorum plenus spiritu
Quae praedixerunt mystica
Fecit nobis pervia
Post quos secunda dispensandi
Verbi Dei primus refulsit gratia.[3]

[1] *Sermo*, cccxxii.
[2] *Ep.* cci., the note in Migne's ed., *P.L.* xxxiii. 927.
[3] The antiphon at the *Magnificat* on the Feast of St. Augustine.

Possidius has left us a touching picture of the Saint's last days. Surely it was fitting that he whose greatest work in many ways was his *Confessions* should meet death with the Penitential Psalms 'pinned on the walls by his bedside,' and lying there 'he gazed at them and read them, and even as he read he shed copious tears.' What more fitting epitaph than the words of the same devoted friend and biographer: 'Throughout his life, up to his last illness, he preached the word of God in the church with joy and with vigour, giving sound counsel out of an intellect unclouded'?[1] Yet there remains another epitaph, one emanating from that Apostolic See which he loved so much, which had at one time—in the person of Pope Zosimus—so misunderstood him :—

We have ever regarded Augustine [wrote Pope Celestine in May, 431] as a man of saintly memory by reason of his life and his merits in communion with us ; no rumour of unworthy suspicion ever besmirched his record. We have long known him as a man of such learning that he was always regarded by our predecessors as one of the greatest of doctors.[2]

* * * * * *

On October 1, 1695, there was discovered in the old monastic church of San Pietro in Ciel d'oro at Pavia a white marble sarcophagus under a brick mausoleum, and in a silver chest lay what was acclaimed as the body of St. Augustine. The identification was at once disputed and the discussion raged for some fifteen years until Pope Benedict XIII published a *Constitution* dated XVII. Kal. October, 1728,[3] in which he gave the details of the translation of the remains of the Bishop of Hippo.

[1] *Vita*, 31.

[2] *Ep.* to the Bishops of Gaul ; *cf.* Denzinger, *Enchiridion*, No. 128 ; to the words of Pope Celestine we may fittingly add those of another Pontiff : 'De libero tamen arbitrio et gratia Dei quid Romana, hoc est Catholica, sequatur et servet Ecclesia, licet in variis libris beati Augustini, et maxime ad Prosperum et Hilarium abunde possit cognosci.' Pope Hormisdas *ad Possessorem*.

[3] F. Beleeli, Prior Generalis totius Ordinis S. Augustini, *Collectio actorum quibus ossa sacra Ticini* (Pavia) *in confessione S. Petri in Coelo Aureo anno* 1695 *reperta esse sacras Sancti Augustini Hipponensis Episcopi exuvias probatum est et novissime judicatum* 1729 *ad SSm. Patrem Benedictum XIII*. Venetiis, 1729.

Briefly, a body of African Bishops expelled by the Vandals took with them the body of the Saint to Sardinia where it was venerated till the opening of the eighth century. When, however, the Saracens invaded the place Luitprand, king of Lombardy, sent an embassy to them, and on the payment of a large sum of money, secured the body which was brought to Pavia and there buried in the neighbourhood of a well. Many miracles were immediately worked at the shrine. But it seems to have fallen into oblivion until, as stated above, the sarcophagus was discovered in 1695, some eight hundred years later. A flood of controversial literature at once followed, and L. A. Muratori went so far as to maintain that the remains were merely those of 'some unknown martyr.'[1] Now, however, the identification is generally accepted[2] and in the church of San Pietro the visitor can see 'the sumptuous Arca di Sant' Agostino adorned with ninety-five statuettes and fifty reliefs executed by Bonino di Campione. On the sarcophagus is the recumbent figure of St. Augustine.'[3]

[1] *Motivi di credere tuttavia ascoso e non iscoperto in Pavia l'anno* 1695 *il s. corpo di Sant' Agostino*, 1730.

[2] Giusto Fontanini, Archbishop of Ancyra, *De corpore Sancti Augustini disquisitio in favore della identita di esso Corpo*, 1728 ; J. Reinkens, *Rélation de la Découverte du corps de S. Augustin*, 1728 ; S. Comi, *Il diritto e possesso del pubblico di Pavia sul deposito e sull' arca di Sant' Agostino . . . contro le opposizione*, 1804 ; J. Germer-Durand, *Le Tombeau de S. Augustin à Pavia*, in *Rev. de l'art chrét.*, 1878, viii. 257 ff.

[3] Baedeker, *Northern Italy*, 1906, p. 204.

IV

ST. AUGUSTINE THE PREACHER

I. His Fame as a Preacher—II. His Audience—III. His Method and Purpose in Preaching—IV. How He prepared his Sermons—V. His Humour—VI. St. Augustine's Eloquence—VII. Editions of His Sermons—VIII. Bibliography.

Quasi sol refulgens, qui dominus dicitur planetarum, et pater luminis super omnia luminaria splendens, delectabilis oculis, ac per omnia respiciens: sic Augustinus Ecclesiam illustravit, gemma doctorum, pater theologorum, suavis eloquio, omnes materias penetrando dilucidans.—St. Antoninus, *Historiarum*, ii. 8.

I—ST. AUGUSTINE'S FAME AS A PREACHER

Those who listen are happier than those who speak. For the learner is humble; but the teacher has to try not to be proud, for fear lest there creep in an unworthy desire to please, and he find himself displeasing God through trying to please men.—*Enarr.* on Ps. l. i. 13.

When an evil-minded person tries to lead you into sin he deservedly incurs the punishment due to a deceiver, even when he does not succeed; so too a faithful preacher of righteousness may be rejected by men; but do not imagine that he will be deprived by God of the reward due to the fulfilment of his duty.—*Contra Cresconium*, i. 7.

Augustine began to preach when only a priest. Though this does not sound strange to us, yet, though it had long been the custom in the East for priests to preach,[1] until Augustine's day only the Bishops did so in Africa. The fact that his Bishop made the newly ordained priest preach caused a good deal of feeling at the time,[2] and even Augustine himself felt bound to

[1] *Vita*, 5; see St. Jerome, *Ep*. ii.
[2] *Vita*, 5.

apologize for doing so : ' We beg you not to refuse to listen to priests who deliver to you the word of God with earnestness and care.' [1] But the practice soon spread, and Augustine writes to the Primate Aurelius to tell him how glad he is that the young priests are in future to preach in the presence of their Bishop. [2] He himself, while still only a priest, preached before the Bishops assembled for the Council of Hippo (A.D. 393). [3]

And people soon realized that a good preacher had risen in Africa ; they came in crowds to hear him and hung upon his words. Preaching on the words, ' They are multiplied beyond measure ' of Ps. xxxix., he says : ' What crowds fill the churches ! They are packed to the walls ; people press on one another ; the mob is almost suffocating.' [4] And again : ' I see in what crowds you have come ; and you see how I am perspiring.' [5] Yet at times he has to lament that ' many are away at the circus,' though he adds, presumably with a smile, that ' even these would, if there came a panic, stand up and make the Sign of the Cross.' [6] On another occasion, the Feast of SS. Peter and Paul, he says : ' I feel somewhat sad, for I do not see so big a congregation as there should be on the feast of the Passion of the Apostles. Did we not know it was their feast, no one could blame us : but if everybody knows it, why so sluggish ? Surely you love Peter and Paul ? Speaking to you, I am addressing those who are not here.' [7] When only a sprinkling turned up for the Feast of St. Laurence : ' You few will have to listen to but a few words, for I am wearied in body and the heat is so great that I cannot say much.' [8] Truth to tell, the Africans were a fickle body : ' I hate to say it, yet I must : you know it is true that a clown makes a greater appeal to you than God does ! ' [9] Still, as a rule the crowds that flocked to hear him were immense ; in fact, when he preached at Carthage

[1] *Sermo*, xx. 4, words spoken after he had finished preaching.
[2] *Ep.* xli. 1 ; see also *Sermones*, xcv.–xcvii., ed. Caillau, XXIV., pp. 116 *sqq.*, spurious sermons ' coram Valerio.'
[3] *Vita*, 21 ; *Sermo*, i. 1 *on* Ps. xxxiv.
[4] *Enarr.* i. 10 *on* Ps. xxxix.
[5] *Enarr.* ii. 9 *on* Ps. xxxii.
[6] *Tract. in Joann.* vi. 1, vii. 1.
[7] *Sermo*, ccxcviii. 2.
[8] *Sermo*, ccciii. 1, cccxix, 8.
[9] *Enarr.* i. 1 *on* Ps. xxxii.

on the *Miserere*, so great was the crowd and so great the noise that he had to beg for ' silence and quiet so that my voice may, after yesterday's efforts, be able to keep up its strength.'[1]

It was the custom for the preacher to sit while the people stood.[2] St. Caesarius of Arles says : ' A few days ago I advised you, nay, in my fatherly solicitude for you I even begged those whose feet were sore, or who were afflicted with some bodily ailment and could not stand, to sit down humbly and in silence when either the Passions (of the Martyrs) or the Lessons were long. But now I notice that some of the ladies think that they ought all to do the same as a regular thing, even women who are in good health.'[3]

Augustine's audience was a mixed one. People came from varied motives, and many took down his sermons as he delivered them,[4] a task of which they did not always acquit themselves too well : ' it is amazing,' says Dom Morin, ' how the manuscripts of this sermon differ even more than usual ; the frequent mistakes and the repetitions of phrases betray either the ignorance or the carelessness of the notary who took it down.'[5] Pagans came,[6] schismatic Donatists came—these latter not always with the purest of intentions ;[7] Roman officials, too—with whom Augustine was always on the best of terms—sat before him.[8] The presence of these more cultivated people was

[1] *Enarr*. i. 1 *on* Ps. l. After the Lesson beginning ' I confess to Thee, O Father, Lord of heaven and earth,' Matth. xi. 25 had been read, Augustine said : ' Yesterday, Sunday, we listened, as you will remember, to the same Lesson, but I wished to have it read to you again to-day because the crowd packed into this narrow space proved too much for my voice which can only make itself heard in complete silence,' *Mai*, cxxvi. 1.

[2] Optatus, *De Schismate Donatistarum*, iv. 5 ; St. Augustine, *Sermo*, civ. 4, ' convenistis, statis, auditis ' ; cccxv. 10, ccclv. 2 ; *De Catechiz. Rudibus*, 19 ; *Tract. in Joann*. xix. 7, cxii. 1.

[3] *Sermo*, ccc. 1, in the *Appendix* to the *Sermons of St. Augustine*, *P.L.* xxxix. 2519. Of course if they did sit down they had to sit on the ground, as St. Caesarius remarks when he goes on to tell them they must stand, *ibid*. The custom of standing during the sermon prevailed in the East also, see St. Chrysostom, *Hom. on Hebrews*, viii. 2.

[4] See *Epp*. xliv. 2, ccxxxviii. 1 ; *Enarr*. i. 1 *on* Ps. l. ; *Enarr*. i. 30 *on* Ps. xciii. ; *De Trinitate*, xv. 27 ; *Proem. to Enarrationes on* Ps. cxviii. ; *Vita*, 7, *Retract*. ii. 67.

[5] Preface to *Denis*, xx., *Miscell*. i. 111.

[6] *Vita*, 7.

[7] *Ibid*. ; *Ep*. xliv. 2, ccxxxviii. 1 ; *Enarr*. i. 1 *on* Ps. li. ; *De Trinitate*, xv. 27 ; *Proemium to Enarrationes on* Ps. cxviii. ; *Retract*. ii. 67.

[8] The happy relations subsisting between Augustine and many of the great Roman officials in Africa is well illustrated by the letters that passed

sometimes disconcerting, for the preacher felt that he must not, while providing for their needs, incur the risk of wearying his simpler but not less valuable hearers [1]—not always an easy matter. Sometimes indeed the presence of unexpected people among the audience induced him to change the subject-matter of his sermon. One day, for example, he saw a Manichaean standing amongst his hearers, and at once entirely changed his sermon, with the gratifying result that the heretic was converted.[2] On another occasion a certain 'mathematicus' (or diviner) was pointed out to him in the church, whereupon Augustine directed his sermon at him.[3]

II—HIS AUDIENCE

Some, though not many, of Augustine's sermons are quite short. At times this was due to the length of the Lessons prescribed for that day; [4] at other times this brevity arose from the state of prostration in which the Bishop found himself.[5] Thus, on one Easter Day his sermon was exceedingly short; he does not say that he is tired, yet we detect a note of weariness in his bitter complaint of the 'number of those who are drunk at this season and of others who are worse than drunk, and who cannot, owing to their licentious lives, sing to-day: "Haec dies quam fecit Dominus."' [6] Here is a complete sermon:—

We are accustomed to hear read the story of the miracles God wrought at the prayers of the Blessed Martyr, Stephen. To-day the 'book' [7] is the sight of this man; instead of a writing here is evidence; instead of paper you have his

between them—for example, *Ep.* cli. to Caecilianus, *Epp.* clii.–clv. to Macedonius, and especially his intimate correspondence with the saintly Marcellinus, *Epp.* cxxviii.–ix., cxxxiii.–iv., cxxxvi.–cxl., cxliii., clxv.–vi., clxix, etc.

[1] See *Enarr.* ii. 1 *on* Ps. xc.

[2] *Vita,* 15; *cf. Sermo,* cccxx., xxxl. 2, ccclii. 1; *Enarr.* i. 1 *on* Ps. cxlvii.; *Mai,* xcv. 2–3.

[3] *Enarr.* i. 22–23 *on* Ps. lxi. 'Virilis in Christo animae praedicator' as St. Paulinus styles him, *Ep.* xciv. 3 *inter Epp. S. Augustini.*

[4] *Sermo,* cccxix. 7.

[5] *Sermo,* cccxx., for instance, takes up but eleven lines; cccxxi. only eight and a half. *Cf. Sermo,* xlii. 1–3, and see below.

[6] *Sermo,* ccxxx.

[7] *Libellus,* a booklet containing an account of St. Stephen's miracles wrought in honour of the Saint.

features.[1] You who remember what you used to see with grief in him, read now in him as he stands before you what will fill you with joy as you look. Give, then, more abundant glory to God, and let what is written in this 'book' be graven too in your memories. You must pardon me if I do not preach you a longer sermon; you are aware of my fatigue. It is due to the prayers of St. Stephen that I was able to do yesterday all I did while fasting and yet not break down, and that I should be able to speak to you at all to-day.[2]

The brief sermons, however, are certainly the exception, for Augustine had, as he himself often acknowledges,[3] a tendency to prolixity;[4] he was not always mindful of his own precept: 'Oportet ut senilis sermo non solum sit gravis sed etiam brevis.'[5] 'A short Psalm but a long Sermon!' he said on one occasion,[6] and after another lengthy discussion he feels compelled to apologize 'loquaci senectuti.'[7]

I may have wearied some of you with all this toil. Still we have finished the Psalm and your weariness has passed at the thought that we have expounded it all. I did think of stopping in the middle, but I feared lest, were your attention once broken, you might not return so readily to hear the other half of the Psalm explained; I felt it better to be a burden to you than to leave the thing half done. There is to be another sermon to-morrow, so come with hungry maws and devout hearts.[8]

Yet people sometimes complained that he was too brief: 'I have wearied some of you; I can see that. Some of you, however, think I have finished all too quickly; I can see that

[1] He had set before them a cripple well known to them all and but recently cured by the intercession of St. Stephen.
[2] *Sermon*, cccxx., eleven lines in the original. The next sermon, cccxxi., is but nine lines in length.
[3] *Enarr*. i. 19 *on* Ps. xxxv.; *cf*. *Tract. in Joann*. v. 20, vii. 24, viii. 13, xi. 15; *De Doctrina Christiana*, iv. 64; *Ep*. lxxxv. 51, etc.
[4] For examples of very long sermons, see *Sermo*, iv. (on Jacob and Esau), ccclxi. (on the Resurrection); *Enarr*. ii. *on* Ps. xxxii.; *Enarr*. i. *on* Ps. xxxv.; *Enarr*. i. *on* Ps. xxxviii.; *Enarr*. i. *on* Ps. xxxix.; *Enarr*. i. *on* Ps. li.; *Tract. in Joann*. xiv., xv., xx., xxxiv.
[5] *Sermo*, cccl. 3.
[6] *Enarr*. i. 15 *on* Ps. cxx.
[7] *Sermon*, cccly. 7.
[8] *Enarr*. i. 19 *on* Ps. xxxv.

too. But the weaker must excuse the stronger and the stronger must pray for the weaker.' [1]

In many country places the ordinary language was Punic, and it was not always easy to find priests who could preach in that tongue. The tragic story of the unworthy Antony, whom St. Augustine had felt compelled to present to the Primate of Numidia as fit to be Bishop of Fussala, had its origin in his search for a priest ' well grounded in Punic.' Augustine did find a capable man, but at the last moment the candidate absolutely refused to accept consecration. As the Primate had come from a great distance Augustine felt bound to provide a substitute on the spot. Hence his unhappy choice of Antony.[2]

Yet Fussala was but forty Roman miles from Hippo [3] where, as we should expect in a Roman Colonia, Latin was the usual medium. But that the ready use of Latin was confined to the towns is clear from a letter in which Augustine tells Novatus, Bishop (apparently) of Sitifis, that he cannot consent to the latter's kinsman, Lucillus, quitting the district of Hippo, ' for he knows Latin well,' [4] and owing to the lack of Latin-speaking priests the work of the Gospel is much crippled in our district (Hippo), whereas in your district that language is not spoken at all.' [5]

Whether Augustine's maternal language was Latin is disputable : ' There was a time when, as an infant, of course, I did not know it. Yet by noticing I learned it, not through fear of punishment, but from my nurse's blandishments, the jokes of kindly-disposed folk and the fun of those who played with me.' [6] He never mentions Punic as though it was a language in which he conversed, though he does quote Punic expressions and proverbs with which many of his hearers were familiar. ' There is,' he says, a ' well-known Punic proverb which, however, I will quote to you in Latin, for you do not all know Punic.'[7] But though unquestionably he always preached in

[1] *Enarr.* ii. 28 *on* Ps. xxxii., *cf.* i. 12 *on* the same Psalm, and ii. 12 *on* Ps. xc.
[2] *Ep.* ccix. 3.
[3] *Ibid.*, 2.
[4] The text is defective, ' Sed cum lingua Latina,' where the verb ' calleat ' seems to have fallen out.
[5] *Ep.* lxxxiv. 2.
[6] *Confess.* i. 23.
[7] *Sermo*, clxvii. 4.

Latin, yet on one occasion at least he says quite suddenly, 'Latine dicam,'[1] as though up till then he had been speaking in some other language (Punic, for instance); yet nothing else in these sermons suggests that he had up to then been speaking anything else but Latin. The same thing occurs in one of his earliest letters where he says: "Labi, effluere et praesens nihil obtinere, id est, ut Latine loquar, non esse.'[2]

These sermons, then, which drew to him the attention of the African people, were delivered in a tongue which cannot have been the vernacular speech of the cosmopolitan crowd that listened to him. No greater proof of the domination exercised by Rome could be found than the fact that all over Northern Africa the language of the conquerors was spoken with an ease and fluency truly remarkable. At the Conference between the Catholics and the Donatists in A.D. 411 speakers on either side poured out floods of Latin oratory absolutely *impromptu*, while the notaries took it all down in shorthand. The Bishops present at this Conference, whether Catholics or Donatists, came from all parts of the country, some even from the furthest corners of Mauretania; yet none of them seem to have found the slightest difficulty in expressing themselves very forcibly indeed in Latin. That very aggressive young man, Vincentius Victor, who ventured to draw his maiden sword against the veteran Augustine, wrote in admirable Latin; yet he hailed from Caesarea in remote Mauretania.[3]

When one scans the many sermons by Augustine which have survived, one wonders how often he preached. It might be an exaggeration to say that he preached every day. Yet, many of his Sermons on St. John's Gospel—the *Tractatus in Joannem*—were delivered on successive days,[4] while of the two Sermons on Ps. lxxxviii., one was preached in the morning and the other in the evening of the same day.[5] Yet on one occasion he remarks that the story of the raising of Lazarus, though often

[1] *Enarr.* i. 10 *on* Ps. xxxv.
[2] *Ep.* ii. 1.
[3] See the many quotations from his writings in St. Augustine's answer to him or the *De Anima et ejus Origine*, in *P.L.* xliv. 475–548.
[4] *Tract.* xix.–xxiii. were delivered on five successive days. *Cf. Tract.* viii. 13; also *Enarr.* i. 19 *on* Ps. xxxv.; ii. 29 *on* Ps. xxxii.; ii. 11 *on* Ps. xxxiii.; i. 19 *on* Ps. lxviii.; i. 23 *on* Ps. lxxx.
[5] *Enarr.* i. 29 *on* Ps. lxxxviii.

read to the people, is rarely the subject of a sermon, 'for unless that Gospel is read to you on a Saturday or a Sunday there is no sermon.'[1] Again, preaching on a Sunday, he refers to 'last Sunday's sermon,' implying, apparently, that there had been no sermon during the week.[2]

There are many instances of sermons being delivered on successive days: 'I know you look upon me as your debtor . . . and your importunity has extorted this sermon from me in spite of my bodily weakness,' he therefore continues his exposition of Ps. ciii. the first part of which he had treated of 'die jam nuper praecedente';[3] and again: 'to-morrow, as you are aware, I owe you a sermon, so help me with your prayers. For you cannot have forgotten my promise; indeed I would not have undertaken to preach except that I wished to be helped by your earnest faith and prayer.'[4] His Low Sunday sermon was on one occasion followed immediately (?), 'ne moras faciamus,' by another, though very brief one, in (?) another church, the Basilica Leontii.[5] 'Yesterday,' he says, 'we showed you how truthful was the Apostle,[6] how then can we explain the Lord's fictitious doings?'[7] His sermon on the anniversary of his consecration was, on one occasion, the third of a series: 'to-day is the third sermon and you have heard those delivered on the two previous days.'[8] These Africans must certainly have loved hearing sermons, for in one sermon Augustine reminds them of what their Bishop (Aurelius) had already preached to them that morning;[9] and again, when preaching on St. John the Baptist, he refers to 'what you have heard already to-day in this morning's sermon.'[10]

As we turn over the pages of the mighty tomes containing Augustine's works and realize that this written or dictated

[1] *Mai*, cxxv. 1.
[2] *Caill.* II. xi. 1; *cf. Miscell. Agost.* i. 353 note.
[3] *Enarr.* ii. 1 *on* Ps. ciii.
[4] *Enarr.* i. 14 *on* Ps. cxxiii.
[5] *Sermons*, cclix. and cclx.; *cp.* cclvii. and cclviii.
[6] *Sermon*, lxxxix. 4; *cf.* Possidius *Indiculus*, 8, on a sermon on St. Paul's rebuke to St. Peter.
[7] 'Finxit se longius abire,' 'He made as though He would go further,' Lk. xxiv. 28.
[8] *Guelf.* xxxii. 1.
[9] *Sermon*, xxiv. 5.
[10] *Frangipane*, viii. 1.

word represents not a tithe of his activity, that his days were often spent in the service of others, in the performance of tasks which must have proved most uncongenial to him, we have to keep reminding ourselves that we are in the presence of a deeply contemplative soul, of one who yearned for solitude where he might occupy himself with the things of God. Still more do we, as we look over his record as a preacher—even as briefly sketched in these pages—find it hard to realize that though preaching must, of course, have been a joy to him, the exercise of a God-given talent, yet he would—had the choice lain with himself—have preferred to lead a contemplative life. Over and over again does he let us into this secret side of his life. Here is one example out of many :—

If I refuse to give out to others ; if I hug my talent, then the Gospel terrifies me. For I might well say : 'Why should I be a nuisance to people ? Why should I keep on saying to the wicked : Give up your wicked ways ; do this, live like this, not like that ? Why, indeed, should I make myself a burden to people ? I have enough to live on. Well, then, I will live my own life as I am bidden, as I am told. I am ready to give an account of what I have received. Why should I be asked to render an account of others too ?' Yet it is always the Gospel that terrifies me. For none can surpass me in desire for a life of unlaborious ease ; to me there is nothing better, nothing more delightful than to occupy myself with the treasury of God, with none to disturb me. That is delightful ; that is a really good thing. But to preach, to argue, to correct, to try and build up, to strive for individual souls ! There you have the real burden, a mighty load, grievous toil. Who would not shrink from it ? Yet, again, it is always the Gospel that terrifies me ! [1]

'It rarely happened,' he says towards the close of his life, 'that, when I was present and a sermon had to be preached to the people, I was allowed to be silent and listen to someone else preaching.' [2]

And his flock listened to him with avidity :—

[1] *Frangipane*, ii. 4.
[2] *Retract. Prologue*, 2.

I note the real avidity you are showing and how ready you always are to listen to me. But there are two things neither of which can be reasonably disregarded ; my bodily weakness and your remembrance of what has been set before you. In the interval, then, go and reflect on what you have heard. Ask yourselves : 'What was it he said ?' In other words, ruminate the food you have taken.[1] And when closing his fourth sermon on Ps. ciii. : 'May our souls, then, bless the Lord, Brethren, in that He has deigned to give me a sermon and the capacity to preach it, and to you has given an intent earnestness in listening. Let each of you recall as best he can what he has heard ; by talking over the sermon between yourselves, recall the mental food you have received and ruminate upon it. It has demanded much toil for me to work this out, much labour to thresh it out with you. May that same toil and labour, then, prove fruitful in you ![2]

It is certainly astonishing to find Augustine writing almost immediately after his conversion :—

To some few people whom He has destined to be rulers in His Church God has granted not merely a courageous expectation of death, but even a joyous desire of it, even the power to face with unruffled mind all the anxieties and labours incident to their work for their Sees. But I can hardly imagine that so great a gift as this is ever granted to people who out of love of temporal dignity aspire to such administrative work ; nor again can I imagine that to such as, though only private folk, seek for a busy life it is ever granted to cultivate a familiarity with death amid noise and bustle, all sorts of comings and goings.[3]

This almost sounds like a presage of what his own episcopal life was to be.

Still, despite their gratifying eagerness, Augustine has to acknowledge that he on his part often found his hearers dull.[4] Sometimes indeed the ignorance they betrayed was amazing.

[1] *Enarr.* i. 19 *on* Ps. ciii. ; *cf. Sermo,* xliii. 5, ccclvi. 1 ; *Enarr.* i. 23 *on* Ps. xxxviii. ; i. 1 *on* Ps. lxi. ; *i.* 1 *on* Ps. lxxxiii ; *De Cataclysmo,* 9 ; *Tract. in Joann.,* ix. 9.

[2] *Enarr.* iv. 19 *on* Ps. ciii. ; *cf. Morin,* xi. 1 and 14 ; *Guelf.* ix. 4.

[3] *Ep.* x. 2, to Nebridius, about A.D. 388.

[4] *De Doctrina Christiana,* iv. 62 ; *Enarr.* iii. 22 *on* Ps. ciii.

He has to explain the difference between 'dolor' and 'dolus,'[1] also to tell them that though 'Deus' and 'diabolus' both begin with 'd,' yet they are not the same thing.[2] Many—perhaps most of them—could not read.[3] Their Latin, too, was often distinctly 'provincial'; still Augustine does not mind that. They can, if they like, say 'floriet' instead of 'florebit.'[4] He himself is not afraid to say 'ossum' for 'os,' for 'it is better to have the schoolmasters laughing at us than that the people should not understand';[5] it is better to say 'fenerat' than the grammatically correct 'feneratur,' for 'what does it matter to us what the schoolmasters think? Better you should understand our barbarism than be left high and dry with our pedantic exactitude.'[6] It is noteworthy that Augustine wrote his *De Agone Christiano* expressly for the benefit of poor Latinists.[7]

The Africans were a demonstrative people, and preaching to them can have been no humdrum affair. They seem to have voiced their approval of what was said to them—perhaps, too, their disapproval—in no half-hearted manner.[8] We have seen how they pointed out the 'mathematicus' who was present at one of Augustine's sermons; we shall see later how demonstratively they beat their breasts when the preacher's words roused them to compunction. On one occasion when he was preaching against Pelagianism and quoted the words 'Exultate cum tremore, ne quando irascatur Dominus,' the audience shouted out. Whereupon the Bishop said: 'I see by your acclamations that you have anticipated me. Your shouts show that you realize what I am going to say.'[9] Similarly, when, preaching on the resurrection of the body, he quoted the words 'that this mortal may be swallowed up by life' (2 Cor. v. 4), his hearers broke out into exclamations. 'You were right to shout,' said Augustine, 'for you know the Scriptures.'[10] Their

1 *Tract. in Joann.*, vii. 18.
2 *Enarr.* iii. 22 *on* Ps. ciii.; *Sermo*, xxxi. 6.
3 *Enarr.* ii. 1 *on* Ps. xc.; *Ep.* xliii. 23; *Retract.* ii. 29.
4 *De Doctrina Christiana*, ii. 21.
5 *Enarr.* i. 20 *on* Ps. cxxxviii.; *cf. De Doctrina Christiana*, iii. 7, iv. 24.
6 *Enarr.* iii. 6 *on* Ps. xxxvi.
7 *Retract.* ii. 3.
8 See *Tract. in Joann.* vii. 6, xviii. 8; *cf.* St. Chrysostom, *Hom. on I. Cor.* xiii. 3.
9 *Sermo*, cxxxi. 5.
10 *Sermo*, ccxcix. 9.

simplicity must sometimes have made the preacher smile. 'Let me give you an example,' he said, 'one which I do not think will be beyond you: When we form letters, it is our mind that first fashions them, and then our hands. Your applause shows that you understood that!'[1]

Now and again the Bishop seems afraid that they are proving restless: 'Perhaps some of you are saying in your hearts, "Oh! If only he would let us go!"'[2] At another time: 'Some of you say, "If only he would stop talking of the sack of Rome!"'[3]

These outbursts of feeling must have been exceedingly disconcerting though we never find a hint that the preacher was put off by them. But at times Augustine felt bound to protest against them: 'Do you not realize that I—indeed all of us—will have to render a strict account to God for your applause? You surely do not imagine that such praise does any honour to me? It is a burden, not an honour.[4] A very strict account indeed will have to be rendered for it. For I am afraid lest when Christ shall come to judge, He may say: "You wicked servants! Gladly did you accept the praises of My people, while holding your tongues about things that meant death to them."'[5] This sermon was preached at Bulla and was outspoken in its condemnation of the misdeeds of the people there.[6]

Augustine may have often found his audience dull, as we have seen. Yet they sometimes proved themselves very quick-witted. For example, when preaching on certain Martyrs 'of whom the first to suffer was Primus and the last Victoria Perpetua,' Augustine exclaimed: 'Brethren, I will with God's help tell you what I feel: In the case of the martyrs love of life was conquered by love of Life,'[7] some of them burst out into acclamations, though others seemingly did not understand, and the preacher had to explain.[8]

[1] *Tract. in Joann.* xviii. 8.
[2] *Sermon*, ci. 4.
[3] *Sermon*, cv. 12.
[4] 'Onerant, non honorant,' see p. 181.
[5] *Denis*, xvii. 9; *Miscell.* i. 89; *P.L.* xlvi. 874–881.
[6] See pp. 243 and 246.
[7] 'Amor vitae amore victus est Vitae.'
[8] *Frangipane*, vi. 2.

We, with our sense of decorum and somewhat straitlaced ways, should probably have felt out of our element amidst an African congregation. What, for instance, should we have thought when, after St. Augustine had been urging the suppression of paganism at Carthage and insisting that this had been effected at Rome, the whole audience shouted out: 'Let us have it at Carthage as it is at Rome!' [1] Northern Africa had a remarkable devotion to St. Stephen the Proto-martyr, through whose intercession many striking miracles had been wrought; [2] and as a consequence Augustine often preached on the Saint's merits, besides frequently alluding to him in other sermons.[3] On one occasion he told them of a miracle which had taken place at Uzala, where his great friend Evodius was Bishop: 'A certain woman had a son, a catechumen, who had suddenly fallen ill, and whom she was unable to assist despite her haste. When he died in her lap, she cried out: "My son who was but a catechumen is dead!"' At this point the audience could not restrain themselves, and at the mention of St. Stephen began to shout out: 'Thanks be to God! Praised be Christ!' When a girl who had been cured (Augustine is referring to another story he had previously told),[4] was led up to the apse and when the people saw her there, they increased their clamour; they said nothing but simply shouted, some from grief, some from joy. When silence was at length procured, Bishop Augustine said: 'I commended this unhappy—nay, previously unhappy—woman to your prayers. We set to work and prayed, and our prayers have been heard. Let our joy be our thanksgiving.' [5]

These little details are convincing proof of one thing, namely that the preacher was always in closest touch with his hearers. He seems to watch their faces just as they watched his. He even seems at times to gauge their very thoughts. He knows at once, and instinctively, whether they are following

[1] *Sermo*, xxiv. 6: 'Quomodo Roma, sic et Carthagine!'

[2] In the Appendix to the *De Civitate Dei* (*P.L.* xli.) will be found a series of narratives relative to the discovery of the remains of St. Stephen, notably the *De Miraculis Sti. Stephani*, where a detailed account of the marvels wrought at Uzala is given.

[3] *Sermones*, cccxiv.–cccxxiv.

[4] *Enarr.* i. 24 *on* Ps. lxxxv.; *cf. Frangipane*, v. 5.

[5] *Sermo*, cccxxii.

him or not. He even catches 'the murmur of those who recognize (the passage from) the Bible.'[1] As we read these sermons—even at this distance of time—they seem almost like a dialogue between preacher and people. He sways them so that we can almost picture them rocking to and fro as he makes point after point. He is not content to think for them, but contrives somehow to think with them.

The Saint's lengthy sermons were full of profound doctrine and must have taxed severely the attention of his hearers. He himself was intensely conscious of this, and he adopted various expedients in order to secure the attention of the less alert among them. At times he plies them with questions which he heaps up so as to force them to realize the gravity of the problem he is discussing.[2] When some doctrinal point is particularly obscure he repeats it again and again. When expounding the theology of St. John's Gospel and having perforce to set before his hearers very subtle points, he was careful at the opening of his next sermon briefly to recapitulate the doctrinal points discussed in the previous sermons. He even went so far as to make the people repeat passages which he was anxious they should make their own. A good example of this occurs in his sermon preached at Carthage immediately before the Conference of A.D. 411. Fearing lest in the excited state of men's minds tempers might break under the strain and the Conference perhaps be wrecked even before it had opened, he preached an exquisite sermon on the beauties of peace, and in the course of it he said: 'Now all say after me: "Charity from a pure heart" (1 Tim. i. 5),' and all his hearers shouted it out after him.[3]

III—HIS METHOD AND PURPOSE IN PREACHING

Augustinum legat omnis qui salutem aeternam adipisci desiderat, humiliter orans misericordiae Dominum ut eundem spiritum intelligentiae legens accipiat quem ille accepit ut scriberet, et eandem illuminationis gratiam adipiscatur, ut

[1] *Sermo*, cccxxiii. 4.
[2] *Sermo*, ci. 9. In his *De Doctrina Christiana*, iv. 39, Augustine advocates this practice.
[3] *Sermo*, ccclviii. 4.

discat quam ille adeptus est ut doceret.—ST. FULGENTIUS, *De Veritate Praedestinationis et Gratiae*, xviii.

But neither his oratorical devices nor his amazing eloquence were the real explanation of the influence Augustine exerted. No one could have listened for any length of time to his expository sermons (for instance to his *Enarrationes* on the Psalms), unless personally devoted to the preacher. This personal affection for himself Augustine desired and encouraged[1] provided it did not stop at himself; he was but the half-way house—a traveller's rest-house, if you like, but not his goal.[2] Hence his unceasing efforts to uplift his hearers, not only by the sublimity of the doctrine he tried to set before them, but also by demanding of them an evergrowing purity of life.[3] In his *De Doctrina Christiana*, he sets out what we might term the theory of preaching, and he sums it up in Cicero's words: 'To teach people is needful, to delight them is a pleasure, to win them is victory.' Or more succinctly: 'Doceat, delectet, flectat.'[4] That Augustine adhered to these principles is evidenced by every sermon he preached.

How did he teach? Out of the Bible. Despite his early distaste for it, he had begun, even before he was baptized, to study St. Paul,[5] and the moment he was ordained he begged for leisure in which to study the Bible as part of a priest's necessary equipment.[6] His Bishop, Valerius, seems to have given him the short period between Christmas and Easter,[7] but Augustine may be said to have devoted the rest of his life to the study of the Bible for the needs of the souls committed to his care.[8] Even so late as A.D. 416, Councils held in Numidia

[1] *Tract. in Joann.* vi. 1; *cf. De Catechiz. Rudibus*, 3–4.

[2] *Ep.* xxii. 9; *Sermo*, iii. 20 (*on* Ps. xxxvi.).

[3] *Sermo*, cccxliii. 9; *cf. Sermo*, cccxxxii. 4. How terribly difficult a task this was will be evident from many sermons which show how widely prevalent were the most gross forms of vice among these Africans. See, for example, *Sermones*, cclxxxviii.–ccxcv. among the sermons falsely attributed to St. Augustine, in *P.L.* xxxix. Appendix; see also A. Degert, *Quid ad mores Afrorum?* 1894.

[4] Cicero, *De Oratore*; *cf. De Doctrina Christiana*, iv. 27. See Francey, *Les idées litteraires de S. Augustin dans le 'De Doctrina Christiana,'* Fribourg, 1920.

[5] *Contra Academicos*, ii. 5–6.

[6] *Ep.* xxi. 3–5.

[7] *Ibid.*

[8] See *Epp.* lxxiii. 5, lxxv. 5, lxxxii. 23, cx. 6, etc.

and Carthage granted him five days of absolute retirement in which he might give himself wholly to this study! A truly generous concession! Probably the assembled Bishops smiled at a request which must have seemed to them singularly naïf coming from one whom they knew to be steeped in the Bible. However, nothing came of the concession: 'It was solemnly entered in the *Acts;* you all agreed to it, in fact you all applauded. And you kept to it for a short space; but your compact was soon rudely broken, and now I am allowed no leisure for the work I want to do; morning and evening I am eaten up with other men's affairs!'[1] His words sound bitter, but they were not meant to be. They were spoken ten years after his request had been made, and occur in the very touching and fatherly address he gave when designating Eraclius as his successor in the See of Hippo. Even then, when his days were drawing to a close, he still asked that some of his burden might be allowed to fall on the shoulders of the younger man: 'And all the people shouted out: "We are pleased at the decision you have come to; we say it twenty-six times."'[2]

But to return to the subject-matter of his preaching. It was the Bible all the time. Its words and expressions flow almost unconsciously from his lips; his stories and illustrations are taken from it; there is not a book of the Bible that he has not commented on in his sermons in some form or another; it is the quarry for all his doctrine; it is 'the word of God' that feeds his soul and out of which he 'provides old things and new' for the spiritual needs of his flock. This is well expressed in the Hymn for his feast:—

Frangis nobis favos mellis
De Scripturis disserens.
Quae obscura prius erant
Nobis plana faciens.

Tu de verbis Salvatoris
Dulcem panem conficis,
Et propinas potum vitae
De Psalmorum nectare.

[1] *Ep.* ccxiii. 5.
[2] *Ibid.*

How Augustine's heart must have ached when he read Jerome's reply to one of his letters : ' If, as the Orator of old said, " silent inter arma leges " (Cicero, *Pro Milone*), how much more true is that of the study of Holy Scripture which calls for so many books, such silence, such care on the part of copyists, and more than all—such peace and tranquillity for those who dictate ! ' [1]

At first sight it might seem strange that an audience apparently so uncultivated as that at Hippo should be able to appreciate sermons which, based as they were on the Bible,[2] demanded of the audience a very intimate acquaintance with the text of Holy Scripture. Yet it is quite evident from a number of passages in Augustine's sermons that his hearers had a very remarkable familiarity with the Bible. Nor was such knowledge confined to the Catholics, for Augustine shows us that people coming for instruction with a view to being received into the Church might be expected to have false notions about the meaning of passages in the Bible, and that this was more especially to be expected amongst the more educated inquirers [3] who in many cases were predisposed to regard the Bible as an unpolished product and quite unworthy the attention of an educated man.[4] This had, of course, been Augustine's own difficulty.[5]

The vast majority of Augustine's hearers, however, must have become familiar with the Bible simply through their Bishop's sermons. For very many of them could not read.[6] The sermons were as a general rule based on passages of Scripture which formed the Lessons for the day. These lessons were read out in no perfunctory manner, and the task of a Lector was no light one. He had to prepare his reading and then ' read it out ' ; ' pronuntiare ' is the expression used for the reading of the Gospel for the day,[7] also ' personante lectore.' [8]

[1] *Ep.* clxv. 2 (*inter Epp. Sti. Augustini*).

[2] For example, *Sermo*, ccxxxii. 1, ccxcix. 2 ; *cf. Contra Litt. Petiliani*, ii. 210.

[3] *De Catechizandis Rudibus*, 12.

[4] *Ibid.*, 13 ; ' No unbeliever but has heard that Christ raised Lazarus from the dead,' *Mai*, cxxv. 1.

[5] *Confess.* iii. 9, *Ep.* civ. 3.

[6] *Enarr.* i. 2 *on* Ps. xc.

[7] Easter Sunday, *Sermo*, ccxxxv. 1.

[8] *Enarr.* i. 2 *on* Ps. cxlvii.

Augustine recommends a Lector to Severus of Milevis on the ground that he had long exercised that office : ' he began to act as Lector in a church which is in my jurisdiction and then in three (? four) other places, at Subsana, Turris, Cizan and Verbalis.' [1]

The intervals between the various orders—technically the ' interstices '—were very long and were legislated for with great precision ; [2] we even read of one who had exercised the office for no less than twelve years ! [3] A Lector had to prepare his reading carefully. Woe betide him, for instance, if he read out uncanonical portions of the Bible in the Church ! When Augustine discovered that a Lector named Privatius had done so—though only once—he refused to have him as a Lector, and he appealed in support of this strong action to the Canons of the Council of Carthage, September, 401.[4] Similarly the Primate Aurelius excommunicated a priest called Quintianus in the Diocese of Badezila for the same offence.[5]

Augustine's *Enarrationes* on the Psalms will serve to illustrate the prevailing practice. The Lector either read out the Psalm sonorously or it was solemnly sung, and sung in such fashion that the people could have their part in it and could be expected to remember what they had just heard or sung.[6] Augustine would then give what was technically known as the ' enarratio,' or running explanation of the text ; though either these have not always come down to us, or very often he did not find it necessary to give such an explanation of the text apart from the sermon which was to follow. On at least one occasion the Lector read out the wrong Psalm : ' We had prepared a shorter Psalm and had bidden the Lector sing it. But at the moment he seems to have been distracted and he read another Psalm. However, we have thought it better to follow the will of God

[1] *Ep.* lxiii. 4. For the Order of Lectors, see St. Cyprian, *Epp.* vi. 6, xvi., xxiii., xxxiii. 4.

[2] *Cf.* Pope Celestine, *Ep.* iv. 4 ; Pope Siricius, *Ep.* i. 13–14 ; Pope Zosimus, *Ep.* ix. 1–5.

[3] Council of Carthage, A.D. 397, can. 44 ; Labbe, *Concilia*, ii. 1175.

[4] *Ep.* lxiv. 2–3.

[5] *Ep.* lix.

[6] Augustine says he is going to speak to them ' on this Psalm which we have heard sung and to which we have made the Responses as it was being sung ' (*Enarr.* i. 8 *on* Ps. xlvi.).

as indicated in the Lector's mistake than to adhere to our original proposal.'[1] On another occasion: 'We never told the Lector to sing this Psalm, but God put into his youthful mind what He thought it would be good for you to hear.'[2] These two Lectors must have felt very uncomfortable!

All this serves to show how carefully the Bishop prepared his sermons and arranged for lessons to be read which should prepare the way for the discourse. People, he remarks, have little idea of what a sermon costs the preacher,[3] indeed, the latter has often to be content to see no appreciable results from his labour.[4] Sometimes people seem to think it a mere trifle to take away a preacher's character![5]

This seems to show that, like all preachers, Augustine had to win his way to the hearts of his people, and that while the majority heard him willingly there were some who set their faces against him. At Hippo he had had to make a determined stand against the orgies which marked the celebration of certain Feasts, even in the churches.[6] Similarly when preaching on the Feast of St. Laurence at Carthage the Bishop opened his sermon by saying: 'Owing to the lack of interest shown there should be no sermon; but on the other hand, we have a duty to the great Martyr.'[7] This 'fastidium' was probably a dumb protest against the campaign the Bishop had instituted against the dancing accompanied by orgies with which the Carthaginians too were in the habit of celebrating the Feasts in the churches.[8]

A good instance of the task assigned to the Lector appears in the two famous sermons Augustine preached in explanation and defence of the lives led by his clergy. At the opening of the second of these he said: 'Although many of you are well acquainted with Holy Scripture, yet in order to recall things

[1] *Enarr.* i. 1 *on* Ps. cxxxviii.
[2] *Sermo*, cclii. 1.
[3] *De Catechiz. Rudibus*, 23. See R. J. Deferrari, *Augustine's method of composing and delivering Sermons*, in *American Journal of Philology*, 1922, Vol. xliii., pp. 97–123, 193–219. On the *Enarrationes in Psalmos* see E. Bouvy, in *Rev. Augustinienne*, 1930, pp. 418–436, where he deals with those on Pss. i.–xxxii.
[4] *Contra Cresconium*, i. 7 and 19.
[5] *Sermon*, ccxcix. 3.
[6] *Ep.* xxix.
[7] *Denis*, xx., xiii. 1, *P.L.* xlvi. 855, *Propter fastidium auditoris.*
[8] *Ibid.*, 4; *cf. Sermon*, cccxi. 5.

to your minds a passage from the Book of the *Acts of the Apostles* shall be read to you so that you may see for yourselves the model which we wish to have followed. And whilst it is being read I want you to be most attentive so that after it is over I may be able to set before you what I want with God's grace to have prepared.' Laurence the Deacon then proceeded to read out Acts iv. 31–35, and when he had finished he handed the book back to the Bishop, who said : ' Now I myself will read to you, for I much prefer to read this Word of God to you than to discuss the question simply in my own words,' and he repeated the same passage. This he presumably did not do because dissatisfied with the way Laurence had read, but in order to emphasize the passage. [1]

But how characteristic of Augustine is the remark that he prefers to read the Bible to his people rather than use his own poor words ! Indeed, if we would picture the Bishop preaching, we must picture him with the Bible—or portions of it—in his hand : ' Listen,' he said, in a sermon on the resurrection of the dead, ' to the Bible itself. For now I will play the Lector's part and not that of a disputant, so that my sermon may be based on the authority of Holy Scripture and not built on sand out of merely human suggestions.' [2] On another occasion, after reading out Gal. vi. 1–10, he said : ' So far I have been playing the Lector. But if we have understood the Lector, what need of any disputant ? ' [3] And once more, when preaching on the Valiant Woman, he said : ' You can see What I am holding in my hands, namely the Bible . . .' referring to Prov. xxxi.[4]

The one object he ever kept before himself in his sermons was to make his hearers think, to make them ponder the most profound mysteries of the Faith. As we read his wonderful *Tractatus in Joannem*,[5] we marvel that he dared put such profound and abstruse doctrine before an audience so uncultured as were many of those who listened to him. Yet he never hesitates to do so, even when he sees that they have not

[1] *Sermon*, ccclvi. 1.
[2] *Sermon*, ccclxii. 25 ; *cp. Ep.* xxix. 3.
[3] *Frangipane*, v. 1–2 ; *Miscellanea*, i. 212–213.
[4] *Sermon*, xxxvii. 1 ; *Miscellanea*, i. 550 ; *cp. Tract.* xxxv. 9 and xl. 1 *in Joann.*
[5] See M. Comeau, ' S. Augustin, exégète du quatrième Evangile ' (1930).

understood. Thus, on the baffling words, 'He that seeth Me seeth the Father also,' John xiv. 8–9, he expounds it as best he can and then ejaculates: 'I warned you that I was going to say something which not all of you would understand!' But can he make them understand? No. He knows that it is beyond him and that nothing save the illumination of divine grace can do so. 'Charity, therefore,' he says, 'begets you, nurtures you, perfects you, fortifies you, so that you may see that the Word of God and His actual 'seeing' are one and the same thing. But there I will stop, for I realize that what I have said may perchance, when thoughtfully weighed, become clear to many of you; wordy repetition will only serve to make it more obscure.'[1] At another time when he had ventured on an exposition of John v. 19, 'The Son cannot do anything of Himself,'[2] he opens his next sermon by saying: 'Yet I have given you no real explanation of that passage, for the simple reason that I do not myself understand any explanation I can give you.'[3] Again, when preaching on the words, 'Salute no man by the way,' he says: 'I see you promptly grasped what I mean; yet I cannot stop there, for you do not all promptly understand. Your remarks show me that some of you grasp it but the silence of the majority shows that they are still puzzling over it. As, however, we are talking of the "way," let us pretend we are on the "way," and let those who are prompt wait for the less prompt, and then let us all walk on together.'[4] Here we get a glimpse of the peculiarly intimate terms which existed between the preacher and his hearers. He takes them into his confidence. You feel that he is groping along with them. He never dominates; he knows no such thing as his own *Ipse dixit;* if the passage of Scripture he happens to be dealing with bristles with difficulties, he is not afraid of letting them see that there are difficulties: 'Attend carefully, beloved, may the Lord assist my will and your expectations so that I may be able to say what I want to say and in the way I want to say it.'[5] And once more: 'I see you

[1] *Sermo*, cxxvi. 15; *cf. Tract. in Joann.* xi., xviii.–xx.; *Sermo*, ccliv. 2.
[2] *Tract. in Joann.* xviii.
[3] *Ibid.*, xix. 1.
[4] *Sermo*, ci. 9.
[5] *Sermo*, xliii. 5.

are listening to me without being bored, and I rejoice that your hearts' palates are healthy and do not reject what makes for your health but receive it with eagerness and retain it with profit.'[1]

And he has a definite purpose in making them think. For he wants to reach their hearts through their understandings; otherwise all preaching is in vain. Hence while he uplifts them, puts before them the profoundest doctrine,[2] and secures their attention in the most amazing fashion,[3] he ever insists that they must have the Holy Spirit in their hearts if he is to do them any good, just as 'the preacher of God's word toils in vain, and as it were merely stands outside, unless he himself hear that word within himself.'[4] Yet, when putting before them the lofty doctrine which he feels they must receive if they are to make progress, he is always afraid of trying them too high. When preaching, for instance, on the incomprehensible nature of God and illustrating the doctrine of the Holy Trinity by the threefold faculties of memory, understanding and will, he says: 'I tell you frankly that when I approached this subject and determined to discuss it with you, I was filled with fear. For I dreaded lest while I should be giving pleasure to some of you who are more capable, I might be wearying those who are not so gifted. Yet I see you listening with deep attention and keenly appreciative of what I am saying, so much so that you not only understand what I am saying but even anticipate what I am going to say. Deo gratias!'[5] This must have been encouraging; yet all this was subordinate to the real object of his preaching, and that was to secure their compunction of heart. 'I heard you, I heard you,' he said, 'when you were beating your breasts';[6] and again: 'I will not burden your hearts any further, I want those hearts to be free to groan, to pray for those, too, who are still deaf and refuse to listen.'[7] After a lengthy sermon on Ps.

[1] *Enarr.* i. 1 *on* Ps. lxi.
[2] *Cf. Sermo*, cccxliii. 9; *Tract. in Joann.* xix. 1.
[3] *Sermo*, xliii. 5; *Enarr.* i. 23 *on* Ps. xxxviii.; *Tract in Joann.* ix. 9; *Enarr.* i. 1 *on* Ps. lxi.; *De Cataclysmo*, 9.
[4] *Sermo*, clxxix, 1.
[5] *Sermo*, lii, 20.
[6] *Sermo*, cccxxxii. 4.
[7] *Tract. in Joann.* xiii. 18, and *cf.* the story of his own sermon at Caesarea, *De Doctrina Christiana*, iv. 53, given below.

xxxviii., he says: 'Consequently, brethren, though I have been a burden to you and caused you bodily toil, put up with it. For I, too, it is true, have had to toil; but after all it is you yourselves who are the cause of your toil. For if I were to feel that you were really weary of my words, I should speedily hold my tongue!'[1]

At the close of many sermons occur the words 'Conversi ad Dominum,' etc.[2] The entire prayer is sometimes given[3] in the form: 'Conversi ad Dominum Deum Omnipotentem, puro corde Ei, quantum potest parvitas nostra, maximas atque uberes gratias agamus; precantes toto animo singularem mansuetudinem Ejus, ut preces nostras in beneplacito Suo exaudire dignetur, inimicum a nostris actibus et cogitationibus Sua virtute expellat, nobis multiplicet fidem, gubernet mentem, spirituales cogitationes concedat, et ad beatitudinem Suam perducat, per Jesum Christum Filium Ejus, Amen.' Only once do the opening words 'Conversi . . .' occur at the close of the *Enarrationes in Psalmos*,[4] but at the end of the whole series of *Enarrationes* the Benedictine editors append it with the prefatory words: 'Oratio quam post singulos sermones atque tractatus dicere consuevit.'[5] But this seems hardly justified, for while some of the *Enarrationes* end with a simple 'Amen,'[6] others end with some words of dismissal which seem to preclude any closing prayer—for example, 'Psalmo peracto proficiscamur'[7] or 'In Nomine Domini crastina die, Ipso adjuvante, reddemus.'[8] Once we have a veritable doxology: 'A Domino, cui est honor et imperium cum Patre et Spiritu Sancto in saecula saeculorum. Amen.'[9]

Many of the sermons falsely attributed to the Saint have a

[1] *Enarr.* i. 23 *on* Ps. xxxviii.
[2] *E.g.*, *Sermones*, cvi., ccxxxiv., cccxxiv., ccclxi.
[3] *Sermo*, lxvii. 10, *c.*, clxxxiii. 4. A variant form is given in *Sermo*, ccclxii: 'Conversi ad Dominum, Ipsum deprecemur pro nobis et pro omni plebe Sua astante nobiscum in atriis domus Suae; quam custodire protegereque dignetur; per Jesum Christum Filium Ejus Dominum nostrum, qui cum Eo vivit et regnat in saecula saeculorum. Amen.' See *Journal of Theol. Studies*, January, 1912, p. 271.
[4] *Enarr. on* Ps. lxxxvi.
[5] After *Enarr. on* Ps. cl.
[6] *Enarr.* ii. 8 *on* Ps. xxxiii.; i. 16 *on* Ps. xlii.; i. 16 *on* Ps. cxlix.
[7] *Enarr.* i. 16 *on* Ps. xxx.
[8] *Enarr.* ii. 14 *on* Ps. xxx.
[9] *Enarr.* i. 20 *on* Ps. cxlvi.

very different closing formula, one of them, indeed, is very like the doxology just given ; but they never hint at the form 'Conversi.' [1] Some of the Saint's closing remarks are quaint in their simplicity, and must now and again have raised a smile. Thus, he breaks off his exposition of a Psalm lest through being too hurried he should only become obscure.[2] At other times he is afraid of tiring them ; [3] indeed, on at least one occasion they were patently exhausted,[4] though more often it was the preacher who was tired.[5] When expounding the very long Ps. lxxxviii., he actually sent his hearers out for a meal and told them to come back in the evening. 'Go out,' he says, 'and take some refreshment, not for your spirits—for your spirits are, I notice, indefatigable ; but go out and give some little refreshment to your bodies, the servants of your souls, so that they may still continue to minister to you ; and when you are refreshed, then come back to your real food.' [6] On another occasion he ended by saying : 'I never noticed how long I had been speaking ! But judging by the fact that we have finished the whole Psalm, judging, too, by the very perceptible smell, I presume I must have preached a very long sermon. The truth is that I cannot keep pace with your eagerness ; it is you who are doing violence ; let us hope your violence will serve to carry by storm the Kingdom of heaven !' [7]

Though devoted, of course, to the needs of his own flock, it would be a mistake to imagine that Augustine confined his preaching to Hippo. As his fame grew, he was in demand everywhere. As we have already seen, he pathetically complained towards the close of his life that he was never allowed to be silent when it was question of a sermon to be preached.[8]

[1] *E.g.*, *Sermones*, x.–xiii., xvi.–xviii., xxii., in *P.L.* xxxvii., Appendix. *Sermo*, xv. in the same Appendix has for its closing formula : 'Conversi ad Dominum misericordiam Ipsius deprecemur, ut desiderium audiendi verbum Dei, quod in nos placatus contulit, et augere semper et conservare dignetur, qui cum Patre et Spiritu Sancto vivit et regnat in saecula saeculorum. Amen.'

[2] *Enarr.* i. 12 *on* Ps. xc. ; *Sermones*, i., ii., vii., viii., xviii., xxiv. *on* Ps. cxviii.

[3] *Sermones* v., x., xv. *on* Ps. cxviii.

[4] *Enarr.* i. 22 *on* Ps. lviii.

[5] *Enarr.* iv. 19 *on* Ps. ciii. ; *Sermo*, cccxx. ; *Tract. in Joann.* xix. 20.

[6] *Enarr.* i. 20 *on* Ps. lxxxviii.

[7] *Enarr.* i. 34 *on* Ps. lxxii.

[8] *Retract.* i. 1 ; *Vita*, 21 ; *De Catechiz. Rudibus*, 10 ; *Enarr.* i. 1 *on* Ps. xxxiv.

The Donatist controversy entailed sermons in various places where the schismatics were strong. Carthage in particular was the scene of many of his sermons ; [1] while he even preached at Caesarea in Mauretania.[2] He must have had to refuse many invitations to preach though we know of only one case in which he had to do so, and then his refusal took the form of the following exquisitely courteous little note :—

To the Blessed and Venerable Brother, and my companion in the Priesthood, Nobilius :—

So great is the solemnity to which you in your brotherly affection invite me that in truth my heart would drag me to you were it not for bodily infirmities. Indeed, I could come were it not for the winter ; and even the winter I could afford to disregard were I a young man ; for then the warm blood of youth would counteract the rigours of the season ; or conversely, were it summer the warmth would compensate for the chilled blood of old age. But now, alas, so long a journey in winter would prove quite incompatible with the pain-wracked old age I have to carry about with me.[3]

From the titles prefixed to some of the sermons, at any rate in certain manuscripts, we learn that *Sermons* i.–ii. on Ps. xxxiv. were preached at Tagaste, the only examples we have of sermons by Augustine in his native town ; [4] *Sermon* cclxxxvi. was preached at Argentarium, as yet unidentified ; [5] *Sermon* lxxxii. bears the title 'Apud Mil. u,'[6] perhaps for Milevis, *cf.* 'Pollianus a Mileo' one of the signatories at the Council of Carthage, A.D. 256 ; [7] *Sermon* x. 'Siniti habitus,' perhaps in Numidia,[8] not far from Hippo Regius.

[1] The *Enarrationes* i.–iii. *on* Ps. xxxvi. were delivered at Carthage ; *Sermo*, xc. and xcii. in the Basilica Restituta there, *Sermo*, clxxiv. in the Basilica Celerina, *Sermo*, clxiv. in the same city, just after the Conference of 411, and many others. See Dom Donatien De Bruyne : '*Enarrationes in Psalmos*' *prêchées à Carthage*, *Miscell. Agostiniana*, ii. 321–325 where he enumerates 34 (? 35) sermons preached there. When we realize the fatigues of the journey thither we can well understand Augustine saying that Carthage meant too much work ! *Ep.* cli. 13, *c.* 414, *cf. De Octo Dulcitii Quaestionibus*, *Praefatio*, *P.L.* xl. 149.

[2] *Sermo ad Plebem Caesareensem ;* see also *De Doctrina Christiana*, iv. 53.

[3] *Ep.* cclxix.

[4] See *Miscellanea Agostiniana*, i. 665.

[5] *Ibid.*, 666.

[6] *Ibid.*, 665.

[7] *De Baptismo contra Donatistas*, vi. 34.

[8] P. Monceaux, *Histoire littéraire de l'Afrique du nord*, vii. 291 ;

IV—HOW HE PREPARED HIS SERMONS

Any preacher who reads St. Augustine's sermons naturally asks how these truly amazing discourses were prepared. For prepared they certainly were. Omitting all question of his prayers beforehand,[1] and forgetting for the moment that we are listening to a master of oratory who had triumphantly carried off the prize for rhetoric against Roman competitors,[2] who had made of the Latin tongue a vehicle for the expression of the profoundest thoughts, forgetting, too, his prodigious memory and his amazing flow of words, we want to know the secret of his preparation for sermons which held Africa enthralled. In a letter to his bosom friend Alypius,[3] already a Bishop when Augustine was only a priest, we are afforded a glimpse of the careful preparation the latter gave to a famous sermon which unfortunately has not been preserved for us.[4] In this sermon he attacked the prevailing custom of holding banquets in the churches and—incredible though it may seem—getting exceedingly drunk. We see that Augustine prepared a number of passages from the Bible bearing on the point, that he read these out himself,[5] and that he then spoke to the people earnestly on the subject.[6] The next day, seeing that some at least were prepared to fight for what they regarded as a time-honoured if not laudable custom, he begged them to conform to the customs in vogue on this point in the Church overseas.[7] The next day the church was crowded with people singing Psalms

Miscellanea, i. 665 ; A Kunzelmann, *Die Chronologie des Sermones der Hl. Augustinus* in *Miscellanea Agostiniana*, Rome, ii. 417–520, Tables, pp. 512–520 ; the views of the Benedictine Editors on the chronology of the Sermons will be found in *P.L.* xxxviii., cols. 10–22 ; see, too, Dom A. Wilmart, *Remarques sur plusieurs collections des sermons de S. Augustin*, in *Casinensia*, 1929, pp. 217–241, also *La collection tripartite des sermons de S. Augustin*, in *Miscellanea Augustiniana*, Bataviae, 1930, pp. 417–449 ; Dom Donatien De Bruyne, *La chronologie de quelques sermons de S. Augustin*, *Rev. Bénédictine*, 1931, pp. 185–193.

1 *Sermo*, lxxi. 8.

2 *Confess*. vi. 6 ; Vita, 1 ; *Contra Litt. Petiliani*, iii. 25.

3 *Ep*. xxix., A.D. 395.

4 *Cf. Sermo*, cclii. 4.

5 *Ep*. xxix. 4–6. See above, p. 158.

6 *Ibid*., 7.

7 *Ibid*., 10.

and saying prayers. The Bishop, Valerius, then told Augustine to preach to them.[1]

Now, nowhere does Augustine suggest that he had committed any part of this sermon to writing. Indeed with one exception it is hard to discover in his writings any suggestion that he was in the habit of writing his sermons. But the one passage we can discover is significant. In his great work on the Trinity he says of a certain sermon he had preached on this dogma: 'I preached it to the people, and after I had preached it I wrote it.'[2] Was this habitual with him? At first sight it would seem incredible that so busy a man should have been able to find time to commit his sermons to writing. But he certainly had copies of some at least of his sermons. For instance, when preaching on John i. 51, he says: 'Some time ago I spoke to you about these Angels who ascended and descended, but in case you have forgotten I will briefly remind you of what I said.'[3] Again he repeats in one sermon eleven lines taken practically word for word from another;[4] while when preaching on Ps. lxviii. he twice refers to a previous sermon on Ps. xxxiv.[5] When St. Paulinus had, as usual, deluged him with questions, among them one which concerned the expression, 'They are full of children,' in Ps. xvi., Augustine replied: 'I have written a brief exposition of that Psalm, one I dictated long ago,' and he proceeds to give his explanation of the words 'after examining the Greek MSS. to discover whether "filiis" is a dative or a genitive, which latter the Greeks employ instead of the Latin ablative.'[6]

On the other hand, he certainly spoke at times simply as the Spirit moved him. For example, when his auditory had shown their disgust at the folk whom the Apostle had, in the Epistle just read to them, described as saying: 'Let us eat and drink, for to-morrow we die,' 1 Cor. xv. 32, Augustine said: 'We will take that as the starting-point of our discussion; it shall

[1] *Ibid.*, 11.
[2] *De Trinitate*, xv. 48.
[3] *Tract. in Joann.* i. 51, vii. 23, where the reference is to *Sermo*, cxxii. 6.
[4] *Sermo*, x. 1, of the *Sermones inediti*, in *P.L.* xlvi. 843 and *Enarr.* i. 1 *on* Ps. cxlix.
[5] *Enarr.* i. 14 and i. 15 *on* Ps. lxviii. refer respectively to *Enarr.* ii. 4 and 3 *on* Ps. xxxiv.
[6] *Ep.* cxlix. 5; *cf. Enarr.* i. 14 *on* Ps. xvi.

be the hinge on which our sermon turns; the rest shall be brought into relation with it as the Lord may deign to suggest to us.'[1] At another time, in a sermon preached presumably at Carthage, he opened his exposition of Ps. lxxxvi. by saying: 'Only just now has our most blessed Father here present with us imposed this sermon on me. So sudden an order would overwhelm me were it not for the prayers of him who gave it; they must sustain me.'[2] Still, he contrived to preach a fairly long and certainly a most beautiful sermon! Yet the same ready preacher could say in effect that he found it difficult to preach to order.[3] Perhaps the clearest light on his method of preparing himself for a sermon is afforded by one he preached on the sin against the Holy Spirit. He says that he has hitherto avoided dealing with this 'most abstruse question, not indeed because I had not many things to say which I had thought out on various aspects of it, nor that I had neglected "to ask, seek and knock" on a point of such moment, but because I was afraid that no words which might occur to me at the moment would adequately express the ideas I was slowly forming on the question.'[4] Here, I think, we have the key to Augustine's preparation for preaching; he prayed much, he thought much, he studied the Bible on the question he wished to treat of, and then, when he felt clear in his own mind, he spoke from the fullness of an illumined mind and of a heart on fire with zeal for the welfare of his flock.

Many may feel that this was all very well for a man like St. Augustine, the master of rhetoric, with his well-stored mind; but what of those whose duty it is to preach but who suffer from a complete lack of ideas? But Augustine himself has forestalled them: 'There are, of course,' he says, 'some who can speak well but who cannot think of anything to say. Now if such people would but take a sermon which has been carefully and thoughtfully written out by someone else, and if, after learning it by heart, they give it out to the people, then—provided they do so in the name of him who wrote it—they do no wrong. And surely this is a useful practice, for many thus

[1] *Sermo*, ccclxi. 1; *cf. Vita*, 15.
[2] *Enarr.* i. 1 *on* Ps. lxxxvi.; *cf. Sermon*, xxiv. 5, *Morin*, i. 1.
[3] *De Catechizandis Rudibus*, 14.
[4] *Sermo*, lxxi. 8.

become preachers of the truth, though they be not "many masters".'[1] Probably every preacher has at one time or another annexed someone else's sermon. How many have publicly acknowledged whence they got it? Cresconius, the bumptious schoolmaster, had jeered at Augustine's 'pseudo-eloquence,' as he dubbed it, but Augustine reminds him that, though a preacher may be flouted by men, yet never by God.[2]

The one thing needful, he insists, is clarity, and he points out how wonderfully clear are the Biblical writers: 'The words they make use of hardly seem to be so much employed by them as to flow spontaneously from the very subject they are dealing with; they flow, like Wisdom, from her own home.'[3] For the sake of securing that clarity of expression he had formed a habit which every preacher and writer has at one time or another intended to form, but which few reduce to practice: 'I meditate,' he says, 'on the Law of God, not indeed "day and night" like the Psalmist, but during the brief moments I can snatch; and lest I should forget the ideas that come to me I pin them down with my pen.'[4] And while he acknowledges that he himself is anxious to please his hearers, even when saying unpleasant things to them,[5] yet he adds the comforting thought that even he is always less pleased with his sermons than are his hearers, for he feels after preaching that he has not really said what he wanted to say nor precisely in the way he wanted;[6] for, as he expresses it elsewhere, the one object of a preacher is 'so to handle his words that the truth may be made clear, may please, may move.'[7] This conviction makes him contemptuous of eloquence falsely so called —'What is the use of a golden key if it will not open the door?'[8] —though he acknowledges that he has known some preachers who, 'though their speech is only so much foam, are yet sound in the faith!'[9] The fact that the Bishop's whole practice was

[1] *De Doctrina Christiana*, iv. 62; see St. Chrysostom, *Hom. on the Epistle to the Hebrews*, iii. 5.
[2] *Contra Cresconium*, i. 7.
[3] *De Trinitate*, i. 5.
[4] *De Doctrina Christiana*, iv. 10.
[5] *Sermo*, lxii. 9; 'Conamur luculenter et delectabiliter vobis dicere.
[6] *De Catechiz. Rudibus*, 3; *cf. De Doctrina Christiana*, iv. 2, 4, 8.
[7] *De Doctrina Christiana*, iv. 61.
[8] *Ibid.*, iv. 26.
[9] *De origine animae*, i. 3.

based on deep-seated principles like these gives additional force to his statement that just as the first, second, third, and indeed all the steps in our journey towards God are humility, so, too, we must endorse Demosthenes' famous dictum that the same applies to eloquence: the first, second, third, and indeed all the stages in it are summed up in the one word 'pronunciation,'[1] for you must get to the hearts of your hearers through their understanding, and how can you do that if they are not clear as to what you are saying?

Preaching he regarded as 'the Lord's table; he who ministers there has no right to defraud the guests, least of all guests so hungry as your eagerness shows you are.'[2]

Not every preacher in Africa was an Augustine. Few, if any, had had his wonderful training. Indeed many of the Bishops seem to have been, if not illiterate, at any rate unpolished. But people who were inclined to criticize their sermons on this score would have met with short shrift from the Bishop of Hippo who says:—

When people who apparently excel in the rhetorical arts wish to become Christians, we have to be more particularly careful in their case to bring home to them the fact that they have to steep themselves in Christian humility. They have to learn not to despise preachers whom they discover to be more careful to avoid mistakes in morals than in speech, who would never dream of putting on the same level cultivated speaking and a clean heart, who in fact prefer the latter to the former. They have to realize that, just as the soul is of more importance than the body, so are ideas more important than words. This will teach them that they have to be just as keen on hearing truth-telling sermons rather than eloquent ones, as they prefer to have friends who are prudent rather than beautiful. They must be made to understand that it is not the voice which reaches the ears of God but the heart's affections. Then they will not sneer when they hear Bishops or ministers using solecisms and barbarous expressions in their prayers to God, or patently not understanding the words they use, or punctuating phrases wrongly. Such things have of course to be corrected so that the people may be able to say 'Amen' to something

[1] *Ep.* cxviii. 22.
[2] *Tract. in Joann.* ix. 9.

they really understand. But those will patiently put up with such things who have learned that, whereas in the courts it is the sound that we praise, in the Church it is the intention. Forensic displays may perchance be 'bona dictio,' never 'benedictio.'[1]

V—ST. AUGUSTINE'S HUMOUR

That Augustine had a deep sense of the humorous side of things appears in all his writings and peeps out in the most unexpected way at times. Always and everywhere he is the preacher. If he writes a letter, it is a sermon; even his controversial works are written from the preacher's standpoint, and, as is only to be expected, this is still more noticeable in his expositions of Holy Scripture. For he is always the teacher *par excellence*, and he teaches by every means at his disposal. Now he had realized that nothing appeals to a man so much as a sense of human nature, of its foibles and its weaknesses; that if you can only make a man smile—even if it be at himself—the battle is half won. Sometimes, however, he failed to win his adversary by these methods. We have an amusing example in his correspondence with St. Jerome. Augustine had received a copy of St. Jerome's *De Viris Illustribus*. But it bore no title, and though someone had suggested that it might be called an 'Epitaphium' since it ended with the words 'ad Pammachium apologeticum et epitaphium,' yet it was hard to reconcile this with the fact that the volume dealt with the living as well as with the dead. He therefore wrote to St. Jerome asking for an explanation.[2] Of course, the sting of his letter lay in the fact that, whereas Jerome had not mentioned the living Augustine, yet the living Jerome had devoted more space to the catalogue of his own works than to any writers save the Apostles and Origen: 'Hieronymus haec scripsi. . . .' Unfortunately Jerome was not conspicuously endowed with a sense of humour, and, to judge by his reply to this letter, he never saw the irony underlying Augustine's question![3] On another occasion Augustine wrote to the hermit

[1] *De Catechizandis Rudibus*, 13.
[2] *Ep.* xl. 2.
[3] *Ep.* lxxv. 3 (*inter Epp. Sti. Augustini*).

of Bethlehem to discover his views on the origin of the human soul, a problem which had always vexed Augustine's mind. In the course of his letter he apologizes for putting a question which, he says, is not half so important as the question how we are going to save the soul we have got. 'It reminds me,' he says, 'of the story of the man who fell into a well full of water. When someone found him in this predicament and exclaimed: "How on earth did you come to fall in there?" the unhappy wight naturally retorted: "Think how you are going to get me out, not how I fell in"!'[1] One has a suspicion that the somewhat sardonic Jerome looked on this as flippant!

The following does not occur in a sermon but in his instruction on catechizing. The Carthaginian deacon Deogratias, for whom he wrote it, must have chuckled when he read it; perhaps he himself used it in his own sermons afterwards:

Some there are who have no desire to be rich or attain to honours and dignities; but they find their happiness in the wine-shop and vice, in the theatre and in the empty games which in the big cities they can enjoy *gratis*. But even such as these spend their poverty on luxurious living, and then, when they have fallen into want, they take refuge in thefts and house-breaking, even in open robbery. Then they are suddenly filled with fears and tremblings; and the man who just before was carolling in the wine-shop now dreams out his woes in gaol![2]

The Bishop's sense of humour allowed him to do and say things which in another less distinguished preacher might have provoked a rebuke. We do not know at what episcopal gathering the following sermon was preached, but certainly the laity must have enjoyed it, though possibly his fellow-Bishops did not:—

My brethren in the episcopate have condescended to visit us and by their presence gladden us. But I cannot imagine why they decline to help a person so tired as I am. I say this to your charity in their hearing so that you who listen may in

[1] *Ep.* clxvii. 2; see Clodomir Delfour, *De narrationibus quae sunt in S. Augustini sermones* (sic), 1892.
[2] *De Catechizandis Rudibus*, 25.

some sort intercede for me with them, and then, when on some other occasion I ask them to preach the sermon, they may do so. Let them dispense what they have got; let them condescend to work rather than make excuses. However, listen to a few words from me though I am very tired and can hardly speak.

He then proceeded to preach on the man who wrapped his talent in a napkin instead of making proper use of it! 'We (Bishops) are dispensers; we give out; you receive. You (he said to the listening laity) cannot give out from that lofty station'—and presumably he pointed to the assembled Bishops —'but you can dispense for us in your own houses. A Bishop is only so called because he is a superintendent, because he exercises watchful care by overseeing. Every one of you should do that in your own homes. . . . If you do so, you are dispensing. You will not be'—did he here point to the assembled Bishops?—'lazy servants.'[1]

Humour, to be effective, must be based on facts; it demands insight, and this Augustine had in a marked degree. For example: 'Do not imagine that heresies are the product of little minds; it takes a big mind to make a heresy; but the bigger the mind the worse these "hills".'[2] Or again: 'A man loves to see another making a fool of himself; but he has no wish to look a fool himself.'[3] Once more: 'Only the wicked grumble at the wicked';[4] or: 'Nothing but his holiness makes a bent and bowed old man beautiful; as a good old man totters along, there is nothing beautiful to look at in his body, yet everybody loves him.'[5] Or, in lighter vein: 'Nothing more unsatisfactory than a thing that rolls away; that is why money is made round, it won't stand still.'[6] What more pithy than his remark about pride: 'How can you be proud unless you are empty? For if you were not deflated, you could not be inflated.'[7]

[1] *Sermo*, xciv. 'Let a man so account of us as of the ministers of Christ and the dispensers of the mysteries of God,' I. Cor. iv. 1.

[2] *Enarr*. i. 5 *on* Ps. cxxiv. Heretics are frequently spoken of as 'hills' by Augustine, *cf*. Ps. lxvii. 16–17; *De Utilitate Jejunii*, ii.

[3] *De Peccatorum Remissione*, i. 66.

[4] *Sermo*, cccii. 16, and *Enarr*. ii. 5 *on* Ps. xv.

[5] *Enarr*. i. 6 *on* Ps. xxxii.; i. 8 *on* Ps. lxiv.

[6] *Enarr*. i. 3 *on* Ps. lxxxiii.

[7] *Enarr*. i. 9 *on* Ps. xcv.

Or when he says of the Donatists that 'a man who does not blush at the thought of his schismatic state can surely have no blood in his body.'[1] Who would forget it when he heard the Bishop describing the death of the soul by saying: 'All men are lamps, for they can be lit and they can be put out. And when those lamps are wise, they shine and are fervent; but if after having been lit they are put out, then they stink!'[2]

His audience must have enjoyed this bit in a sermon: 'Look at a gymnast, for example. There you have a man who with immense pains has learned to walk on a tight rope; suspended, he keeps you in suspense![3] But now turn your gaze on Him who does far more spectacular things. Did he learn to walk on a tight rope? No! He walked on the sea! Forget your theatre, then, for a moment and fix your gaze on Him who is our "Rock"; no tight-rope-walker He, but a sea-walker.'[4]

These shrewd touches, whether in his sermons or in his writings, are a perpetual joy to the reader; for example: 'When once you have fallen into the hands of a poor doctor, you are afraid to trust yourself to a good one!'[5] There must have been a smile in church when he said: '"Your hair wants cutting," says a grave old gentleman to a love-sick youth, "you have no business to come in here with hair as long as that!" But the young man knows that there is someone who is fascinated by those locks of his.'[6] 'Riches are dangerous,' he says, 'they have a knack of clinging. When there is a glut of honey, it is not for nothing that a bee has wings; for the honey might kill her if it stuck.'[7] It is 'better to be small and healthy with Zacheus than big and feverish with Goliath.'[8] Again: 'Your most insignificant members are the hairs of your head. . . . Yet, if the hairdresser cuts your hair badly, you are angry with him because he did not cut it evenly!'[9]

[1] *Ep.* lxxxvii. 6.
[2] *Tract. in Joann.*, xxiii. 3.
[3] 'Pendens te suspendit.'
[4] 'Non funambulum sed mariambulum' (*Enarr* i. 9. *on* Ps. xxxix.).
[5] *Confess.* vi. 5.
[6] *Enarr.* i. 7 *on* Ps. xxxii.
[7] *Ep.* xv. 2.
[8] *De Bono Conjugali*, 29.
[9] *De Utilitate Jejunii*, 8.

Augustine had learned the value, too, of brief, pithy sentences which, though not precisely humorous, focussed attention and, because so brief, were calculated to remain in the hearer's memory. It is remarkable how many of these apothegms were concerned with the subject of faith: thus of the Martyrs: 'They saw something with their minds, with the result that they cared nothing for what they saw with the eye of the body; for in them was the eye of faith, an eye that gazed on the future so that they despised the present. But a person whose eye for things that are future is put out dreads things that are present and never attains to things that are future.'[1] Again, on the words: 'Many shall come from the East and from the West': 'Whither shall they come? Where they may believe, there they come. For to come is to believe';[2] while to the man who demands intellectual proof before he will believe: 'You do not understand that so you may arrive at belief; but you believe so that you may arrive at understanding.'[3]

How succinct, too, are the words: 'That we should deserve the vision of God depends on our faith; but that vision itself is the reward of our faith.'[4]

How many preachers could afford to say to their congregations when preaching on 'And the Word was made flesh and dwelt among us': 'If God, the Word, had done this only, namely become flesh, such humility would have been incredible. But blessed are they who believe that incredible thing, for our faith is based on incredible things. The Word of God became grass, He died and rose again; God was crucified! Incredible!'[5]

And yet again:—

Let everybody preach Christ when occasion offers, and he is at once a martyr.[6] For sometimes a person, though not suffering persecution, dreads being put to shame. He may have, for example, to live amongst pagans and he is ashamed of being known as a Christian. But if ashamed of a man he

[1] *Denis*, xxiv. 4.
[2] *Mai*, vi. 3.
[3] *Guelf*. xi. 4.
[4] *Cas*. II. cxiv. 3, 'Meritum visionis, fides est; merces fidei, visio est.'
[5] *Mai*, xxii. 1; 'All flesh is grass,' Isa. xl. 6.
[6] Or a 'witness.'

lives with how can he expect to withstand a persecutor? So, preach Christ wherever you can, to whom you can and as you can. It is faith that is demanded of you, not eloquence; let your faith speak for you, and then Christ will speak. For if faith abides in you, then Christ too abides in you.[1]

Once more, on the words: 'He must increase, but I must decrease': 'May God, then, increase, but man decrease. Yet how does the Perfect increase? What can be lacking to God so that He may increase? God increases in you when you understand Him.'[2]

As an example of how the Bishop himself 'preached Christ' by word of mouth we may take the following:—

In some such sort as this does the Lord our God, our Saviour, address us: 'Oh, ye men! I made man right, but he has gone astray. You left Me and, left to yourselves, you perished; but I am going to seek that which has perished.' 'You left Me,' He says, 'and so you lost life *and the Life was the Light of men*. See what you left when you all perished in Adam! *The Life was the Light of men*. What 'Life'? *In the beginning was the Word, and the Word was with God, and the Word was God*. Life was, then; but you were prostrate in death. I, the Word, had not whereby I might die; nor had you men whereby you might live. Since Christ, our Lord, deigns to permit it, I have made His words my own; if He makes use of mine how much more should I make use of His! Speaking to us, then, in silent fashion, and appealing to facts, Christ our Lord says to us: 'I had not whereby I might die; you men had not whereby you might live. Let us then enter into a compact: I give to you; do you give to Me. From you I take death; do you receive Life from Me. Rouse yourselves: see what I am giving and what I wish to receive in return. In glory in heaven, on earth I received from you humiliation; I, your Lord, received from you *the form of a servant*, from you I received wounds; I, your Life, received from you death. I, the Word, became flesh that so I might die. When with the Father I had not flesh; I took of your clay[3] the means of making presents to you'—for the Virgin Mary was of our clay; from

[1] *Guelf*. xix. 2.
[2] *Guelf*. xxii. 5.
[3] 'Massa.'

her Christ took our flesh, that is from the human race—' From thee I took flesh whereby I might die for you ; receive then from Me the life-giving Spirit whereby you may live with Me. Finally, by that which was yours I died ; live then by that which is Mine.'[1]

Once more, this time on our Blessed Lady, on the words :—

' Whosoever shall do the will of My Father who is in heaven, he is My brother and sister and mother ' ; Did not the Virgin Mary do the will of the Father, she who believed by faith, conceived by faith, who was chosen to be the means whereby our Salvation should be born amongst us men, who was created by Christ before ever Christ was created in her ? Beyond all question Holy Mary did the will of the Father and therefore for her it was a greater thing to have been Christ's disciple than to have been Christ's mother ; indeed, not only a greater thing but a happier thing for her. Mary, then, was blessed because even before she brought Him forth she carried her Master in her womb. . . . Holy Mary, then, blessed Mary, then ; yet is the Church something better than Mary the Virgin. Why ? Because Mary is but a part of the Church ; a holy member of it indeed, an outstanding member, a super-excellent member ; yet with all that, still a member of the whole Body.[2]

Yet again, on the value of the orthodox faith :—

Why do you rejoice when you hear ' The Father is greater than I ' ? Rejoice still more when you hear ' The Father and I are one.' See how the Catholic faith steers its course midway between Scylla and Charybdis just like a ship in that famous strait between Sicily and Italy. On one side rocks ready to rend her, on the other a whirlpool ready to swallow her. On one side Sabellius : ' One, He said, not two, the Father and the Son.' There you have the shipwreck ! On the other side Arius : ' Two, he said ; one greater, the other less, there is no equality in nature there ! ' There you have the whirlpool ! But do you steer your way between the two and so keep on the right track. Not without reason are Catholics styled

[1] *Denis*, v. 5.
[2] *Denis*, xxv. 7, *P.L.* xlvi. 937–938.

'Orthodox,' for the Greek word 'orthodoxon' is the Latin word 'straight.'[1]

Every sermon contained a great deal of doctrinal exposition, but this always had its moral application. These moral applications were couched in brief and pithy form and are interspersed here and there, thus compelling attention. We give some of them, taken at random: 'Once you begin to be bad,' he says to his catechumens, 'you fancy everybody else is bad. But it is a lie. Don't you believe it!'[2] On one occasion he tells, with a malicious sort of glee, of an interpretation of 'Let not thy left hand know what thy right hand doth,' an interpretation, he says, 'so absurd and laughable that had I not come across many who held to it I should not have mentioned it: they say that the "left hand" is a man's wife, and this on the ground that wives are apt to hold so fast to the housekeeping money!'[3] When Augustine proved that the most precious bodily possession people had were their eyes, yet that these were nothing in comparison with their minds, his hearers all applauded.[4] 'No need to accuse the devil of everything that goes wrong; a man can be his own devil!'[5] 'Better Job on his dunghill than Adam in his paradise!'[6] 'What more expressive symbol of emptiness than the talkativeness of frogs?'[7] 'How ashamed you would be if you were to discover that your wife had loved you only for your money! Worse still if when you became poor she thought of committing adultery!'[8] 'No one long defers a good dinner!'[9] These are not mere 'obiter dicta,' they crystallize all that he has been saying. People would carry them away with them and repeat them to one another.

The Bishop of Hippo well knew the value of examples and

[1] *Guelf*. xi. 4. Precisely the same will be found in *Tract*. xxxvi. 9 and xxxvii. 9 *in Joann*.
[2] *Guelf*. xviii. 2.
[3] *De Sermone Domini in monte*, ii. 7.
[4] *Guelf*. xx, 1–2.
[5] *Frangipane*, v. 5.
[6] *Denis*, xxi. 7.
[7] *Frangipane*, i. 5; St. Augustine was fond of this remark, *cf*. *Enarr*. i. 27 *on* Ps. lxxvii.; 'rana, loquacissima vanitas.'
[8] *Enarr*. i. 10 *on* Ps. liii.
[9] *Sermon*, lxxxii. 14.

illustrations, and he uses them freely. They are all drawn from the daily life going on around him. There is not one but would appeal to his hearers. 'The snow melts so quickly, yet if it escapes the action of the sun it crystallizes and nothing will melt it. There you have the hardened sinner. Some of you are familiar with this illustration, but you must not grumble at that, for I am giving it for the sake of those unfamiliar with it.'[1] 'I have said it very often, but as it is an apt illustration I will repeat it: When someone treads on you in a crowd, it is your foot he treads on, he has not harmed your tongue. Why is it, then, that your tongue cries out: "You are treading on me"?'—and he goes on to argue from this unity of our bodily members to our unity with Christ our Head.'[2] When you place a curved line on a level pavement, he says, it will not harmonize, it does not fit; so with the will of God; it is level, while our wills are crooked.[3] If you light a fire, the smoke ascends and spreads; but the more it spreads the thinner it gets till it disappears altogether; so the sinner will vanish, as the Psalmist says.[4] Many of his audience would appreciate his picture of the veteran soldiers: 'who have toiled so long in their military service, who have lived among wounds for so many years, who began to fight when they were but youngsters but who only get out of the army when they are old men; yet to gain a few days of repose in their old age, when their old age has itself begun to crush men whom no wars succeeded in crushing—what hardships they have put up with, what journeys they have made, how much cold and heat, how much privation, what wounds they have received, through what dangers they have passed!'[5] No doubt many a man groaned in sympathy when he heard his Bishop saying: 'How many come and say "the Government has taken all my property, and I shall die in penury!" How few come and say "Christ has taken away my property so that I may never die at all"!'[6] In his treatise, *De catechizandis rudibus*, a most practical manual

[1] *Enarr.* i. 2 *on* Ps. cxlvii.
[2] *Sermo*, cclxi, 14; *Tract.* in *I. Joann.*, i. 8.
[3] *Enarr.* i. 17 *on* Ps. xliv.
[4] *Enarr.* ii. 12 *on* Ps. xxxvi.
[5] *Enarr.* ii. 16 *on* Ps. xxxvi.
[6] *Sermo*, cccii. 5.

on how to instruct people, he insists on the advantage of such illustrations : I sometimes say ' something totally unexpected and out of the way and thus stave off a man's weariness. But this,' he adds, ' must be done briefly.'[1]

The following is interesting as an example of the pains Augustine took to provide practical illustrations of doctrinal points : he is talking of the yoke of Christ which we have to bear if we would be saved :—

> A person carrying a heavy burden seems weighed down, while one with a light one is less weighed down ; still both are weighed down. But one who carried none at all seems to walk with his shoulders delightfully free. Now it is not like that with Christ's burden ; we have to carry it if we would be lifted up ; if you lay it down your burden becomes all the heavier. Nor, Brethren, should you deem this impossible. It is possible, perhaps, to discover an illustration of this, something which will enable you to see in material fashion what I am saying, though the illustration is itself marvellous, well nigh incredible. My illustration is taken from birds. Now every bird carries its own wings. Watch a bird, then, and note how it folds its wings when it lights on the ground, how its wings then rest and the bird lays them along its sides. Now do you imagine the bird is burdened by them ? Let it lay aside its burden and it promptly falls ; the less that bird bears its burden the less is it able to fly. Would you, out of compassion, remove that burden ? No, if you want to show it compassion you will leave it alone.[2]

This humorous lightness of touch appears at every turn. Even when carrying on an acrimonious controversy he intersperses remarks which must have made his most hardened opponent smile—unless he were a Donatist, for no Donatist seems to have had any vestige of a sense of humour. Thus, when he tells Julian the Pelagian that his very ink ought to have blushed as he penned a certain statement,[3] or when he remarks that ' one healthy man can much more readily put up with two sick men than two sick men can put up with

[1] *De Catechiz. Rudibus*, 19.
[2] *Caillau*, II. xi. 6.
[3] *Contra Julianum*, iii. 26.

one another,'[1] he hoped to raise a smile on Julian's face as he read, while the facetious remarks in his sermons were calculated to put his audience in a good humour. This is, of course, the only legitimate argument for humour in a sermon, and Augustine shows his shrewd knowledge of human nature when he employs it in various ways to suit the capacity of his hearers. A woman, for instance, would smile with appreciation when he said : 'How mothers scrub their children in the bath, but for their health's sake ! And how the children cry out under their hands ! '[2] A man would chuckle when he listened to his Bishop describing a scolding wife :[3] 'Everybody has a home of his own so as to secure some rest. But supposing even in his home there are troubles, where can he find rest ? Outside are unfriendly people, inside a scolding wife.' 'You know well,' he says again, 'how unwillingly husbands go home when there is a scold there. So they go to the market-place instead, and there they are happy. Still, the time does at length come when they must go home, and then they grow gloomy. For they know they are going to grumblings, murmurings and complaints, to a home where everything is upside down. For you cannot have an orderly home when there is no peace between husband and wife ; much better, then, they say, to keep on wandering round the market-place ! '[4]

A preacher who has to speak to the same people again and again, year in and year out, must needs repeat himself at times. One of the many marvels of St. Augustine's life as a preacher is that in the thousand and more sermons of one sort or another that have come down to us he does so rarely repeat himself. Yet he had no hesitation about doing so if he thought it opportune. In fact, as he points out, one has to do so when instructing converts : 'The constant repetition of the same familiar things and the presentation of them to beginners is often a source of weariness.' 'But,' he adds, 'frequently it happens that when we have often to pass by some beautiful spot in the town or in the country we do not experience any particular pleasure simply because we have seen it so often, yet when we

[1] *Enarr.* ii. 5 *on* Ps. xxv.
[2] *Enarr.* ii. 20 *on* Ps. xxxiii.
[3] *Enarr.* i. 5 *on* Ps. xxxv.
[4] *Enarr.* ii. 8 *on* Ps. xxxiii. See J. Vérin, *S. Augustini auditores* (1870).

show it to someone who has never seen it before, our delight in the old familiar sight is renewed owing to the pleasure the visitor feels in what to him is a novelty!'[1] Still the more practical question is not so much whether the preacher is bored as that the audience be not bored by hearing an old sermon. Augustine faces this squarely. When about to explain Ps. xlvi., he warns his hearers: 'I am going to say what you already know. Yet, none the less I may be able with God's help to afford you a certain pleasure in hearing what you have already heard again and again if you will but take the hint and will ruminate over what you are going to hear again.'[2] When Severus of Milevis was staying with him and declined to preach himself but insisted on Augustine doing so, the latter may have been taken unawares. Yet, if he was so, he succeeded in preaching a very long and a very wonderful sermon on Ps. cxxxi. But he started by warning his hearers: 'You must not listen to it all as though you were but beginners; you must help me by listening to things you have heard already; it should not be necessary for me always to say something new. The real point in that we have got to *be* "new"; our old material must not prove a hindrance to us; for we have got to grow and make progress.'[3]

Augustine felt, too, that such repetitions had a real utility:—

It is good for you to be reminded of things you are wont to hear each year; for just as it is not enough to read once something that is written, so neither is it enough to have but a single exposition of something you do not understand. Those of you, then, who have already heard what I am going to say and who have understood it, who bear it in mind and remember it well, must listen patiently.

Augustine then goes on to discuss, as he did every Easter, the meaning of Christ's 'Noli Me tangere' to the Magdalen.[4] Again:—

[1] *De Catechiz. Rudibus*, 17.
[2] *Enarr.* i. 1 *on* Ps. xlvi.; *cf. Enarr.* ii. 1 *on* Ps. cx.
[3] *Enarr.* i. 1 *on* Ps. cxxxi.
[4] *Guelf.* xiii. 1.

Many of you know what I am going to say. But those who do know must put up with the delay; for when two are walking on the road and one goes fast while the other is slower, it is up to the fast walker to secure that they both keep together; for he can wait for the slower man. The person, then, who knows what I am going to say is like the fast walker and must wait for his slower companion.[1]

Some repetitions are on a large scale. Thus one passage of twenty-two lines on the yoke of Christ appears in two sermons, even such a play on words as 'non onerat sed honorat sarcina Christi' appearing in both. This particular 'pun' would seem to show that the 'h' was aspirated.[2]

See especially the repeated use of certain happy illustrations: 'put me up on your horse,' asks the child. 'Folly,' says his father, 'he would only crush you,'[3] and so does Almighty God in His superior wisdom decline to grant some of our petitions. Quoting the Bible from memory, as he must generally have done, we are not surprised to find a misquotation occurring more than once, as, for example, when, apropos of the cure of the woman with the issue of blood, he adds that the disciples *marvelled*,[4] a detail not to be found in the Gospels. Another illustration often repeated is that of the doors by which the devil tries to obtain an entry into the soul: cupidity and fear.[5]

Of the priests who sent the Magi to Bethlehem but did not go themselves to worship there he says that they 'are like milestones which indeed show the traveller the way but themselves remain fixed and immovable.'[6]

Whether he hesitated about repeating his sermons or not, he certainly did not hesitate about repeating and emphasizing the doctrinal points and conclusions arrived at in the preceding sermons. This is very noticeable in his sermons or *Tractatus*

[1] *Guelf.* xv. 3; *Denis*, xviii. 1; *Enarr.* ii. 1 *on* Ps. xc.; *Sermon*, ccl. 3.

[2] *Mai*, cxxvi. 12 and *Caill.* II. xi. 6, 'tam similis quam ovo ovum' remarks Dom Morin, *Miscell.* i. 259; *cp. Denis*, xvii. 9; *P.L.* xlvi. 881; *De Sermone Domini in monte.* For other repetitions see *Mai*, xvi. 4 and *Enarr.* i. 2 *on* Ps. lxxiv.; *Mai.* xvi. 1 and *Enarr.* i. 3 *on* Ps. xci.

[3] *Morin*, xvi. 3; *Sermon*, lxxx. 7.

[4] *Guelf.* xiii. 1; *Tract.* xxvi. 3 *in Joann.*; but not in *Guelf.* xiv. 2, xxiv. 1; *Mai*, xcv. 6, xxv. 3; *Morin*, vii. 1.

[5] *Mai.* xii. 4; *Caill.* II. vi. 5; *Morin*, xv. 5; *Enarr.* i. 10 *on* Ps. xxx.

[6] *Sermon*, cxcix. 2, cccli. 11, ccclxxiii. 4.

on St. John's Gospel. The fact that his audience grew and that people were present who had not heard the earlier sermons,[1] explains this in part ; but his main reason for such repetition was his determination to teach them the mysteries of the faith by hammering them in with repeated blows.

VI—ST. AUGUSTINE'S ELOQUENCE

That Augustine was eloquent goes without saying. Even the Donatists allowed that ; in fact they tried to make their people believe that he was nothing but a rhetorical dialectician.[2] His training as a pleader had been severe and his phenomenal success had very nearly ruined him. He himself has told us what it cost him to give up the profession of rhetoric, also how ashamed he was of the triumph he won when competing for the chair of rhetoric at Milan and indulging in lying flattery of the Emperor.[3]

Had Saul never become St. Paul, what would have been his place in the world's history ? He would certainly have left his mark on the world ; he would have outrivalled Nero in his fanatic hatred of Christianity, would have been a precursor of some of those terrible Roman Prefects whose names and deeds are enshrined in the *Acts* of the early Martyrs. Had Augustine of Tagaste, Carthage, Rome and Milan never become the neophyte of Ambrose, the hermit of Cassiciacum, the Superior of the monastery at Tagaste, and finally Bishop of Hippo and the greatest Doctor of the Western Church, what would he have been ? Certainly famous as a speculative philosopher. More certainly still a renowned pleader in the courts, an advocate whom everyone would have been anxious to retain ; a rhetorician, a mighty orator, a man who, as Archbishop Trench somewhere expresses it, made of the Latin tongue a weapon of amazing pliability wherewith to charm the souls of men But though his conversion did not silence him—nothing

[1] *Tract.* ii. 1. Naturally enough more were present on Sundays than on weekdays (*Sermo*, cxxviii. 6). Augustine felt the difficulty of this when he preached his second sermon on Ps. xxxiii. (*P.L.* xxxvi. 307). Sermons were, of course, more frequent on Sundays, even with this indefatigable preacher, *cf. Tract. in Joann.* vii. 24, viii. 13.

[2] *Contra Cresconium*, i. 1, 16.

[3] *Vita*, 1 ; *Confess.* vi. 6 ; *Contra Litt. Petiliani* iii. 25.

could have done that—yet it certainly did succeed in changing the orator and the rhetorician into the humblest of preachers. For, surprising though it may sound, the spectacle of the Bishop of Hippo in the pulpit must have afforded men a lesson in humility. 'Indeed,' says Possidius, 'I deem that they profited the most from him who had the opportunity of hearing him and seeing him in the church, and more especially such as were familiar with his life amongst us.'[1] What must his hearers have felt when they heard their saintly Bishop unashamedly confessing in the pulpit at Carthage the enormities of the life he had once led in their midst?[2] What did they feel when they listened to his wonderful prayers for the divine guidance? 'All this I have said in order to bring out the real difficulty of this problem; you realize how grave it is, well-nigh insoluble [he is discussing Christ's words to the Magdalen: "Noli Me tangere"]. May the Lord, then, help me to solve it! May He who deigned to set us the problem answer it Himself! Whatever suggestion He may offer me I will share it with you. If any among you has a better interpretation, then let him teach me; I am only a teacher in so far as I am receptive of teaching.'[3] So, too, when they heard him saying: 'Our whole strength lies in humility; for pride is but a brittle thing . . . humble people are like a rock; it is true that a rock is under our feet, but it is solid. Whereas proud men—what are they? They are but smoke. . . . They mount, but they vanish.'[4]

From the day he became Bishop, Augustine regarded himself as the servant of his flock.[5] There is henceforth no striving after eloquence; the rhetorician has disappeared. The Scriptures, once despised, have become the daily food of his soul.[6] The classical writers he loved so much[7] are laid aside, though their words, learned in his infancy, still rise spontaneously to his lips. Instead of those heathen authors he now

[1] *Vita*, 31.
[2] *Enarr.* iii. 19–20 *on* Ps. xxxvi.
[3] *Sermo*, ccxliv. 4.
[4] *Enarr.* i. 3 *on* Ps. xcii.
[5] See *Epp.* lxxv. 5, lxxxii. 23, cx. 6.
[6] *De Doctrina Christiana*, iv. 11; *cf. Sermon*, li. 6.
[7] *Ibid.*, iv. 10; *cf. Epp.* ci. 3, cxviii. 2 and 9.

reads Gregory and Basil, Chrysostom of Antioch, Cyprian, Optatus, Ambrose and Jerome, besides a host of others whose works are now lost.[1] These, he says, are the great men who 'not merely by word of mouth while here on earth, but by the writings they left to posterity, were strenuous defenders of the Catholic Faith';[2] they were and still are 'praeclara Catholica lumina.'[3] 'They did not all live at the same time, but God, at different periods and in places far removed from one another, raises up, as seems to Him wise and expedient, faithful and outstanding ministers, even though few.'[4] These great teachers Augustine read assiduously for the sake of his people. For he knew that a trust had been committed to him; that he was the instrument of One greater than himself, One to whom he will have to give an account of the souls of many.[5] Hence the extraordinary simplicity of his sermons. At times they are even rugged, rough-hewn. For they are the spontaneous outpourings of a heart on fire to other hearts which he would fain see as enkindled as himself.

Had anyone asked St. Augustine in what the essence of good preaching consisted, I fancy he would have referred his questioner to a passage which occurs in a context where one would least expect it.

Now there is something that I want to say for the sake of some of my brethren and most dear friends, who have, quite unconsciously, a Pelagian taint in them. For they imagine that their exhortations to lead good and holy lives are only effective when—since dealing with men and asking a man to do something—they make the whole depend on man's powers unaided by the gifts of God, and regard it as produced solely by the exercise of man's free will. As though one's free will could do anything to perfect a good work unless first freed by the gift of God. They do not realize that it is owing to the gift of God that they by their free will exhort men to undertake to lead a good life, stimulate the sluggish, kindle the frigid, correct the evil, convert people who have turned away from

[1] *Contra Julianum*, i. 5–32, ii. 14–15, 19–20, 26–29; *cf.* especially *Ep.* cxlviii. 10.
[2] *Contra Julianum*, ii. 31.
[3] *Ibid.*, ii. 35, iii. 3.
[4] *Ibid.*, ii. 37.
[5] *Vita*, 19.

God, and tranquillize rebellious wills. For it is only by this gift of God that they can persuade men to accept their persuasions. If they do not produce these effects in men's wills, what are they doing? Why speak at all? Why not leave people to their own free will? If however they do produce the above results, can it be true that a man by speaking produces such effects in another's will, and that God does nothing in that same will by His assistance? For no matter what gift of speech a person may have, no matter if by his skill in dispute and by the agreeable way in which he expresses himself he is able to sow the seeds of the truth in a man's will, foster in him love of God, root up his errors by teaching him and by his exhortations rouse him from sloth, it will always remain true that 'neither he that planteth is anything, nor he that watereth, but God who giveth the increase' (1 Cor. iii. 7). In vain does a man toil with all his might from without unless the Creator works in hidden fashion from within. It is in the hope that this letter of mine to your Excellency may speedily come into the hands of people who have such ideas that I have thought fit to make these few remarks.[1]

But though the rhetoric and the eloquence have gone, there remain traces, inevitable ones, of the training of years. We see it in his love of a neat phrase, in his habit of playing on words, in his rhyming phrases which defy translation. But even this was subordinate to the one end he had in view, the teaching of his people. The rhymes, the undying phrases, the puns—as we should call them—all are meant to help his people to remember, to fix a thought so that they shall never forget it. It would be a grave mistake to regard these happy turns of speech as mere quips, as a means of raising a laugh. They always have a sting in them. In this they resemble the Parables, at first sight so plain yet so full of deepest significance when we ponder them. Examples could be multiplied indefinitely, but a few will suffice. Those familiar with his *Rule* will recall the pithy phrase, 'Melius est enim minus egere quam plus habere,'[2] which enshrines the whole idea of the vow of poverty. How perfectly, too, he has expressed his own

[1] *De Bono Viduitatis*, 22, a treatise penned in A.D. 414 when Pelagius' notions were just beginning to attract attention.

[2] *Regula ad Servos Dei*, 5, *in P.L.* xxxii. 1380.

state of soul when, after telling us of his study of Plato, he says : 'Garriebam plane quasi peritus, et nisi in Christo Salvatore nostro viam Tuam quaererem, non peritus sed periturus essem.'[1] What more succinct than this on St. Peter's denials : 'Petrus flevit amare qui novit amare';[2] or this definition of gluttony : 'Ita nescit cupiditas ubi finitur necessitas';[3] or his comment on that last meal by the sea-shore : 'Piscis assus, Christus passus';[4] or on Pilate's *Quod scripsi scripsi*, 'clamoso silentio';[5] or on the Donatist pseudo-martyrs : 'Non eorum mirantur mortes sed recordantur mores.'[6] How better contrast St. Peter and St. Cyprian—whom the Donatists exalted at the expense of the former—than : 'Magnus Cyprianus orator, sed prior Petrus piscator, per quem postea crederet non tantum orator sed et Imperator.'[7] The profound statement, 'In Novo Testamento patent quae in Veteri latent,' is worthy of Augustine, but though the idea recurs frequently I have never been able to discover a nearer approach to it than : 'Quanquam et in Vetere Novum lateat, et in Novo Vetus pateat.'[8] How better describe the patient than by saying : 'Patientes malunt mala non commitendo ferre, quam ferendo committere'[9]—a passage which St. Thomas has made his own ?[10] The Baptist's advice to soldiers was practical (Luke iii. 14), and so was St. Augustine's : 'Milites non militia sed malitia prohibet benefacere.'[11] Once more on St. Peter's fall : 'Non terruit ungula sed una oppressit muliercula.'[12] Finally, when dealing with certain delicate matrimonial questions, he apologizes for his veiled expressions by saying : 'Necessitas loqui, honestas circumloqui cogit.'[13]

[1] *Confess.* vii. 26.
[2] *Sermo*, ccxcv. 3.
[3] *Contra Julianum*, iv. 70.
[4] *Tract. in Joann.* cxxiii. 2.
[5] *Ibid.*, cxvii. 5.
[6] *Ep.* clxxxv. 12.
[7] *Tract.* vii. 17 *in Joannem*.
[8] *Quaestiones in Heptateuchum*, II. lxxiii.; *cf. Contra Adversarium Legis*, 34; *De Catechizandis Rudibus*, 8; *Sermo*, clx. 6, ccc. 3, etc. For the style in the Sermons, *cf.* F. di Capua, *Il ritmo prosaico in S. Agostino*, *Miscellanea Agostiniana*, Rome, ii. pp. 750–764.
[9] *De Patientia*, 2 and 5.
[10] *Summa Theol.*, II.–II. Q. cxxxvi. art. 1, ad. 2.
[11] *Sermo*, cccii. 15.
[12] *De Tempore Barbarico*, 8.
[13] *Contra Julianum*, v. 19.

Eloquence of course has its due place, as Augustine himself insists in no uncertain way in his *De Doctrina Christiana*, the fourth book of which might be called his 'Manual of Preaching.' But this eloquence has to be severely disciplined. 'The eloquent are listened to with pleasure,' he says, 'but the wise are heard with healthful results to the soul.'[1] 'A man speaks wisely in proportion as he is steeped in Holy Scripture.'[2] 'You have only said a thing well when you have said it truly; a preacher must not be a slave to words; rather should they be his servants.'[3] For Augustine this was the true test of eloquence. For since the sole object of eloquence is to persuade,[4] it has to be by turns humble and accommodating,[5] temperate or restrained, and forceful.[6] Holy Scripture provides us with examples of all these aspects of eloquence: St. Paul is accommodating and restrained by turns, even when writing to the Galatians;[7] at times, too, he indulges in ornate language even to them.[8] To the Romans he writes 'ornate,'[9] to the Corinthians 'granditer' or forcefully[10] as occasion demands. Yet, ornate speech is, Augustine confesses, comparatively rare in the Bible.[11] What, indeed, he asks, have we preachers to do with ornate language? We can leave that to those who deliver panegyrics, unless, of course, we can make it conducive to the higher purpose of making men love virtue.[12] Great preachers like St. Cyprian and St. Ambrose afford us examples of the use of all these aspects of eloquence. Cyprian and Ambrose are accommodating when speaking—the former of the use of the 'mixed chalice' (which he wished to enforce despite the decay of the practice),[13] Ambrose when treating of the Holy Spirit, because of the profundity of the doctrine.[14] And both these writers combine ornate language

[1] *De Doctrina Christiana*, iv. 8.
[2] *Ibid.*, 7.
[3] *Ibid.*, 61.
[4] *Ibid.*, 55.
[5] *Ibid.*, 52.
[6] 'Grandis.'
[7] *Ibid.*, 39.
[8] *Ibid.*, 44.
[9] *Ibid.*, 43.
[10] *Ibid.*, 42.
[11] *Ibid.*, 41.
[12] *Ibid.*, 55.
[13] *Ibid.*, 45; St. Cyprian, *Ep.* lxiii.
[14] *Ibid.*, 46.

with their restrained speech when treating of the glory of holy Virginity,[1] though at times they use forceful language (granditer), even on this subject.[2]

Of the appropriate use of forceful language Augustine gives us an example from his own experience : 'I remember how on one occasion I wanted to dissuade the people of Caesarea in Mauretania from civil war or, what was even worse than civil war, mob-rule,[3] for not merely the ordinary citizens, but relatives, brethren, fathers and their children used on the occasion of some annual feast to arm themselves with stones and form into opposing camps ; this would last for several days on end and everyone tried to kill at least one person. So I spoke as forcefully as I could . . . nor did I fancy I had gained my object when I heard them applauding me, but only when I saw them weeping. Their applause showed they had understood and were pleased with what I said ; their tears showed that they were sincerely affected.'[4] Apropos of this applause from his hearers Augustine remarks that what he terms 'eloquentia submissa,' or an eloquence which accommodates itself to the temperament of the audience at the moment and to the nature of the subject treated of, is the only true natural eloquence : 'more especially when it has about it a certain unsought and natural beauty, a certain unstudied rhythm which seems, in a sense, to spring from the subject itself which we are handling. Eloquence such as this rouses such applause that it hardly seems to be "accommodated".'[5]

This enables him to formulate the statement that, 'if a preacher wants to speak eloquently, he must aim at being heard intelligently, gladly and submissively ; not indeed that these three effects are to be assigned to three different kinds of

[1] *Ibid.*, 47, 48.
[2] *Ibid.*, 49, 50.
[3] 'Catervatim.'
[4] *De Doctrina Christiana*, iv. 53. As Augustine here says that this event took place eight years previously and we know that his visit to Caesarea was made in A.D. 418 (see *Sermo ad Plebem Caesareensem*), this last book of the *De Doctrina Christiana* must be referred to 426 ; consequently it represents the matured thought of one who had then been preaching for some five-and-thirty years.
[5] *Ibid.*, 56 ; see A. Zurek, *De Sancti Augustini praeceptis rhetoricis*, Vienna, 1905.

eloquence, as though to be listened to intelligently means that you speak in an accommodating fashion, to be listened to gladly means that your eloquence is restrained, and to be listened to submissively means that you speak forcibly ; but rather that one should always aim at these three effects together.' [1] Finally, ' restrained pulpit eloquence, then, has its own beauty, while spurning unbecoming embellishments. Nor does it aim simply at pleasing one's auditory ; that we can leave to professional rhetoricians. But even when it praises or blames and urges people to seek after and cling to what is good, and avoid and loathe what is bad, it still desires to be listened to submissively. Yet, if not listened to intelligently, then neither pleasurably. Consequently, intelligent, pleasurable and submissive attention have all three to be aimed at, though the first thing is to secure people's pleasurable attention.' [2] ' When, then, you talk of eloquent, true and wise preaching, you can only mean that in accommodating your speech to your hearers and your subject-matter you use appropriate words, so that in your restrained eloquence your words yet glow, in your forceful speech they are vehement, while the things you speak of are true and what your hearers need to know. And if some cannot do all three things, at any rate let them say with wisdom what they cannot say with eloquence, rather than say with eloquence what they cannot say without folly.' [3]

Needless to add that Augustine insists that the preacher's greatest asset is his own personal life : ' Many are good hands at saying what they themselves do not practise, though they would do good to a far greater number of people if they but did what they say.' [4] But for once we must disagree with Augustine. For he says—as, of course, he would—that the picture of the true preacher of the Word of God which he has here drawn is not a picture of himself : ' Thanks be to God that in these four books I have not sketched myself as I am, for I fall short of this ideal in many respects ; but I have outlined as best I can what he should be who aims at " labouring, not

[1] *Ibid.*
[2] *De Doctrina Christiana*, iv. 57.
[3] *Ibid.*, 61.
[4] *Ibid.*, 60.

for himself alone but for others, in the sound—that is, in the Christian—doctrine he sets forth." '[1]

But despite his self-restraint the Saint does allow us now and again a glimpse of his oratorical powers. For though his sermons are, as a rule, examples of calm, methodical exposition, sometimes he is forceful, even vehement. For example, on the passage: 'I go not up to this festival. . . . But after His brethren had gone up He also went up to the feast.'—John vii. 8–10:

> 'Christ lied, then,' [says one]. 'Where?' I ask. And he answers: 'When He said, "I go not up to this festival."' Now I would like to examine that passage to see whether, after all, He did not lie. Or, better, since I have no manner of doubt but that He did not lie I shall either study that passage and understand it or I shall put it on one side precisely because I do not understand it. But in neither case shall I say that Christ lied. Now on the supposition that I do not arrive at an understanding of it I shall go away in a state of nescience; and it is surely preferable to fail in knowledge than in piety; preferable not to pass a rash judgment. . . . Let us see, then, where it is that you say that He lied. You answer: 'When He said, "I go not up to this festival."' . . . But now supposing someone said, 'Christ never said that!' how would you convince him that Christ did say it? Why, you would open your book, you would find the place, you would point it out to that man, and with full and complete confidence you would smack the book and say: 'Here, take it for yourself and read it, you have the Gospel in your hands. . . .' And then supposing the other says, 'The Gospel tells us what you say He did not say'; I should answer: 'So then, you believe that Christ says it because the Gospel says so! Truly I marvel that you should prefer to say that Christ lied rather than say that the Gospel lied!'[2]

It would demand too much space to quote more, so we must be content with a few references.[3] How rare, however, are

[1] *Ibid.*, 64.
[2] *Sermon*, cxxxiii. 6.
[3] See, for example, his sermon on the Ten Virgins, *Sermo*, xciii., and note the peroration at the close, No. 17; see, too, *Tract. in Joann.* lxxxv. 2, xcii., xciii. 1–2, cxvii. 3; also his eloquent reiteration of the words, 'Ad Te omnis caro veniet,' *Enarr.* i. 5 *on* Ps. lxiv.

these hints of a power which, had it not been Christianized (bound fast to the chariot of Christ), would have thrilled the pagan world! There is a saying attributed to Augustine—though it has always evaded one's search—to the effect that, had he had the offer of the fulfilment of three wishes, he would have asked to see The Word of God Incarnate, to have witnessed the Roman Empire in its glory, and lastly to have listened to St. Paul thundering in the pulpit. The first wish we can all make our own; the second is more doubtful. But the third will be echoed—and applied to Augustine—by everyone who has read and pondered his Sermons. Well did his biographer, Possidius, say after giving a summary account of the Saint's writings: 'I however think that men profited more by seeing him actually present, witnessing especially his life amongst us and hearing him preaching in the church.'[1]

In Migne's Latin Patrology, vols. xxxviii.–xxxix. (*S. Augustini Opera*, v.) give 396 Sermons about the authenticity of which there is no question. Vol. xxxix. contains in addition (*a*) Fragments of sermons preserved in quotations by Eugippius, Ven. Bede, Florus[2] and John the Deacon, cols. 1719–1736; (*b*) cols. 1735–2354 contain 317 sermons of doubtful authenticity if not certainly spurious. In vol. xl., 1159–1168: two sermons apparently adapted from St. Chrysostom; one on the Creed, another on Easter Eve, followed by four *Ad Neophytos*.[3] There then follow seven sermons with the interesting titles: On the Vanity of the World, On Contempt for the World, On the Profit of Discipline, On Obedience and Humility, On Charity, On Prayer and Almsgiving, and again On Almsgiving. Last of all come 76 Sermons to the Brethren in the Desert; but some of these are but fragmentary.

Among the authentic sermons we must reckon the 124 *Tractatus in Joannem*, *P.L.* xxxv. 1379–1976, also the 10 *Tractatus in Epistolam Joannis ad Parthos, i.e., in Im. Epistolam Joannis, ibid.*, 1977–2062. Then there come the *Enarrationes in Psalmos*, though not all of these were actually preached; they number 207 on the 150 Psalms.[4] Further, in *P.L.* xlvi. 817–940,

[1] *Vita*, 31.
[2] *P.L.* xxxix. 1723 ff.
[3] See *Miscellanea*, i. p. 5.
[4] On many of the Psalms there are two *Enarrationes;* on Pss. xxxii.,

25 Sermons first published by Michael Denis, Vienna, 1792;[1] *ibid.*, cols. 845–1004, 10 Sermons published by Octavius Fraja Frangipane, Rome, 1819;[2] *P.L.* xlvii. 1189–1248, four Sermons published by Angelo Card. Mai, Rome, 1842.[3]

Thus the Benedictines of the Congregation of St. Maur—whose work is that preserved in the above-named volumes of Migne's *Latin Patrology*—knew of 737 sermons which were certainly St. Augustine's and, in addition to the Fragments, 332 others of more or less doubtful genuineness. To the above must be added the 39 others incorporated in Migne's edition of St. Augustine as given above, making in all a grand total of no less than 1,108 sermons attributed at one time or another to the Bishop of Hippo, but of which little more than half were really his.

Since 1683, when the labours of the Maurists came to a close, 640 more sermons have been brought to light and attributed by various sponsors to St. Augustine. These fall into twelve collections, and have been very carefully studied by Dom Germain Morin, O.S.B., who published his critical conclusions in *Miscellanea Agostiniana, Testi e Studi, pubblicata a cura dell' Ordine Eremitano di S. Agostino nel XV Centenario dalla morte del Santo Dottore*, Vol. I., *Sancti Augustini Sermones post Maurinos Reperti*, Roma, 1930.[4]

Of these twelve collections of Sermons four are wholly rejected by Dom Morin 'nullus in eis sermo reperiatur qui tantillum habeat auctoritatis,'[5] and out of the 640 claiming St. Augustine as their author he will only allow the claims of 138.[6] Of the collections by Denis and Frangipane we need not say more, they will be found in Migne, see above. But the most notable collection in point of size is that published by Caillau and Saint-Yves, *Sermones cclxix.*, Paris, 1836 and 1842,

xxxiii., xxxvi., there are three; on Pss. xxx. and ciii. we have four; on Ps. cxviii. no less than thirty-two.

[1] Morin regards all of these as genuine save Nos. i. and x.; *cf. Miscell.* i., p. 10.

[2] Morin rejects No. x. 'in dubium vocandus videtur,' *Miscell.* i., p. 167.

[3] All are repudiated by Morin, *Miscell.* i. 277–284.

[4] Dom Morin had published the Thirty-four Sermons found in *Codex Guelferbitanus 4096* in 1917 and other Sermons in the *Rev. Bénédictine*, 1890–1929.

[5] *Miscellanea*, i., p. viii.

[6] *Ibid.*

though they only claim authenticity for 169 of these, and even of that number Morin rejects all but seven![1] Cardinal Mai published in 1852 *Sermones CCII*, which he attributed to St. Augustine.[2] But here again Morin is severe: 'illas solum denuo edere visum est quarum auctoritas in dubium revocare nequit,'[3] and he eliminates all but 26 which appeared for the first time in Mai's *Bibliotheca*. Another collection was that of Franciscus Liverani who published in 1863 his *Spicilegium Liberianum*—he was a Canon of St. Mary Major, the 'Liberian' Basilica—which included 10 sermons assigned to St. Augustine, but in Morin's words: 'Vix duo invenias qui ad Augustinum re vera pertineant.'[4]

The next list is that of the editors of the *Bibliotheca Casinensis*, vols. i.–iii., 1873–1877. Many sermons and fragments are assigned to St. Augustine, but a large proportion of these have appeared in collections already given, and Morin only admits four as new and genuine.[5] We then come to Dom Morin's own discoveries: *Sermones quos diversis temporibus hucusque edidit Germanus Morin*. These comprise 34 sermons from *Codex Guelferbitanus 4096* already published by Morin in 1917;[6] also 17 others published from time to time in the *Rev. Bénédictine*, 1890–1929.[7]

Finally we have thirteen Sermons published at various times between 1913 and 1929 by Dom A. Wilmart in the *Rev. Bénédictine*, the *Rev. d'Ascétique* and the *Journal of Theological Studies*.[8] To these are appended some 'Additamenta' or Fragments.[9]

[1] *Ibid.*, p. 242. Referred to in these pages as *Caillau*.
[2] *Nova Patrum Bibliotheca*, I. 1852. Referred to as *Mai*.
[3] *Miscellanea*, i. 284.
[4] *Ibid.*, p. 389.
[5] *Ibid.*, p. 400. Referred to as *Cas*.
[6] *Ibid.*, pp. 441–585. Referred to as *Guelf*.
[7] *Ibid.*, pp. 589–663.
[8] *Miscellanea*, i. pp. 673–715.
[9] *Ibid.*, pp. 716–719; see A. Wilmart, *La Collection tripartite des Sermons de S. Augustin*, in *Miscellanea Augustiniana*, Nijmegen, 1930, pp. 418-449; see, too, by the same author, *Remarques sur plusieurs collections des sermons de S. Augustin*, in *Casinensia*, pp. 21–241.

VIII—BIBLIOGRAPHY

J. M. Ashley, *St. Augustine the Preacher : Fifty short Sermons founded upon Select Passages*, 1877.

Baker and Bickersteth, *Preaching and Teaching according to St. Augustine ; being a new translation of his ' De Doctrina Christiana,'* iv., and *' De Catechizandis Rudibus,'* 1907.

M. I. Barry, *St. Augustine : the Orator : A Study of the Rhetorical Qualities of St. Augustine's Sermones ad Populum*, 1924.

A. Berger, *Histoire de l'éloquence Latine*, 1872.

A. Lezat, *De Oratore Christiano apud S. Augustinum*, 1871.

G. Longhaye, *S. Augustin, prédicateur*, 1888.

Sermons on Selected Lessons of the New Testament, by St. Augustine, 2 vols., Oxford, 1854, ed. by E. B. Pusey.

A. Regnier, *De la latinité des Sermons de S. Augustin.*

J. Sparrow Simpson, *St. Augustine the Preacher*, 1912.

J. Stalker, *The Place of St. Augustine in the History of Preaching*, in *Expositor*, December, 1921.

J. Verin, *S. Augustini auditores*, 1870.

V

ST. AUGUSTINE THE LETTER-WRITER

I. The Subject-matter of His Letters: Their Length—II. Dictation and Copyists—III. Letters that went Astray—IV. Editions and Translations of the Letters.

I—THE SUBJECT-MATTER OF HIS LETTERS; THEIR LENGTH

To a hard-worked man the post is to-day a ' necessary evil.' It was much the same in Augustine's day, though we may find it hard to believe it. His surviving correspondence comprises no less than two hundred and seventy-four letters, of which the vast majority were written, or rather dictated, by himself, while the remainder were addressed to him. Nowadays many would smile at such a modest total and say that they themselves receive and write ten times as many in the course of a single year. But Augustine's correspondence occupies no less than one thousand and thirty-four closely written columns in Migne's *Latin Patrology*.[1] He would never have dignified the ' snippets ' we write with the title of ' letters,' *notatiunculae* would more probably have been his term for them. His own ' letters ' are often veritable treatises, running to a prodigious length, and we can in fancy picture him walking up and down his room thinking out loud and dictating. To act as his secretary can have been no easy task!

Our Victorian parents would tell us that we have little or no idea of letter-writing, and would point with scorn to the hastily written notes with which most of us are content to-day. But the correspondents of the fourth and fifth centuries would, we fancy, look askance at the productions of the early Vic-

[1] *P.L.* xxxiii. For the Chronology of the Epistles see *P.L.* xxxiii. 13–48, for a series of arguments for assigning dates to them. But the most recent work is the last volume of Goldbacher's critical edition of the Epistles of St. Augustine, *C.S.E.L.* lviii. See, too, Dom Donatien De Bruyne, *Les anciennes collections et la chronologie des épîtres de s. Augustin*, *Rev. Bénédictine,* 1931, 284–295.

torians. For there is no question but that the letters of the great men of those early centuries were polished efforts. Take any letter you like of St. Augustine's and analyse it, and you will feel that the above is no exaggeration. How meticulously careful he is in his opening address to his correspondent! The latter's titles are correctly and carefully given; the reason for writing is stated; apologies for not having answered sooner are ample—when called for; the arguments are marshalled with precision; there is not a word that can hurt the most delicate susceptibilities, even when a rebuke has to be administered; there are no banalities, no talk about the weather, no complaints about the writer's health. But what impresses most is the marvellous balance of the sentences. You feel they are 'constructed,' not simply thrown on to the paper. There is a cadence about them which compels admiration; for these letters are marvellous examples of rhythmical prose. And this becomes still more wonderful when it is realized that these letters were dictated; they are not the work of a writer weighing his sentences, erasing and re-writing, polishing and polishing again. In fact so striking is the cadence of Augustine's prose that editors are beginning to feel that its presence or absence provides us with a valid test in case of disputed readings, whether in the letters or in any other of Augustine's works.[1]

Augustine even encourages his correspondents to write long letters :—

You see [he writes to Volusianus] what a long letter I have written you! If, then, you are really interested and feel that such discussion between us is of value, do not feel bound to tie yourself down to the customary narrow limits allowed in letters. You are familiar with the tremendously long letters the men of old were wont to write when dealing with problems which could not be briefly handled. And even if those writers of quite another class of literature than ours had not indulged in long letters we can justify our own long letters by recalling some of our own Christian writers who in such a matter are

[1] This has been well brought out by F. di Capua in *Miscellanea Agostiniana*, ii., pp. 607–764, especially pp. 652–655; see Sister W. Parsons, *A Study of the vocabulary and rhetoric of the letters of St. Augustine*, Cath. University, Washington, 1923; also C. J Balmus, *Etude sur le Style de S. Augustin*, 1930.

more deserving of imitation. Look, for example, at the length of the Letters the Apostle wrote; think too of the massive productions of those who have written commentaries on those same Epistles. Do not be afraid, then, to put me many questions if they occur to you.[1]

A few examples will show the length to which some of Augustine's own letters ran. Some of them indeed are veritable treatises and though they may not rank as *opera* they are certainly *opuscula.* One, for example, on Roman ritual practices, takes up fifteen columns in Migne's edition;[2] another, on the impudence of the Donatists, covers fourteen;[3] his reply to various questions put by Januarius, twenty-three;[4] his famous letter to Vincent the Rogatist—a member of one of the sects into which Donatism split up—occupies twenty-six columns;[5] a letter to Deogratias on Paganism, fifteen;[6] another on re-Baptism, also fifteen;[7] the wonderful treatise on Prayer, in the form of a letter to a widow named Proba, thirteen;[8] while one on the New Testament and its spirit occupies no less than thirty-seven columns.[9] St. Jerome was sometimes almost as diffuse; one of his letters to Augustine takes up thirteen columns,[10] while Augustine's reply fills another sixteen.[11] Augustine himself remarks of his treatise *De Remissione Peccatorum* that it has insensibly grown into a treatise.[12] Over and over again do we find him apologizing for his prolixity, yet it is a comparatively short letter which closes with the remark: 'I have unconsciously written at great length, in fact I almost forgot my work!'[13]

At the same time there was a valid reason for this prolixity. It was not simply garrulity, but was done of set purpose. In

[1] *Ep.* cxxxvii. 19.
[2] *Ep.* xxxvi.
[3] *Ep.* xliii.
[4] *Ep.* lxxv.
[5] *Ep.* xciii.
[6] *Ep.* cii.
[7] *Ep.* cviii.
[8] *Ep.* cxxx.
[9] *Ep.* cxl.
[10] *Ep.* lxxv.
[11] *Ep.* lxxxii.
[12] *De Remissione Peccatorum,* iii. 23.
[13] *Ep.* clxii. 9.

his sermons he keeps on recurring to the same points again and again and he repeats his arguments because he wanted to make sure that his auditory really had grasped things. This repetition is, perhaps, most noticeable in his treatises, sermons and letters against the Donatists, more perhaps in the treatises than in the sermons or letters. In his introductory remarks to each treatise he explains why he does this. For example :—

In replying to people who dissent from us and have strayed from the Rule of Truth we have often to deal with points on which we have written over and over again. Yet I deem it profitable to do so, both for the sake of those less alert minds which discover a fresh truth when they hear an old one differently expressed, also because it is worth while to multiply copies of discussions and so not merely secure that it can be a treasure-trove to those who can appreciate it, but afford a chance of at least one reaching somebody who would not otherwise be interested.[1]

And again :—

If the obligation of replying to opponents compels me to repeat things I have already said in other volumes—though I shall do so as little as possible—people who have read and possess those other volumes ought not to find this burdensome. For first of all, needful instruction has to be repeated again and again for minds less alert, and secondly, when the same points are presented frequently and from different angles this proves helpful even to minds more richly endowed, it makes it easier for them to learn and provides them with abundant material for discussion. For I am well aware of the annoyance a reader feels when he comes across a knotty problem in some book he is reading and for the solution of it is referred to some other book which perhaps he does not possess.[2]

Here, however, we are concerned more especially with Augustine's letters. Their varied character will appear from

[1] *De Unico Baptismo*, 1.

[2] *De Baptismo contra Donatistas*, ii. 1 ; *cf. Contra Cresconium*, ii. 1, 49 ; iii. 1 ; *Contra Litt. Petiliani*, ii. 1 ; *Contra Gaudentium*, i. 1, ii. 1 ; *De Baptismo contra Donatistas*, ii. 1, vi. 8, vii. 1 ; *Retract.* ii. 43, 51, 52, 60, 85.

the multiplicity of subjects with which they deal. Of those treating of theological matters, strictly so-called, eight concern the Holy Trinity, there are four on the Divine Attributes, three on Predestination, four on the Beatific Vision. There are twenty on different aspects of the Incarnation ; thirty-six on man—that is seven on Original Sin, two on the resurrection of the body, five on the soul and its origin, three on the end of the world, two on man's final happiness, nine on free will, eight on grace. Ten letters are occupied with general questions regarding the Bible, twenty-seven with the interpretation of specific passages.

Of his polemical letters some deal with the Pagans, others with the Manichaeans and Arians, forty-one with the Donatists, twenty-nine with the Pelagians. There are ten on the Catholic Church, seven on toleration of sinners, nine on Church rites, ten more on Bishops and priests. Many letters deal with the moral aspects of the Christian life in general ; various virtues are discussed in thirteen letters, various vices in twenty-two ; while thirteen others may be described as purely philosophical.

Augustine's correspondents wrote from all parts of the Mediterranean world : St. Paulinus from Italy, St. Jerome from Palestine, others from Spain, while his fellow-Bishops in Africa constantly appealed to him for help, instruction and advice. In addition to these regular correspondents, magistrates and officials, Pagans and Christians of every walk in life, widows and widowers as well as married folk, saints and sinners of every type, all appealed to Augustine of Hippo.

The arrival of the post with the accumulated letters and books, with requests for advice, with appeals from officials who realized the influence wielded by the Bishop, with letters, at times rather patronizing, from wealthy Pagans, must have been an event in the Bishop's household. Probably Augustine did not get letters every day, but if we could in imagination take a peep at his desk we should find, first of all, a lengthy letter from his revered friend St. Paulinus of Nola, who writes—as always—in conjunction with his wife Theresia. They have just received copies of Augustine's treatises against the Manichaeans and are filled with delight at the news of his elevation to the Episcopate. They hail him with extravagant praise :

'Thou art truly the salt of the earth; by you are our hearts salted lest they be misled by the world's errors. Thou art a lamp fittingly set on the Church's candlestick.'[1] Augustine in reply acknowledges that the news of his elevation is true, but he says: 'I cannot bear it with equanimity, for were I to do so no one could with equanimity bear with me. What has happened in my case is marvellous, yet true.' But he deprecates their eulogies: 'In your letter you have overwhelmed me with such praises that were I to reply to them in kind and deem it scant praise it might sound as though I did not believe you. I am indeed ashamed to believe so much good of myself; but I should feel more ashamed were I not to believe you!'[2] The next letter is from a lady who is weary of life and seeks consolation; she gets it—briefly. Yet there is one sentence in Augustine's answer which must have made this apparently curt reply worth having:—

I fancy that even when we are in districts remote from each other and are thus separated in body, we should find that if we could but divine one another's thoughts we are in reality far closer together than if we were sitting side by side and looking silently at each other, betraying by no outward indications our inmost feelings, by no bodily movement the spirit within us. That shows you that everyone is more present to himself than two people can be to each other, more known to himself than he can ever be to someone else.[3]

Another letter is from the illustrious Count Boniface. He had taken a vow of celibacy, but now he has gone and taken a wife; he writes to defend himself.[4] Yet another is from the reigning Pope, Innocent I, the friend of St. Jerome and of St. Exuperius; he writes on the Pelagian question.[5] Another day brings a letter from one who is later on to be Pope Xystus; he needs instruction on the same vexed question.[6] Finally, there come two letters of a very different type, though there must

[1] *Ep.* xxv. 1.
[2] *Ep.* xxvii. 3.
[3] *Ep.* cclxvii.
[4] *Ep.* clxxxix. and ccxx.
[5] *Ep.* clxxxiv.
[6] *Ep.* cxci. and cxciv.

have been many of the same kind in the Bishop's post-bag. The first is from a Bishop asking him to come—and by implication—to preach, for the dedication of his new church. This the busy Bishop of Hippo has to refuse, but we have seen how delicately he puts his refusal.[1] The other letter is from a girl who sends him a present of a new tunic which she had made for her brother, a deacon, who has now, however, unfortunately died. Augustine thanks her for it, 'more especially since you fancy it will be no small comfort to you if I were to wear the tunic you had made for your brother, God's minister. Therefore, before writing to you I put it on.' He writes her quite a long letter, ninety-four lines, full of consolation :—

> There is no cause in his case for protracted sorrow but rather for everlasting joy. I, it is true, am wearing the garment your brother could not wear, and that is some comfort to you ; how much greater and more solid comfort should you not derive from the thought that he for whom it was made now needs no corruptible garment [2] but will be clothed with immortality and incorruption ? [3]

II—DICTATION OF LETTERS ; NOTARIES AND COPYISTS

We are not to suppose, of course, that all this voluminous correspondence was laboriously penned by Augustine himself. Dictation, as is evident from a multitude of allusions, was the general practice. For instance, Augustine remarks that there have been brought to his notice 'certain things either dictated or written against himself by the Donatists.'[4] Similarly St. Paulinus puts questions to Augustine which, he says, 'occurred to me whilst dictating this to you.'[5] Augustine says that he dictated his volumes on the Holy Trinity[6] and, as a proof of his

[1] *Ep.* cclxix., given above, p. 163.
[2] 'Incorruptibili' in the text of Migne.
[3] *Ep.* cclxiii.
[4] *Retract.* ii. 19, 67 ; *Epp.* cxxxvii. 1, cxxxix. 3, clxxi., etc. It was on his deathbed that St. Ambrose dictated his exposition of Ps. xliii. *Vita* xlii. Origen says to Africanus : 'He who toiled with me in the dictation of this letter salutes you,' *Ad Africanum* 16, *P.G.* xi. 84, and St. Jerome : 'After reading a number of commentaries on Gal. ii. I summoned a notary and dictated,' *Ep.* cxii. 4.
[5] *Ep.* cxxi. 14.
[6] *Ep.* clxxiv. 1.

personal interest in him and his questions, he tells his correspondent Pascentius that he has not merely dictated his lengthy answer but has taken care to sign it himself.[1] When writing—perhaps somewhat impatiently—to Evodius who was greedy for replies, he says : 'You are asking a good deal of a man who is very busy ; and what is worse, you seem to fancy that my replies can be hurriedly dictated ; whereas the subject-matter is so difficult that answers have to be written or dictated with the greatest care ' ; he adds somewhat maliciously—and one can almost see him smile as he says it, and his amanuensis must have smiled too—' perhaps even then they can hardly penetrate such brains as you are possessed of ! '[2]

In Augustine's own case it is possible that writing was a difficulty, for at the opening of his *Soliloquy*, written at Cassiciacum in the early part of A.D. 387, he says that his 'health makes him shrink from the labour involved in writing ' while at the same time he does not like to dictate a 'soliloquy ' which, as the term implies, presupposes solitude. However he makes up his mind to set it down in writing.[3]

Letters and treatises were, of course, written on parchment. Augustine, for instance, tells Dioscuros that in preparing his answers to the latter's queries he had 'annotated the margins of the parchment on which Dioscuros had written.'[4] Copies, however, seem to have been made on paper sheets (*schedae*) ; the difference between these two materials is pointed out by St. Optatus.[5] When the famous Conference between the Catholics and the Donatists was staged at Carthage in A.D. 411, the stenographers[6] sat round and took everything down in short-hand. One of the tricks made use of by the Donatists was to talk so much that the notaries filled up their note-books so quickly that not only did fresh notaries with fresh material have to be brought in on two occasions, but the resulting bulk of material was so huge that, as the wily Donatists had hoped

[1] *Ep.* ccxxxviii.
[2] *Ep.* clxii. 1.
[3] *Soliloquium*, i. 1, *P.L.* xxxii. 869.
[4] *Ep.* cxviii. 34 ; *cp. Ep.* xxiv. 6.
[5] *De Schismate Donatistarum*, vii. 7 ; 'secundo loco est charta, secundo loco membranae,' *P.L.* xi. 1101 ; *cp.* St. Augustine to St. Paulinus, *Ep.* xxxi. 2.
[6] For the employment of such notaries see *Epp.* xliv. 2, clviii. 2, etc.

would be the case, it proved impossible to reduce it to readable form in the given time. Hence delays which very nearly wrecked the meetings. That these notaries made use of a species of shorthand is clear from the complaint lodged by Petilian, one of the Donatist delegates to the Conference, that neither he nor anybody else could be expected to understand the ' notes ' until they were written out in full on sheets.[1]

As regards the practice of dictating instead of writing with one's own hand, it seems that in the case of letters it was the etiquette to write with one's own hand, and on parchment, to people in a superior station of life. But when writing to equals or inferiors letters almost invariably appear to have been dictated and written on paper. We have an instance of this in the case of a letter sent by Augustine and Alypius in their combined names to a certain Maximus or Maximinus, a physician who had recently been converted from Arianism. In the course of their letter they set forth the Catholic doctrine on the Holy Trinity at considerable length and urge him to continue instructing in the true faith those who come in his way.[2] But apparently the convert either never received the letter or failed to acknowledge it. Augustine and Alypius therefore wrote to the latter's Bishop, Peregrinus, asking him to find out whether their letter has done any good. They add that as they had written on paper they are now afraid lest the physician has perhaps taken offence at what he may have regarded as a slight.

> Tell him, then, that we are in the habit of writing lengthy letters to intimate friends—not only to layfolk, but to Bishops too—in the same fashion as we wrote to him. We do this so that these letters may be written more speedily ; also because when reading letters it is more easy to hold paper (than parchment). He may not be aware of our practice and may therefore think he has been slighted.[3]

Dictation, of course, demanded the services of secretaries or, as the Romans called them, notaries. The business man

[1] *Gesta Collationis*, ii. 43, *P.L.* xi. 1358.
[2] *Ep*. clxx.
[3] *Ep*. clxxi.

of to-day dictates his correspondence to a typist, who takes down his words of wisdom in shorthand and then hammers them out on a typewriter. Though Augustine and his contemporaries had no such mechanical aids as typewriters they certainly had shorthand writers who were known as *tachygraphoi* or 'quick-writers.' Origen bewails the absence at Caesarea of the *tachygraphoi* he has been accustomed to have in the schools at Alexandria.[1] St. Gregory of Nyssa laments the dearth of such scriveners in Cappadocia and says that his work against Eunomius is held up on that account.[2] St. Jerome voices the same complaint : 'Here in this district we experience a real dearth of notaries skilled in Latin.'[3] Notaries skilled in Greek were not lacking at Antioch however, for Eusebius tells us that a certain Malchion held a discussion with Paul of Samosata and had it all taken down by notaries ; it was from this verbatim report that he was afterwards able to secure the condemnation of Paul.[4] St. Augustine's sermons were taken down in the same fashion.[5]

These notaries formed a class apart. The extent to which their services were enlisted is really amazing. For example, they were called in as a matter of course to take down the informal and private discussions held at Cassiciacum. But they are not even named nor referred to in any way. They were simply machines and were presumably paid so much an hour for their work.[6] They seem to have taken their notes on wax tablets and then transcribed them later in full.[7] At other times they seem to have taken their notes on paper (*schedae*) and then written them out in full, apparently on parchment.[8]

That these professional notaries or scribes were sometimes very inefficient was only to be expected. St. Jerome complains in vigorous terms of the miseries arising from having to dictate to people who presumably did not understand what they

[1] *Praef*. in Tom. vi. *in Joann.*, *P.G.* xiv. 199.
[2] *Adv. Eunomianum*, i.
[3] *Ep*. clxxii. 2, ccii. 2 (*inter Epp. Sti. Augustini*).
[4] *Hist. Eccles*. vii. 29.
[5] *Vita*, by Possidius, 7 ; *Retract*. ii. 67 ; *Ep*. ccxxxviii. 1 ; *Enarr*. i. 1 *on* Ps. li. ; *De Trinitate*, xv. 27.
[6] *De Ordine*, i. 27 and 30.
[7] *De Ordine*, i. 30 ; *cf*. St. Basil, *Ep*. ii. ; St. Cyprian, *Vita*, 12.
[8] *Gesta Collationis*, ii. 58–70, *P.L.* xi. 1361.

heard.[1] When a certain lady named Seleuciana had written to St. Augustine on the subject of St. Peter's baptism and repentance Augustine replied by sending back to her the letter she had written, for 'if you will look at it carefully you will see that I am only replying to what I actually found in it. Unless the notary took his notes incorrectly or transcribed them wrongly, I cannot understand the mentality of a man who, while acknowledging that the Apostles were baptized, says that Peter was not.'[2]

A business man to-day takes copies of his letters before he sends them out. He does it by a machine. Augustine, of course, had no machine for this purpose; but no letter seems to have left his desk until it had been copied, and probably copied many times. For the post was then a precarious matter and the letters of those days were—as in the Victorian age—precious things. They were not dashed off but carefully and laboriously framed. When a letter was received from a person of position it was read again and again and communicated to all who might be interested in it: 'I have read your letter,' says Augustine to St. Paulinus . . . 'the brethren, too, have read it and rejoiced beyond measure.'[3] When letters were of real importance they were learned by heart.[4] It must have been much the same when some Church was privileged to receive a letter from St. Paul; a fact which serves to explain how his letters came to be so carefully preserved despite the fact that the Apostle's autographs have disappeared.[5]

It is difficult for us, at this distance of time, when, too, we rely so largely on mechanical contrivances, to realize how extensive was this practice of laboriously copying not merely letters but books and documents of all sorts. Indeed there was no other method of multiplying copies of important works. And though letters might at first sight seem to fall into a different category as being more ephemeral in character, yet literature was not then the raging flood that it is to-day; men had no newspapers or fiction wherewith to occupy their minds

[1] *On* Abdias, *P.L.* xxv. 1117–1118.
[2] *Ep.* cclxv. 1.
[3] *Ep.* xxvii. 2.
[4] St. Cyprian, *Ep.* lxxv. 4.
[5] Coloss. iv. 15–16.

or waste their time; letters, too, such as those with which we are here concerned, had a very real importance, either by reason of their subject-matter or from the eminence of the person who sent them.

Moreover, the very fact that copying was the sole medium for securing a number of copies, the fact, too, that the task of copying was in the hands of a professional class and that there existed no such thing as copyright, made it necessary that important letters should be copied before being sent out, lest the writer should be accused later on of saying what he never had said. Hence St. Paulinus takes for granted that St. Augustine will have by him a copy of the letter he has written to him (Paulinus), for he asks him to copy it out again and send it to him:—

> If [he says] you have a copy on paper of your comparatively brief letter, which, however, was full of instruction on the faith, the one you wrote to me on the resurrection of the body when you were wintering at Carthage, I beg you will send it to me, or even write it afresh—an easy matter for you. For even if no copy exists—since a brief note like that may not have been deemed worthy of retention on your crowded shelves—re-write it for me out of the well-stored treasury of your mind.[1]

Similarly Augustine tells Nectarius to read once more his own letter, and he proceeds to quote extracts from what he himself had previously written to Nectarius.[2] Again, when writing to St. Jerome, the latter is presumed to have by him copies of what he had written to Augustine,[3] just as Laurence clearly had a copy of that letter of his to Augustine which led the latter to pen his *Enchiridion*.[4] Augustine, perhaps, thought that a woman might be more remiss in this matter, for we remember that he thought it prudent to send Seleuciana a copy of her own letter to him in case she had not kept one.[5]

And as with letters so with books. Toilsome copying was the only means of multiplying them. St. Jerome, for instance,

[1] *Ep.* cxxi. 14.
[2] *Ep.* civ. 5.
[3] *Ep.* lxxxii. 30; *cf.* cii. 2; *De Dono Perseverantiae*, 23.
[4] *Enchiridion*, 3.
[5] *Ep.* cclxv. 1, see above, p. 205.

says that he has had sent to him ' on sheets ' (in *schedulis*) the writings of a certain Annianus on the origin of the soul ; [1] while Augustine suggests to his somewhat exigent correspondent Evodius that if he really does attach such importance to what Augustine has written he had better send someone over to copy out his *Enarrationes* on Ps. lxvii., lxxi., and lxxvii., also the first five books of his *De Civitate Dei*, as well as the two letters—really treatises—which he had written to Jerome on the origin of the soul and on a passage in the Epistle of St. James, also his letter or treatise *De Natura et Gratia*.[2]

Alypius must have been a great copyist. When Julian the Pelagian had added eight books to the four he had already written against Augustine and which the latter had answered (in *De Nuptiis et Concupiscentiis*, i.),[3] Alypius ' came across these eight at Rome, and though he had not then copied them all, he sent me five of them when an opportunity presented itself and promised to send the remaining three as soon as possible.' [4] Work done at such speed was often badly done. Much of the difficulty Augustine had with Julian of Eclanum arose from the fact that he had to rely on defective copying of what Julian first wrote.[5]

When Augustine asked St. Paulinus for the loan of a copy of Eusebius' *Ecclesiastical History*, Paulinus replied that he had not got a copy himself but that finding Domnio, a relative of his at Rome, possessed one, he has asked Alypius and Evodius to transcribe it and ' send on the parchment copy to Carthage . . . lest Domnio should be too long deprived of his own copy.'[6] Augustine, too, seems to have had on hand plenty of copies of his anti-Pelagian treatises, for he is in a position to provide copies for the monks at Adrumetum ; these latter already possessed copies of St. Cyprian's *De Oratione*.[7]

Small wonder that mistakes crept in when every copy of a book had thus laboriously to be made by hand, more especially

[1] *Ep.* ccii. 2 (*inter Epp. Sti. Augustini*).
[2] *Epp.* clxix. 1, 13.
[3] *Praef. in Opus Imperfectum contra Julianum ; De Nuptiis et Concupiscentiis*, ii. 1 ; *Ep.* ccvii.
[4] *Ep.* ccxxiv. 2.
[5] See *Ep.* ccvii. ; *Contra Julianum, Opus Imperfectum*, i. 64, 71, etc.
[6] *Ep.* xxiv. 3 (*inter Epp. Sti. Augustini*) ; *cf. Ep.* xxv. 5.
[7] *Ep.* ccxv. 2–3.

when such copies were made by professional copyists who had little or no understanding of what they were copying. St. Jerome complains of the already corrupted state in which he found his first correction of the Latin *Psalter*.[1] Similarly St. Augustine finds that his own volumes on *Infant Baptism*, already in the hands of many, are sorely in need of a correction of the text, but he finds himself quite unable at the moment to give the necessary time to the work.[2] It was the same with his most important work on the *Trinity*, the uncompleted volumes of which had been filched by someone from his room and were then circulating in a mutilated state.[3] It was partly through fear of similar mishaps that he kept back for so long his *De Genesi ad Litteram* and his *De Civitate Dei*.[4]

We have already drawn an imaginary picture of the contents of St. Augustine's incoming post; from the detailed account of the proceedings at the Conference of A.D. 411, referred to above, we can form some notion of what St. Augustine's outgoing post must have looked like. At the opening of the second day of the Conference 'the parchment volume containing the sheets, with the notes partly copied out, as well as the notebooks containing the records (of the previous session), all of them sealed and the whole wrapped in linen, were brought in for judicial inspection.'[5] When, then, Augustine sent to Aurelius the Primate a copy of a portion of his work on the *Trinity*[6] it was almost certainly written on parchment, and was probably wrapped up much as this bulky volume of the records of the first day of the Conference; presumably, too, it would have been sealed. But before it left Augustine's hands not one but many copies would have been made. Some of these he sent to other friends,[7] some he would keep by him for reference, others he would place in the library he was so industriously accumulating.

[1] St. Jerome, *Ep.* cvi.

[2] St. Augustine, *Ep.* cxxxix. 3, *cf. Ep.* ci. 1.

[3] *Ep.* clxxiv. Gennadius, *Script. Eccles.* lxiv., tells us that the same fate befell St. Vincent of Lerins' *Peregrini adversus Haereticos*.

[4] *Epp.* cxliii. 4, clix. 2, clxii. 2, clxix. 1.

[5] *Gesta Collationis*, ii. 53, *P.L.* xi. 1360.

[6] *Ep.* clxxiv.

[7] *E.g.*, to Marcellinus, *Ep.* cxliii. 4. 'In ea domo quae dicitur domus episcopii,' *Sermon*, ccclv. 2.

If the Bishop of Hippo, then, was busy writing, his household must have been kept busy copying. And when the ships were seen coming into the port his disciples' activity must have been redoubled. For the Bishop would be certain to have letters to send off, and these, as well as the letters coming in, would have to be copied. The episcopal palace must have hummed with dictation! Then there would be the packages to be made up and sealed while messengers kept coming from the quay insisting that the boats could wait no longer.[1]

III—LETTERS THAT WENT ASTRAY

Sometimes, though rarely, we have to complain that letters have gone astray in the post; yet we still continue to trust it. But to 'trust the post' in the fourth century was heroic. You wrote a letter—or, more correctly, you composed a treatise—and then you waited for a messenger, or, if its destination was overseas, you waited for a boat. In Augustine's case, as with St. Paul, the facts generally seem to have been the other way round; he heard a messenger was leaving or a boat sailing, and he at once sat down to pen or rather to dictate an immense letter.[2] Often he had to finish his letter simply because the patience of the messenger was exhausted or because the wind was favourable and the shipmaster refused to wait any longer.[3] And when these letters did start on their journey it was quite problematical whether they would reach their destination, though Severus was astonished to find a letter reaching him the very day it was written: 'vere miror, eodem die venit quo scriptum est.'[4] Presumably letters did as a rule travel safely, else people would not have written. But the laments that reach us about letters that have gone astray are eloquent.

'I have no idea,' writes Augustine to Cresconius, 'when this my reply will reach you, but I do not give up all hope.'[5] In this particular instance, however, the anticipated delay was

[1] *Ep*. civ. 1, *cf*. xxxviii. 3, etc.
[2] *Epp*. xcvi. 1, xcvii. 3, cx. 1, cxlix. 1, etc.; St. Jerome, *Ep*. cxii. 1.
[3] *Ep*. lxxx. 1.
[4] *Ep*. cix. 3.
[5] *Contra Cresconium*, i. 1.

hardly due to the post so much as to the gulf then existing between the Catholics and the Donatists, a gulf which made it difficult for the one party to learn what the other had written.[1]

How disheartening it must have been for two such devoted correspondents as St. Augustine and St. Paulinus when a letter written by the latter in A.D. 408–9 [2] only reached Augustine in 410,[3] while Augustine himself seems to have been unable to get a reply through till 414![4] In that reply he says that he is taking advantage of the fact that a Deacon, Rufinus, is sailing shortly from Hippo, and that he will in consequence entrust the letter to him :—

Your letter, in which you asked many questions and helped me to realize how much room there was for such questions, in which, too, you taught me much by your very questions, has reached me. But the reply I at once sent has not, so I gather from your letter, reached you. I cannot at this moment recall what answer I gave to your questions, nor could I discover a copy of your letter when I looked for it. Yet I am certain I answered some points and that I only failed to answer them all because the messenger was in such a hurry. At the same time I sent you, in accordance with your request, a copy of the letter I wrote to you from Carthage on the resurrection of the body. I send you now another copy of that letter, also a copy of another which I feel cannot have reached you, since in your present letter you put questions which I am quite sure, from the copy I have kept, that I had answered in that second letter. Through whom I sent that letter I have no idea. But your own letter to which mine was an answer was forwarded to me by our people at Hippo when I was staying with our colleague, Bishop Boniface. I did not see the messenger myself but I did reply without delay.[5]

These and similar delays were often due, it is true, to the inadequate postal arrangements, as, for example, when a parcel of books sent to Augustine from Caesarea in Mauretania in the summer of A.D. 418 apparently reached him at Hippo only in

[1] *Cf. Ep.* xii.
[2] *Ep.* xcv.
[3] *Ep.* cxxi.
[4] *Ep.* cxlix.; see p. 206.
[5] *Ep.* cxlix. 1–2.

the autumn of the following year.[1] One has an uneasy suspicion, however, that Augustine was sometimes himself to blame; for he seems to have been untidy at his desk. More than once he has to plead guilty to being unable to find letters he knows he has received or copies of letters he has sent. We have just seen an instance of this in his correspondence with St. Paulinus.[2] So, too, he writes to Marcellinus: 'The letter you sent me by Bishop Boniface I got, but when I was going to answer it I could not find it.'[3] On at least two occasions he has to make the same confession to Evodius: 'your letter,' he says, 'has unaccountably gone astray, and though I have looked for it everywhere I cannot find it.'[4] But Evodius must have been a fatiguing correspondent, though always a welcome one; he felt he had discovered a gold mine in the Bishop of Hippo and therefore took every opportunity of putting questions to him. Perhaps St. Augustine may not have been sorry to have mislaid these missives! But it was probably the fault of the post and not of Augustine that only two out of three letters written to him by Oceanus reached him.[5]

Letters, as we all know to our cost, are often apt to be misleading. The written word does not always faithfully express the writer's mind, or the mind of the recipient happens at the moment not to be attuned to the mind of the writer. Hence misunderstandings which are most difficult to remove, especially when the sole means for so doing are further letters which only too often entangle the correspondents still more. When five minutes' conversation would have set the matter at rest, five years of correspondence may only lead to embittered feelings on both sides. The embroilment becomes deeper if by chance a letter which was the key to the whole position happens not to reach one of the correspondents.

It would be difficult to find a more tragic instance of this

[1] *De Anima et ejus Origine*, i. 1; for similar delays see *Epp*. civ. 1, clxvi. 1, ccii. 2, etc.; see A. E. Desjardins, *Les Tabelarii, courriers porteurs de dépêches chez les Romains*, 1878.
[2] *Ep*. cxlix. 2.
[3] *Ep*. cxliii. 1.
[4] *Ep*. clix. 1, though it is perhaps the same letter which is referred to in both instances.
[5] *Ep*. clxxx. 1.

than the correspondence between St. Jerome and St. Augustine.[1] The latter had written to Jerome about the year 394–5, when, that is, Augustine himself was still only a priest.[2] He had entrusted it to his friend and disciple Profuturus, but he, when just on the point of sailing, was made Bishop of Cirta or Constantina and died shortly after.[3] In this letter Augustine had, in the name of the entire African Church, begged Jerome to continue his translation of the Bible on the same lines as he had employed in his edition of *Job*, wherein, by means of certain signs, he had shown where the Latin text differed from that of the Septuagint, for even Augustine himself failed to see the object of translating afresh from the Hebrew.[4] But what interests him even more is a *Commentary on the Epistle to the Galatians* which is, so he understands, St. Jerome's work. Augustine is dismayed to find Jerome saying in that Commentary that St. Peter's accommodation to Jewish prejudices, for which St. Paul 'withstood him to the face,' was a polite fiction. He feels that if that is a sound explanation it can only mean that the Biblical writers set down what was not true, and he fails to see where, if once such a concession be made, we are to draw the line. For any heretic who dislikes some doctrine

[1] This correspondence has been published separately in the *Florilegium Patristicum*, Fascic. xxii., ed. Geyer and Zellinger, *SS. Eusebii Hieronymi et Aurelii Augustini Epistulae Mutuae*, ed. Jos. Schmidt, Bonn, 1930. In Migne's *Latin Patrology* all the letters which passed between St. Jerome and St. Augustine are given in the respective volumes of their letters. But it involves a great deal of toil to discover among St. Jerome's letters one numbered, for instance, *Ep.* xxxix. in St. Augustine's correspondence, and *vice versâ*. The following tables, then, may prove useful :—

A. *St. Jerome to St. Augustine.* (Among Jerome's Letters), cii., ciii., cv., cxii., cxv., cxxxiv., cxli., cxlii., cxliii. (Among Augustine's Letters), lxviii. *c.* A.D. 402–403, xxxix. 397, lxxii. 403–404, lxxv. 404, lxxxi. 405, clxxii. 416, cxcv. 418, cxxiii. 410, ccii. 419.

B. *St. Augustine to St. Jerome.* (Among Jerome's Letters), lvi., lxvii., ci., civ., cx., cxvi., cxxxi. (*a*), cxxxi. (*b*). (Among Augustine's Letters), xxviii., *c.* A.D. 394–395, xl. 398, lxvii. 402, lxxi. 404–405, lxxiii. 404–405, lxxxii. 405, clxvii. 415. See H. Lietzmann, *Zur Entstehungsgeschichte der Briefsammlung Augustins*, 1930.

[2] *Ep.* xxviii. (Jerome lvi.).

[3] *Ibid.*, 1, *Ep.* lxxi. 2 ; *De Unico Baptismo*, 29 ; St. Paulinus rejoices in the fact of his elevation to the Episcopate, *Ep.* xxxii. 1 (*inter Epp. Sti. Augustini*), see, too, Augustine's letter to Profuturus where, *Ep.* xxxviii. 3, he seems to refer to the same fact. Evodius, *Ep.* clviii. 9, tells of a vision he had had of Profuturus who foretold him things that actually came to pass.

[4] *Ep.* xxviii. 2.

could always feel free to say that on that point the Biblical writers were untruthful.[1] He concludes by assuring St. Jerome of Profuturus' competence and adds that he is sending some of his own writings to Jerome. About the year 397 came a very brief letter from St. Jerome [2] in which he says that he had written in the previous year and sent his letter by Asterius, but he makes no reference to Augustine's letter (*Ep.* xxviii.). Evidently he had not received it. To this Augustine immediately replied.[3] He begins by asking what title St. Jerome's work, which we now know as *De Viris Illustribus*, should bear.[4] He then passes to the question with which he had dealt in the letter (*Ep.* xxviii.) which Jerome had not received. Is an ' officious lie,' he asks, such as Jerome had attributed to St. Paul, conceivable in Holy Scripture ? He urges that St. Peter was induced to do as he did with a view to conciliating the Jews, that in this he was wrong and that St. Paul told nothing but the truth when he said that Peter so behaved ; otherwise the authority of the written word comes tottering to the ground.[5] Consequently he beseeches Jerome to sing a recantation, παλινωδία.[6] He then explains that he had sent his previous Letter (*Ep.* xxviii.) by Profuturus, but that the latter had been prevented from sailing, and so the letter never went.[7] Finally he refers to a letter he has received from Jerome on the subject of Origen and he makes certain suggestions about the *De Viris Illustribus* :—

There came into my hands a short time ago a book of yours, the title of which I do not know, for the volume did not indicate this on its front page as is usual. The Brother who had it suggested that it ought to be called *Epitaphium*. I could have supposed that you would have agreed with that title had the volume contained accounts of the lives or writings only of people already dead. But since it gives details of many who were living at the time you wrote it and some of them still survive—I cannot but wonder whether you really would agree with that title.[8]

[1] *Ibid.*, 3–5.
[2] *Ep.* xxxix.
[3] *Ep.* xl.
[4] *Ep.* xl. 3 ; see p. 169
[5] *Ep.* xl. 7.
[6] *Ibid.*, 7.
[7] *Ibid.*, 8.
[8] *Ep.* xl. 2.

The sting of this lay in the fact that Jerome had not included Augustine among the famous writers, whereas he included himself and had written somewhat bombastically : *Hieronymus . . . haec scripsi* with a lengthy account of his life and works, the whole closing with the words : 'Multaque alia de opere prophetali quae nunc habeo in manibus et necdum expleta sunt.'[1]

Then began the unfortunate embroilment between these two great men. Augustine writes, about A.D. 402, that he understands Jerome has received his letter and he can only attribute the lack of a reply to some hindrance.[2] But he is dismayed by a rumour that Jerome has heard that Augustine had written a book against him and had actually sent it to Rome. This, he takes his oath, is false.[3] To this letter Jerome replied at once.[4] He accepts Augustine's statement but says that copies of some such letter had been brought to him by a certain Sysinnius and that that letter—to judge by 'the style and the handwriting, ἐπιχειρήματα,' seemed to me to be Augustine's. But Jerome was particularly annoyed that the writer should have begged him to sing a recantation of his statements about the 'officious lie' in Galatians ii ; here he is clearly referring to Augustine's actual letter (*Ep.* xl. 7). At the same time Jerome protests that he is perfectly ready to accept Augustine's statement on oath and he writes very graciously. The tragedy, of course, lay in the fact that the original letter on the subject (*Ep.* xxviii.), the one which Profuturus should have conveyed to Jerome and which contained a detailed discussion of the whole question without any reference to a recantation, had never reached Bethlehem. Naturally enough it never entered into Augustine's mind that his request for a recantation could have been regarded by Jerome as '*a book*' against himself, and sent to Rome rather than to Jerome direct.[5]

The correspondence was not resumed till A.D. 405 when

[1] *De Viris Illustribus*, cxxxv.
[2] *Ep.* lxvii. 1. This embroilment has always interested writers on Church History ; there exists an anonymous publication, probably dated 1510, entitled *Discordantiae Sanctorum doctorum Hieronymi et Augustini*.
[3] *Ibid.*, 2.
[4] *Ep.* lxviii. *c.* A.D. 402–403 (Jerome *Ep.* cii.).
[5] *Ep.* lxxxii. 33 : 'libri nomen ab illa epistola discernebam.

Augustine wrote to Jerome by a Deacon called Cyprian. He has clearly not had Jerome's letter just referred to (*Ep.* lxviii, Jerome cii.). He now says he has written two letters to Jerome, but since he has had no reply he can only suppose either that Jerome has never had them or that he himself has not received Jerome's replies. He therefore (*Ep.* lxxi.) sends fresh copies and explains that the first of these letters he had sent by Profuturus, who however had never set sail, as he became a Bishop and died almost immediately.[1] As this first letter of the series (*Ep.* xxviii.) was, as Augustine here states, written when he was still only a priest and, therefore, about A.D. 395–6, ten years have elapsed since he despatched it. In his fresh letter Augustine reopens the question of the Septuagint and the advantage of translating, or rather correcting, the existing Latin text by it ; he instances the case of the Bishop of Oea or Tripoli who had read out from the pulpit the story of Jonas and the gourd according to Jerome's translation from the Hebrew, with the result that there was an uproar on the part of the people who complained that that was not the text of *Jonas* to which they had been accustomed.[2] Augustine ends by warmly congratulating Jerome on his correction of the Latin *New Testament* by comparison with the Greek text.[3]

To this Jerome replied, A.D. 403–4.[4] He has several letters from Augustine ; one unsigned, through Sysinnius, one sent through Profuturus, and another by somebody else. The first-mentioned letter was the unfortunate one (*Ep.* xl.) in which Augustine had asked Jerome to sing his recantation, but which was only intelligible in the light of the first letter (*Ep.* xxviii.) which Profuturus was to transmit and which Jerome now, after ten years, saw for the first time in the fresh copy Augustine had just sent him.[5] Up till that moment Jerome had accepted Augustine's sworn statement that he had not written a book against him nor sent any thing of the sort to Rome. But now all his suspicions are renewed :—

[1] *Ep.* lxxi. 2.
[2] *Ibid.*, 3–5.
[3] *Ep.* lxxi. 6.
[4] *Ep.* lxxii. Aug. (cv. Jer.).
[5] *Ep.* lxxi. 2.

I can only marvel that so many people should tell me that that very letter (*Ep*. xl.) is in circulation in Rome and in Italy, and yet has never reached me to whom alone it was addressed. This is all the more difficult to understand in view of the fact that Sysinnius tells me that he himself saw it amongst other treatises of yours, not in Africa nor in your hands, but, practically five years ago, in an island in the Adriatic ! [1]

Jerome adds that many folk in Palestine are insisting that Augustine is nothing but a popularity-hunter and that he looks on Jerome with contempt. He himself has not answered the letter, partly because uncertain whether it really was Augustine's, partly because he had no wish to enter into controversy with one who was a Bishop, but more particularly because he thought it was heretical ! [2]

As I wrote before, either send that letter signed with your own hand or stop worrying an old man hiding in his cell. . . . You take your oath that you never wrote that book against me and that you never sent to Rome the letter you didn't write ! Then how is it that other people come and tell me of your criticisms of me ? How is it that Italy has copies of what you never wrote ? How can you possibly ask me to reply to letters you never wrote ? You keep on urging me to correct things I have written and bidding me sing a recantation. . . . Either say clearly that it is not your book—if it isn't—and stop asking me to answer letters you didn't write, or if the letter really was written by you then acknowledge it like a man. . . . I repeat once more : you are provoking an old man, you are prodding a person who doesn't want to talk, you are trying to show off your learning ! . . . I am not saying that there is anything in your writings which I should think blameworthy. To tell the truth I have never read them seriously. The only examples we have here are your *Soliloquies* and your *Expositions* of some of the Psalms ; in the case of the latter I could point out to you discrepancies between your interpretations and those of the old Greek Commentators—that they also differ from my interpretation is of no importance, for I am of no importance.[3]

[1] *Ep*. lxxi. 1.
[2] *Ep*. lxxi. 2.
[3] *Ep*. lxxii. 5.

It is perhaps unfair to the glorious St. Jerome to present but snippets from such a letter. For, bitter though it is, it is interspersed with kindly remarks, which, alas, are immediately discounted by unkindly ones. How the gentle soul of Augustine must have felt all this! It all seemed so uncalled for. And to tell Augustine that he was a popularity-hunter and was showing off! But worse was to come. In the same year, 404, Augustine wrote saying that he hoped Jerome had by now received his answer (*Ep.* lxxi.) to the letter in which the latter had complained about the attack he supposed had been made on him (*Ep.* lxviii.). At the time of writing Augustine knows nothing of the terrible letter at which we have just been glancing but which was probably finding its leisurely way to Africa at the moment. He apologizes fully without attempting explanations beyond saying, 'the carrier neither took it to you nor returned it to me.' But he seized on the opportunity afforded by Jerome's comparison of himself to a goaded ox which can kick [1] to try to pacify the irascible old man by saying: 'Old in body, yes; but not in mind: if, then, I have done wrong I present myself, kick me hard!' [2] Yet withal Augustine is dignified in his reply. He feels, and justly, that he has been unfairly handled; yet he sweeps all that on one side and instead of recriminating he pays St. Jerome the most delicate compliment imaginable:—

I find so much food for thought in those of your letters that have reached me that I would gladly, were it possible, give up all my own studies and work side by side with you. But since that is out of the question I am thinking of sending to you one of my sons here in the Lord so that he may be our teacher later on, on the supposition, that is, that you answer my letter. For I have not, nor can I ever hope to have such a knowledge of Holy Scripture as you possess. And the little I do have, I expend wholly on God's people. As for devoting myself with any real diligence to studies other than those which make for the instruction of my flock, that is wholly precluded by ecclesiastical preoccupations.[3]

[1] *Ep.* lxviii. 2 (Jerome, *Ep.* cii. 2).
[2] *Ep.* lxxiii. 4.
[3] *Ep.* lxxiii. 5.

Jerome could hardly be said to have written a charitable letter. Yet how delicately Augustine insinuates this :—

I cannot think you would have been angry unless I had omitted to say something I ought to have said, or had not fittingly expressed what I did say. Yet it ought not to be surprising that we know one another so much less than our intimate friends and relatives know us, and on whose charity I find it easy to throw myself whole-heartedly, especially when worried with the scandals of this world. In their love of me I find repose without anxiety. For in that affection I find God. On Him, then, I cast myself without trepidation ; in Him I find repose without anxiety.[1]

More than once in the course of this letter Augustine bewails the rupture which had then come to a head between Jerome and Rufinus, those two fiery spirits !

After reading the preceding letter it is hard to resist a smile when one turns to the next one, addressed to the priest Praesidius who had undertaken to secure that Jerome shall get the letter :—

That you may clearly understand how to write to him [Jerome] in my defence I am sending you copies of my letters to him, also of his to me. When you have read these your prudence will make you realize the moderation I have felt it incumbent on me to observe ; you will be aware, too, of the agitated state of his mind and will see that I have good reason to be afraid of it.[2]

Meanwhile a further letter from Jerome was on its way, a terrible one. Both servants of God were probably writing to one another at the same time. What Augustine must have felt when he read what Jerome now wrote can easily be imagined. For Jerome says that he has just received at one and the same time ' three letters, or rather three small books.' These were *Epp.* xxviii., xl. and lxxi., and in them Jerome discovers criticisms of his own writings. He writes in haste, as the

[1] *Ibid.*, 10 ; ' In Quem me securus projicio, et in Quo securus requiesco ' ; *securus* was always Augustine's favourite expression after his conversion, the word, of course, means *sine cura*, hence ' without anxiety.'
[2] *Ep.* lxxiv.

messenger only came to him three days before he was due to sail.[1] He begins mildly, acknowledging that Augustine is not seeking his own glory but Christ's, yet he adds : 'I pass over the blandishments with which you try to soften your criticism.'[2] After explaining that the title *De Viris Illustribus* is an adequate one, he at once passes to the crucial question : whether St. Paul really meant that St. Peter did accommodate himself to the Jews at Antioch, or whether—as Jerome has said in his *Commentary on Galatians*—the whole thing was a piece of pretence. On this point, he says that Augustine ought before criticizing him to have noticed Jerome's prefatory note to the effect that he had read Origen, Didymus of Alexandria, Apollinaris of Laodicea—who, he confesses, had just left the Church, Alexander, an old-time heretic, Eusebius Emissenus and Theodorus Heracleotes : 'I read all these, and when I had got them all into my head I called a notary and dictated, whether my own thought or theirs.'[3] Here he breaks off to give a summary of the position adopted by Augustine, and then says—rather sneeringly, I am afraid : 'You are a Bishop known throughout the world. You had better set out your view and get all your colleagues in the Episcopate to agree with you. But, of course, I, in my little hut, in the midst of my monks, my fellow-sinners, dare not lay down the law on these great matters.'[4] Then, after pointing out that St. John Chrysostom and the great writers he has cited had held the same opinion as himself,[5] Jerome insists that St. Peter well knew that the Gentiles were to be received into the Church directly and not through the door of the Synagogue (Acts x.–xi., xiv. 26, xv. 1–12), also that St. Paul was fully cognisant of St. Peter's position as Primate (Gal. i. 18, ii. 1–2, 14).[6] He then argues that, like St. Peter at Antioch, St. Paul consistently pretended to show the same compliance with Jewish prejudice, he instances his circumcision of Timothy (Acts xv. 41, xvi. 1–3) and his observance of the Nazarite ceremonial (xxi. 23–26) ; he

[1] *Ep*. lxxv. 1.
[3] *Ibid*., 2.
[3] *Ibid*., 4.
[4] *Ep*. lxxv. 5.
[5] *Ibid*., 6.
[6] *Ibid*., 7–8.

adds, too, that St. James himself had urged a similar compliance (xxi. 17–26).[1] Both Paul, then, and Peter 'dissimulated.'[2] Finally Jerome does not hesitate to say that Augustine's notion that on certain points it was still legitimate to observe the Mosaic Law, is simply Ebionism,[3] and calls on him, as 'being a Bishop, a Doctor in the Church of Christ,' to prove his assertion.[4] He protests against Augustine

stirring up illiterate folk who venerate you as a Bishop and who, on listening to you thundering in church, are apt to despise a mere priest and laugh at me, who am now decrepit and drawing towards the close of my life. You ought to go and look for people whom you can teach or correct: for, separated as we are by stretches of land and sea, your voice hardly reaches me here. And even when you write letters they are sent to Italy and Rome before being sent to me to whom they should have been sent.[5]

This last passage is certainly savage; his renewed sneers, too, at St. Augustine's *Enarrationes in Psalmos* are unworthy: either the earlier Commentators, he says, found certain passages in the Psalms too difficult—in which case it was an impertinence on Augustine's part to try and do what they could not do, or—if their expositions were satisfactory, then Augustine's become superfluous.[6] He closes with the petulant words:—

Do you who are still young (Augustine was fifty in that year and St. Jerome perhaps sixty, with another sixteen years of life before him) and who have reached episcopal dignity, be content to teach your own flock and enrich Rome with new fruit from Africa. For me it suffices to whisper to the few poor people who will listen to me and read me in a corner of the monastery.[7]

One cannot without grief contemplate the feelings of the gentle Augustine when this dreadful letter reached him. He

[1] *Ibid.*, 9–10.
[2] *Ibid.*, 11.
[3] *Ibid.*, 12–14.
[4] *Ibid.*, 15.
[5] *Ibid.*, 18.
[6] *Ep.* lxxv. 20.
[7] *Ibid.*, 22.

had so immense a reverence for Jerome's scientific Biblical equipment; he had for so long envied him his life of comparative leisure and scholarly ease; he had so repeatedly written begging for his help towards a better understanding of that Word of God which was the food of his own soul and which he was ever striving to appreciate better and better that so he might be able therewith to feed his own hungry flock—and all he gets is vituperation! They are both Saints in heaven now and 'known even as they are known.' Augustine, we are well assured, would tell us now—as he probably said to himself at the time—that Jerome's bitterness gave him an opportunity for practising humility. And Jerome? It was probably in the following year, 405, that he wrote an apology.[1] Not a very gracious one, it is true, but one that certainly cost the Hermit of Bethlehem a good deal of self-humiliation. Augustine seems to have received this apology at the same time as he got Jerome's letters written in the previous year (*Epp.* lxxii. and lxxv.).[2] He writes back as sweetly and patiently as ever, but does not shrink from re-stating his arguments against the notion that St. Peter only pretended to accommodate himself to Jewish prejudices. Scripture alone cannot lie, not even Jerome—he adds with a spice of malicious glee—would claim exemption from error in his own writings.[3] Nor, again, would Jerome himself condescend to any *dissimulatio*; therefore neither would Peter or Paul.[4] He insists that the precise question is not what Peter or Paul did, nor whether they were right or wrong in what they did, but whether what is 'written' was written truly or falsely.[5] He then discusses the arguments whereby Jerome had tried to prove that both the great Apostles consistently practised some sort of 'dissimulation' with regard to the observance of the Jewish law; to commend the authority of the Sacred Books and Rites of the Old Testament does not mean that for us Christians they are the sources of our salvation;[6] the Old Testament has to be read indeed, but it is not

[1] *Ep.* lxxxi.
[2] *Ep.* lxxxii. 1 and 36.
[3] *Ibid.*, 3, 7, 22, 24.
[4] *Ep.* lxxxii. 4.
[5] *Ibid.*, 7, 11, 15.
[6] *Ibid.*, 9.

meant to be reduced to practice in all points.[1] The Synagogue has to be buried indeed, but with honour.[2] St. Jerome had regarded the Mosaic ceremonial Law as *vivifica* till the coming of Christ, when it became *mortifera* ; Augustine would insert a third period, that, namely, between the coming of Christ and the full promulgation of the Law of Grace, during that interval observance of the Jewish Law would be neither *vivifica* nor *mortifera* but *mortua*.[3]

Moreover, Augustine countered Jerome's argument from authority very neatly. For of the former's seven Doctors he rejects Apollinaris and Alexander as, on Jerome's own confession, heretics, while Jerome himself has on various occasions denounced Origen and Didymus. To the three remaining: St. Chrysostom, Eusebius Emissenus and Theodore Heracleotes, Augustine opposes St. Cyprian and St. Ambrose, and, by an amusing *tour de force*—St. Paul himself![4] Nor does Augustine withdraw his request for a recantation by Jerome, though he does not now press it. Nowhere in his letters did Jerome ever sing that 'recantation' about this *dissimulatio*, but when writing later on against the Pelagians, he remarked that rarely is a Bishop without some fault, and he adds that, according to St. Paul, even St. Peter was blameworthy : 'who then could grumble,' he asks, 'if he finds that he lacks something that not even the Prince of the Apostles had,' viz., blamelessness ?[5]

To Jerome's bitter remarks about Augustine, the Bishop, the latter made a rejoinder which could not be bettered : 'Though, in accordance with the honorific terms the use of which is now consecrated in the Church, a Bishop is superior to a priest, yet in many things is Augustine inferior to Jerome ; and no inferior should decline or contemn correction by his superior.'[6] How delicate, too, and yet how dignified the closing words of his apology :—

[1] *Ibid.*, 15.
[2] *Ibid.*, 16.
[3] *Ibid.*, 15–22.
[4] *Ibid.*, 23, 24.
[5] *Dialogus cum Pelagianis*, i. 22, *P.L.* xxiii. 516, a recantation which Augustine was quick to note, *Ep.* clxxx. 5, though he generously made no comment on it.
[6] *Ep.* lxxxii. 35.

I certainly did write that I had never sent a book to Rome against you. But I wrote that because I never took your word 'book' as referring to my 'letter.' Hence I could not imagine what gossip you had been hearing. And that letter itself I certainly never sent to Rome, but to you. Nor did I ever dream of it as being 'against you,' for I felt I had written it in the spirit of true friendship, whether as a suggestion or with a view either to your correcting me or I you.[1]

In conclusion Augustine expresses himself as convinced by Jerome's arguments in favour of translating direct from the Hebrew rather than merely correcting the Latin text by the Septuagint.[2]

No further letters passed between Augustine and Jerome till, in A.D. 410, there came a very brief note of salutation from Jerome[3] just after the capture of Rome by Alaric. It is characteristic of the two men that their intense hatred of heresy did more to bring them together than their equally passionate love of the Bible. It is no injustice to St. Jerome to say that he had come to look on the Bible as his own peculiar property! He had fought so magnificent a fight for securing as pure a text as possible; he had for years toiled in the obscurity of Bethlehem, far removed from the scholars of the day; yet from the rest of the world he seemed to meet with nothing but criticism, and what was only too often ignorant and invidious criticism. When Augustine's incisive, and in fact compelling questionings about the validity of his statements regarding the conflict of the Princes of the Apostles at Antioch reached him he had just completed his magnificent translation of the whole Hebrew Bible. Was it unnatural, then, that he should regard those letters with suspicion, more especially when there were rumours that the influential Bishop of Hippo had actually written a treatise against him and had not informed him of the fact? Worse still: this same African Bishop—who knew practically nothing of Hebrew, and who seemed to have no idea of what the Septuagint version really was—was actually writing to him and urging him to drop his lifelong task of

[1] *Ibid.*, 33.
[2] *Ibid.*, 34.
[3] *Ep.* cxxiii.

translating from the Hebrew just when that monumental work had been completed! The truth is that these twin giants were poles asunder in their outlook on Holy Scripture: Bethlehem wholly occupied with the text, Hippo with its exposition for the needs of souls.

It was inevitable that St. Jerome should look upon Augustine as little more than a popularizer, as a preacher rather than a scholar. No one would have granted this more readily than Augustine himself. To him the tragedy was that they could not combine their forces. He devoured everything that Jerome wrote, for he looked upon him as a veritable mine of information. Indeed it is amazing that Augustine should, despite the distance that separated them, have had in his possession so many of St. Jerome's works. He had his *Commentaries on Jonas*,[1] *Isaias*[2] and *Daniel*,[3] also his *Adversus Jovinianum*[4] and *Adversus Rufinum*,[5] he had read Jerome's *Quaestiones Hebraicae in Genesim*,[6] also his *Chronicon*,[7] he knows the *Exposition* of Psalm xciii. by that 'vir in Scripturis doctissimus,'[8] his translation of *Job* from the Hebrew[9] as well as his correction of its Latin text by the Septuagint,[10] he prefers Jerome's translation of Amos vii. 14–15 and quotes it with the eulogy:[11] 'In our own days the priest Jerome, a most learned man and skilled in all three languages, has translated the Sacred Scriptures into Latin, not from Greek but from Hebrew.'[12]

At the same time we must not forget the very real work done by St. Augustine himself in his efforts to secure as perfect a text as possible of Holy Scripture, see, in particular, Dom Donatien de Bruyne, *S. Augustin, Reviseur de la Bible*, in the *Miscellanea Augustiniana*, 1931, ii. 521 ff.

[1] *Ep*. clxvi. 6.
[2] *Ep*. cxlviii. 7.
[3] *Epp*. cxcvii. 1, cxcviii. 1; *De Civitate Dei*, XX. xxiii. 1.
[4] *Ep*. clxvi. 2.
[5] *Ibid*., 5.
[6] *Quaestiones in Heptateuchum*, I. xxvi.
[7] *De Civitate Dei*, XVIII. viii. 1.
[8] *Ep*. cxlviii. 14.
[9] *Ep*. lxxi. 3.
[10] *Ep*. lxxv. 19.
[11] *De Doctrina Christiana*, iv. 15–16.
[12] *De Civitate Dei*, XVIII. xliii.

In the spring of A.D. 415 Augustine sent to Jerome two important letters, one on the ever-recurring question of the origin of the human soul,[1] the other proposing an interpretation of James ii. 10. Twenty years have elapsed since they first exchanged letters and now both are old men :—

Though you are much older than I am, yet I, too, am an old man and I now write for your advice. For when it is a question of learning something no age seems to me too old. Old men, it is true, ought rather to be teaching than learning ; still it is better to learn than to teach what you do not know. There is nothing I find harder to put up with in all my anxieties over complicated questions than the fact that we are so far apart that I can hardly send you letters or receive yours save at intervals, not of days or months, but of years.[2]

He then states the various opinions current on the origin of the soul. Since this problem is intimately connected with the Pelagian views on grace and free will, which were then beginning to be ventilated both in east and west, Augustine sets out with great clearness the views Pelagius was busy propagating : 'opinions which I have never (before) heard or read of anywhere.'[3] The letter on James ii. 10 need not detain us save for Augustine's eulogy on St. Jerome's work in general : 'I ought gladly to learn from anybody things which it is no gain not to know. How much more fittingly, then, should I beg information from one from whose teaching, in the Lord's Name and with His help, Latin ecclesiastical literature has benefited to an extent hitherto unheard of ?'[4] To these two letters Jerome replied very briefly :—

I have not been able to reply now to your most learned letters, full as they are of wonderful eloquence . . . but you have stated, and with admirable clarity, all that could be said, and have supported it from the fountains of Holy Scripture. Permit me, then, to praise somewhat your genius, for you and I discuss questions in order to learn. . . . My sole wish is to love you, to look up to you, venerate you, marvel at you and

[1] *Ep.* clxvi.
[2] *Ibid.*, 1.
[3] *Ibid.*, 23.
[4] *Ep.* clxvii. 21.

uphold what you say as though I had said it myself. As a matter of fact in my *Dialogue* just published I have, as was only fitting, made honourable mention of you. . . . May Christ the Lord keep you in health and make you mindful of me, O truly holy and blessed Father.[1]

Here is the truly 'honourable mention':—

The holy and eloquent Bishop Augustine recently wrote two books on Infant Baptism in opposition to your heresy . . . and a third against people who say, like you, that a man can avoid sin without the grace of God, also a fourth to Hilary in opposition to your teaching. He is reported to have written others too which he addressed to yourself personally, but they have not yet reached me. No need, then, for me to continue. For either my words would be superfluous, or if I did wish to say something fresh it would have already been better said by that man of great intellect, Augustine.[2]

One is inclined to exclaim: *Quantum mutatus ab illo!* Yet after all it is the real Jerome who is here displayed. He has but four more years of life and he has mellowed. The sneers and criticisms which had so embittered him in the old days are now things of the past and he has discovered that in Augustine the Church had her greatest champion against a heresy which was saddening Jerome's declining years almost as much as it was to darken the fourteen years remaining to Augustine. Two years later Jerome wrote again, a note of some fifteen lines, breathing the deepest affection for Augustine: 'Always,' he begins, 'do I hold your Reverence in the honour which is your due, and I love the Lord our Saviour who abides in you. . . . I let no hour pass without mentioning your name.'[3] This was written in A.D. 418, when the Pelagian heresy had, mainly through Augustine's unremitting efforts, been officially condemned. The last letter was written the year after, in 419; 'with all due affection and veneration to Bishops Alypius and Augustine . . . since through your labour and toil the heresy of Coelestius has been slain.'[4] Perhaps these were the last words penned by the Hermit of Bethlehem; if so, it is

[1] *Ep.*, clxxii. 1–2.
[2] *Dialogus adv. Pelagianos*, iii. 19.
[3] *Ep.* cxcv.
[4] *Ep.* ccii.

gratifying to think that they were addressed to one whose gentleness and charity had finally triumphed.

When these last two letters reached Augustine we do not know. But when in A.D. 420 he wrote to Bishop Optatus on the question of the origin of the soul he had not then had an answer to his letters to Jerome (*Epp.* clxvi.–clxvii.) on that subject and on James ii. 10. It may well be that when he did ultimately get the answer (*Ep.* clxxii.) he had already learned of the death of Jerome.

In the year 421 when Pelagius, through the united efforts of the two Saints, had already been condemned three years, Augustine had to take up his pen against Julian the Pelagian, who had jeered at the great names invoked against him. This led St. Augustine to pen one last tribute to the hermit of Bethlehem :—

You should not despise holy Jerome on the ground that he was a priest. For he was learned in Greek and Latin, in Hebrew too ; and, passing from the West to the East, he lived even to a decrepit old age in the Holy Places and in the Holy Scriptures, and he had read all or nearly all who—whether of the East or the West—had written on Ecclesiastical doctrine.[1]

Pope Gelasius, writing in A.D. 493 to the Bishops of Eastern Italy to complain of the negligence of which some of them were guilty in conniving at the existence of Pelagian doctrines in their midst, mentions with indignation the fact that anyone 'should, even in the presence of the clergy, blacken the memory of Jerome and Augustine, those guiding lights for all the Church's teachers.'[2]

IV—EDITIONS AND TRANSLATIONS OF ST. AUGUSTINE'S LETTERS

M. H. Allies, *Leaves from Saint Augustine*, 1886.

J. H. Baxter, *Select Letters*, in the Loeb Classical Library, 1930.

St. Augustine : Letters, translated by J. C. Cunningham, 1872.

In the *Translation of the Works of St. Augustine*, ed. by Marcus Dod, 1871–76, vols. vi. and xiii., contain the *Letters*.

A. Goldbacher, *Ueber Handschriften der Briefe des Augustinus*, 1873.

S. Aurelii Augustini Hipponiensis Episcopi Epistulae, recensuit A. Goldbacher, 1872–1923. These five volumes in the Vienna Corpus occupied the editor during his whole life ; the fifth volume gives his *Preface* and *Indices*.

T. R. Glover, *Life and Letters in the Fourth Century*, Cambridge University Press, 1901.

Keenan (Mary Emily) Sister, *The Life and Times of S. Augustine as revealed in his Letters*. Washington, 1935.

[1] *Contra Julianum*, i. 34.

[2] Given in *P.L.* xlv. 1771.

VI

ST. AUGUSTINE AND THE WORLD OF NATURE

I. His Interest in Men and Beasts—II. In Birds and Insects—III. In Reptiles and Fishes—IV. The Key to this Interest in Nature.

I—ST. AUGUSTINE'S INTEREST IN MEN AND BEASTS

There is this to be gained from the hidden works of God: they are not so clear that we can hold them cheap; yet, though we do not comprehend them, they do not therefore cease to compel our admiration (*Contra Julianum*, vi. 17).

There are, alas, few to-day who read St. Augustine's Treatises on *Genesis*.[1] But those who do so are aware of the profound speculations on the created works of God which he had been for so many years revolving in his mind, and which he set down in writing with so much caution and after so much delay. It is not with these profound principles, however, that we propose to deal here, but rather with what we may style their raw material—the daily observations and the acute—though to our minds often very naïve—remarks to which they gave rise. Some will perhaps be apt to imagine that a purely speculative philosopher and theologian like Augustine can have nothing interesting to tell us concerning the animal world. But though it would be idle to expect from him anything in the shape of a zoological treatise, we can hardly imagine that a mind so acute and so observant as his should have failed to be impressed by the African flora and fauna which were presumably far more plentiful in his day than they are now.

[1] St. Augustine wrote *De Genesi adversus Manichaeos* in A.D. 389, or before his ordination as a priest (*Retract.* I. x.); four years later, 393, he wrote *De Genesi ad Litteram, Opus imperfectum.* The outcome of these preliminary efforts was his *De Genesi ad Litteram;* this he began after commencing his *De Trinitate*, but he finished it before the last-named work, on which he was occupied off and on from about 400 to 416 (see *Retract.* II. xxiv. 1; *Epp.* xliii. 4, clix. 2).

As a matter of fact, Augustine had a devouring curiosity. He seems to have been a man who asked endless questions, one who, whenever he came across a person of experience in any department of knowledge, religiously 'picked his brains.'

For example, he has evidently consulted his medical friends about the structure of the brain. 'It has been pointed out,' he says, 'that it has three ventricles: an anterior one, whence all feeling; another behind, at the neck, whence all motion; a third between the above two, and here memory dwells'; he adds that 'knowledge of these facts is due to the discovery that injuries to those various parts result respectively in loss of feeling, movement or memory.'[1] He has very clear ideas, too (derived, as he expressly says, from physicians whom he has consulted), about the functions of the nervous system and the relation between the nerves and the spinal cord.[2] Naturally enough, he regards the arteries as air-passages—as indeed the very term 'artery' implies, and as was naturally suggested by the fact that the arteries empty themselves at death.[3]

Human monstrosities interest him enormously. He tells us, for instance, of Polyphemus and other deformed men 'whose portraits are depicted on the esplanade (*via maritima*) at Carthage.'[4] Curiously enough, he seems to have regarded the Cynocephalus—or Dog-headed baboon, so familiar to London visitors of the Zoo at 'Monkey-hill'—as a human being, though he acknowledges that 'its bark indicates a beast rather than a man.'[5] One wonders, however, whether Augustine can really have seen a specimen himself; had he done so, it seems incredible that he should ever have taken it for a member of the human species. He has heard too of Pygmies, of one-legged men who had no knee-joint, and 'yet were marvellously swift of foot';[6] he tells us, too, of a web-footed man at Hippo Diarrhytus,[7] while he is much impressed by St. Jerome's account of what we should call 'Siamese twins'—'born,'

[1] *De Genesi ad Litt.* vii. 24.
[2] *Ibid.*, vii. 20.
[3] *De Genesi ad Litt.* vii. 20; *cf. De Anima et ejus Origine,* iv. 6.
[4] *De Civitate Dei,* XVI. viii. 1.
[5] *Ibid.*
[6] *Ibid.*
[7] *Ibid.* XVI. viii. 2.

says Jerome, 'in our day at Lydda.'[1] In his discussions with medical men he seems to have come across instances of professional jealousy familiar to us in these days, for he seems to be talking of people whom we are too apt to speak of as 'bone-setters' when he remarks: 'I often hear that the most skilled physicians are, when it comes to the use of the knife and of manipulation, frequently surpassed in amputating or manipulating limbs by others less skilled; they call this "surgery."'[2]

Dissection too, even vivisection, were quite familiar ideas to him. 'Medical men, those whom we dub "anatomists," have examined the limbs, veins, nerves, bones, marrow, even the vital interior parts of men, by dissection; they have even done so in the case of living people for so long a time as such were able to remain alive under the hands of those who rummaged about inside them! This they have done with a view to discovering the nature of the human body.'[3] He was much impressed, too, by 'a story I heard from older men who said that they had known and actually witnessed the case of Fundanius, a professor of rhetoric at Carthage, who through an accident lost an eye, but when after his accident he begot a son the latter too had only one eye.'[4]

Augustine's interest in diseases appears in his minute account of certain miracles, especially in the famous section in *De Civitate Dei*[5] which he devotes to this subject. Dropsy, phthisis and elephantiasis seem to have been familiar complaints in Africa, and while they often baffled the physicians, their unexpected failure to kill sometimes proved equally baffling to them.[6]

He is well aware that gout arises from intemperance and is often transmitted to one's descendants.[7]

We might at times be tempted to think the great Doctor excessively credulous, when, for example, he remarks that, though nothing can break those diamonds 'which so many

[1] *Enchiridion*, 87, *cf*. St. Jerome, *Ep*. lxxii. 2.
[2] *De Musica*, i. 9.
[3] *De Anima et ejus Origine*, iv. 3.
[4] *Contra Julianum*, vi. 16.
[5] *De Civitate Dei*, XXII. viii.
[6] *Sermo*, lxxvii. 14.
[7] *Contra Julianum*, *Opus imperfectum*, ii. 177.

people here have,' yet 'it is said that goat's blood melts them.'[1] But these marvels he accepts because they are told him by people whom he cannot suppose to be lying. As no one had come to him from the Antipodes, he had nothing to go by but his reason when discussing whether there can be such places: 'The stories they tell of "Antipodes" or people living on the other side of the earth, where the sun is rising when with us it is setting, and where their footsteps are, as it were, up against ours, present no grounds for our belief.'[2] He evidently regards the 'Antipodes' as people rather than places; indeed, that is the meaning of the word. If the 'Fundamentalists' of Tennessee ever light on this passage, it would gladden their hearts!

One would have liked to hear Augustine's comments on the enormous dragon encountered by Regulus when attacking Carthage. Orosius gives a most vivid account of it, and seems to have no difficulty in 'swallowing' it despite the assertion that it was one hundred and twenty feet long![3]

We probably imagine that love of dogs is a very modern thing, and perhaps that is true of the craze for dogs with which we are familiar. But only one who appreciated a dog could have said as Augustine did when discussing Jephte's vow to sacrifice whatever first came out to meet him on his return from victory: 'Cattle are certainly not in the habit of coming out to meet a victorious general; but, however it may be with other animals, dogs certainly do come out to meet their masters and fawn upon them, and then run along home in front of them.'[4] Dog-lovers will also appreciate the pithy remark that, 'no matter how alike two people may be, yet if they cannot speak each other's language and so exchange thoughts, their likeness is not much assistance to them; in fact, a man would far sooner take a walk with his dog than with a foreigner with whom he cannot converse.'[5]

The modern touch of the following is irresistible:—

I do not now go to see the dogs chasing a hare in the

[1] *De Civitate Dei*, XXI. iv. 4.
[2] *Ibid.*, XVI. ix.; *cf.* Lactantius, *Instituta*, iii. 24.
[3] *Historia*, IV. viii. 11–15.
[4] *In Heptateuchum*, vii. 49.
[5] *De Civitate Dei*, XIX. vii.

theatre, but if I come across such a sight in the country it does sometimes distract me, even from profound thoughts, and the chase draws my attention. And unless Thou dost speedily admonish me by showing me my weakness, or by compelling me to lift up my thoughts to Thee by reason of that very spectacle, or make me despise the whole thing and pass on my way, my mind becomes dull and empty. Supposing, however, when I am sitting at home I watch a lizard catching flies, or a spider wrapping up the incoming victims in its net, and I grow intent upon the spectacle ? Does the fact that these are but tiny animals make any difference ? [1]

Indeed if St. Augustine had not loved dogs, his disciple Orosius would not have written to him as he did when penning the opening passage of his *History* :—

Although in a great household there are many different kinds of animals useful for domestic purposes, dogs are not among the least important. For they alone have qualities implanted in them by nature that make them enjoy being urged on to some task set them and yet at the same time from a certain innate habit of obedience they, because they are trained, wait expectantly until by some nod or sign permission is given them to undertake it. They possess qualities in which they surpass other brutes just in proportion as they become kin to rational beings ; for they can distinguish, they can love, and they can serve. Thus, while they can distinguish between their masters and strangers, they have no hatred for those they pursue, though they are jealous for those they love. And while they love their masters and their homes, it is not merely owing to some purely natural bodily aptitude that they watch over them ; for they guard them assiduously with an earnestness sharpened by their love.[2]

Nor was Augustine's curiosity mere inquisitiveness. It had, as we shall see more fully later on, a very definite object. Here we shall only note that it grew in part out of his study of the

[1] *Confess.* x. 57.

[2] *Historiarum adversus Paganos*, I., *Prologus*, 3–6. Orosius then compares himself to Augustine's little dog, for he has faithfully, lovingly and watchfully performed the task committed to him, namely of preparing this 'History.'

Bible and his defence of its truth. For the Bible is full of natural history, and to some minds its statements about the animal world seem puerile. This view Augustine could not endure. Hence, when discussing the question of the giants so often mentioned in the sacred text, he tells us that, when walking one day with some companions along the seashore at Utica, they discovered ' a man's molar tooth of such immense size that we felt that, had it been broken up into a number of teeth of the size of those with which we are at present furnished, it would have made a hundred of them. I fancy it must have belonged to a giant.'[1] The sceptic will laugh and say that in all probability it was an elephant's tooth. But then the Bishop of Hippo was not precisely a fool. The same desire to defend statements in the Bible made him inquire into the possibility of procuring sheep coloured at will by the method Jacob employed. It is one with which stock-breeders are thoroughly familiar. But Augustine investigated the subject, and he quotes ' Soranus, a noted medical writer,' who also had gone into the question.[2]

In his sermons he frequently went to the animal world for illustrations. ' We, of course, are not surprised,' he remarks, ' that human beings should love their children, for even wild beasts love their young ; the asp, the tiger, the lion, all love their offspring. There exists no animal which does not purr over its little ones ; they may frighten men, but they cherish their young. When the lion roars in the forest, none dare pass through ; but when it creeps into the lair where its cubs lie, it leaves its ferocity behind it.'[3] ' No one,' he remarks, ' can get a load on to a camel by coaxing it ; you have to make it kneel down.'[4] We have all noticed how a horse can twitch its skin at any given point and thus get rid of a troublesome fly ; Augustine too had noticed this, and he had learned that some animals can even get rid of a spear in this way.[5] He has also noticed, and marvelled at the fact, that some animals ' can, even when tiny, run about at once and can recognize their

[1] *De Civitate Dei*, XV. ix.
[2] *Contra Julianum*, v. 51 ; *cf. Retract.* ii. 16.
[3] *Sermo*, cccxlix, 2.
[4] *Caillau*, xix. 5, *Miscell.* i. 268.
[5] *De Civitate Dei*, XIV. xxiv. 1.

own mothers ; nor do they need any external help to find their mother's breasts but, stowed away in some hidden receptacle in their mother's bodies, they find them with extraordinary ease.'[1] This almost looks as though he was familiar with some of the marsupials, though so far as we know these were confined to Australia.

The farmyard, too, furnished him with apt illustrations, and we can picture the African peasantry grinning when he said : ' Do you never notice how even among dumb animals, which are irrational and have no such thing as spiritual charity but only a carnal and natural affection, the young with great affection demand milk from their mothers' udders ? And although, when he sucks, the youngster makes a veritable assault on his mother's udder, yet it is better for her that it should be so than that he should not suck or not demand what love owes him. We often see quite well-grown calves butt at the cows' udders ; indeed, they sometimes almost lift them off their feet by their violence ; yet their mothers never retort with a kick ; nay, if the young ones do not come to suck, their mothers low till they come to the udder.'[2]

This curiosity of his was in no sense morbid. It was accompanied by close observation. For while he watches, he is thinking and asking himself questions. So much so that at times we almost feel a regret that he did not devote himself to scientific inquiry. Indeed, had he not been Augustine the Bishop of Hippo and Pastor of his flock, he might well have anticipated Fabre of the Landes of France. ' You must surely have noticed,' he says on one occasion, ' how carpenters and woodcutters always hit the same spot when using an axe, their blows fall precisely where their minds meant them to fall. When we try to do the same, we fail and the axeman laughs at us.'[3]

True scientific investigation was, of course, still in the womb of time. Yet, at times Augustine comes very near it ; he almost anticipates Pasteur when he tells us of his experiments on the flesh of a peacock. Someone had told him that it was

[1] *De Peccatorum Remissione*, i. 69.
[2] *Tract. in Ep. Joannis*, ix. 1.
[3] *De Musica*, i. 9.

incorruptible, a statement which seemed to him incredible. So he set to work to test it.

Who, save God, the Creator of all things, made the flesh of a dead peacock incorruptible ? I had heard it stated but felt it incredible. It happened, however, that a cooked peacock was brought to table at Carthage, so I had a certain portion removed from the breast and ordered it to be carefully preserved. After a considerable time, when any other flesh would, even after being cooked, have putrefied, it was brought out and set before us, yet there was nothing in any way offensive in the smell. So we put it away again for more than a month, but with the same result. Then we put it away again for a year, with the same result save that it seemed to have shrivelled and dried up somewhat.[1]

Note that he realizes that allowance had to be made for the fact that it was cooked.

II—IN BIRDS AND INSECTS

Birds, especially birds that could talk, appealed to the Saint. 'Blackbirds, parrots, ravens and pies,' he says, 'are often taught by people to express sounds which they do not in the least understand.'[2] The nightingale's song charms him : 'We all agree, don't we, that in the spring-time the song of the nightingale is exquisite, most melodious and sweet ; it seems to fit in with the season. Yet, you would never maintain that, since this birds sings so beautifully, it must therefore be skilled in the liberal art of music . . . nor would you expect it to answer your questions about its song or about the greater or lesser intervals it makes.'[3] And again : 'What exquisite modulations, what dulcet tones, fill the air when the nightingale pours forth its lay ! Could the soul of that tiny bird so spontaneously and at will pour forth such sounds, unless they were by some vital motion impressed on its bodily frame ?'[4]

Though very far from regarding birds or animals as mere

[1] *De Civitate Dei*, XXI. iv. 1.
[2] *De Anima et ejus Origine*, ii. 3.
[3] *Contra Epistolam Manichaei*, 20.
[4] *Enarr*. ii. 1 *on* Ps. xviii.

mechanisms, Augustine realizes that their actions are due to instinct rather than to reason. At the same time he finds it hard to draw a sharp dividing line between some of man's faculties and those of the animal world. Thus, he states as a simple fact that sparrows know the difference between black and white, though how he could prove that it is not easy to see.[1] He has noticed, too, what memories animals have: 'Beasts of burden pass through places they know without making any mistake; the wild animals find the way to their lairs; dogs recognize their masters' bodies and sometimes when they are asleep they keep murmuring, at times they even break out into barks. But they certainly could not do these things unless they retained some memory of things they had seen or of sensible experiences received through the medium of their bodies.'[2]

'But who would dream,' he asks, 'of assigning a higher place to the brute creation than to mankind on the ground that the sense-perceptions of the former are so much more keen? Look at the sagacity of a hound which discovers a wild animal by a sense of smell so acute that he actually leads a man to its capture. Now surely that is not due to some intellectual prudence but solely to the possession of keen bodily senses? Or look at the vulture which flies to an exposed corpse from a distance whence it could not see it (*improvisa longiquitate*). Think, too, of the eagle which, though flying at a great height, yet—so they say—sees a fish swimming at a great depth beneath the waves, and with beak and talons violently wrenches it from the water. Realize, too, the number of animals which spend their lives amid growths fatal to their health yet never touch the things that would harm them; whereas we men hardly learn by experience what to avoid and we are afraid of many quite harmless things simply because we have never tried them.'

He has noticed, too, what perhaps few naturalists realized until recently when bird-watching has become almost the fashion. 'Even in some animals that have not reason, for example, in some species of birds, their marriage is a sort of

[1] *De Musica*, i. 5.
[2] *De vera religione*, 79.

partnership : their nest-building is a social task performed together, they take it in turns to brood over their eggs, and they share the work of feeding the young ones.' [1]

The ' pelican of the wilderness, the raven in the house [Revised Version : ' an owl of the waste places '], the sparrow all alone on the housetop ' (Ps. ci. 7–8), naturally afford scope for St. Augustine's exegetical gifts. ' Three birds,' he says, ' three places : the pelican, the owl, the sparrow—the wilderness, the waste places or ruins, the housetop. . . . What is the pelican ? Born in the wilderness, particularly by the Nile in Egypt, to us it is not familiar . . . but the owl dwells in the ruins, while as for the sparrow on the housetop, well you all know him ! ' But Augustine is particularly interested in the pelican : ' We must not pass over what we are told, nay what we even read, about this bird. We shall make no rash assertions, but shall simply state what those who have written on the subject would have us know. Listen then, and if you think it true, accept it ; if not, then reject it. Now, they say that this bird kills its young with repeated blows of its bill, and then mourns over their dead bodies in the nest for three days ; that then the mother-bird inflicts grievous wounds on herself and pours her blood on her offspring which thereupon come to life again. Perhaps it is true, perhaps it is false.' [2] Since Augustine's principle in interpreting the Psalms is that all is to be referred either to Christ the Head or to the Church His Body, he takes the pelican as Christ and applies the foregoing in the way rendered familiar to us by St. Thomas' lines :—

Pie Pellicane, Jesu Domine, me immundum munda Tuo Sanguine,
Cujus una stilla salvum facere totum mundum quit ab omni scelere.

Is this foolish credulity ? Yet how careful Augustine is. The authority for the story is very great ; yet still, it sounds incredible. He tells it, therefore, with every reserve, and

[1] *De Nuptiis*, i. 5.
[2] *Enarr.* i. 8 *on* Ps. ci. See *De Anima et ejus Origine*, iv. 33, where Augustine evidently identifies the pelican with the phœnix.

leaves it to his hearers to accept it or not. But of the application he is certain. Christ the Lord is represented by these three birds : 'Pelicanus nascendo, nycticorax moriendo, passer resurgendo.'

The eagle, the king of birds, of course appeals to him. It may or may not be true, but he would like to believe that 'the eaglets are held in their father's talons for the sun's rays to beat upon them, also that, if they so much as let an eyelid quiver, he repudiates them as bastards.'[1] The crow must, of course, have been a familiar sight in Africa, and its hoarse croak a wonted sound. 'There are many folk,' says Augustine, 'who dream about conversion but they put it off ; such people remind one of the crow which cries "*cras*, *cras !*" (to-morrow, to-morrow !)' But what does Augustine mean by the 'cornicula'? If the jackdaw, then there would seem to have been none in Africa. For when Dioscuros was terrified lest, when he came to Africa, people might put him puzzling questions about the teachings of Cicero, Augustine reassured him by saying : 'You would as soon hear jackdaws (*corniculas*) in Africa as hear questions of that sort here.'[2]

The picture of a hen with her chicks, used by Our Saviour as a portrait of Himself, naturally appeals to the Bishop of Hippo : 'The hen is the Divine Wisdom who took flesh to gather His chicks. Look at a hen with her plumage all fluffed out, her wings let down, her voice quavering, broken, tired and low as she gathers together her chicks !'[3]

Elsewhere he returns to the same picture, but adds :—

But if you saw some other kind of bird and were ignorant whether it had a nest or not you could not tell (by its appearance) whether it had either eggs or chicks. Yet you have only to look at a hen to know at once—even without seeing either eggs or chicks—by its note and its carriage, that it is a mother.

What a naturalist Augustine would have made ![4]

When Julian the Pelagian had objected to the notion that the pains of childbirth were a penalty paid for sin and urged

[1] *De Gestis Pelagii*, 18 ; see Tertullian, *De Anima*, 8.
[2] *Ep.* cxviii. 9.
[3] *Sermo*, cv. 11 ; *cf. Tract.* xx. *in Joann.* 7, and *Enarr.* i. 5 *on* Ps. xc.
[4] *Denis*, xiii. 6 ; *P.L.* xlvi. 859.

that the same argument would prove animals had been guilty of sin since they too cried out when bearing, Augustine retorted :—

Did any animal ever tell you whether their cries then were signs of joy or signs of pain ? When hens are going to lay, their cries sound more like joy than pain. And when they have laid they emit just the same kind of cry as when they were terrified. Besides, observers will tell you that some birds, doves for instance, lay in complete silence.

Few hen-wives would agree that the cry a hen emits after laying is just the same as when the bird scuttles away frightened ! [1]

Again : has any sportsman or any gamekeeper ever noticed that the partridge is peculiarly quarrelsome ? I have asked several, but none can explain why Augustine says more than once that this is the case. 'There is a certain type of heretic,' he remarks, 'whom I should call—like the partridge—"a quarrelsome animal." For, as bird-catchers know, the partridge is captured through its love of fighting.' [2] This, of course, is true of many birds during the mating season, but why the partridge should be thus singled out is a mystery.

Nor is it only the human race, his fellow-men, or the beasts of the field or the birds of the air, that interest him. The insect world, too, had its fascinations. He has noticed (*observatum est*) that many 'are born, whether in the water or on the land, which are sexless.' Whence he argues that 'the seminal principle is not in them but in the elements whence they spring.' [3] Spontaneous generation was, of course, a first principle in those days, as indeed it was with many till the days of Pasteur ; even now old rustic fishermen will assure you that the pike is begotten of the reeds by the water-side ! St. Augustine takes it for granted ; in fact, he uses it as an argument for the possibility of Christ's birth of a virgin. [4] His great friend, Evodius, who drew from him this argument, is peculiarly naïve on the subject.

[1] *Contra Julianum, Opus imperf.* vi. 26.
[2] *Sermo*, xlvi. 29 ; *Contra Faustum*, xiii. 12.
[3] *De Genesi ad Litt.* iii. 19 ; similarly he knows that mules are sexless, *De Anima et ejus Origine*, iv. 33.
[4] *Ep.* cxl. 21, clxi. 1–2.

'Mares,' he says, 'conceive by the wind, ducks by the water, hens by the dust. . . .' In fact, he says, 'I have heard that the spider's web is an instance of virginal conception.' He is puzzled, too, by the presence of a grub in the very middle of an apple; he concludes that it originated there.[1] Can we blame these men of old? After all, they had none of our perfected methods of investigation, nor is it very long since the majority of men believed the same, and even more amazing things.

Here in England we see ants, tiny things, seemingly innocuous. But it is far otherwise in Africa where they are a stern reality, a menace at times. But to Augustine they were peculiarly interesting, and suggest an excellent moral, just as they had long ago done to the Wise Man: 'Go to the ant, thou sluggard!'[2] 'When times are prosperous,' says Augustine the preacher, 'a man should harvest the word of God and lay it up in his inmost heart, just as the ant stores away her summer's toil in the depths of her tortuous nest.'[3] It is somewhat striking that he has not more to say about bees than he has. He states as an elementary fact that they spring from the bodies of oxen.[4] He seems to imagine that their young are produced from the wax,[5] and fancies them sexless.[6] But he speaks of 'the many wonderful facts about bees which we can witness with our own eyes, though reason, which men and Angels (not men and animals) have in common, far transcends the marvellous sense with which these irrational things are endowed.'[7]

How interested Augustine and his friends were in the marvels of the insect creation appears from the following. 'I remember when we were boys,' said Evodius, 'how we used to marvel at the way in which a lizard's tail would continue to wriggle after it had been cut off.' Augustine replies by telling him how, 'when recently we were in the country in Liguria, the young students who were with me saw lying on the ground in a shady

[1] *Ep.* clxi. 1–2; *cf. De Moribus Manichaeorum*, ii. 63–64.
[2] Prov. vi. 6, xxx. 25.
[3] *Enarr.* ii. 11 *on* Ps. xxxvi. and i. 1 *on* Ps. lxi.
[4] *De Moribus Manichaeorum*, ii. 63; *De Trin.*, iii. 13.
[5] *De Genesi ad Litt.* ix. 18.
[6] *De Civitate Dei*, XV. xxvii. 3; *De Trinitate*, iii. 13.
[7] *De Gestis Pelagii*, 18.

place a creeping beast with a great number of feet, as long, I should say, as a worm. It is a common beast, but what I am going to tell you about it was entirely new to my experience. For one of the students accidentally cut the animal in two; whereupon the two separated portions of the body immediately wriggled away in opposite directions and with such swift motion of the feet and with such wholly undiminished effort that one might have thought that there were now two animals instead of one. Terrified at this extraordinary sight and anxious for an explanation of it, they brought the exceedingly lively broken portions to where Alypius and I were sitting. We were no less astonished than the students at seeing these separated portions run in all directions on the table, and we noticed that, when you touched one of them with a twig, it twisted itself up towards the seat of the pain, but the other portion seemed insensible of this; in fact, it continued its own independent movements. We tested it in every possible way; we even cut up the worm—or rather the worms—into a number of sections, yet they all kept moving about, so that, had we not known that we had done it, and had not the fresh wounds been evident, one would have supposed that they had been born separately and that each had always led its own independent existence.' [1]

The scorpion, 'which smites with its tail' and is a scourge in Africa, fascinates him. Apropos of the words, 'Will he for an egg give him a scorpion?' Augustine quaintly remarks: 'They come out from their holes and sting horribly, but the hens kill and eat them, so that they pass into their bodies and there they turn them into eggs.' [2] Even such torturesome insects as the hosts of flies and fleas have an interest for him. The flies come to a light, cockroaches shun it: 'Muscas lucipetas, blattas lucifugas.' [3] The fly-flapper, 'muscarium,' was in perpetual use save in Numidia where there was no need of it. [4] 'Who fashioned limbs for the flea and the gnat? Who gave them their due proportions, their life and their movement?

[1] *De Quantitate animae*, 62; discussion of this—to us familiar—phenomenon continues in the following sections, 63–64.

[2] *Sermo*, cv. 7 and 12.

[3] *Contra Faustum*, xix. 24.

[4] *Sermo*, xlvi. 39.

Take any tiny beast you can think of, and study the methodical arrangement of its parts and its animated movements. See how it shrinks from death and fights for life, how it seeks for pleasure and shuns pain, how it exercises its different sense-organs and has its own peculiar movements. Who planted in a mosquito that dart, that weapon, whereby it sucks up blood ? What a tiny duct it has for absorbing it ! Who indeed arranged all these things ? Who made them ? Are you stupefied at these tiny things ? They praise their Great Maker.' [1]

The locusts, of course, Augustine knew, though he does not seem actually to have witnessed the clouds of these devastating insects. 'Historians tell us that the swarms of locusts in Africa were prodigious even after it had become a Roman Province ; they say they ate up the fruits and the very leaves from the trees, and were then hurled into the sea, a huge incalculable cloud of them ; and that, when dead and cast up on the shore, they produced so great a plague that in Massinissa's district alone 800,000 people perished and many more in neighbouring countries. They even say that at that time out of thirty thousand young people at Utica only ten remained.' [2]

III—IN REPTILES AND FISHES

Augustine's curiously observant mind did not confine itself to men, birds, beasts and insects ; the reptiles too appealed to him. He remarks, for instance, that 'we can see for ourselves how the chameleon by " a quick change " varies the colour of its body in accordance with the colour it sees.' [3] The crocodile has now disappeared from Northern Africa,[4] but mosaics from Hadrumetum and the seaboard show that it must have been common in Augustine's day ; indeed Julian the Pelagian must have been familiar with that reptile when he quoted the statement of a certain Albinus to the effect that 'the crocodile is the only animal which can move the upper portion of its mandibles, and that, while fire destroys everything else, to the salamander it is but a joke.' [5] When commenting on this

[1] *Enarr*. i. 10 *on* Ps. cxlviii.
[2] *De Civitate Dei*, III. xxxi.
[3] *De Trinitate*, xi. 5.
[4] Tissot, however, *Géographie comparée de l'Afrique du nord*, i. 329, says that crocodiles still exist in the lakes of Mauretania.
[5] *Contra Julianum*, vi. 16.

Augustine makes no remark about Albinus' crocodile, but says that as for the salamander ' to whom fire is a joke ' he can see no more difficulty in its immunity from the effects of fire than in the fact that Aetna, while ever burning, is yet never consumed.[1]

When treating of the powers of memory, a subject which interested him immensely, he will not hear of the notion that reptiles have no memory, but refers those who doubt it to the writings of people who have kept aquaria and ' have noted many wonderful things ' about fish. In fact he adds that he himself has personally proved that fish have memories, and he tells of the fish in a pool at Bulla Regia which were regularly fed and which fought for the food offered them, with the result that ' when people walk along the banks, the fish too gather in numbers, swimming to and fro in expectation of food.'[2] In England, though we see frogs we hardly ever hear them. But in Africa the ' bellow ' of the huge bull-frogs is a familiar sound, especially when rain is threatening. It forms a sort of diapason to the storm. What better definition of a frog, then, could be framed than Augustine's ' loquacissima vanitas,' a ' talkative emptiness ' ?[3]

He is astonished, too, at a fish's capacity for swimming unharmed amongst the rocks in a swirling stream, and quotes what was apparently a well-known adage, *Piscis bonus, pia est fides*, as though illustrative of this fact.[4]

In his *De Genesi ad Litteram* Augustine had concerned himself solely with the problem of the metaphysical constitution of the Universe ; theories about its physical constitution do not seem to have interested him much at any time. He has heard, however, of the atomic theories which were then current, but he has scant sympathy with them :—

Grant that there are such things as atoms ; grant that by their fortuitous concurrence they drive on and move hither and thither. Will it follow that by the same fortuitous concurrence these atoms make things, modify their form, give them definite

[1] *De Civitate Dei*, XXI, iv. 1.
[2] *De Genesi ad Litt.* iii. 12.
[3] *Enarr.* i. 27 *on* Ps. lxxvii. ; i. 11 *on* Ps. xcv.
[4] *Sermo*, cv. 6.

shape, polish them so as to make their colours gleam, endow them with a quickening soul ? Surely, none of these things can be done save by the art of Divine Providence ! But to realize that presupposes that a person is prepared to see with his mind rather than his eyes, and that he will ask his Maker to help him to do so.[1]

The foregoing gleanings from Augustine's writings will have served to show us something of his love for and interest in the animal world. If we turn now for a moment to his fellow-Africans, the people in whose midst he lived and worked and for whose salvation he was ever toiling, we shall see what a gulf separated him from them. They too were keenly interested in the fauna which teemed everywhere ; but theirs was the fascination of the hunter. Nowhere do we find any hint that the animals excited any other interest in their minds. 'What are your interests ?' asked the Bishop in a sermon. 'Eating and drinking, luxurious living, gaming and hunting. And what a crowd of evils follow in their wake ! Of course, we know well that these things are pleasant. Who would question it ? But the observance of God's law is a greater pleasure : "The wicked have told me of pleasures, but of none compared to Thy Law." '[2]

The predominant love of hunting and sport to which also St. Augustine has referred is fully borne out by the series of mosaics to be found on the stairway in the British Museum as you go from the lower to the upper Egyptian Rooms. These hail from North Africa, especially from Carthage. Here we have hunting scenes depicting a stag, a boar and a leopard, while an ostrich is being driven into a net which, curiously enough, appears to be worked from a boat. Then come vivid pictures of a man on horseback lassoing a deer, of another rider and his hound in pursuit of a deer ; in another picture the hound has a spiked collar, though at the moment he is only chasing an innocuous hare. The fishing scenes are perhaps the most thrilling. In one we see an angler with a rod and line, fishing from a boat while a dolphin disports itself

[1] *Ep.* cxviii. 31 ; *cf. Ep.* iii. 2, also Lactantius, *Epitome*, 36, and Origen, *Contra Celsum*, iv. 75.

[2] *Tract. in I. Joann.* x. 6, the Old-Latin version of Ps. cxviii. 85.

hard by ; in another Nereus is riding on a triton, and has an escort of dolphins ; in another we have a basket containing the angler's ' catch,' a fine bream, two octopuses and what is presumably a squid.

These mosaics are but the scanty relics picked up by Nathaniel Davis some eighty years ago. But the innumerable mosaics preserved to-day in various museums of North Africa afford us glimpses of what a Carthaginian house of St. Augustine's day must have looked like. For there we see pavements of what must in many cases have been private houses, pavements on which Augustine and his disciples may well have walked, pictures that were constantly before their eyes. In one, for instance, we have a huge octopus attacking two dolphins at once, while the packed crew of the good ship *Fortuna Redux* with her ten oars look on. Another gives a picture of Jonas, but—as always on the Mediterranean littoral—it is not a whale which ejects him, but a dragon armed with terrific teeth. Another flooring depicts Virgil composing his *Æneid*, the work Augustine loved so much and of which he used at times to read half a book a day ; hard by the poet stands a figure bearing a tragedian's mask. Then comes another fishing scene wherein the net is held up by corks and a dolphin has got entangled in it, while one of the netsmen has just been bitten by a crab. Once more we are shown a fisherman's ' catch ' for the day—more probably for the night, for his bag includes a huge conger eel ; another big fish, wonderfully drawn, is seen slipping out of the basket. This fisherman, by the way, was no dry-fly expert, but carries a trident for spearing his prey while cherubs riding on dolphins gaze at him. The most realistic picture of all however is one of a crocodile which has succeeded in getting a donkey half-way down his throat while the animal's masters were otherwise engaged. These latter, on discovering what is happening, rush up and fasten ropes round the donkey's legs and then proceed to tug with all their might ; meanwhile a hippopotamus looks on superciliously. One wonders what value the rescued ass would have. Perhaps the hippopotamus was thinking the same !

Among the many animals depicted in these mosaics are

hares and panthers, among the birds, eagles and peacocks, and, of course, the inevitable centaur. All these are drawn with amazing fidelity despite the unhandy nature of the material. Nor are portraits of men and women wanting, for we have pictures of Virgil, Ganymede, the Emperor Antoninus Pius, Faustina, and last but not least the Good Shepherd.[1]

In the sermon quoted above, St. Augustine referred to gaming ; cut in the rock at Timgad, the ancient Thamugadi, may be seen what was perhaps a gaming-table with the enigmatic inscription [2] :—

QUIEVER	VENARI	OC ANAS	LAVARI
	LUDERE		RIDERE
	OCC EST		VIVERE [3]

The Africans had only too faithfully copied their Roman masters in their love of the theatre and the games, and St. Augustine is never weary of denouncing them for this : ' Sometimes,' he says, ' the spectators inspect themselves, and then condemn themselves for going. We are glad to say that this has happened in many cases. There was a time when we, too, sat on those benches and went mad like the rest. How many perchance are sitting in the theatre at this moment who will however be one day not only Christians but even Christian Bishops ! ' [4] On one occasion the Bishop of Bulla asked Augustine to preach in his church. The Bishop must have asked him to speak openly against the theatres there, for certainly Augustine never preached a more vehement sermon on the subject. It was apparently the feast of the Seven Maccabee Brethren and their mother :—

Contrast [he said] that holy spectacle with the pleasures and delights of the theatre. There your eyes are defiled, here your

[1] For these and similar examples see the *Musée de Tebessa*, ed. Gsell, 1902, the *Musée Lavigerie*, ed. Delattre, 1899, the *Musée de Philippeville*, ed. Gsell, 1898, the *Musée de Sousse*, ed. Gauckler, 1902, etc.

[2] Given in Boisvillard, *Timgad*, pp. 20–21.

[3] Presumably, ' This is a duck.'

[4] *Enarr*. i. 7 *on* Ps. cxlvii. ; for similar laments over the theatres see *Enarr*. i. 11 and 23 *on* Ps. lxxx. ; i. 1 *on* Ps. xxxii. ; i. 1 *on* Ps. l. ; *Confess*. i. 16, iii. 2, *De Moribus Manichaeorum*, 72, etc.

hearts are cleansed. Here the spectator deserves praise if he but imitate what he sees ; there he is bad, and if he imitates what he sees he becomes infamous. . . . You look at a clown, you watch a pantomime. And I might well say to you, 'You are like that ! and do not be angry with me for saying it !' Ye brethren of Bulla, in practically every city of yours round here your youthful piety has become dumb. Are you not ashamed that you are now almost the sole practitioners of vices that can be bought with money ? . . . Sometimes there may even come here strangers in search of such commodities and you say to them, 'What are you looking for ? Clowns, harlots ? You can have them both at Bulla !' Are you proud of that ? If so, your satisfaction is possibly a greater crime. Brethren, I say it with the most profound sorrow : for this all the neighbouring cities condemn you in the sight of men and before God's judgment seat. In my city of Hippo, where such vices are by now practically extinct, evil-livers of the type I have just mentioned are hired from here. Perhaps you will reply that you are only doing what is done at Carthage ? Then because at Carthage there exists a large proportion of holy and religious-minded people the great crowd of those otherwise-minded in that huge city is to take that fact as an excuse for all the rest ! Yet at Carthage they could truthfully say : 'The pagans do it ! The Jews do it !' Yes, but those who do so in this city are Christians. . . . Now then, when the Games are on here do you Christians stay away and then see if the result is not such a solitude at the Games that sin itself will have to blush. Make up your minds, then, you Christians, and do not go near the theatre ! [1]

And in a sermon preached at Carthage :—

What harm is wrought by a debased curiosity, by the idle 'concupiscence of the eyes,' by your eagerness for the inanities offered in the theatres, by the mad follies of the races, all of them conflicts which bring no reward ! The charioteers do, it is true, strive for some kind of prize ; but the spectators who wrangle over those charioteers—what prize do they win ? Yet you are delighted with a charioteer, with a huntsman, with an actor ! Is it possible that a debased exhibition can please a good man ? [2]

[1] *Denis*, xvii. 7 ; *P.L.* xlvi. 879. For the moral corruption of Carthage see Mommsen, *Provinces*, ii. 341, and Augustine, *Enarr.* i. 13 *on* Ps. ciii.
[2] *Denis*, xiv. 3.

And again at Carthage: 'Have you never noticed how when people dissipate all their substance on actors, while giving nothing to the poor, all men's mouths are filled with their praises?'[1]

IV—THE KEY TO THIS INTEREST IN NATURE

No one will suppose that this curiosity of St. Augustine's was purely idle, the offspring of a merely inquisitive mind. We have seen already that it was in part due to his desire to vindicate the truth of the Bible even in such insignificant details as its references to nature. But Augustine was motived by something even more profound than that, as perhaps the following extracts will show.

As early as A.D. 387, the year of his conversion, we find him in the course of the Dialogue *De Ordine* giving us the following remarkable description:—

We rose in the morning, and after our daily prayers set out for the baths. But just as we were passing the gate, we spied two cockerels preparing for a lusty combat and felt constrained to watch them. For when one loves something, one's eyes are ever on the look-out for anything that may afford even a fleeting glimpse of that Reason which controls and governs all things, whether they are conscious of it or not—that Reason which ever draws in its train those who love It, and bids them seek It wherever and however It would have us seek It.[2] You have an instance of It in these very birds. Look at those heads so eagerly thrust forward; look at their swollen combs; note the terrific blows they deal; see how cleverly they evade each other! Yet, though bereft of reason, not a single movement of theirs but has its grace. Why is that? Surely because there is a Reason above them directing it all. And when the battle is over, then listen to the victor's pæan of triumph, his proud crow! His very limbs all seem concentrated on that last cry of exultant domination. And the vanquished one! Why, his very wings droop, his very gait is unsightly, even his voice is dismal. Yet, in all this there is

[1] *Frangipane*, v. 5; *cp. Enarr.* i. 13 *on* Ps. cii., *Ep.* cxxxviii. 14.
[2] Compare St. Thomas, 'Ubi amor, ibi oculus' (*De Dilectione Dei*, 14).

something strangely beautiful, because all is in harmony with nature's laws.[1]

Here we have the key to Augustine's intense curiosity. It is not the facts of nature of which he is enamoured so much as the Law, the Reason, the Mind behind those facts. In a word, it was God, the Author of nature, whom he was for ever seeking ; God ' who cannot be wholly unknown to men ; for such is the might of the true Godhead that He cannot be hidden from a rational creature who uses his reason. Save for a very few whose nature is wholly depraved, the entire human race acknowledges God as the Author of the world.'[2] And it is easy for us to know God, ' for He who made us is more nigh to us than are the many things that He has made.'[3]

Some people, in order to discover God, read books. But there is a great book : the very appearance of created things. Look above you ! Look below you ! Note it ; read it. God, whom you want to discover, never wrote that book with ink ; instead He set before your eyes the things that He had made. Can you ask for a louder voice than that ? Why, heaven and earth shout to you : ' God made me ! '[4]

For, as he says elsewhere :—

True wisdom means to subordinate things created to their Creator ; distinguishing carefully the building and the Builder, the work and its Artificer. A person who confuses the artificer with his handiwork understands neither the artificer nor his art ; whereas one who realizes the difference between them is filled with true wisdom.[5]

Yet, by a fatuity ever recurrent, ' while God would lead a man to His own likeness by warnings, teaching, exhortations and corrections, man not only does not follow after that likeness but tries to make God to his own image ! '[6] An anticipation of Voltaire ! But even then who shall describe God ? ' He is

[1] *De Ordine*, i. 25 ; *cf*. ii. 12.
[2] *Tract*. cvi. *in Joann*. 4.
[3] *De Genesi ad Litt*. v. 34–35.
[4] *Mai*, cxxvi. 6.
[5] *Sermon*, cclii. 10.
[6] *Sermo*, xlvii. 5.

beyond our words; it is easier for us to say what He is not than what He is.'[1] Yet, that same ineffable God is our possession: 'Behold God has become your staff; on Him a man leans with all security (*securus*), for He never gives way. Say then with all security: "He is my possession." . . . Say it with security, love Him with security, hope in Him with security.'[2] For, once more, 'He says: "Here I am; I am present with thee. What do you want of Me? Whatever I may give you will be of no value compared to Me. So take Me Myself, enjoy Me, embrace Me. You cannot do so wholly now, but hold on to Me by faith, and thus will you cling to Me, and all your burdens I will remove from you."'[3] This is the consummation of the dignity of man: 'I ask you O rational soul, are you not somewhat less than God? And so much less that, apart from God, there is nothing better than you!'[4] Hence in God alone is the final repose of the human soul: 'I feel, then, that it is on God that I can throw myself with all security, that in Him I can rest with tranquillity.'[5]

Passages like the foregoing could be multiplied indefinitely, but they suffice to show how the one absorbing thought with Augustine was God whom he saw mirrored in nature: 'The Creator who is Almighty, whom no human words can adequately describe, who in His tiniest works is great,'[6] of whom finally a man must feel that, when he passes from a consideration of nature and begins to think of God in as worthy fashion as it is given to man to do, 'he will discover that God can only be praised by the voiceless words of the silence of the heart.'[7] Thoughts like these this true shepherd of souls consistently kept before his people so as to raise their minds to higher things.

Your very bowels [he said, when writing against Faustus the Manichee who had such unworthy notions anent the human

[1] *Enarr.* i. 12 *on* Ps. lxxxv.; *cf. De Ordine*, ii. 44: 'summus ille Deus qui scitur melius nesciendo.'
[2] *Enarr.* ii. 17 *on* Ps. xxxii.; *cf.* i. 4 *on* Ps. xxxvi.
[3] *Enarr.* ii. 9 *on* Ps. xxxiii.; *cf.* ii. 16 *on* Ps. xxxii.
[4] *Contra Epistolam Manichaei*, 43.
[5] *De Genesi ad Litt.* iv. 29.
[6] *De Genesi ad Litt.* ix. 18.
[7] *Sermo*, cccxli. 9.

frame], your very bowels, your very vitals in your fleshly frame, the harmonious interaction of every part of your being, your limbs (each of them with its due task), your organs of feeling (each of them with its own definite place and function, its due mode and measure, its corresponding details, its proper weight) —all these point to God as their Artificer, to Him of whom it is truly said : ' Thou hast arranged all things in measure, number and weight.' Whence else could all these things have been derived save from Him on whose unity every measure depends, to whose wisdom all beauty is due, from whose law all order flows ? [1]

Once more :—

' Blessed are the clean of heart, for they shall see God.' God, then, has promised to show Himself to us. Let us reflect on what that beauty of His must be ! He made all these beautiful things that you see and love. If they are beautiful, then what must He be ! If they are great, how great must He be ! From a consideration, then, of these things which we love here, let us rather yearn for Him, and, despising these other things, let us love Him. [2]

Even the sight of a lion-tamer—probably not a rare one in those days of the games and the amphitheatre—affords Augustine an opportunity for driving home a truth : ' How wretched the darkness of the human soul when a man knows how to tame a lion, yet not how to direct his own life aright.' [3]

Those who have read and pondered the ' Confessions,' and wandered with Augustine through the maze of his intellectual difficulties, who have marvelled at the apparent crudity of the ideas he had at one time cherished regarding the nature of God whom he deemed material,[4] must marvel more at the way in which he, from the moment he was baptized, stepped into the fullness of the Catholic faith and the fullness of its philosophical expression. When he penned those ' Confessions,' *c.* A.D. 400, only thirteen years after his Baptism, his growth in knowledge of God is already amazing ; [5] as the years go by

[1] *Contra Faustum*, xxi. vi.
[2] *Enarr.* i. 9 *on* Ps. lxxxiv.
[3] *De Natura et Gratia*, 47.
[4] *Confess.* vii. 1.
[5] *Ibid.*, ii. 12 ; iv. 16–17 ; vii. 16.

and he slowly elaborates the treatises *De Genesi ad Litteram* and *De Trinitate*, we can see how he had penetrated into the mysteries of the Godhead, has become almost ' comprehensor ' and not simply ' viator,' so that we can understand how St. Paulinus could, in a letter written in A.D. 410, say : ' Te, qui vides quasi per Deum, interrogavi.' [1]

He has, of course, arrived at this knowledge by his prayer and communion with God, by his unceasing study of Holy Scripture, but also by that study of the book of nature of which we have seen something in our earlier pages. That book of nature had become to him the most convincing proof of God's existence :—

With the sole exception of the Prophecies, this very world by its orderly series of changes, its mobility, the wondrous beauty of its display, bears the most convincing, albeit silent, witness to the fact that it has been made, and that it could only have been made, by One ineffably and invisibly mighty, ineffably and invisibly beautiful.

The philosophical expression of these sublime truths could hardly be better expressed than in the following :—

Though ineffable and never by men to be expressed to men save in terms of time and space, He who made us is more nigh to us than many other things which also are made. For ' in Him we live and move and have our being ' (Acts xvii. 28). Indeed, many of those other things are strangers to our minds ; wholly corporeal, they are wholly different from us. Neither can our minds see them in the Godhead—in those very ideas, that is, in accordance with which they have been fashioned. Hence we cannot, even were we able to perceive them otherwise than through the medium of our bodily senses, duly appreciate their number, size, and character. In reality, too, these things are far removed even from our bodily senses, for they are always at a distance from us, separated from our sight and touch by the fact that other things come between us and them, or are even set over against them. Hence, far more toil has to be expended if we would discover them than if we would discover their Maker. And to discover Him in the

[1] *Ep.* cxxi. 14. See T. E. Lacey, *Nature, Miracle, and Sin : A Study of St. Augustine's conception of the natural order*, 1916.

tiniest thing that is, and give Him joyous welcome, is far more important for the devout soul than to comprehend the entire Universe.[1]

Hence, this Prince of Philosophers and Theologians can dare to pronounce that even corruption has its beauty.

The outer man is corrupted either by the progress of the interior man or by his own failure. Corruption by the progress of the interior man is meant to secure his complete re-formation into something better, his restoration to pristine integrity at the last trump, never more to corrupt or be corrupt. But corruption through his own failure means that he is hurled into beauties still more corruptible—into the harmony, that is, of penalties. Wonder not that I speak of ' beauties,' for nothing that is in order is without beauty.[2]

In truth, for Augustine all things were beautiful since made by God.

When we compare small things with great, we call the former by different names. For example, because in the human figure there is greater beauty, a monkey's beauty is by comparison ugliness, so that thoughtless people are misled and deem a man beautiful and a monkey ugly. They are oblivious to the perfect proportion in a monkey, the equal length of his arms on either side, the harmony of his members, his bodily completeness, and other points which it would take too long to enumerate.[3]

We must needs acknowledge that a man in tears is better than a worm full of joy. Yet, I could discourse at great length and with strict adherence to truth about the beauty of a worm. I could dwell upon its shining colours, its smoothly rounded body, the perfect harmony between the joints in front, those in the middle and those behind ; I could point out how all these, even in that lowly form of nature, preserve a sense for unity ; no one portion but is duly proportioned to every other.[4]

[1] *De Genesi ad Litt.*, v. 34.
[2] *De Vera Religione*, 77, in *P.L.* xxxiv. 156.
[3] *De Natura Boni*, 14–15.
[4] *De Vera Religione*, 77.

VII

THE CRIME OF SCHISM

I. A Brief Sketch of the Donatist Schism and of some of its Leaders—II. The Appalling State of divided Christian Africa—III. Schism is always 'Sacrilege'—IV. To remain in Schism is a Question for the Individual to Settle—V. Pride is its Root—VI. The Mental Torpor induced by Living in Schism—VII. The Problem of Disestablishment—VIII. Heresy and Schism defined—IX. The Donatists resented being called 'Heretics'—X. They claim to be 'Catholics'—XI. But have no real Understanding of the Church—XII. Schismatics and the Sacraments.

> 'Fugite, O miseri, execranda Novati
> Schismata, Catholicis vos reddite populis.
> Una fides vigeat, prisco quae condito templo est.
> Quam tenet cathedra Petri.'
>
> St. Prudentius, *Hymn on St. Hippolytus.*

I—A BRIEF SKETCH OF THE DONATIST SCHISM

The story of the Donatist schism has often been told.[1] Its remote origin was a meeting at Cirta or Constantine in Numidia, towards the close of the Diocletian persecution in A.D. 305, when Silvanus was simoniacally elected Bishop of that See.[2] When, in A.D. 311–312, the See of Carthage fell vacant the clergy elected Caecilian without waiting for the arrival of the Numidian Bishops of whom some had taken part in the nefarious election at Cirta. The chagrin of these latter on finding the election over was fostered by an intriguing woman, Lucilla, who induced them to disregard the newly-elected Caecilian and bribed them to choose a certain Majorinus as Archbishop of

[1] St. Optatus, *De Schismate Donatistarum*, c. A.D. 366, i. 13–28. See, too, John Chapman, O.S.B., in the *Catholic Encyclopaedia*, *s.v. Donatists*, also in the *Catholic Dictionary*.

[2] St. Optatus, *l.c.* i. 14; St. Augustine, *Epp.* xliii. 3, liii. 2, lxxvi. 2; *Breviculus Collationis*, iii. 27, 31; *De Unitate*, 43; *Contra Cresconium*, iii. 30.

Carthage.[1] These simoniacal schismatics attempted to justify their action by maintaining that Caecilian—or at least one of his consecrators, Felix—had been guilty of surrendering copies of the Bible during the Diocletian persecution.[2] Such betrayal of his trust rendered him, so they maintained, incapable of conferring valid Orders.[3] The case was referred to Rome, where, A.D. 312–313, it was decided, in default of any evidence the schismatics could produce, that Caecilian was not guilty, and that, anyhow, his election was valid.[4] A series of appeals followed and the case was once more gone into thoroughly at the Council of Arles, October, 314.[5] The same decision was arrived at and was reiterated by Constantine in 316.[6] The schismatics proved obstinate, however, and it was not till A.D. 348 that the then Archbishop of Carthage, Gratus, could return thanks in Council for the restoration of peace to the Church.[7]

This peace unfortunately lasted but a short time. For, on his accession in 361, Julian the Apostate allowed the exiled schismatics to return, and he handed over to them the Catholic churches and their property in North Africa.[8] Then began a reign of terror which was to last off and on till A.D. 412, when, as the result of a three days' Conference between the Donatist and Catholic Bishops, the Emperor Honorius condemned the former to exile unless they returned to the Catholic Church.[9] The schism then died out.

The keynote of the schism was the Donatist claim to exclusive sanctity, a claim based on the alleged fact that they alone had refused to condone the crime which they falsely attributed to

[1] St. Optatus, *l.c.*, i. 10, 19, 22, vii. 5 ; St. Augustine, *Epp.* xliii. 14–15, lxxxviii. 1, xciii. 13. Hence the expression 'Pars Majorini' given to the Donatists at first, *cf.* St. Augustine, *Breviculus*, iii. 24.

[2] St. Augustine, *Breviculus*, iii. 42 ; *Epp.* liii. 4, lxxxviii. 3, cxli. 10–11 ; *cf. P.L.*, viii. 715, xliii. 780.

[3] *Contra Epistolam Parmeniani*, ii. 28.

[4] *Breviculus*, iii. 24 ; *Ad Donatistas post Collationem*, 33 ; *Epp.* xliii. 15–16, clxxxv. 47 ; St. Optatus, *l.c.*, i. 23–24.

[5] *Epp.* xliii. 20, cv. 7 ; *Breviculus*, iii. 27. For the date see C. H. Turner, in the *Journal of Theol. Studies*, April, 1926, p. 283.

[6] *Contra Epistolam Parmeniani*, i. 10 ; *Contra Cresconium*, iii. 68.

[7] For the date 345–348 see Hefele-Leclercq, *Histoire des Conciles*, ii. 185.

[8] St. Optatus, *l.c.*, ii. 16–17 ; St. Augustine, *Epp.* xciii. 12, cv. 9, cviii. 18 ; *Contra Litt. Petiliani*, ii. 184, 203, 205, 224.

[9] Jan. 30, 412, see below, pp. 350–51.

Caecilian, or at least to his consecrators, as well as to other Bishops, hoping thereby to cloak the fact that they had themselves been guilty of that very crime. 'This,' says Augustine, 'is clearly the root of the whole matter; You claim to be just, and maintain that others are wicked, and that it is unfitting that the just should consort with the wicked.'[1] Yet the presence of criminals among the Donatists was an undisputed fact; [2] equally undisputed was the existence of many saintly Catholic Bishops,[3] not to speak of saintly folk among the laity.[4] Moreover, to insist that the true Church should consist of saints alone was to make the Church an invisible body,[5] to mistake it for that 'Church without spot or wrinkle' of which the Apostle speaks as a thing of the future, of the next world, not of this.[6] How preposterous the claim that Africa alone—and only Donatist Africa at that—was holy! '"We are the good odour of Christ," says St. Paul,[7] but you Donatists say: "Africa alone breathes forth a sweet odour, the rest of the world stinks!"'[8] How ridiculous a statement when the Donatists had such concrete criminal examples amongst them as Optatus, the Donatist Bishop of Thamugadi, 'under whom Africa groaned for ten years.' This unmitigated blackguard—no milder terms will do justice to his case—was the scourge of Africa. He was commonly spoken of as 'satelles Gildonis,'[9] or the 'satellite' of that Count Gildo who conspired against Honorius towards the close of A.D. 397 with a view to bringing Africa under Arcadius, but who was in the following year slain by his own brother, Mascezel, acting with the help of Italian troops.[10] St. Augustine speaks of him as not only 'fur sed raptor'[11] and says that by his crimes this unworthy Bishop did more harm than any 'Traditor' who surrendered the

[1] *Sermo*, xlvii. 16, *cf. Enarr.* i. 5 *on* Ps. x.
[2] *Ep.* clxxxv. 12, 25–27.
[3] *Contra Epistolam Parmeniani*, ii. 8.
[4] *De Moribus Ecclesiae Catholicae et Manichaeorum.*
[5] *Ep.* clxxxv. 38.
[6] Ephes. v. 27; *cf. Collatio*, iii. 4.
[7] 2 Cor. ii. 14–15.
[8] *Enarr.* ii. 2, *on* Ps. xxi.
[9] *Contra Epistolam Parmeniani*, ii. 34; *Contra Litt. Petiliani*, ii. 209; *Contra Cresconium*, iv. 31–32.
[10] See Pallu de Lessert, *Vicaires et Comtes de L'Afrique*, ii. 257.
[11] *Contra Ep. Parmeniani*, ii. 18; *Contra Litt. Petiliani*, ii. 53–55, 237.

Sacred Scriptures to the persecutors.[1] His violence towards the unhappy Catholics was such that the municipal archives were full of protests lodged by the latter against him.[2] The Donatists tolerated him and his enormities lest they should, by excommunicating him, drive him into schism and so split up their 'party.'[3] After his defeat he died in prison,[4] and Petilian was not ashamed to accuse Augustine of having compassed his end.[5] For ten years, says Augustine, this man had 'made Africa to groan,'[6] and had been a stumbling-block even to the Donatists, who had at all costs to uphold their claim to exclusive sanctity.

An even more flagrant contradiction to such a claim lay in the incredible enormities perpetrated by the bands of Circumcellions.[7] 'How illogical,' exclaimed Augustine, 'to propose tests to discover the sinners amongst you when by their very presence in your midst they have—on your own principles—contaminated you!'[8] But to Augustine's thinking a far more damning proof of the Donatists' lack of 'sanctity' was 'the very fact that by deliberately choosing to remain in schism you show that you have not the Holy Spirit and therefore cannot be holy.'[9]

It was not till some fifty-five years after the formal declaration of the schism in A.D. 311 that the crushed and downtrodden Catholic remnant was in a position to take up the pen against the Donatists. Then, when Julian the Apostate had been dead three years, there appeared, in A.D. 366, the *De Schismate Donatistarum*,[10] by St. Optatus of Milevis. This was a scathing

[1] *Contra Ep. Parmeniani*, ii. 2.
[2] *Contra Cresconium*, iii. 49.
[3] *Contra Litt. Petiliani*, ii. 156; *cf.* i. 10, 26, iii. 48; *Contra Cresconium*, iii. 49.
[4] *Contra Ep. Parmeniani*, ii. 8.
[5] *Contra Litt. Petiliani*, iii. 48.
[6] *Ep.* xliii. 24, *Contra Ep. Parmeniani*, ii. 4, 8, *Contra Litt. Petiliani*, ii. 120.
[7] *Contra Litt. Petiliani*, ii. 94; *Ep.* clxxxv. 26–27; see below, p. 261.
[8] *Ep.* lxxxvii. 1.
[9] *Ep.* clxxxv. 42, 46, 49–50.
[10] There were probably two editions published, one about A.D. 366, containing Bks. i.–vi.; another under Pope Siricius, *c.* 385, Bks. i.–vii.; *cf.* Monceaux, *Histoire de la littérature chrétienne*, p. 126, also *S. Optat. et les premiers écrivains Donatistes*, in Vol. v. of the above, 1920. A very good English translation appeared in 1917: *The Work of St. Optatus against the Donatists*, translated with Notes by O. R. Vassall Phillips, C.S.S.R.

indictment, and until he was able to secure documents later than those used by Optatus, St. Augustine made great use of the latter's treatise. But, so far as we are aware, Optatus' apologetic work fell flat. The Donatists certainly read it, but it is doubtful whether they really understood it. At any rate, when, at the final Conference of A.D. 411, the President acceded to their insistent demand that a certain passage from this treatise by St. Optatus should be read out, it was found to say precisely the opposite of what they wanted, to the vast amusement of all but themselves.[1] Of the five-and-twenty years which elapsed between the appearance of St. Optatus' treatise and St. Augustine's ordination in 391 we have no record. But Augustine, immediately on his ordination, threw himself into the fray. He felt that so long as these unhappy divisions persisted, there could be no peace in Christian Africa, indeed, no progress in the spiritual life of the people.

His first step was to compose an *Abecedarius* or A.B.C. of the controversy. The Saint's own title for this production was *Psalmus contra partem Donati.*[2] For it was a metrical composition intended to be committed to memory as a convenient summary of the facts and principles involved,[3] but it served a double purpose. For first of all it provided the members of the Catholic minority with a species of armoury when disputing with their schismatical neighbours ; secondly, if Augustine's hearers really did take the trouble to learn it, his task in the pulpit would be rendered much easier. For he would now be able to preach to them on the subject of the schism without any anxiety lest the facts and principles he would have frequent occasion to refer to should be outside their cognizance or only shadowy memories. We must picture him, then, teaching this species of Catechism of the schism day by day, and insisting on his flock learning it. Indeed, it is clear from a study of his sermons and his audience that as the various points dealt with in this *Abecedarius* came up in the course of the sermons on

[1] *Collatio cum Donatistis*, iii. 531–537 ; *Breviculus Collationis*, 38 ; *Ad Donatistas, post Collationem*, 54 ; *Ep*. cxli. 8.

[2] Given in *P.L.* xliii. 23–32 ; *cf. Retractations*, i. 20.

[3] Petilian appears to have adopted the same method, perhaps in imitation of Augustine, for his people knew by heart many extracts from his Encyclical Letter, see below, and *De Unitate*, 1.

the schism which he preached between the years 391 and 420 his audience kept repeating the familiar phrases of their A.B.C. Nor, to judge by their frequent exclamations during his sermons, did they do this *sotto voce* but out loud, so that there must have been a continuous murmuring of many of its sentences, more particularly of the ever-recurring refrain with which it opens :—

> ' Omnes qui gaudetis de pace, modo verum judicate,' or
> ' All ye who rejoice in peace, at least now judge rightly ' ;

and again : ' Jam, fratres, finiatur error, et simus in unitate,' or

> ' Brethren, let error now be put away and let us live in peace ' ;

or : ' Dissentiebant sacerdotes in tota Africana parte ;
Sacerdotes transmarini possent inde judicare :
Quid curritis ad schisma, et altare contra altare ? ', or

> ' The clergy throughout Africa disagreed ;
> But surely the clergy overseas could thereon have judged ?
> Why, then, rushed ye into schism and set up altar over against altar ? '

once more : ' Quasi vos aliquis vetet jàm recedere ab errore.
Sed superbia vos ligavit in cathedra pestilentiae,' or

> ' As though anyone forbade you to quit your error !
> It was your pride that bound you fast " in the seat of scorning " '[1]

and : ' Scitis Catholica quid sit, et quid sit praecisum a vite :
Si qui sunt inter vos cauti, veniant, vivant in radice,' or

[1] Written about A.D. 394, these words were almost prophetic. For at the Conference of A.D. 411 the Donatists refused the courteous invitation of Marcellinus the Tribune to be seated ; they refused, they said, to ' sit in the seat of scorners,' quoting Ps. xxv. 4. Their words, remarks St. Augustine, seemed almost like an echo of the Pharisee's ' Noli me tangere ! ' *Sermon* xcix. 8 ; *cf. Collatio*, i. 144, *P.L.*, xi., Mansi, *Concilia*, iv. The result of this boorishness on the part of the Donatists was that the whole assembly of about 800 persons had to stand from early morning till late at night for two out of the three days, the session on the second day being but a brief one. Later the Donatists endeavoured to explain their conduct as being merely a precaution lest anyone should say they had been bribed ! *Ad Donatistas post Collationem*, 7 ; *cf. Breviculus Collationis*, ii. 1.

'Well ye know what the Catholic Church is, and what it is to be cut off from the Vine ;
Are there any thoughtful men among you ? Let them come and find life in the Root.'

and lastly : 'Numerate sacerdotes vel ab ipsa Petri sede,
Et in ordine illo patrum quis cui successit, videte :
Ipsa est petra, quam non vincant superbae inferorum portae,' or

'Reckon up the Priests from the days that Peter sat,
And in their ancestral ranks note who to whom succeeded;
For that is the Rock o'er which the Gates of Hell shall ne'er prevail.'

During the twenty-nine years which followed, from A.D. 391–420, Augustine, in sermons, letters and treatises, assailed from every angle the arguments commonly used by the Donatists. And though not afraid to employ sarcasm, irony, invective and all the dialectical weapons of which he was master, he relied more than all on persuasion. Hence a series of eloquent appeals to their good sense and to the wretched state to which their attitude of uncompromising hostility had reduced Africa. More particularly did he feel that if only the leaders on either side could meet in open and frank discussion, the disagreement between the two parties would soon be at an end.[1] Nothing was further, however, from the minds of the Donatist Bishops ; they refused all Augustine's overtures,[2] so that things seemed at a deadlock.

But the campaign thus inaugurated had an unexpected effect. For, not content with their possession of the churches and property of the Catholics whom they had ousted, the Donatists took the offensive after a fashion peculiarly their own. Determined to check the progress of the Catholic body which was causing them much uneasiness, and apparently only too well aware of the insecurity of their own position, they, with the

[1] *Epp*. xliii. 1, lxxxviii. 7, 11, clxxxv. 25–26 ; *Contra Cresconium*, iii. 49, v. 3, 80 ; St. Optatus, *l.c.*, i. 4.

[2] *Ep*. cv. 2, 13 ; *Contra Cresconium*, ii. 1, iv. 80 ; *Contra Litt. Petiliani*, i. 1, ii. 1 ; *Contra Julianum*, iii. 5.

assistance of roving bands known as 'Circumcellions,'[1] ravaged the countryside and committed a series of outrages, even of murders, which made the very existence of the Catholics precarious. When at length the Imperial authorities were forced to take cognizance of this state of affairs, and Honorius published, in A.D. 405, an Edict in which he insisted on Unity in the Catholic Faith,[2] the Donatists only increased their enormities. This led the Catholic Bishops to renewed efforts to secure a conference between themselves and their opponents, efforts which were finally crowned with success when, in A.D. 410, a further Edict from the Emperor arranged such a conference for the following year. At this famous meeting which lasted three days, the Donatists could produce no valid arguments in favour of their schismatical position, and were consequently disestablished, deprived of their ill-gotten property, and, in many cases, driven into exile.

In previous chapters we have often had occasion to mention some of the leading Donatists; a brief account of the more famous among them will help towards an understanding of St. Augustine's handling of the question of schism.

PARMENIAN succeeded Donatus in the Donatist See of Carthage *c.* A.D. 355, and died in 391.[3] St. Optatus calls him a 'peregrinus,' meaning apparently that he came from some other diocese than that of Carthage[4]; there seems to have been some well-known flaw in his Orders, at any rate Optatus calls on him 'to blush' for them[5]; he had certainly been 're-baptized' by the Donatists.[6] Gifted with a rugged eloquence he wrote a violent attack on the Catholic Church which produced a reply in St. Optatus' *De Schismate Donatistarum.* Optatus shows up Parmenian as somewhat dull, distinctly illogical in his arguments, rather crafty, even sly, very prolix, and at times brutal.[7] He knew, says Optatus, that

[1] *Epp.* lxxxviii. 8, xciii. 2, cv. 5, cviii. 18; *Vita* by Possidius, 4, 10, 12; St. Optatus, *l.c.* iii. 4.

[2] *Codex Theodosianus*, ed. Mommsen and Meyer, xvi. v. 38.

[3] Optatus, *l.c.*, i. 10; Augustine, *Retract.*, ii. 17; *cf. P.L.*, xi. 363, *Contra Ep. Parmeniani*, iii. 18.

[4] Optatus, ii. 4, 7, iii. 3.

[5] *Ibid.*, ii. 7, iii. 3.

[6] *Ibid.*, ii. 7.

[7] *Ibid.*, i. 5, 9, ii. 18, iii. 7, iv. 9, v. 1; St. Augustine, *Contra Ep. Parmeniani*, i. 1, ii. 19, 32–35, iii. 3–7.

he had no case against the Church.[1] Optatus betrays no knowledge of the Epistle of Parmenian which St. Augustine assailed in *Contra Epistolam Parmeniani*, *c.* A.D. 400, when Parmenian had been dead nine years. That Epistle must, then, have been written somewhere between A.D. 370 and 391, and it is hard to believe that when he penned it Parmenian had not seen and read Optatus' work. That did not prevent him, however, from publishing what was evidently a violent attack on a famous fellow-Donatist, Tychonius, who had ventilated ideas which would, if carried to their true conclusion, have wrecked the Donatist position. This brought St. Augustine into the arena with his *Contra Epistolam Parmeniani*, a treatise which—though it was far from being his first work against the schismatics [2]—established the Bishop of Hippo as an antagonist who would have to be reckoned with.

Parmenian was succeeded by PRIMIANUS, A.D. 391; he presided over the Donatist party at the Conference of A.D. 411, though he was practically a nonentity and left all the disputation to PETILIAN of Cirta and EMERITUS of Caesarea in Mauretania. The former was Augustine's most bitter opponent. In fact he seemed obsessed by an almost insane hatred of him.[3] Possibly his own sad story, preserved for us by Augustine himself, had something to do with this: 'When the Donatist faction was dominant at Cirta they seized one of our laity, a catechumen, a man born of Catholic parents and called Petilian. Him they handled savagely; and when he ran away they searched for him and discovered him in hiding; they dragged him out stricken with terror; they baptized him to his dismay; they ordained him against his will.' [4] In due course this

[1] Optatus, *l.c.*, i. 9.

[2] *E.g.*, *Epp.* xxiii., xxxiii.–xxxv., xliii.–xliv., besides several works now lost.

[3] One sample of his language about Augustine must suffice: 'You wicked persecutor! Cloak yourself in goodness how you will; wage war against us with whatever kisses of peace you like; seduce men by whatever talk of Unity you choose, you who to this present moment art ever a deceiver and a misleader: it will always remain true that you are a child of the devil and betray your parentage by your morals!' quoted by St. Augustine, *Contra Litteras Petiliani*, ii. 38; *cf.* iii. 11, 17, 19, 20, 30; *De Unitate*, 24.

[4] 'Vim fecit nolenti, scrutatus est fugientem, invenit latentem, extraxit paventem, baptizavit trementem, ordinavit nolentem,' *Sermo ad Plebem Caesariensem*, 8.

unhappy man became a pleader in the courts and finally Donatist Bishop of Cirta or Constantina. He used to boast of his eloquence, even going so far as to style himself the 'Paraclete.' [1]

Though none of his writings has come down to us, Petilian was a voluminous writer. Amongst other works, he addressed a species of Encyclical *Ad Presbyteros et Diaconos Donatistas adversus Catholicam* of which lengthy extracts can be recovered[2] from Augustine's refutations of various portions of it as they came into his hands. This answer Augustine termed *Contra Litteras Petiliani.* Augustine also refers to a Treatise by Petilian on the Maximianist secession from the Donatists [3] as well as to an *Epistola de Ordine Partis Donati,*[4] but both of these have perished. The same fate befell his *De Unico Baptismo,* in which he tried to prove that it was absurd to charge the Donatists with re-baptizing since—as Catholic Baptisms were null—it was impossible to re-baptize them. Augustine gave the same title, *De Unico Baptismo,* to his refutation of this pamphlet.

Chosen by his party as one of the seven Donatist delegates at the Conference of A.D. 411, Petilian had every opportunity of airing his eloquence. And he surpassed himself. For he spoke no less than one-hundred-and-fifty-three times in the three days; indeed, probably far more often, for the *Acta* of the third and crucial day have for the most part perished. We do know, however, that he was so fatigued by his own oratory that he had perforce to stop speaking owing—so he said—to hoarseness.[5] Perhaps Petilian's temper contributed as much as anything else to the rout of the Donatists in this tournament. Not unjustly does Francis Baldwin say of him: 'Versutior fuit causidicus, et forensium cautionum atque cavillationum peritior, quam causa postularet.' [6]

The last prominent figure among the Donatist leaders

[1] *Contra Litt. Petiliani,* iii. 19; *cf. ibid.,* ii. 239.

[2] For an attempt at such a reconstruction, see P. Monceaux, *Revue de Philologie,* xxx. (1906), pp. 218–243, and xxxi., pp. 28–44.

[3] *Contra Litt. Petiliani,* iii. 42–45.

[4] *Ep.* liii. 1, 2 4.

[5] *Collatio,* iii. 541, in Marcellus' summary of the contents; the actual *Gesta Collationis* only takes us down to iii. 281. The *Gesta* will be found in *P.L.,* xi. with the *Opera* of St. Optatus.

[6] *Historia Donatistarum, P.L.,* xi. 1441.

remains: EMERITUS, the Bishop of Caesarea in Mauretania. Somewhere between A.D. 406 and 411 Augustine addressed a letter to him which has been preserved,[1] though it was not the first he had sent him[2]; he wrote to him as 'one who had received a liberal education' and whose persistence in schism was therefore all the more surprising. 'I have but one question to put to you,' he says: 'Is your Church or ours the true Church of God?' Augustine knows that this question will not be answered any more than the questions he had put in his previous letter, but he feels bound to free his own conscience by making this straightforward appeal to one 'who is, as I am given to understand, a good man and a well-educated one.' There was no answer.

As far back as A.D. 394 the Donatists had held a famous—or rather an infamous—Council of their sect at Bagai,[3] and had thundered forth anathemas against the Maximianists who had seceded from the parent stem. This exceedingly turgid document was said to have emanated from the pen of Emeritus[4] whom Possidius speaks of as 'doctus, eloquens et praedicatus'[5]; but apart from Augustine's letter to him this is all we know of Emeritus previous to the Conference of A.D. 411 when he was one of the Donatist delegates and played a prominent, though elusive and purely obstructionist part in the discussions. He complained of the badly punctuated reading of one of the documents adduced,[6] also of the fact that the *Acta* had been taken down in shorthand and were therefore illegible[7]; at one point in the discussion he declared that he was no good at following an intricate argument, but he speedily showed that he could do so when he wished to. And while protesting that he was only going to say a few words he contrived to make several very lengthy and indeed eloquent

[1] *Ep.* lxxxvii.
[2] *Ibid.*, 6.
[3] No less than three-hundred-and-ten Donatist Bishops were present, *Contra Ep. Parmeniani*, i. 18, ii. 7, *Contra Cresconium*, ii. 15, iii. 16, etc. For the actual Decree then drawn up, see *Contra Cresconium*, iii. 22–25, 59, iv. 38–39, 45; *Enarr.* ii. 20 *on* Ps. xxxvi., etc.
[4] *Ep.* cviii. 15, *De Gestis cum Emerito*, 10–11, etc.
[5] *Vita Augustini*, xiv.
[6] *Collatio*, iii. 255; *cf. Breviculus Collationis*, ii.
[7] *Ibid.*, ii.

speeches.[1] At length, however, the long-drawn-out proceedings came to an end and Marcellinus the President pronounced sentence in due course—disestablishment for those Donatists who should refuse to give up their schismatical state.

Some little time after this Augustine again wrote to Emeritus, begging him to reconsider the question : Which was the True Church ? [2] But, as before, no answer was forthcoming. Seven years after the Conference, however, they did meet, and under peculiar circumstances. For in A.D. 418 the reigning Pontiff, Zosimus, sent Augustine on a commission to Caesarea of Mauretania, Emeritus' See.[3] Here he met his old antagonist in the street and straightway asked him to accompany him to the church where he was about to preach. Emeritus accepted with such promptitude that Augustine even thought he might be willing at last to make his submission and be reconciled to the Church. The scene must have been a striking one. For after the preamble to the Conference of A.D. 411 had been solemnly read out, Augustine addressed them all on the events of that great Conference. And all the while Emeritus, formerly Bishop of that very city, and perhaps exercising his functions in that very church, stood before him. What were his feelings ? A very large proportion of his former flock has already gone over to the Catholic Church and now he is standing where formerly he had sat and preached to his people ! Suddenly he hears Augustine addressing him personally : 'Brother Emeritus, you are here, and you were also at the Conference. If you were defeated then, why have you come here now ? If you maintain that you were not defeated then, will you tell us why you think that ? ' [4] Emeritus looked up and said : 'The *Acta* of that Conference show whether I was defeated or not, whether I was overwhelmed by authority or by arguments.' 'Then why have you come in here ? ' repeated Augustine. 'To say what you want me to say,' was the cryptic reply.[5] 'But,'

[1] *Collatio*, iii. 45, when he tried to instruct the President on the proper method of conducting the enquiry ! *Ibid.*, 114, 157, 188, 200, 225–226, 260, 262, 266.

[2] *Retract*, ii. 48.

[3] *Vita*, xiv. ; *Retract*. ii. 51 ; *cf*. *Epp*., cxc.–cxciii.

[4] *De Gestis cum Emerito*, 3.

[5] Was this simply a sneering question ?

retorted Augustine, 'what I want you to say is why you have come. I would not have asked you that had you not come.'

Emeritus' only reply was to say to the notary, who was taking it all down: 'Do' (fac). What he meant by that it is impossible to say as he refused to open his lips again. 'He had nothing to say. Like a dumb man he listened to the whole of my sermon on the one question of the Maximianists which I set out before him.'[1] Augustine closed with an eloquent appeal for Unity: 'For this,' he said, 'we toil and sweat. For this we incur danger from the Donatist weapons and the sanguinary fury of their Circumcellions. . . . I have spoken at great length though I am worn out . . . and still our Brother stands there obstinate! He mistakes his cruel fortitude for constancy! For him let us pray.'

II—THE APPALLING STATE OF DIVIDED CHRISTIAN AFRICA

In the course of the thirty years' contest St. Augustine, who was, of course, the champion on the Catholic side, had to ponder deeply the theoretical as well as the practical character of schism. We are not concerned here with the steps he took to secure its removal, but solely with the ideas he had, in the course of years, formed on the real nature of schism and its gravity.

What most grieved the Bishop was the appalling state to which this wholly unjustifiable schism had reduced Northern Africa. St. Optatus had already pointed out the fatal divisions in families which thence resulted: 'Call to mind how the members of Mother Church have, through you, been separated from one another. For never yet have you been able to pervert an entire family. Either the wife goes off and the husband remains, or both parents are misled and their children decline to follow them, or while a brother stands fast his sister goes

[1] *Retract.* ii. 51. Possidius adds the interesting detail that Emeritus would not 'answer to this exhortation even on the urgent appeal of his relatives and fellow-citizens who undertook to return to his communion, even though it involved the loss of their property and their means of livelihood, if only he would show the hollowness of the Catholic assertions.' *Vita*, xiv.

astray.'[1] St. Augustine is equally eloquent on the point. He begs for a general return to Unity in order that

> our unhappy populace, which believes in Christ, may be able to have in common not only their meals but also the Table of Christ. Have we never to grieve at the sight of husband and wife who, for the sake of mutual faith in their bodily union, swear—both of them—by the Name of Christ, yet rend the Body of Christ by the separate Communions they make ?[2] 'Unity is put to flight,' he cries, 'and husband goes to church here and wife there ; the husband says, "keep unity with me, for I am your husband," but she : "I will die where my father died before me.'" 'In every thing else,' he continues, 'men agree, save at Christ's altar, where they disagree.'[3] And again : 'children have one father's home, not one Heavenly Father's home !'[4]

So, too, when a certain Donatist refused to accept a young man as a son-in-law unless he consented to join their 'party,'[5] Augustine not unnaturally exclaimed : 'If you cannot accept the account of what the originators of the schism did at Cirta (A.D. 305) or at Carthage (311–312) you can at least believe the testimony of your own eyes which see what is going on all round you.'[6]

And how unhappy many of these schismatics were ! 'Why,' asks Augustine, 'do they prowl round outside, yet cannot make up their minds to enter ? Because,' he answers, 'it is the wheel of time they love, not eternity ; hence they refuse to embrace the truth.'[7] But, as he repeatedly tells them, they never will understand until they do enter : 'If they would get rid of their confusion of mind they must take refuge in Catholic truth ; they will find no solution of their difficulties so long as they are entangled in the crime of schism.'[8]

But, alas, the Donatists had the fatal habit of preoccupation

[1] *De Schismate Donatistarum*, iii. 10.
[2] *Ep.* xxiii. 5 ; *cf.* xxxiii. 5 ; *Sermo*, xlvi. 15, 21.
[3] *Ep.* cviii. 17–18.
[4] *Ep.* xxxiii. 5.
[5] *Sermo*, xlvi. 15.
[6] *Ep.* xliii. 25.
[7] *Enarr.* ii. 11 *on* Ps. xxx. 14.
[8] *Contra Epistolam Parmeniani*, ii. 20 ; *cf. Contra Litt. Petiliani*, i. 24.

with things that did not really matter; they occupied themselves with trifles of Biblical interpretation which only served to obscure the real issue [1]; they kept harping on the historical side of the question, to the neglect of the principles. This proved their stumbling-block throughout, and it came to a head in the Conference of A.D. 411, when the decision might truly be said to have been given against them by default, simply because they neither could nor would come to the point.

The plight of the Donatist laity was indeed a pitiable one. Their Bishops either did nothing or published violent and unworthy diatribes against the Catholic Church. But as a rule they preferred to keep silence, for they well knew that they had no case. How pathetic, then, the excuses offered by the laity for remaining where they were! 'We are quite safe if only we follow our Bishops!' 'How often,' adds Augustine, 'do heretics say this when convinced of the patent truth! And they go on to say: "We are the flock; it is for our pastors to render an account of us!" Indeed, they will have to give an account—a dreadful one—of your deaths!' concludes Augustine.[2]

Nor was it the Christian body alone that suffered owing to the schism. The effect on the pagans can easily be guessed. St. Augustine was dismayed by the fact that whereas 'the Church had reached such a pitch of glory that no pagan dared speak ill of her, yet they still had this argument, "Why do you disagree among yourselves?"' [3] Hence he urges the Catholics to try and convert the heathen in their midst by affording them 'such an exhibition of harmony that they may be led to peace and unity in the worship of God.' [4]

But seemingly all the Bishop's efforts were in vain. The Catholics felt too crushed, the pagans were indifferent onlookers who were somewhat amused, the Donatists themselves had crystallized in schism. Most of them had been born in it and hardly realized the horror of their position. In vain did

[1] *Contra Cresconium*, iv. 33; *Enarr*. i. 8 *on* Ps. x.
[2] *Sermon* xlvi. 21; *cf*. Optatus, *l.c*. v. 3.
[3] *Sermo*, xlvii. 28; *cf*. *ibid*., No. 18.
[4] *De Utilitate Jejunii*, 10, *P.L*., xl. 713; *cf*. *De Civitate Dei*, XVIII. xv. 2; St. Ambrose, *Epp*. xvii.–xviii., *P.L*., xvi. 96–97; St. Vincent of Lerins, *Commonitorium*, 31.

the Saint warn them that though not now dramatically punished as in the case of Core, Dathan and Abiron, schism would most certainly be punished hereafter,[1] that if they deliberately remained in it Hell would be their portion [2]; that it must mean the loss of eternal life [3]; and—even here on earth—a steady withering away: 'Where they fall, there they stay; and where they are separated off, there they wither away. . . . Yet all the while, wheresoever they are, there is the Catholic Church, as you see here in Africa where your sect is; though the converse is not true, *viz.* that wheresoever the Catholic Church is, there are you, too, or any other sect.' [4] As St. Optatus had told them thirty years and more before: schism produces nothing new,[5] but it does mean fighting against the known truth.[6] A fatal folly! An incredibly foolish procrastination which can only end in that most awful thing, a deathbed in deliberate schism.[7] You are dismayed, says Augustine, if you cut your finger,[8] horrified when a man suffers some bodily wound [9]; but when the soul dies—as it is on the way to do when in schism—you feel no dismay [10]; for you are 'amputated,' nay 'self-amputated' members of the body.[11]

III—SCHISM IS ALWAYS 'SACRILEGE'

In Augustine's eyes schism is always 'sacrilege':—

Why did you separate? Why perish in the sacrilege of this accursed schism? [12] You are all equally guilty and criminal; not so much by reason of the crimes committed by some among you—crimes which some commit but which others condemn; but you are all guilty of the crime of schism; from that

[1] See Optatus, *l.c.*, i. 21; *cf.* Nbs. xvi.
[2] *Epp.* cxli. 5, clxxiii. 6; *Enarr.* i. 16 *on* Ps. liv.
[3] *Epp.* xliii. 21, cxli. 5.
[4] *Contra Cresconium*, iv. 73 and 75.
[5] *L.c.*, i. 11.
[6] *Ep.* xciii. 10.
[7] *De Baptismo contra Donatistas*, i. 11; *Contra Epistolam Parmeniani*, ii. 25; *Sermon* ccclviii. 3.
[8] *Ep.* clxxxv. 42.
[9] *De Baptismo contra Donatistas*, i. 11.
[10] *Contra Epistolam Parmeniani*, i. 14, ii. 25.
[11] *Contra Cresconium*, iii. 77; *cf. Ep.* liii. 1, clxxxv. 44.
[12] *Contra Litt. Petiliani*, ii. 180; *cf. ib.* 146; *Ep.* li. 5, lxxxvii. 1; *De Baptismo contra Donatistas*, ii. 5, 6, 9.

appalling sacrilege none of you can pretend that he is free so long as he refuses to enter into communion with the Unity of all the nations—unless, of course, you prefer to say that Christ lied in what He said of the Church spread throughout all the nations of the world (Luke xxiv. 47).[1]

Though the wound caused by schism is an invisible one, he says elsewhere, it is none the less grave, indeed, it should inspire greater fear than a patent sore.[2] To be a schismatic is a worse crime than to surrender copies of the Bible to the persecutor[3]; it involves the murder of the soul,[4] or, as St. Thomas expresses it, 'est peccatum maximum in proximum'[5]; it is a huge evil[6]; no words can exaggerate it[7]; the schismatic builds on sand[8] because at the best he is in a state of uncertainty.[9]

IV—TO REMAIN IN SCHISM IS A QUESTION FOR EACH INDIVIDUAL TO SETTLE FOR HIMSELF

Not only is schism illogical in its inception, but an illogical starting-point must inevitably result in a whole series of illogical positions. The logical consequence of the illogical basis of Donatism—namely that they alone were 'holy'—should have been that the moment a person realized that some member of his 'sinless' party was a sinner he himself was bound in conscience to leave them, partly to escape personal contamination, but much more because, on the principles of the 'party,' it could no longer be the true Church. To this delightful impasse Augustine returns again and again. For the crimes prevalent among the Donatists were too notorious to be ignored by the most outrageous partisan amongst them.

[1] *Contra Litt. Petiliani*, ii. 221; *cf. Contra Epistolam Parmeniani*, ii. 5 *Contra Gaudentium*, i. 49.
[2] *Contra Ep. Parmeniani*, i. 14.
[3] *De Baptismo contra Donatistas*, iii. 3.
[4] *Contra Litt. Petiliani*, ii. 46.
[5] *Summa Theol.*, 2da. 2dae. xxxix. 2 *ad* 2dm.
[6] *Contra Cresconium*, iv. 26.
[7] *Contra Litt. Petiliani*, ii. 20 and 54.
[8] *Ibid.*, ii. 247.
[9] *De Baptismo contra Donatistas*, i. 4.

'If,' he asks, 'those among you who are not criminal are disgusted at the crimes of other members and try to convince themselves that other folks' sins are no concern of theirs, then why remain in a disastrous schism which is itself a crime in which you all share?'[1]

Augustine was not indulging in mere dialectics. The point he wished to make was that whether to remain in schism or to quit it was a question every individual had to decide for himself. I can understand you, he writes to Emeritus of Caesarea, when you say that had you excommunicated the notorious Optatus there would have been a schism in your 'party' since he would have drawn many away with him; 'but what makes you guilty in the eyes of God is that, though feeling that Optatus should be tolerated in your communion rather than incur the risk of the terrible evil of splitting up your "party," you yet continued to remain in the evil wrought by your predecessors when they split up the Church of Christ.'[2]

Over and over again does Augustine insist that whereas the question: Which is the True Church? does not depend on the goodness or badness, the virtues or vices of individual members of any particular Communion[3]—for their personal failings are no reflection on the Church which they thus disgrace—yet the same does not hold good of 'the crime of schism'; for schism is essentially an individual question, one which each man has to settle for himself.[4] So strongly does he insist on this fundamental point that Monceaux thinks that for the Bishop of Hippo 'persons count for more than principles,'[5] perhaps a pardonable exaggeration! At the same time St. Augustine does not pretend that it is an easy thing to break the shackles of long habit: 'to persevere along a path of unaccustomed rectitude, to break the bonds of wrong habit with which one has become familiar through long usage, that demands real strength, though with God's help no one need ever despair.[6]

[1] *Contra Epistolam Parmeniani*, ii. 19.
[2] *Ep.* lxxxvii. 4; *cf. Contra Gaudentium*, i. 49.
[3] *De Unico Baptismo*, 26.
[4] *Contra Ep. Parmeniani*, ii. 19; *De Unitate*, 3; *Ep.* lxxxvii. 4, 9; *cf. De Gestis cum Emerito*, 4.
[5] *Histoire littéraire de L'Afrique du Nord*, vii. 129.
[6] *Ep.* lvi. 2.

Not every sin in word or deed is to be called the sin against the Holy Spirit, but only some sin that is definite and peculiar, namely that hardness of heart whereby to the close of his days a man refuses to obtain the remission of his sins in the Unity of that Body of Christ which is quickened by the Holy Spirit.' [1] How appalling a thing to be classed among such as 'call themselves Christians yet are not really so, but merely people whom the Church has but partially digested, its dung, like all heretics and schismatics, fruitless twigs lopped from the vine, straws blown from the threshing-floor by the winnowing!' [2] How terrible to rank among those whose 'sole bond of union is that while disagreeing with one another they are in agreement against Unity' [3]; how degrading to feel that by force of their very principles—the rejection of authority and the right to separate—they must inevitably 'wither away' [4] since the process of disintegration goes on unceasingly as first one and then another 'sect,' another 'branch,' another 'reform' starts to mangle and further break up the parent stem! 'Why should not Parmenian,' asks Augustine, 'gather round him men like-minded with himself and so start a sect of "Parmenianists," like those many crumblets scattered throughout Africa and broken off from the original crumblet?' [5] This actually had been done by the Claudianists,[6] the Urbanists,[7] and the Rogatists—whom Augustine dubs 'brevissimum frustum de frusto majore praecisum' [8]; but the most notorious, indeed tragic, instance of this was the case of the Maximianists, whose secession in A.D. 493–494 may be said to have sounded the death-knell of the Donatists [9]: 'Some in one place, some in another, but

[1] *Ep.* clxxxv. 49.

[2] *Ep.* liii. 1, clxxxv. 44; *Sermo*, v. 1, 3.

[3] *Sermo*, xlvii. 27.

[4] 'Branches broken off, drawing no sap from the root, lying prone each of them where it fell and there withering away.' *Contra Cresconium*, iv. 73, 75.

[5] *Contra Ep. Parmeniani*, i. 9.

[6] *Contra Cresconium*, iv. 9–11, 73; *Enarr.*, ii. 20–22 *on* Ps. xxxvi.; Claudius was one of the Donatist Bishops in Rome, St. Optatus, *l.c.*, ii. 4, and was at the Synod they held there in A.D. 374, Mansi, *Concilia*, iii. 626.

[7] A sect in Numidia, *Contra Cresconium*, iv. 73.

[8] *Ibid.*, and especially *Ep.* xciii. to Vincent the Rogatist.

[9] The best summary of their complicated story will be found in *De Gestis cum Emerito*, 9; *cf. Contra Ep. Parmeniani*, i. 6; *Contra Cresconium*, iv. throughout.

each of them holding up for our admiration their own peculiar shreds of views (praesumptionum) or rather their amputations of doctrine, they with a wicked pride repudiate the root-stock whence they were lopped.' [1] All that these sects could do was to support one another in their refusal to give in, [2] occupying themselves with the things that do not count, [3] while resisting a truth of which they were perfectly well aware. [4] Fancy dying in that state ! ' Were you to depart this life separated from the Unity of the Body of Christ,' he writes to Felicia, ' your virginal integrity would avail you nothing,' [5] for, as he wrote to the Donatists after the Conference of A.D. 411, ' Whosoever shall have separated himself from the Catholic Church, no matter how praiseworthy such a person may fancy his life has been, yet for that one crime of having cut himself off from the Unity of Christ he shall not have eternal life, but the wrath of God shall abide with him for ever.' [6] When Gaudentius of Thamugadi wrote and told Augustine that he and all his flock were gathered together in their church and were going to set it on fire and perish in the flames rather than surrender to the demands of the Emperors and accept the Catholic faith, Augustine pithily replied that many had discovered that a schism was hardly worth the loss of their property and had consequently thought better of it ; he therefore suggests that Gaudentius and his companions might well ask themselves whether any schism was worth dying for. [7] To Petilian he wrote that the only means of obtaining ' the full and Catholic Unity of the Church is to be in her ' [8] ; and to Parmenian, that the only interpretation of the passages of Scripture which the Donatists alleged in their defence was the Catholic one ; it alone would satisfy all requirements, ' but not so long as people remain enmeshed in schism.' [9]

[1] *Contra Cresconium*, iii. 77.
[2] *Sermo*, xlvii. 27.
[3] See above, p. 268.
[4] *Ep*. xciii. 10.
[5] *Ep*.ccviii. 7.
[6] *Ep*. cxli. 5 ; *cf*. *Ep*. clxxvi. 3 ; *Enarr*. i. 16 *on* Ps. liv.
[7] *Contra Gaudentium*, ii. 8.
[8] *Contra Litt. Petiliani*, i. 24.
[9] *Contra Ep. Parmeniani*, ii. 20.

V—PRIDE IS THE ROOT-CAUSE OF SCHISM

But the real root of the schism was—at least on the part of its leaders—pride, the pride of

carnal-minded men seeking their own honour or losing patience; there was a way out, and they took it—the way of separation. . . . Swelling with pride they knew not what tolerance meant, in other words they had no charity. . . . How promptly they fell away the moment the Church did something they did not like! How unwilling they were to surrender their own dignity; how ready even to die for its retention! They want to keep the people under their feet, therefore they will not allow them to return to the Unity of Christ.[1] And again: The one mother pride bore them all; just as our one Mother, the Catholic Church, bore all the Christian faithful throughout the world.[2]

Augustine is here referring, of course, to those who inaugurated the schism, to those whose doings showed so little reflection, such an overweening sense of their own importance.[3] But what distressed him so much during the course of his long campaign was that the leaders of the schism in his own day, men who had never known the originators of the present miserable state of things, were unchanged in mind, were, in fact, as proud, as unwilling to see the truth as had been Donatus himself or the original conspirators at Cirta. 'You cannot help seeing,' he says, 'that what I am saying is true; had you any charity you would rejoice with the truth.' Christ, he pointed out, had said of the tares, 'Suffer them to grow till the harvest'; but the Donatist leaders insisted on the immediate expulsion of those whom they reputed wicked:—

You labour with all the words at your command to make men believe that the wheat has perished everywhere in the field save in your tiny little plot! You would make Christ a liar and yourselves the only truth-tellers. Yet in so doing

[1] *Sermo*, iv. 33–34; *cf*. xlvii. 16.
[2] *Sermo*, xlvi. 18; *cf*. xlvii. 16; *Contra Epistolam Parmeniani*, i. 8; *Ep*. xxxiii.; *Enarr*. i. 3 *on* Ps. xlix.
[3] The 'Tauri et vaccae' of Ps. lxvii. as Augustine calls them, *Enarr*. i. 3 *on* Ps. xxxix.; *cf*. *Ep*. cv. 1.

you are acting against your own consciences ; for no one can cast even a superficial glance at the Gospel and then dare to say in his heart that among all those nations who—practically unanimously—say ' Amen ' and sing ' Alleluia ' there are no Christians. Rather than admit that ' the party of Donatus, which is not in communion with the ' Orbis terrarum,' was in error, you, if an Angel from heaven—one who can see the entire world—were to assure you that outside your communion there really were no innocent or good people, would, without a shadow of doubt, rejoice at the wickedness of the human race and boastfully declare that yourselves had always maintained that truth—even before you knew it.[1]

VI—THE MENTAL TORPOR INDUCED THROUGH LIVING IN SCHISM

How was it that the schism lasted so long, roughly speaking, from A.D. 311–411 ? St. Augustine gives an answer, tragic in its simplicity :—

When plain and evident truth came home to the ears and hearts of men, the quicksands of unhappy custom sucked them in and they preferred to resist any authority, any arguments, rather than yield to the truth. This resistance took the form either of persecuting their opponents or of lapsing into torpor.[2]

In many sermons and letters as well as in his more formal treatises Augustine deals with the violent persecution of the Catholics by the Donatists, but what particularly disturbed him was the state of mental torpor and inertia into which the schismatics had fallen. ' Sometimes,' he says, ' we meet sluggish-minded people who in answer to our arguments mutter ' :

It is all true, master ; it is all true ; and I have no answer to give you. And when we say : ' Well, but then why not act on that ? ' they answer : ' Oh, my father died among them,' or ' my mother lies buried among them.' To this we, of course, say : ' Yes, but you are talking of people long dead and buried, whereas you yourself are alive, you have a tongue

[1] *Contra Litt. Petiliani*, ii. 174 ; *cf. Ep.* lxxxix. 6, xciii. 1.
[2] *Ep.* lxxxix. 6 ; *cf. Ep.* xliii. 27 : ' You groan about it yet you still cling to it ! '

and can talk to people. Now you say your parents were Christians belonging to "the party of Donatus"; perhaps their parents, too, were Christians. But their grandparents, or at least their great-grandparents, were certainly pagans. Yet those of them who became Christians, did they, when they reflected that their parents had been pagans, shrink into themselves and shirk the truth? Did they cling to the authority of their dead parents? Did they not prefer the living Christ to their dead parents? If, then, you see before your eyes the true Unity and know that outside of it you will die eternally, why prefer to follow your dead parents, dead to you and to God? What can you say to that?' The only answer they make is: 'It is true, I have nothing to say. But what can I do?' Truth to tell, some strange species of custom has got such people in its grip. They have become lethargic; vexed with conflicting diseases, they will die in their sleep![1]

VII—THE PROBLEM OF DISESTABLISHMENT

The truth is that the schism had become a tradition in Africa. So much was this the case that when St. Augustine reproved Macrobius, the newly-consecrated Donatist Bishop of Hippo, for re-baptizing a Catholic Sub-deacon who had gone over to him in a fit of petulance, Macrobius answered that he was bound in duty to receive such as came to him and to give them the faith they asked for. But when Augustine asked him to explain the case of the Maximianists who had seceded from the main Donatist body, Macrobius replied that 'as a newly-consecrated Bishop it was not for him to sit in judgment on the doings of his fathers but to stand by what he had received from his predecessors.'[2] This sounds like, and possibly was, a becoming modesty, though it is hard to believe in the modesty of a young Bishop who, on finding himself installed in the same See as the venerable Augustine who had been Bishop there for thirteen years, dared to flout him on so grave an issue as the re-baptism of one of the latter's Sub-deacons.

Yet this action on the part of Macrobius was in keeping with

[1] *Sermo,* ccclix. 8; *cp. Ep.* cviii. 2: 'Nothing can justify you in holding on to what you know to be a bad cause.'
[2] *Epp.* cvi.–cviii.

the attitude generally adopted by the Donatist Bishops. For these men were not fools. Were they, then, knaves? Augustine has no doubt on the point: 'You,' he writes to Cresconius, 'believed your lying Bishops'[1] who knew in their secret hearts that they had no case against the Catholics.[2] This, as Augustine insists, particularly appeared in their persistent refusals to meet the Catholic Bishops in conference. And certainly the result of the Conference finally forced upon them, in A.D. 411, by the Emperor Honorius shows that their worldly wisdom was justified in this respect. The same want of candour in debate characterized all their dealings with the Catholic leaders. Petilian of Cirta and Emeritus of Caesarea proved themselves past masters in the arts of obstruction and evasion of the truth in the Conference of A.D. 411. These schismatic Bishops were determined that their flocks should not learn the truth.[3] For though not the originators of the schism, they had inherited it—with its emoluments: 'retention of their dignities is the root of their state of separation,' said Augustine.[4] Did their flocks once grasp the true position, disestablishment stared these intruders in the face. At all costs, then, they must not be allowed to learn. The same lack of straightforwardness appears in the case of the more educated among the Donatist laity. Hence Augustine felt bound to say to Cresconius:—

I do not say you would not see my argument; rather have you declined to touch it; for the more carefully and closely you scrutinized it the more afraid you were to touch it . . . you shrewdly felt it best to pass it over in silence as though I had never said it.[5]

This haunting fear of disestablishment, of the loss of all the immense property of the Catholic Church in Africa unjustly

[1] *Contra Cresconium*, iii. 26; *cf. ibid.*, 27, 36–38. In fact deliberate lying had been the policy of the original schismatics at Cirta in A.D.305, at Carthage in 311–312, and in their series of appeals to Constantine, *ibid.*, iii. 67.

[2] *De Baptismo contra Donatistas*, ii. 16.

[3] *Contra Cresconium*, iii. 26–27, 37–38, 67; *Enarr.* ii. 2, 29 *on* Ps. xxi.; *Contra Ep. Parmeniani*, i. 3, etc.

[4] 'Causa principatus sui se separat,' *Enarr.* i. 7 *on* Ps. x.; *cp. Contra Gaudentium*, ii. 59; *Epp.* xciii. 15, cv. 9, clxxxv. 36; *Contra Litt. Petiliani*, ii. 132, 203, 224. Three years after the Conference a Council of thirty Donatist Bishops refused to consider disestablishment.

[5] *Contra Cresconium*, ii. 22; *cf. ibid.*, 23 and iv. 9.

handed over to them by Julian the Apostate, A.D. 361–363, is the key to the attitude of the Donatist Bishops. What sadder spectacle than that of the disinherited, disestablished, disendowed Emeritus wandering in the year 418 through the streets of Caesarea where he had once dwelt as its venerable Bishop ? [1] It was this uncompromising attitude of theirs which compelled Augustine to secure their attendance at the great Conference of A.D. 411. Not that he was desirous of humbling the Bishops or the clergy. It was the interests of the people that he had at heart : ' It is not acute and clever disputing that we want on this question which has the populace in its grip.' [2] Here we have the true explanation of what many have chosen to regard as an uncalled-for change of mind on Augustine's part when he came to see that the laws against heretics could and should be applied to the Donatists who, to save their own skins, persisted that they were really only schismatics and therefore did not fall under the Imperial laws against heretics. ' The whole question,' he says to Petilian, ' comes to this : are not you malefactors, you whom the " Orbis terrarum " upbraids with the sacrilege of so terrible a schism, you who sweep on one side all discussion on the subject and only urge what is not to the point, you, who, while you live like bandits, boast that you die as martyrs ? ' [3]

VIII—HERESY AND SCHISM DEFINED

Augustine was, of course, well aware that invective and declamation—however eloquent—would never break down the schism nor bring conviction to erring minds. Hence his appeal throughout his long campaign was to principles, or rather to a single principle—the Church of Christ, the ' Corpus Christi ' which is as much a dogma, as profound a mystery as the Caput Ecclesiae ' or the Incarnate Christ Himself. ' Where s the Church ? ' he asks, ' with you or with us ? ' [4] And ' what does schism mean but separation from that " Corpus

[1] See above, pp. 264–266.
[2] *De Unitate*, 9 ; *cf. Ep.* xxxiii. 5.
[3] *Contra Litt. Petiliani*, ii. 164.
[4] *Contra Litt. Petiliani*, ii. 37, 189.

Christi " which is as divine and essential a thing as its Head the " Verbum Incarnatum " Himself ? '[1] It was idle to pretend that either schismatics or heretics really belonged to the Church ; for the Church was essentially a visible conspicuous thing, the ' city set upon a hill ' which all could see if they wished. If they wished ! That was the source of all the trouble. ' I know which is the Catholic Church. You know it, too,' he writes to Maximinus the Donatist Bishop of Sinitum near Hippo, ' or if you do not know, then look for it ; it can readily be discovered by such as will look for it.'[2] As a matter of fact Maximinus did ' look for it ' and found the pearl of great price, indeed he had to pay a heavy price for his conversion.[3] But the Donatists as a body declined to look for the Church, in fact, as Augustine pithily remarks, they preferred to turn their gaze to quarters where they knew the Church was not to be looked for.[4] They seemed actually to want to remain in schism : ' the sole reason for your separation is the crazy desire for a sacrilegious schism—appetitus sacrilegi schismatis.'[5] In vain, he urges, do you claim that you believe everything that we believe ; you can do that and yet be schismatics.'[6] Augustine questions indeed whether they really do believe, whether they are not simply living on a congeries of opinions : ' their chief grudge against the Catholic Church is that she bids those who come to her believe ; whereas heretics boast that they impose no such yoke of belief, but open up to their adherents the sources of doctrine . . . they try to win the crowd by an appeal to reason.'[7] What a tragedy that men should be content with the uncertain and the hazy when they can have the certain and the patent for the asking : ' In things that concern our salvation a man sins gravely, if only because he is preferring the uncertain to the certain.'[8]

But we [says St. Augustine] believe in Holy Church, assuredly

[1] *Cp. Enarr.* ii. 3–4 *on* Ps. xxx., iii. 1 *on* the same Psalm ; i. 14 *on* Ps. xxxiv., iii. 4 *on* Ps. xxxvi., i. 4 *on* Ps. lxi. ; *Ep.* clxxxv. 50, etc.

[2] *Ep.* xxiii. 2.

[3] *Ep.* cv. 2, 4, 17 ; *Civ. Dei*, XXII. viii. 7.

[4] *Contra Cresconium*, iii. 73 ; *cp.* St. Optatus, *l.c.*, i. 6.

[5] *Ibid.*, 39.

[6] *De Unitate*, 7.

[7] *De Utilitate credendi*, 21 ; *P.L.* xlii. 79.

[8] *De Baptismo contra Donatistas*, i. 4.

the Catholic Church ; for even heretics and schismatics style their assemblies ' churches.' But whereas heretics violate the faith by their false ideas about God, schismatics, by their wicked separation, cut themselves off from fraternal charity. Hence neither do heretics belong to the Catholic Church, for it loves God ; nor do schismatics, for the Catholic Church loves its neighbour.[1]

' Heretics,' he says, ' are united with good people in this world, not by the bond of the One Church or the One Faith, but solely by the bond implied in their title of " Christian " [2] ; and he adds that ' when people ask in what heretics differ from schismatics, the answer usually given is that it is not divergence in the faith that makes people schismatics but a breach in the bond of union.' [3] He then goes on to explain that not all heretics or schismatics are actually separated from the Church :

For if he holds false beliefs about God or on some point of doctrine which concerns the substance (aedificationem) of the faith, so that his mental attitude is not simply that of a man who hesitates because he is still searching for the truth but rather that of one holding firmly to his beliefs, in fact differing in no way from the opinions and errors of the sort of man who knows everything—then he is a heretic and is really outside the Church, though so far as external appearances go, he may seem to be in it. As a matter of fact the Church has many hidden heretics in her midst, people, that is, who do not so obstinately maintain their false views as to draw the attention of others to the fact—if they do so they are, of course, expelled. Similarly, those who envy good people and seek opportunity to drive them out of the Church or to degrade them, or who —when their crimes are made evident or their own attention is called to them—are prepared to cause disturbances in the Church or even go so far as to convene separate meetings, such folk are already schismatics and are really in heart separated

[1] *De Fide et Symbolo*, 21.

[2] *Quaestionum Septemdecim in Matthaeum*, qu. xi. 1 ; *P.L.* xxxv. 1367 ; the authenticity of this work is disputed though it would seem on insufficient grounds ; see the *Admonitio Maurorum*, *ibid.*, 1363, also G. Bardy in the *Rev. Biblique*, October, 1932, p. 527.

[3] *Ibid.*, 2.

from the Church, even though, owing to the fact that their crimes are hidden or no occasion for separation has presented itself, they may still remain members of the Church so far as external behaviour goes.[1]

With the Luciferians, for example, says Augustine, we do not quarrel on the score that they repeat Baptism, but

> because they have cut themselves off from Unity and prefer to be called 'Luciferians' rather than 'Catholics.' . . . No one can fail to realize how abominable a crime they commit in being content thus to be cut off from the Root. Moreover, a particularly detestable feature in their case is that they quarrel with the Catholic Church on a point which is peculiarly characteristic of Catholic holiness. For what more striking feature than its mercy can we find in the Catholic Church? She, like a true Mother, would never disdainfully trample on her erring children nor be slow to pardon them when they repent. With good reason does Peter, out of all the Apostles, act in the person of the Catholic Church—for to this Church were the Keys of the Kingdom of Heaven given when bestowed on Peter. Hence when the Lord asked him: 'Lovest thou Me?' that question was put to all. The Catholic Church, then, ought readily to pardon her children when they repent and are re-established in devotion to her; for to Peter himself, who acted in her person, pardon was extended when (his faith) wavered in the sea, when through carnal affection he wanted the Lord not to suffer, when with his sword he cut off the servant's ear, when he thrice denied the Lord Himself, when he failed through superstitious dissimulation; but, repentant and re-established, he came at last to the glory of the Lord's Passion.[2]

The same holds good, Augustine insists, of the Cathari

> who deny that the Church can forgive all sins. Miserable people! For while in Peter they refuse to recognize the Rock, and will not believe that to the Church were committed the keys of the Kingdom of Heaven, they have let those keys fall from their own hands.[3]

[1] *Ibid.*
[2] *De Agone Christiano*, 32.
[3] *Ibid.*, 33.

Technically speaking, schism, as Augustine well knew, is not heresy. A man may—in theory at least—be in schism yet hold no heretical tenets.[1] But in practice schism inevitably shades off into heresy: 'You are a schismatic by your sacrilegious separation,' Augustine writes to Gaudentius in the final stages of the controversy, 'but you are a heretic by your sacrilegious teachings'[2]; again, to Petilian: 'Our whole object is to preserve you from becoming heretics . . . for your disagreement with us and your divided state make you heretics; whereas peace and unity make you Catholics.'[3] This is set out by St. Thomas with his usual succinctness:—

Heresy is of its very nature opposed to faith, but schism is of its very nature opposed to the unity of ecclesiastical charity. Since, then, faith and charity are different virtues—although whoso lacks faith lacks charity—so, too, schism and heresy are distinct vices; and while a man who is a heretic is also a schismatic, the converse is not true. Hence St. Jerome says: 'This is, I deem, the difference between heresy and schism: heresy means holding some perverted dogma, schism means separation from the Church.' Yet [continues St. Thomas] just as loss of charity leads to loss of faith . . . so, too, schism leads to heresy; and his conclusion is that: 'At first sight and from one angle schism appears to be a different thing from heresy; yet there is no schism which does not fashion for itself some heresy—for example, that it is right to have left the Church.'[4]

Schism, then, though distinct in nature from heresy, yet tends of its very nature to become heresy since it is in effect the repudiation of a cardinal doctrine, namely the indivisible Unity of the Church. Further still, as the bond of union with the head is relaxed and the principle of authority lost sight of, men cease to feel that it is a grievous thing to hold views condemned by that authority, with the inevitable result that the schismatic's hold on the very Creeds themselves becomes tenuous. Moreover, no sect or schismatic body can afford to

[1] St. Optatus, *De Schismate Donatistarum*, i. 10.
[2] *Contra Gaudentium*, ii. 10.
[3] *Contra Litt. Petiliani*, ii. 219.
[4] *Summa Theol.* 2da. 2dae. xxxix. 1 *ad* 3m.

stand alone ; it instinctively seeks support from others similarly situated, as it were from companions in misfortune. So with the Donatists : they turned to the East and to the Arians ; when, for example, St. Augustine had a discussion with Fortunius, the Donatist Bishop of Tubersicum, the latter tried to palm off on him the *Acts* of the Arian Council held at Philippolis as being the genuine *Acts* of Sardica, arguing that since the name of Donatus of Carthage figured there as one of the signatories he must have been in communion with the Universal Church.[1] As a matter of fact, however, the Donatists were, as Augustine acknowledges, but little infected by the Arian heresy.[2]

IX—THE DONATISTS RESENTED BEING CALLED 'HERETICS'

As Augustine's influence waxed and that of the schismatics waned, the latter grew more and more anxious about their position, and as their fears intensified so did the controversy become more and more acrimonious. The Bishop of Hippo never had any doubt but that schismatics were *ipso facto* heretics, at least by implication. But as the various points under discussion came up again and again he was able to formulate his ideas with growing clearness and precision. Naturally enough the Donatists bitterly resented being dubbed 'heretics' ; they insisted that they were only schismatics, people who had been compelled for conscience' sake to separate from the main body of the Church ; they even seem to have gloried in the idea of being in schism, as though—in modern parlance—there was something rather 'chic' in being a 'schismatic' ! But the real cause for anxiety on their part lay in the fact that if they were to be regarded as heretics, then they fell automatically under the penal laws enacted against such people by, among others, Valens, Gratian and Valentinian, in A.D. 376, and in 381 and 389 ; they particularly feared the Edict of Valentinian, Theodosius and Arcadius, June, 392, which imposed a fine of £10 in gold on all heretics ; this was followed in July by a threat of deportation, while a series of similar

[1] *Ep.* xlvi. 6 ; *Contra Cresconium,* iii. 38.
[2] *Sermo,* clxxxiii. 9 ; *Ep.* clxxxv. 1.

Edicts appeared in 394–395 forbidding heretics to ordain or to teach and comprising under the term 'heretics' all who assailed the Catholic faith.[1]

The Donatist, Parmenian, who succeeded Donatus the Great in the See of Carthage in A.D. 355, and against whom St. Optatus had published his *De Schismate Donatistarum*, had emphatically protested against the term 'heretic' being applied to his 'party,'[2] and the same protest was voiced by Cresconius the 'Grammarian' who resented Augustine's attack on Petilian, the Donatist Bishop of Cirta, and especially the way in which Augustine had therein spoken of 'the sacrilegious error of these heretics,'[3] referring, of course, to the Donatists. 'You only have "heresy,"' Cresconius urged, 'when people follow divergent views,' and he instanced the Arians, Manichaeans and Novatians. He then ventured to formulate definitions of heresy and schism: 'heresy,' he said, 'is a sect of men who follow different opinions; schism is the separation between men who hold the same opinions. . . . Between us, then, for whom Christ died and rose again, there is but one religion and the same Sacraments; there is no diversity in our Christian observances. Ours, then, is a schism, not a heresy.'[4]

Augustine fully conceded the distinction. It was no new one, for it had appeared in a Council held by St. Cyprian in A.D. 256,[5] and Augustine himself had repeatedly used it, though with much greater precision than as formulated by Cresconius. In a letter to Emeritus, the Donatist Bishop of Caesarea, somewhere between A.D. 406 and 411, Augustine had said: "The only thing we urge against you is your crime of schism which

[1] See below, *Toleration*, pp. 299 ff, and *Codex Theodosianus*, ed. Mommsen and Meyer, XVI. v. 4, 7, 19, 21, 22, 24–28, 30, and iv. 3–6. In fact, as St. Augustine declares, the Donatists were driven to claim the title 'Catholic' precisely in order to escape the penalties inflicted on heretics. 'You said you were "Catholics" so that you might escape those very laws which you yourselves made use of to oppress others.' *Contra Litt. Petiliani*, ii. 132.

[2] Optatus, *l.c.*, i. 10.

[3] *Contra Cresconium*, i. 1.

[4] *Ibid.*, ii. 4.

[5] Lucian, Bishop of Castrum Galbae, gave it as his opinion that 'heretics clearly do not hold the full confession of the faith; nor can schismatics be considered spiritual physicians, since by quitting the One Church they have put themselves in foolish opposition,' quoted by St. Augustine, *De Baptismo contra Donatistas*, vi. 22.

you have turned into a heresy by wickedly persevering in it.'[1] But he now took up Cresconius' challenge and with pitiless logic drove home this definition in a way that must have made the unlucky 'Grammaticus' wince:

As a matter of fact [says Augustine] I rather prefer that distinction between heresy and schism which regards the latter as a recent split in a community owing to some difference of opinion—for, of course, you cannot have a schism unless those who cause it adhere to divergent opinions—whereas *heresy is a schism grown old.* But why should I labour this point when the definition you have offered me is such a priceless gift that if you and yours will agree to stand by it I would prefer to call you schismatics rather than heretics. For if people who make a schism have one and the same religion, the same Sacraments and the same Christian observances as those from whom they have separated, then that you should re-baptize (people who go over to you) becomes still more deserving of condemnation; for if your religion, Sacraments and Christian observances are the same as ours, there can be no room for a different Baptism. . . . Moreover, you certainly are heretics from the very fact that you remain in your schism which has grown old . . . and assuredly you are guilty of sacrilegious error when you not only cut yourselves off from Christian Unity but do a wrong to, and cut yourselves off from, the Christian Sacraments which, on your supposition, are identical with ours.[2]

'Heresy is a schism grown old!' Here you have the crystallized formula, one tacitly endorsed by St. Thomas, as we have seen. Yet on this Paul Monceaux, than whom no one has made a more profound study of Donatism, makes the strange comment:

Explication curieuse, mais de circonstance, et dont Augustin lui-même ne pouvait être satisfait. Elle s'accordait mal avec

[1] *Ep.* lxxxvii. 4. How consistently Augustine held to this opinion may be gauged from a series of statements covering the years A.D. 400–417: *Ep.* lxi. 1, cxli. 5, clxxxv. 1; *Contra Faustum*, xx. 3; *Contra Gaudentium*, ii. 10; *De Baptismo contra Donatistas*, i. 2–3; *Sermones*, ccl. 2, clxxxiii. 9, ccl. 2, cclxx. 7; *De Unico Baptismo*, 4; *Contra Litt. Petiliani*, ii. 164; *Enarr.* i. 1 *on* Ps. x., ii. 28 *on* Ps. xxi., etc.
[2] *Contra Cresconium*, ii. 9–10.

la réalité, avec les faits, notamment avec les édits d'union : car l'union directe, sans rétractations des doctrines, eût été sacrilège ou impossible, si le schisme des Donatistes avait été vraiment une hérésie. Augustin le savait bien ; et, dans la suite, pour amadouer les dissidents, il ne devait pas craindre de leur répéter encore qui'ils étaient séparés seulement de l'Eglise par le schisme. Mais il raisonnait içi en politique, qui voulait justifier à tout prix l'assimilation prononcée par la loi, et qui, par surcroit, voulait expliquer son propre changement de tactique.

But surely by coming over to the Church these converted Donatists were *ipso facto* surrendering the sole heretical tenet here alleged against them, namely that it was lawful to continue in schism ?

Monceaux continues :

S'il tenait tant à transformer en hérétiques les schismatiques africains, c'est qu'il commençait à désespérer d'arriver au but par les moyens pacifiques, et que l'hérésie tombait sous le coup de la loi, de lois multiples et sévéres.

This change, then, M. Monceaux regards as due to the series of deceptions Augustine had experienced, to the way in which his hopes had been repeatedly dashed. Once more :

C'est vers l'année 400 que l'on saisit la transition : non pas encore d'une politique de liberté à une politique de contrainte, mais d'un principe à l'autre . . . il affirmait que ce recours légitime était utile, parfois nécessaire.[1]

But Augustine had repeatedly drawn the same distinction : ' Schism, unless I am mistaken, means that men think the same and follow the same rites as others ; but they prefer to split up the congregation. Whereas a sect means that its followers think very differently from the rest and have set up for themselves a very different form of Divine worship.' [2]

[1] *Histoire littéraire de l'Afrique*, vii. 221–223.

[2] See above, p. 285, note [1]. *Contra Faustum*, xx. 3, *c*. A.D. 400 ; *cf. De Unitate*, 55 ; *Contra Epistolam Parmeniani*, i. 16 ; *Contra Litt. Petiliani*, ii. 184 ; *Ep*. li. 3.

X—THE DONATISTS CLAIMED TO BE 'CATHOLICS'

The Donatists, of course, claimed to be 'Catholics.'[1] But to substantiate this claim they had perforce to shut their eyes to the derivation of the word.

> You fancy [Augustine writes to Vincent the Rogatist] that you have said something very clever when you explain the term 'Catholic' as meaning, not the being in communion with the 'Orbis terrarum,' but the keeping of all God's commandments and the possession of all the Sacraments. You thereby seem to suggest that we rely on the term 'Catholic' when we wish to point to the Church spread throughout all nations; whereas what we rely on is God's promise and the number of patent prophecies emanating from the Truth Itself, though I agree, of course, that the Church may also be justly termed 'Catholic' on the ground that it really does hold to that entire body of truth of which some shreds are discoverable in the various species of heresies.[2]

This notion that 'Catholicism' meant the possession of all the Sacraments was dear to the Donatists. At the Conference of A.D. 411, St. Augustine had insisted that 'the Christians of Africa are not only called but really are "Catholics," since, by being in communion (with the Orbis terrarum) they prove how truly "Catholic" they are. For "Catholon," he said, means "according to the whole," whereas people separated from the whole and merely contending for a part broken off from the whole can lay no claim to that title.'[3] To this Gaudentius, the Donatist Bishop of Thamugadi, at once retorted: 'These people fancy the term "Catholic" refers to Provinces or Nationalities, whereas it really means what is plenished with all the Sacraments, something perfect and without spot; it has nothing whatever to do with Nationalities.'[4]

[1] A claim made, of course, by all heretics and schismatics, as Augustine is never weary of pointing out, *e.g.*, *Contra Epistolam Manichaei quam vocant 'Fundamenti,'* 5; *De Vera Religione*, 12; *De Utilitate credendi*, 19; *cf.* Lactantius, *Instituta*, iv. 30.

[2] *Ep.* xciii. 23. The Rogatists were so called from one Rogatus, who had seceded from the main Donatist body 'brevissimum frustum de frusto majore praecisum' as Augustine describes the sect. *Ibid.*, 24.

[3] *Collatio*, iii. 101; *P.L.* xi. 1381.

[4] *Ibid.*, 102; *cf. Breviculus Collationis*, iii. 3.

Before the Conference closed, the Donatists made one last despairing effort to secure for themselves the coveted title 'Catholic.' For when the President, Marcellinus, had had occasion to rule that 'the Catholic party must explain' some point, Adeodatus, a Donatist Bishop, shouted out: 'Write down that it is we who are the Catholics'; an outburst which drew from Fortunatianus, the Catholic Bishop of Cirta, the crushing retort that their own Donatist Archbishop, Primianus, had himself, in the official mandate delivered to the Donatist delegates to the Conference, styled them 'Donatists' and not 'Catholics.'[1]

Nine years later, when explaining to Augustine that he and his flock were preparing to commit suicide in preference to surrendering their church and property to the Catholics as the Imperial Edict of A.D. 412 had decreed, the same Gaudentius endeavoured to show from St. Cyprian that the Donatists really were Catholics. We do not know what passages from the great African he adduced in support of his statement, but St. Augustine retorted by quoting from St. Cyprian's *De Unitate Ecclesiae*:

> The Church, filled with light from the Lord, spreads its rays throughout the world; and though that light remains one, it is everywhere diffused, while the one body remains unbroken. With teeming fertility that tree sends its branches throughout the whole earth; that Church pours forth its spreading streams in ever-widening circles; its Head is One; its origin one; its Mother one.[2]

Can the schismatics, asks Augustine, point to anything in their sect corresponding to that historic fact? Yet, he adds, in those words of Cyprian, 'you have the reason why the Church is in Greek called "Catholic." For ὅλον in Greek means "whole" or "universal," whence "throughout the whole" is in Greek καθ'ὅλον, whence, too, the term "Catholic." If you knew that, why did you pretend you did not?'[3]

The wily ex-lawyer, Petilian, failed to come to the support of his colleague, Gaudentius, when he made the above-quoted

[1] *Collatio*, iii. 122–123.
[2] *De Unitate Ecclesiae*, 5; *cf. ibid.*, 7 and 11.
[3] *Contra Gaudentium*, ii. 2.

statement about the meaning of the term 'Catholic.' Perhaps this was because on this very point he had had a taste of Augustine's logic some years previously. For when he had assailed the Catholic Church in a species of Encyclical, and Augustine had answered it,[1] Petilian attempted to refute him, and tried to argue that it was the so-called 'Catholics' who were in schism, not the Donatists: 'If,' he said, 'you insist that it is you who hold to the Catholic Church, I must remind you that "catholicos" means in Greek "the only one" or "the whole." Now you are not in the "whole," for you have become a "party."'[2] To this Augustine had replied: 'My knowledge of Greek is scanty, practically nil; but even so it is no impertinence on my part to say that I know that ὅλον does not mean "one" but "whole," and that καθ'ὅλον means "according to the whole," whence the Catholic Church derives its title. To call yourselves "Catholics" is almost the same as calling me 'Petilian,' a statement I could not refute except by laughing because I should presume you were joking, or by grieving at what I could only take to be a proof that you had gone mad. Indeed the latter seems the only possible solution; for I can see you are not joking. So I must leave it to you.'[3] To this Petilian had no answer save abuse.[4]

We have unfortunately no remains of the Donatist anti-Catholic literature save what can be reconstructed from Augustine's replies to their assaults. But their attempts at meeting the challenge thrown down by the Catholics included such statements as that the Catholics were not 'the Church,' urging in support that the 'Orbis terrarum' was not in communion with the Catholic body in N. Africa, a patent falsehood[5]; also that there were parts of the world in which there were no Catholics; they insisted, too, that the patent existence of various sects showed that the boasted Catholic Unity was

[1] *Contra Litt. Petiliani*, i. See the *Admonitio Maurorum* in *P.L.* xliii. 243.
[2] *Contra Litt. Petiliani*, ii. 90.
[3] *Ibid.*, 91. See also *Ep.* xciii. 22–23, 49; *Sermons* ccxxxviii. 3, ccxliii. 2; *Enarr.* i. 19 *on* Ps. cxlvii.; *Tract.* xcviii. 5 and cxviii. 4 *in Joann.*, etc.
[4] *Ibid.*, 92; *cf. De Unitate*, 3; *Tract.* cxviii. 4 *in Joann.*
[5] *Ep.* xliv.; *Contra Cresconium*, iii. 70; *Contra Litt. Petiliani*, i. 25; *De Unitate*, 11.

somewhat fictitious.[1] And while conceding that they themselves were but ' a little flock,' they urged that very fact as an argument in their favour : the truth, they said, lies more often with the few than the many.[2] While conceding, too, that they had quitted the present-day Church, they maintained that they had only done so because it was degenerate ; while they themselves were one with the primitive Church.[3] Similarly, while allowing that the earlier Roman Pontiffs had been good men, they maintained that the same could not be said of the later ones ; they referred, of course, to such Popes as Miltiades, Marcellus, Marcellinus and Silvester whom Petilian roundly accused of having connived at the surrender of copies of the Scriptures during the Diocletian persecution.[4] Curiously enough the Donatists never seem to have thought of condemning such Pontiffs as Liberius or Damasus.[5] Then, again, besides insisting on their claim to an exclusive sanctity, they pointed to their so-called martyrs,[6] and maintained that the fact that they had to undergo persecution was a proof that theirs was the true Church in accordance with our Lord's promise : ' Blessed are they that suffer persecution,' to which Augustine, of course, replied by pointing to the omitted words ' for justice sake.' [7] Finally they protested that, whatever the theoretical aspects of the case, the fact remained that all true Christian faith and practice was to be found in their ' party.' [8]

XI—THE DONATISTS HAVE NO REAL UNDERSTANDING OF WHAT IS MEANT BY THE ' CHURCH '

The real difficulty with these unhappy people, who had not originated but inherited their schismatical state, and who were —many of them at least—in good faith, was their inability to grasp the real meaning and character of the Church. St. Optatus had, long before St. Augustine, pointed this out :

[1] *Contra Cresconium*, iii.
[2] *Ibid.*, iii. ; *Contra Gaudentium*, ii.
[3] *Contra Litt. Petiliani*, ii. 202.
[4] *Ibid.*, ; *cf. De Unico Baptismo*, 27.
[5] *Contra Julianum*, vi.
[6] See *Epp*. xlviii. 9, lxxvi. 4, lxxxvii. 2, lxxxix. 1, clxxxv. 16 ; *Sermons*, cxxxviii. 2–3, cclxxxv. 2, cccxxv. 2 ; Optatus, *l.c.*, ii. 14.
[7] *Ep*. cviii. 14 ; *ad Donatistas, post Collationem*, 21–23.
[8] *Enarr*. ii. 14 *on* Ps. lxxxviii.

'Christ,' he said, 'is the Bridegroom of one Church only . . . and when in the *Canticle of Canticles* He praises one only He thereby condemns the rest; for apart from that one Church, the true Catholic Church, other churches may indeed be reckoned as such by heretics, but they are not really so.' And Optatus concludes: 'You have no true conception of what is meant by the "Church," hence your state of confusion.'[1] Optatus readily conceded, however, that being 'schismatics,' that is, 'cut off' from the original trunk of the Church, the Donatists had certain affinities with the parent stem, that, in fact, all that was worth having in such separated bodies was derived from the Church: 'You and we,' he says, 'share the same Church-practices, read the same Lessons, have the same faith, the same mysteries of the faith, the same Sacraments'[2]; and, as he says elsewhere, the same Scriptures.[3] As for the Sacraments: 'those which you have not changed are approved by us in proportion as you have them.'[4] Cresconius, the Donatist Grammarian, had, as we have seen, strongly insisted on the same fact: 'We have one and the same religion and the same Sacraments; there are no differences in our Christian observances.'[5] But while in fundamental agreement with him on this point St. Augustine feels bound to say: 'I cannot entirely agree with what you say, for you have most certainly not got the Christian Church, neither have you Christian charity.'[6] He goes on to point out that when converted and repentant 'the first thing they will receive is the Church herself, and with her, peace, charity and unity through the Holy Spirit who is the true and invisible source of the Church.'[7]

It must be confessed that such failure to realize the true nature of the Church was only to be expected when people had been living in schism for close upon one hundred years. 'You can meet with people to-day,' says Augustine, 'a person for instance, born in the Donatist sect, who though he knows

[1] *De Schismate Donatistarum*, i. 10.
[2] *Ibid.*, v. 1.
[3] St. Optatus, *l.c.*, vi. 2; St. Augustine, *Ep.* xliii. 21, cxxix. 3; *Sermo*, iv. 31.
[4] *Ep.* lxxxvii. 9.
[5] *Contra Cresconium*, ii. 12.
[6] *Ibid.*
[7] *Ibid.*, 19.

where he was born, yet has no idea what the Church is.'[1] It must be remembered, too, that the schismatics formed the large majority of the Christians ; the Catholic body had only just began to raise up its head after long years of suppression ; their churches and property were in the hands of the alien party who regarded the insignificant Catholic flock with contempt. So much was this the case that a Donatist Bishop of Hippo could with impunity forbid the bakers in the town to bake for Catholics[2] ; and when, through the influence of St. Augustine, the Catholics began to grow in prestige and numbers the Donatists could, without any fear of interference by the civil authorities, send their roving bands of Circumcellions to ravage and burn their farms, even to murder their helpless owners.[3] Moreover, as the number of those who passed over to the Catholic Church steadily grew, the Donatist leaders took alarm. They disregarded all efforts made to secure public or even private conferences between the representatives of the two sides[4] ; they persistently threw dust in the eyes of their people and evaded their inconvenient enquiries by subterfuges and evasive answers[5] ; 'they even say to their flocks : "Do not speak to the Catholics, have nothing to do with them, do not listen to them."'[6] Hence Augustine felt bound to state again and again that it was not the populace but their leaders who were in fault[7] since these latter deliberately kept their flocks in ignorance of what they in their inmost hearts knew to be the truth[8] ; hence he urges the Donatist laity to insist on an answer from their leaders on the points at issue[9] ; but the latter, he fears, will, unfortunately, pretend not to know the facts of the case[10] :—

[1] *Enarr.* ii. 8 *on* Ps. xxx.
[2] *Contra Litt. Petiliani*, ii. 184.
[3] See *Epp.* xliii. 24, lxxxviii. 1, cv. 3–4 ; *Contra Cresconium*, iii. 69, iv. 60–61, 77 ; *Contra Litt. Petiliani*, i. 26, ii. 201 ; *Vita*, 10 ; *Breviculus Collationis*, iii. 21–22 ; *Enarr.* ii. 18 *on* Ps. xxxvi.
[4] *Contra Ep. Parmeniani*, i. 11, 14, 17–18 ; *Epp.* xxiii. 6–7, xxxiii. 2, xliii. 1, 6, 24, cviii. 14, cxli. 2–3, etc.
[5] *Contra Cresconium*, iii. 26–27, 37–38, 67 ; *Enarr.* i. 3 *on* Ps. xlix. ; *Ep.* lxxvi. 4, etc.
[6] *Enarr.* i. 9 *on* Ps. lvii.
[7] *De Unitate*, 9 ; *Enarr.* i. 39 *on* Ps. lxvii.
[8] *Contra Cresconium*, iii. 26–27, 37–38, 67 ; *Enarr.* i. 3 *on* Ps. xlix.
[9] *Ep.* lxxvi. 4.
[10] *Contra Cresconium*, ii. 22–23, iv. 9 ; *Contra Litt. Petiliani*, ii. 184.

We have [he laments] made them our enemies because we tell them the truth, because we have been afraid to hold our tongues, because we have dreaded ceasing to urge them. . . . For they themselves see what harm they do ; they see that they have no reply to what we say. They throw dust in the eyes of illiterate folk.[1]

Truth to tell, the Donatists, especially their Bishops, hated the Catholic Church—because they feared her. They seem to have suffered from an ' inferiority complex.'

XII—SCHISMATICS AND THE SACRAMENTS

The Holy Spirit is the ' soul ' of the Church ; ' the Holy Spirit alone vivifies its body,' [2] ' its own peculiar but invisible source is the Holy Spirit,' [3] the Sacraments and the Creed are but the outward shell ; ' unless nourished by the inward Spirit it is idle to boast of the shell.' [4] The veritable schismatic, then, the man who is deliberately outside what he knows to be the True Church, cannot possess the Holy Spirit. Therefore even if the Sacraments of the sect to which he belongs are validly administered—that is by validly ordained ministers—they cannot possess that informing Holy Spirit who alone renders them efficacious.

Hence Augustine concludes a detailed discussion of St. Paul's analogy between the Church and the human body by asking :

What else does ' to expire ' mean but to lose the ' spirit ' ? If a limb be amputated, does the spirit follow it ? Yet you can still recognize it as a limb ; it is still a finger, a hand, an arm, an ear ; in other words, it retains, even apart from the body, its form or figure—but not its life. So, too, with a man separated from the Church. If you ask for his Sacraments you find them. Baptism ? He has it ; the Creed ? He has it.

[1] *De Baptismo contra Donatistas*, ii. 16 ; *cf. Contra Cresconium*, iii. 26–27, 37–38, 67.
[2] *Ep.* clxxxv. 46.
[3] *Contra Cresconium*, ii. 19.
[4] *Sermon* cclxviii. 2.

The form or figure, then, is there ; but, unless 'informed' by the spirit, in vain do you boast of the figure.' [1]

Similarly, when preaching on the Holy Spirit at Pentecost : 'Those are wholly strangers to this gift of the Holy Spirit who hate the bond of peace, who hold not to the society of Unity.' [2] Hence he is not afraid to say that even in the case of good-living people :

The mere fact of their separation condemns them [3] ; you are one with us in Baptism, in Creed and in the rest of the Lord's Sacraments ; but in the spirit of Unity and the bond of Peace, and lastly in the Catholic Church itself, you are not one with us. If you would but receive these latter, then the aforementioned Sacraments would not come to you afresh ; though they would then begin to avail you.[4]

The Donatist position on the validity and—as they illogically concluded—the licitness of the Sacraments conferred in their sect was, to repeat, simply stated in Cresconius' formula : 'You and we have one and the same religion, one and the same Sacraments ; there is no difference in our Christian observances.' These false notions, assiduously promulgated by the Donatists in self-defence, compelled the Bishop of Hippo to formulate the Church's position on the point. His teaching is stern and uncompromising in its logic ; but the gentle Augustine would never have expressed it as he did, and repeated it, too, year by year with insistence, had he not been convinced of its truth. In reply, then, to the above statement by Cresconius, he said :

I cannot quite agree to that statement. For since you have not got the Christian Church you cannot have charity. I frankly recognize your Sacraments, but at the same time I reprobate and repudiate the contradiction whereby you repudiate among Catholics the very Sacraments which you have retained in your schism. The Church unreservedly

[1] *Ibid.*, *cf.* cclxix. 2–3.
[2] *Sermon* cclxxi. ; *cf.* ccclix. 5.
[3] *Ep.* cviii. 20.
[4] *Ep.* xciii. 46.

acknowledges the existence among you of Sacraments which are really her own; they do not cease to be hers because they happen to be with you. Remember that with you those Sacraments are adventitious (aliena); but when the Church to which they really belong shall have received you, amended, then those Sacraments which, when merely adventitious, made for your destruction, will make for your salvation.[1]

The Donatists seem to have been unable to see the difference between a Sacrament validly and licitly administered and a Sacrament validly but illicitly administered. To them it seemed a contradiction to admit—as the Catholics always had done—the validity of their Sacraments and at the same time deny their efficacy. Hence their Bishops said openly to their flocks that if they went over to the Catholics they would have to submit to a fresh Baptism, and to their clergy that they would have to submit to a fresh Ordination; for this, they thought, was the only logical conclusion from the Catholic position. And when the Catholics taunted them with re-baptizing those who had been baptized in the Catholic fold, the Donatists retorted that the Catholics ought, if logical, to do the same.

St. Augustine repeatedly faces this question:

Both these (Baptism and Orders) are Sacraments, and therefore neither of them can be repeated in the Catholic Church. If, for example, any of their leaders come over from that sect and are for the sake of peace received after correcting their schismatical error, and if, further, it seems advisable that they should continue to exercise the same functions as before, they are not re-ordained, for their Orders remain intact, just like their Baptism. For the fault lay in their state of separation—now set right in the peace of Unity—not in the Sacraments which are everywhere the same. If, on the contrary, the Church judges it advisable that any of their Bishops who come over to the Catholic Church should not be allowed to exercise their functions, their Sacramental Orders are not taken from them, but remain intact. In the case of such Bishops, then, there follows no Imposition of hands, lest any indignity should thereby be offered to the Sacrament, not to the individual

[1] *Contra Epistolam Parmeniani*, ii. 28.

man. . . . For it is one thing not to have a Sacrament at all, another to have it to one's prejudice ; yet another to have it for one's salvation.[1]

Similarly in his formal treatise, *De Baptismo contra Donatistas :*

We do not say to schismatics : ' Do not confer Baptism,' but ' Do not confer it in schism.' Nor do we say to people who are going to be baptized by them : ' Do not receive it,' but ' Do not receive it in schism.' If, however, in a case of extreme necessity a person cannot find a Catholic from whom to receive Baptism, and if while safeguarding his Catholic peace he approaches someone who is not in Catholic Unity with the object of receiving from him what he would—had he been able—have received in Catholic Unity, then were he to depart this life we could not regard him as anything save a Catholic. Moreover, were he to recover his health and present himself in person to the Catholic body which he had never quitted in his heart, then we should not only refuse to condemn him for what he had done, but should without hesitation, and in all truthfulness praise him for it ; and this on the ground that he had all the while believed in his heart that God was present with that Church where Unity was preserved, also because he had made up his mind not to depart this life without that Sacrament of Baptism which was, he knew, God's, and not man's, wheresoever he might find it.[2]

Sacraments administered or received in a state of schism, then, were in some respect shorn of their efficacy : ' While readily admitting that schismatics have a valid Baptism, we do not allow that it avails them ; on the contrary, it harms them ' ; again, ' Unless in communion with the Church Baptism cannot avail ' ; and once more : schismatics

have to be taught that even Baptism in its integrity avails them nothing so long as they obstinately refuse to be set right. This does not mean that the integrity of their Baptism is destroyed by their perversity in refusing to be set right, nor that being set right rectifies their Baptism ; but that the moment they lay aside their bad dispositions, the Baptism they have

[1] *Contra Epistolam Parmeniani*, ii. 28.

[2] *De Baptismo contra Donatistas*, i. 3 ; *cf*. 18, iii. 19, 21 ; *Sermons* xxxvii. 27, lxxi. 32–33, cclxviii. 2, cclxix. 2–3 ; *Sermon* viii. 2–3 ; *P.L.* xlvi. 839 ; *Enarr*. ii. 19 *on* Ps. xli. ; *Ep*. lxxxvii. 9.

already received—up till then for their destruction—begins to avail for their salvation [1];

'outside the Church Baptism can be in you but it cannot avail you' 'inesse potuit, non prodesse.' [2] This last phrase is constantly on his lips [3] as a convenient summary of a doctrine which he is perpetually inculcating.[4]

Augustine wrote in the same sense against Petilian:

Without fellowship with the Church and the holy bond of Unity and the supreme gift of charity, neither he from whom an evil spirit is driven out nor he who is baptized can gain eternal life, any more than people who by reason of their fellowship with us in the Sacraments seem to be in the bosom of the Church yet by their bad lives show that they are not really so.[5]

And even more emphatically to Cresconius:

To start a schism from the Unity of Christ, or to be in schism, is an immense evil. It is absolutely impossible that Christ should be to one who is in schism the source of—I do not say his 'faith'—but of his sacrilegious error; impossible, too, that one who is in schism should have his roots planted in Christ or that Christ should be his source and his Head.[6]

Once more:

We admit the integrity of the Sacrament (of Baptism) wherever it may be found, but outside the Unity of the Church it will not avail for the irrevocable remission of our sins.[7]

[1] *De Baptismo contra Donatistas*, v. 5; *cf. Contra Litt. Petiliani*, i. 25, iii. 46; *De Unico Baptismo*, 8; *Ep.* xciii. 46.
[2] *Contra Cresconium*, iv. 76; *cf.* iii. 27.
[3] 'Dicimus Baptismum et illic esse, sed non dicimus et prodesse, imo vero dicimus et obesse,' *Contra Cresconium*, i. 27; *cf.* iii. 27, iv. 46; *De Baptismo contra Donatistas*, ii. 11, iii. 21, v. 5.
[4] *Contra Cresconium*, ii. 15, 16, 19, 42; *cf. ibid.*, i. 31, 40; *Ep.* lxxxvii. 9; *De Baptismo contra Donatistas*, i. 4, iii. 22, iv. 6, v. 5, 9; *Contra Litt. Petiliani*, i. 25, iii. 46; *De Unico Baptismo*, 8. Note especially: 'Fatemur . . . tunc ei prodesse incipere cum transit ad corpus Christi, quod est Ecclesia Dei vivi.' *Contra Cresconium*, ii. 34.
[5] *Contra Litt. Petiliani*, ii. 178.
[6] *Contra Cresconium*, iv. 26.
[7] *De Baptismo contra Donatistas*, iii. 22; *cf.* vii. 87 and *Ep.* cxli. 13.

Lastly:

The Lord's Supper (he is commenting on Luke xiv., the parable of the Great Supper) is the Unity of the Body of Christ, not only in the Sacrament of the altar, but in the bond of peace.[1]

* * * * * *

It is only when we have grasped St. Augustine's views on schism and its enormity that we can approach with unprejudiced minds the question of his attitude on Toleration.

[1] *Ep.* clxxxv. 24.

VIII

ST. AUGUSTINE 'REX PACIFICUS' OR THE MODEL OF TOLERANCE

I. The Opposite View is generally held—II. Brief History of the Donatist Schism—III. Imperial Repressive Laws up to A.D. 400—IV. African Conciliar Action, A.D. 393–401—V. St. Augustine's Letters: His Attitude on Repression, A.D. 393–402—VI. Conciliar Action, A.D. 403–404—VII. The Edict of Unity, A.D. 405; Epistles lxxxvi. and lxxxix., A.D. 405–406—VIII. Decrees issued, A.D. 407—IX. Conciliar Action, A.D. 408; Epistle xciii.—X. Imperial Decrees, A.D. 408–409; Epistle C., A.D. 408–409—XI. The Edict of Tolerance, A.D. 409; Its Withdrawal; the Conference of A.D. 411; Epistle cxxxiv.—XII. Further Decrees, A.D. 412–415; Epistle cxxxix.—XIII. Epistle clxxxv., A.D. 417; the Meeting with Emeritus, A.D. 418; Epistle cciv., A.D. 420; the Case of Gaudentius.

I—VIEWS GENERALLY HELD

The literature on the question of Toleration is, of course, immense, and much of it has, by what we may justly term the irony of events, centred round the name of St. Augustine; more especially has this been the case since the attacks of men like Theodore Beza,[1] Bayle, [2] Leibnitz [3] and Voltaire.[4] Le Clercq (Joannes Clericus or 'Pherepon') too, and Erasmus have had their share in belittling the great Doctor.[5]

A more moderate tone appears in such works as those of Havet,[6] Tanon,[7] Creighton [8] and Nickerson.[9] But such

[1] *De Haereticis a Civili Magistratu puniendis*, 1554, a translation of which into French appeared in 1560.

[2] Bayle has a treatise on 'Compelle intrare,' *Opera*, ii. pp. 1–154, 1686; this drew a reply by Brueys: *Réponse aux plaints des protestants contre les moyens que l'on emploie pout les réunir a l'Eglise*, 1686.

[3] *De la Tolérance des religions*, 1692.

[4] *Traité sur la Tolérance*, 1764.

[5] See below, pp. 318, 341–2.

[6] *L'Hérésie et le bras séculier au moyen age*, *Œuvres*, ii. 115 ff., 1881.

[7] L. Tanon, *Histoire des tribunaux de l'Inquisition de France*, 1893.

[8] *Persecution and Tolerance*, 1895.

[9] *The Inquisition: a political and military study of its establishment*, 1923.

summary pronouncements as the following from Boissier, de Cauzons and Martin need considerable qualification :

'Augustine had no mercy on the Pagans ; they had persecuted, and now it was their turn. But he hesitated about calling in the State in Religious quarrels.'[1] Similarly de Cauzons : 'he passed unconsciously from civil to religious penalties ; from disturbers of public peace to heretics.'[2] So, too, G. Martin : 'he was always in favour of forcible repression of schism ; but he did not at first hold that the laws should compel abjuration and a formal profession of faith, though after the Council of Carthage in 404 he agreed to this.'[3]

A more unfair account of St. Augustine's attitude on the subject could hardly be framed than that given by Lea :

Augustine entreats the Prefect of Africa not to put any Donatists to death because if he does so, no ecclesiastic can make complaint of them, for they will prefer to suffer death themselves rather than be the cause of it to others. Yet Augustine approved of the imperial laws which banished and fined them and deprived them of their churches and of their testamentary power, telling them that God did not wish them to perish in antagonism to Catholic unity. To constrain anyone from evil to good, he argued, was not oppression but charity ; and when the unlucky schismatics urged that no one ought to be coerced in his faith, he freely admitted it as a general principle, but added that sin and infidelity must be punished.[4]

Again : 'Even Augustin (*sic*) could see nothing to soften his heart in the enthusiastic ardour with which the Donatists endured, and even courted, martyrdom.'[5]

Yet of those same pseudo-martyrs and their supporters Augustine could say with truth : 'Corpora praecipitatorum cum honore colligunt . . . ad eorum tumulos se inebriant . . . ut se praecipitent "Deo laudes" clamant ; in ore "Deo

[1] G. Boissier, *La Fin du Paganisme*, 2nd ed., i., p. 71.

[2] de Cauzons, *Histoire de l'Inquisition en France*, Paris, 1909, i., p. 179.

[3] J. Martin, *S. Augustin*, 1st ed., 1901, p. 379 ; 2nd ed., 1907.

[4] H. C. Lea, *History of the Inquisition*, i. 214, and he refers to *Ep*. c., as Donatum, *Ep*. cxxxix., ad Marcellinum, *Ep*. cv. 13, *Enchir*. 72, *Contra Litt. Petil*., ii., 83 ; see below, p. 347.

[5] *Ibid*., i., p. 211 ; he refers to, indeed quotes, *Ep*. clxxxv. 12 and St. Cyprian, *De Unitate*, 3.

laudes," in factis Deo odibles,'[1] Again, Lea says: 'The African Church repeatedly asked the intervention of the secular arm to suppress the Donatists.'[2] A most unjust, because an unqualified, statement.

In the minds of some, then, Augustine was a relentless persecutor; others—with a fuller knowledge of the documents—deny this but maintain that he welcomed the Imperial laws when they came and, while he did not ask for them, insisted on their rigid application; others, again—while feeling that neither of the above conclusions do full justice to the facts—hold that his policy was short-sighted and regrettable. But what are the facts? We have several sources of information: the Letters of the Bishop of Hippo on the subject; the Imperial laws themselves, and the action taken by the Fathers of the African Church in the various Councils held at Carthage.

II—BRIEF HISTORY OF THE SCHISM

To arrive at a just estimate of the Imperial and Ecclesiastical action against the Donatists we must bear in mind the history of the schism.[3] Formally inaugurated in A.D. 311, though really originating in the disgraceful scenes at Cirta during the Diocletian Persecution, 303–305, when Silvanus was simoniacally elected to that See, the schism had gone from strength to strength despite Constantine's thunderings against it in his Edict addressed to Dracilian, September 1, 326, when he had declared that 'the privileges granted for the sake of religion are only intended for those who adhere to the Catholic law. We mean heretics and schismatics not only not to profit by the said privileges but to be restrained and made subject to various disabilities.'[4] From that date until the accession of Julian the Apostate in A.D. 361 the schismatics

[1] *Sermo de Natali S. Cypriani, inter Sermones inediti*, ed. Morin, 1930.

[2] Lea, *l.c.*, i. 2–5, and he cites in proof of this, *Ep*. clxxxv. 7, *Contra Crescon.*, iii. 46, 47; *Vita*, xii; see below, pp. 310, ff.

[3] See above, pp. 254 ff.; *cf. Epp*. xxiii., civ. 4; *De Civitate Dei*, XXII., viii. 6.

[4] Privilegia quae contemplatione religionis indulta sunt, Catholicae tantum legis observatoribus prodesse oportet. Haereticos autem atque schismaticos non solum ab his privilegiis alienos esse volumus sed etiam diversis muneribus constringi et subjici. *Codex Theodosianus*, XVI., v. 1.

had been in partial, if not complete, disfavour, and their leaders had been sent into exile.[1]

But when the policy of Julian restored them to favour they returned in triumph and commenced a series of persecutions of the Catholics to which Augustine makes feeling reference on many occasions.[2] With the appearance of St. Optatus' polemic in A.D. 366, or three years after the death of Julian, and still more with the appearance of St. Augustine on the scene when, as Possidius wrote : ' Africa began to lift up its head,' [3] the scene changed and the schismatics found that they were no longer to have things all their own way. But the change was a very gradual one despite the efforts of such champions as Optatus and Augustine. The latter had preached innumerable sermons against the schism and by the end of the century had published treatise after treatise in which he set forth the facts of the case ; but he found that he was up against a company of ' passive resisters ' in the Donatist Bishops who were in possession and who tacitly ignored his efforts so long as they could, and who soon passed from passive resistance to active persecution of the Catholic body.

From the very outset of his campaign Augustine had realized that the only effective way to end the schism was for the opposing parties to meet and discuss the situation. But to all his advances the Donatists turned a deaf ear.[4] Meanwhile the harm done was immense. Families were divided : ' unhappy folk who all believe in Christ, who at home share their food in common, cannot meet at Christ's table.' [5] The pagans openly jeered at the spectacle of a ' divided ' Christendom,[6] and not unnaturally refused to become Christians. Moreover, the schismatics had never hesitated to appeal to the civil authorities against the Catholics whenever occasion offered.[7] It was

[1] St. Augustine, *Ep.* cv. 9.
[2] *Contra Julianum Pelagianum*, iii. 5.
[3] *Vita*, 7.
[4] *Epp.* xxiii. 6–7, xxxiii. 2, etc.
[5] *Epp.*, xxiii. 5, xxxiii. 5, cviii. 17–18 ; St. Optatus, *De Schismate Donatistarum*, iii. 10 ; St. Augustine, *Sermo*, xlvi. 15.
[6] *Sermo*, xlvii. 18, 28 ; *De Utilitate Jejunii*, 10 ; *Civitate Dei*, XVIII., li. 2.
[7] For the whole series of these appeals, see *Ep.* cv. 8–9 ; *cp. Epp.* liii. 5, lxxxviii. 5, clxxxv. 7 ; *Breviculus Collationis*, iii. 26 ; *Ad Donatistas post Collationem*, 55 ; *Contra Cresconium*, iii. 34, 67–68, 81, 83, etc.

owing to an infamous appeal of this sort to Julian the Apostate in A.D. 361 that they secured their return from a well-merited exile and succeeded in dispossessing the Catholics.[1] True, they had already begun to share the fate of all schismatics and were rapidly splitting up into factions which were all at one another's throats: 'tiny crumbs broken off from a bigger crumb,' as Augustine dubbed them.[2] But this process of attrition could only be a slow one. Further, there were the marauding bands of the Circumcellions, who pillaged and murdered as they chose; whose immoralities [3] and drunken habits [4] were notorious, who made a cult of suicide,[5] and of whom the Donatists made use in their assaults on the Catholics.[6] The Donatist Bishops denied this emphatically, but Optatus had long before pointed out that the schismatic Bishops were the real leaders of these bands,[7] and Augustine himself constantly speaks of the Circumcellions and the Donatist clerics as combined forces.[8] With their cry of 'Deo laudes' [9] which struck fear into everyone who heard it, with their clubs which they christened 'Israels,' [10] and with their swords [11] they made the countryside a place of horror. The Government seemed paralysed, and though repeated laws were passed against them, these remained a dead letter.[12] Quite, apart, too, from their share in the enormities perpetrated by these brigands who in Augustine's phrase 'live like robbers, die like Circumcellions,

[1] *Ep.* xciii. 12, cv. 9; *Contra Litt. Petiliani*, ii. 205. For the atrocities they committed on their return, see St. Optatus, *l.c.*, ii. 17.

[2] *Ep.* xciii. 24, clxxxv. 32; *Enarr.* ii. 26 *on* Ps. xxi., ii. 20 *on* Ps. xxxvi.

[3] See for peculiarly gross instances of this, *Contra Litt. Petiliani*, iii. 37, 40, 43, also ii. 61, 195.

[4] *Sermo*, xvii. 2–3, xlvii. 17, cli. 4, ccxxv. 4, cclii. 4; *Epp.* xxii. 6, xxix. 5, xciii. 48–49; *Contra Litt. Petiliani*, ii. 78, 93, 174, 195, 233; *Contra Cresconium*, iv. 77, etc.

[5] *Epp.* xliii. 24, clxxiii., clxxxv. 12, cciv. 2; *Contra Litt. Petiliani*, ii. 197.

[6] *Contra Litt. Petiliani*, ii. 110; *cp. Ep.* xliii. 24.

[7] *De Schismate Donatistarum*, ii. 18–19, iii. 4.

[8] *Ep.* c.; *Contra Cresconium*, iv. 60; *Contra Litt. Petiliani*, ii. 184.

[9] *Contra Litt. Petiliani*, ii. 146, 186; the Catholic war-cry was 'Deo gratias,' *Enarr.* i. 6 *on* Ps. cxxxii.

[10] *Enarr.* i. 5 *on* Ps. x., i. 11 *on* Ps. xcv.; *Contra Litt. Petiliani*, ii. 110, 144, 195, 222.

[11] *Ibid.*, 222.

[12] *Ep.* lxxxviii. 8. This was particularly the case after the death of Stilicho, August 23, 408, when the Donatists maintained that his laws immediately lapsed.

and are venerated as martyrs,'[1] many of the Donatist leaders had been guilty of the gravest enormities,[2] were notorious drunkards and flagrantly immoral. Some of them had actually committed murder and gloried in the fact.[3] They had threatened Augustine with the same fate,[4] and but for an interposition of Providence he would have fallen into the ambush prepared for him.[5]

Such threats of course left the Bishop unmoved. His personal welfare was of little moment. What did concern him deeply was the spiritual welfare of his flock. We have already seen how strong were his feelings regarding the nature and effect of schism.[6] For one thing it blinded people ; in particular it had blinded the Donatist leaders : 'This is blindness of heart,' he tells Petilian, 'and if you do not recognize this blindness in yourselves, that is a still greater blindness.'[7] Hence the obstinacy [8] of the Donatist Bishops, an obstinacy which led them deliberately to keep their people in ignorance and to lie of set purpose when the Maximianist case should have compelled them to face certain awkward facts.[9] Who could blame the populace when they heard their Bishops stoutly maintaining that the Catholics were wrong? Why should they even dream that they were lying? A patent instance of this had been the case of Cresconius, the schoolmaster. He had a certain amount of education, and was overwhelmed by Augustine's ruthless dissection of the Maximianist secession from the main Donatist body and the illogical steps taken by the schismatic Bishops to rectify the scandal.[10]

[1] *Ep.* lxxxviii. 8, cv. 5 ; *Contra Litt. Petiliani*, ii. 184.

[2] For their treatment of the Catholic clergy, see *De Unico Baptismo*, 19 ; for their desecration of churches, altars and chalices, St. Optatus, *l.c.*, ii. 20, 24, 26, vi. 1, 5 ; of nuns, *ibid.*, ii. 19 ; and for their general brutality, see *Epp.* xxxv. 4, lxxxviii. 8, cv. 1, 4, 17, clxxxv. 15 ; *Contra Cresconium*, iii. 50. So awful were these atrocities that at the Council of Carthage held in September, 401, a letter was read from Pope Anastasius bidding the African Bishops publish them abroad, Labbe, *Concilia*, ii. 1651.

[3] *Contra Gaudentium*, i. 25–26.

[4] *Ep.* cv. 1, A.D. 409.

[5] *Vita*, Auctore Possido, xii.

[6] See pp. 255 ff, above.

[7] *Contra Litt. Petiliani*, ii. 152.

[8] *Epp.* lxxxix. 6, xciii. 1.

[9] *Contra Cresconium*, iii. 26–27, 37–38, 67.

[10] *Contra Cresconium*, ii. 17, iii. 17–18, iv. 35–37, 41–42, 46, 48, 51.

He applied to the Donatist leaders for a true statement of the facts and then proceeded, as he thought, to pulverize Augustine. Naturally enough it never entered into the mind of Cresconius that his Bishops were deliberately lying.[1] But this, as Augustine proceeded to show, was what they had always done from the very outset of the schism.[2]

After all, who shall blame them? Their very livelihood depended on their retaining their hold on their people. For they were intruders, and they knew it well. The churches and property they held were not theirs, but belonged to the Catholics whom they had ousted,[3] from whom they had filched it by their disgraceful appeal to the apostate Julian when they hailed him as 'one with whom justice alone held sway.'[4] Disestablishment faced them; for the Emperor Honorius had in March, A.D. 400, ordered that their infamous appeal to Julian should be fixed up in conspicuous places as a warning to the Donatists and a pledge of goodwill towards the Catholics. These leaders, then, were fighting against the known truth: 'You know,' says Augustine, 'where the truth lies, but owing to your hateful obstinacy you are fighting against a truth perfectly clear to you.'[5] Yet once more: it was not so much with these blind guides that Augustine was concerned as with the people yet halting between two sides; he is weary, he says, 'of ingenious arguments on a question which concerns the people'[6] and which is keeping people out of the Church[7] and endangering their eternal salvation; for deliberately to remain in schism means hell in the end.[8]

[1] *Ibid.*, iii. 58, 35–37, 42, iv. 44, 46, 48–49; *Ep.* clxxxv. 32; *Sermo*, xlvii. 22.

[2] *Contra Litt. Petiliani*, ii. 184, 203, 205, 208, 224.

[3] *Ep.* xciii. 12, cv. 9, cviii. 18; *Contra Litt. Petiliani*, ii. 224; St. Optatus, *l.c.*, ii. 16.

[4] Arcadius et Honorius. Hadriano, Praef. Praet: Rescribtum quod Donatistae a Juliano tunc principe impetrasse dicuntur, propositi programmate celeberrimis in locis volumus anteferri et gesta, quibus est hujusmodi allegatio inserta, subnecti, quo omnibus innotescat et Catholicae confidentia stabilita constantia et Donatistarum desperatio fucata perfidia. Ravenna, February 25, 405 Stilichone et Aurelio Conss; *Codex Theodosianus*, ed. Mommsen, i. 867; *cf. Ep.* cv.; *Enarr. on* Ps. xxxvi. 18; St. Optatus, *De Schismate Donatistarum*, ii. 16; Mansi, *Concilia*, iii. 373.

[5] *Ep.* xciii. 10.

[6] *De Unitate*, 9.

[7] *Sermo*, xlvii. 28; St. Vincent of Lerins, *Commonitorium*, 31.

[8] *Ep.* cxli. 5, clxxiii. 6.

III—IMPERIAL REPRESSIVE LAWS UP TO A.D. 400

Before examining the Imperial laws which follow we must draw attention to a feature in the case which is always overlooked by those who pretend to be scandalized at St. Augustine for urging legal action against the Donatists. They fail to realize that during the greater part of the fourth century Imperial fulminations against heresies of every kind were almost the order of the day, and that a whole series of enactments against the Manichees,[1] the Eunomians,[2] sectarians in general [3] and renegade Catholics [4] appear in the *Theodosian Code*, also against the Novatians, Priscillianists, Arians and Jews. Imperial action, then, against the Donatists was only to be expected, indeed had all along been taken by the civil authorities independently of the Church. The Ecclesiastical authorities, however, were very slow indeed to endorse such action, and, as we shall see, did their best to modify it.

In the face, then, of such scenes of violence as those depicted above, the Imperial authorities could not be expected to keep silence. In A.D. 365 Valentinian and Valens enacted a penalty for making a Christian act as porter in a heathen temple.[5] In the years 373 and 377 appeared decrees against the practice of re-baptizing.[6] In 376 (perhaps 378) heretical meetings were to be suppressed 'in quibus falso religionis obtentu altaria locarentur,' [7] an echo perhaps of Optatus' 'altare contra

[1] March 2, 372, May 8, 381, March 31, 382, July 21, 383, May 17, 399, February 12, 405—where they are coupled with the Donatists ; *Cod. Theod.*, XVI. v. 3, 7, 9, 10, 35, 38. For these Edicts and Decrees from A.D. 377 onwards, see *Ep.* li.

[2] January 10, 381, July 19, 381, July 25, 383, December 3, 383, January 21, 384, May 4, 389, June 20, 394, March 13, 395, April 21, 396, April 22 (?), 396, March 4, 398, July 6, 399 ; *ibid.*, v. 6, 8, 11, 12, 13, 17, 23, 25, 31, 32, 34, 36.

[3] June 4, 388, June 24, 388, July 9, 394, July 26, 394, March 13, 30, 395. It is not impossible that the three last-named were due to the Donatist and Maximianist troubles of 393–394 ; *ibid.*, v. 15.

[4] May 2, 391, May 20, 383, May 21, 383, May 11, 391, March 23, 396, April 7, 426. We have to be careful to distinguish between 'Law,' ἐπικρίμα, and 'Edict,' διαταγμα, the latter denoting rather a declaration of policy which a new Governor is going to adopt, see Cicero, *In Verrem*, i. 42 ; *cf.* Roussel in *Syria*, 1934, 46.

[5] *Codex Theodosianus*, XVI. i.

[6] *Ibid.*, vi. 1–2 ; *cf. P.L.* xi. 1180–1181, cliii. 805–806 ; Augustine, *Epp.* xxvii. 8, cv. 12.

[7] *Ibid.*, v. 4.

altare.'[1] Between A.D. 381 and 396 some dozen pronouncements against as many different kinds of heretics appeared, their meetings were forbidden, nor were they to be allowed to make wills or testaments, while magistrates negligent in carrying out these enactments were to be punished.[2]

In A.D. 392 an even more stringent decree was published by Valentinian, Theodosius and Arcadius: people ordaining or receiving Orders among heretics were to be fined £10 in gold, the place of meeting was to lapse to the Treasury, its hirer to pay £10 in gold, or—if he pleaded poverty—to be flogged, while heretics claiming to be ministers of religion were to be fined the same sum of £10.[3] In July of that year, 392, the same Emperors pronounced sentence of exile against disturbers of Catholic peace,[4] while in 394 they renewed their sentence against Ordinations, adding a prohibition against heretical Confirmation.[5] In the July of that same year they went even further: 'Lest heretics should in their crazy folly continue to perpetrate (the enormities) which they are found to have committed they are to be forbidden to teach or to learn their false precepts, nor are their Bishops to dare to promulgate a faith which they have not got or to ordain ministers which themselves are not.'[6] In the following year Arcadius and Honorius forbade all heretical meetings and prohibited any of their leaders from being styled 'bishops'[7]; these Emperors renewed, too, all the enactments of their father, Theodosius, against heretics,[8] and in the following September they declared that 'under the heading "heretic" and subject

[1] Optatus, *l.c.*, i. 15, 19; Augustine, *Ep.* xliii. 4, 17, 24. The Donatists washed down altars which had been used by Catholics, Optatus, *l.c.*, vi. 1; Augustine, *Ep.* cviii. 14; *Psalmus contra Partem Donati*, 17, 24, etc.

[2] *Codex Theodosianus*, XVI. v. 6–36.

[3] *Ibid.*, v. 21; *P.L.*, xi. 1192. This fine of £10 in gold only affected such Donatists as indulged in acts of sabotage, and was well known to everyone, *Epp.* lxvi. 1, lxxxviii. 7, cv. 4; *Contra Epistolam Parmeniani*, i. 10; it was first imposed by Theodosius the Elder; *cf. Contra Cresconium*, iii. 51; *Ep.* clxxxv. 25; *cf. P.L.* xi. 806.

[4] *Ibid.*, iv. 4. 'Deportatione dignus est, qui nec lege generali admonitus nec competentia emendatus et fidem Catholicam turbat et populum'; edicts to the same effect were published January 29, September 11, November 19, 404.

[5] *Ibid.*, v. 22.

[6] *Ibid.*, v. 24.

[7] *Ibid.*, v. 26.

[8] *Ibid.*, v. 25.

to all the penalties enacted against them, come all such as are found deviating from the norm and rule of the Catholic religion even on minor points '[1]; in the November they insist that no heretic is to be allowed to serve in any law office.[2]

Pallu de Lessert points out that the penalty of 'interdiction' was very rare in Africa; that that of 'relegation'—when a man was allowed, however, to keep his patrimony—was almost unknown there: that exile was rarely inflicted[3]; but that 'deportation' was a common punishment for the Donatists.[4] It was certainly the ordinary procedure under the Vandals, see Victor Vitensis, *De Persecutione Vandalica*.[5]

In A.D. 398 Arcadius and Honorius declared that:

> If anyone shall have committed such a sacrilege as to break into Catholic churches, deal violently with the clergy and ministers, or treat the service or the place itself injuriously, as, from letters received from the rulers, magistrates, officials and those notaries known as 'Stationarii,' we learn has been done, such a one must be brought before the chief authorities, etc. The Governor of the Province must realize that those convicted of or pleading guilty to such injuries done to the priests and ministers of the Catholic Church and to the service and place itself must suffer capital punishment. If, however, the violence of the crowd is such that because they are armed or the local situation renders it difficult for the civil authorities to act even with the assistance of the magistrates and the landed proprietors, then letters should be sent by the magistrates in Africa to the Count of Africa asking for military assistance, and at the same time informing him of this law, lest people guilty of such crimes should go unpunished. Given at Milan, April 25, 398.[6]

This pronouncement directly affected the Donatists, and when, on February 26, 400, there appeared a declaration rescinding

[1] *Ibid.*, v. 28. 'Haereticorum vocabulo continentur et latis adversus eos sanctionibus debent succumbere, qui levi argumento judicio Catholicae religionis et tramite detecti fuerint deviare.'

[2] *Ibid.*, v. 29.

[3] But *cf. Ep.* cci. 1.

[4] See the Decree of November 11, 408, *Codex Theodos.*, XVI. v. 52, 54.

[5] Pallu de Lessert, *Fastes de la Numidie*, ii., p. 120. See, too, de Cauzons, *L'Inquisition*, I., ch. ii., art. iii.: *Punition de l'hérétique par l'empire romain*.

[6] Given in *P.L.* xliii. 807–808; *Cod. Theod.*, XVI. ii. 31.

the Act whereby Julian the Apostate had handed over to them the Catholic churches in Africa,[1] they must have felt that their long reign was nearing its end. That Imperial notification declared that 'The rescript which the Donatists are said to have asked for at the hands of Julian then reigning is to be replaced by the accompanying Notice which is to be set up in frequented places, and the Records containing that alleged proceeding is to be attached to it so that all may realize the firm confidence and constancy of the Catholics and the despair and lying perfidy of the Donatists, February 26, 400.' [2]

The above declaration by Arcadius and Honorius is notable for the threat of 'capital punishment' for such as are 'convicted or who plead guilty to injuries done to the priests and ministers of the Catholic Church.' Yet in the Edict of Union of February 12, 405, there is no mention of capital punishment, though 'still more severe measures' are threatened.[3] In A.D. 412 Honorius and Theodosius declare that only the 'wonted Imperial clemency saves them from capital punishment, and that that same clemency will not be shown if they persist in their crimes,' [4] and further on in the same decree 'they must realize that those convicted or pleading guilty will be liable to capital punishment.' [5] St. Augustine seems, too, to endorse the idea that the Donatists were liable to capital punishment when he writes to Donatus the Proconsul in A.D. 408–409, begging him not to condemn them to death.[6] So, too, he says that the Council held at Carthage in 404 deprecated capital punishment for them.[7] Yet writing against Petilian, *c.* A.D. 400, he says: 'I can recall no Imperial law condemning you to death,' [8] and again: 'no royal law orders

[1] In their appeal to Julian they had dared to speak of the Apostate as one 'with whom justice alone finds place,' words on which Augustine remarks that this means 'calling Julian's idolatry and apostasy "justice,"' *Contra Litt. Petiliani*, ii. 203; *cf.* Optatus, *l.c.*, ii. 16. The appeal is given in *Cod. Theodos. De Haer.* 37; *cf. P.L.* xliii. 802.

[2] *Cod. Theodos.* XVI. v. 37; *cf. Ep.* xciii. 12; *Contra Gaudentium*, i. 24; *Enarr.* ii. 18 *on* Ps. xxxvi.

[3] See p. 329, below.

[4] *Constitutiones Sirmondianae*, xiv., given in Haenel's ed. of the *Codex Theodos.*, p. 468.

[5] *Codex Theodos.*, XVI. ii. 31, Haenel, p. 1500.

[6] *Ep.* c.

[7] *Ep.* clxxxv. 26; *Contra Cresconium*, iii. 55, 57.

[8] *Contra Litt. Petiliani*, ii. 46.

your death ' [1]; and he repeats this more emphatically in A.D. 420, when he says to Dulcitius the Tribune: 'No law gives you the right to use the sword ("jus gladii") against them; in none of the Imperial constitutions which you have to carry out is it anywhere laid down that they are to be put to death.' [2] In fact he challenges Petilian to prove that any Donatist has been slain.[3] Whatever the explanation of this seeming contradiction Tanon is certainly right when he says: 'The Theodosian Code meant death for heretics, but we have no proof of its systematic and continued application at this time.' [4]

IV—AFRICAN CONCILIAR ACTION, A.D. 393–401

To appreciate aright the next series of Decrees we must discover what line of action the African Bishops in their frequent Councils thought would be advisable in this crisis. The famous Council of Hippo was held in the autumn of A.D. 393, and Augustine, not yet a Bishop, was present as the preacher. He had already inaugurated his campaign against the schism, and the Church in Africa felt that in him they had found the champion of their cause. Canon xxxvii. of that Council runs:

> As for the Donatists, it was agreed to consult our Brethren and fellow-Priests Siricius and Simplicianus [5] about those baptized as such simply when children, and ask whether a step which they had not taken on their own initiative, but which was solely due to their parents' errors, should, on their being converted to the Church through God's good purpose, preclude them from promotion to the ministry of the altar.[6]

This decision was motived in part by the lack of clergy which the depleted African Church was then experiencing, but Rome and Milan apparently failed to appreciate the difficulties and

[1] *Ibid.*, 191.
[2] *Ep.* cciv. 3.
[3] *Contra Litt. Petiliani*, ii. 46.
[4] *Histoire des tribunaux de l'Inquisition de France*, 1893, p. 128.
[5] Siricius was Bishop of Rome, Simplicianus had succeeded St. Ambrose at Milan.
[6] Mansi, *Concilia*, iii. 924–925; given in *P.L.* xi. 1192 and xliii. 807.

did not endorse the decision arrived at at Carthage. But the case was serious. Consequently the African Fathers renewed their request nine years later, when they met at Carthage in June, 401. Their statement is of interest: Aurelius the Primate proposed that one of their number should be sent over

to point out to Anastasius, Bishop of the Apostolic See, and to Venerius of Milan, our grave difficulties, complaints and needs; for those Sees have forbidden what we are now going to propose. We want them, therefore, to suggest some way in which to meet our common danger. For such is the dearth of clergy, such the plight of many churches, that it is hard to find even an illiterate deacon, let alone officials of higher degree; for if even deacons are not easy to find, still less those in higher Orders. We can no longer, then, turn a deaf ear to the daily complaints of so many half-starved flocks; if we do not speedily discover some relief for them we shall have to give a terrible account to God for innumerable souls that are perishing; excuses will not avail us with Him.

Now in a previous Council [1] you unanimously agreed with me that men baptized as children among the Donatists, at an age, that is, when they could not realize the baneful results of their errors, but who on arriving at the use of reason have acknowledged the truth, repudiated their errors and returned to the Universal Church, and who were, therefore, in accordance with ancient practice, received by the imposition of hands, should not be debarred from admission to Orders by reason of their original error. There may be, it is true, some of their clergy who are desirous of passing over to us with their flocks,

[1] See Canon xxvii. of the *Breviarium Hipponense*: 'It was also agreed that since it had been decided in previous Councils that no Donatist should, on being received into Unity by us, be allowed to retain his clerical status, but should, for the sake of that salvation refused to no one, rank among the laity; yet such is the dearth of candidates for Orders from which the Church in Africa is suffering—some places are wholly without clergy—that, while adhering to the existing decision, exception should be made in the case of such as could be shown either never to have re-baptized or to be desirous of passing with their flocks into Catholic Communion. . . . It was agreed, however, that this point should not be settled until the Church overseas had been consulted.' Mansi, *Concilia*, iii. 924. The Ballerini questioned the authenticity of this Canon on the ground that Denis the Little, in his edition of the *Codex canonum Ecclesiae Africanae*, gives under Canon XLVII. merely the decree about Donatist children. But later the Ballerini found sufficient MS. authority for maintaining the genuineness of the Canon.

but who still cling to their Orders. . . .[1] But this point should, I think, be referred to the consideration of the brethren abovementioned, so that when they have prudently weighed our suggestion they may let us know what they think. At present we are content to ask them to agree, if they think fit, with our suggestion about ordaining those who were baptized as children.[2]

The Council next met in the September of that same year, 401. First of all the reply of 'Anastasius, the Bishop of the Roman Church,' was read :

In it he exhorted us with all the sincere solicitude of paternal and fraternal charity not to keep silence about the wicked plots of the heretical and schismatical Donatists who so grievously assail the Church in Africa. We thank God for deigning to inspire His good and holy Bishop with such care for the members of Christ's body who, though in a different part of the world, are yet compacted together in one body.

After stating that their sole preoccupation was to deal pacifically with the Donatists, the Conciliar Fathers agreed that with this end in view, local magistrates should be asked to procure reliable information concerning the Maximianists.[3]

Then, after carefully weighing everything that seemed to make for the welfare of the Church, we, with the help and inspiration of God's Holy Spirit, decided to deal as pacifically as we could with the aforesaid Donatists, even though they are, owing to their dissensions, cut off from unity with the body of the Lord. We agreed that we would do everything possible to make all those who throughout the African Provinces are entangled in that communion and sect realize in what a deplorable state of error they are. It was therefore decided to send letters from this Council to the Magistrates in Africa, asking them to extend to our common Mother the Catholic Church such help as the civil government can give in support of Episcopal authority. In other words, we asked them to use

[1] The text seems corrupt : 'qui amore honoris aut persuadent ad vitam aut retinent ad salutem.'

[2] *P.L.* xliii. 808–809.

[3] See below for their object in asking for this information.

their judicial authority and their Christian diligence to discover the precise facts in those various places where the Maximianists—who had seceded from the Donatists—had obtained possession of the basilicas, and having done so, to draw up a public record of them so as to secure the necessary accurate knowledge of the facts.

Then, since Anastasius has apparently acceded to their request about Donatist children, they ask for a further concession, namely that convert Donatist clerics may be allowed to exercise their clerical functions.

It was then decided to send letters to our Brethren and fellow-Bishops, especially to the Apostolic See now presided over by our venerable brother and colleague Anastasius, to inform him that, for the sake of the Church's peace and profit, Africa sorely needs that some concession should be made in the case of such Donatist clergy as wish, when once converted, to pass over into Catholic Unity: they should, always in accordance with the will and discretion of the Catholic Bishop of the district if he considers such a step conducive to Christian peace, be allowed to retain their clerical status. This was certainly the practice in the first days of the schism; the case of many, if not of practically all the African churches where this error started, is proof of it. Not that we desire a reversal of the decision arrived at on this point by the Church overseas; our suggestion would only apply to such as desire to pass over to the Catholic Church in such fashion that no rending [1] of unity could thence result. We think that through such men the cause of Catholic Unity would be enormously strengthened owing to the patent example of fraternal charity they would give in their own districts. The decision arrived at in the Council held overseas, namely that no one ordained in 'the party of Donatus' but now converted and wishful to pass over into the Catholic Church should be allowed to retain his clerical status, should not be allowed to stand in their way. All we want to do is to take precautions to safeguard Catholic Unity.[2]

[1] Reading 'concisio' a variant for 'compensatio.'

[2] Council of Carthage, September 12, 401. *P.L.* xliii. 809; Mansi, *Concilia*, iii. 774.

The final decision was to send preachers, armed with reliable information (see above) on the treatment meted out to the Maximianist seceders, who should preach among the Donatists and try to open the eyes of the populace to the inconsistencies of their leaders :

Finally we decided that representatives from amongst us should be sent to preach to the Donatist Bishops—where there are such—as also to the laity : that peace and unity without which we cannot attain to the salvation that is in Christ. These preachers should help people to realize that they have no just ground of complaint against the Catholic Church ; more particularly they should show them, on the written authority of the municipal records, how their own people dealt with the Maximianist seceders from their body. For herein they have a proof from heaven—if they will but see it—that those original seceders from the Church acted just as wickedly in thus seceding as they now loudly proclaim that the Maximianists have done in seceding from their own body. Yet out of that very body of separatists whom they so emphatically condemned in their plenary Council [1] they have re-admitted some, allowed them to retain their full clerical status, and have agreed to recognize the Baptisms administered by these men when in a state of condemnation and excommunication ! This fact should open their eyes to the folly of fighting against the peace of the Universal Church when they do such things for the sake of the peace of the 'party of Donatus'; the folly, too, of saying that while they themselves are not to be held contaminated when, for the sake of peace, they now enter into fellowship with people thus reinstated, yet (we) the Catholic Church—no matter how far removed she was from the scene—was contaminated by her fellowship with people whose guilt even their contemporary accusers were unable to prove.[2]

[1] The Donatist Council of Bagai, A.D. 394, here termed 'plenary' because so spoken of by the Donatists in the decree then drawn up 'universalis concilii ore veridico damnatos esse cognoscitis'; *cf. Contra Cresconium*, iii. 59, and 'plenarii concilii ore veridico,' *De Baptismo contra Donatistas*, ii. 17.

[2] Council of Carthage, September 12, 401 ; *P.L.* xliii. 810. Canon cxxiii. in the *Codex canonum Ecclesiae Africanae* runs as follows : 'If in the principal Sees any Bishop is found negligent in dealing with heretics he should be approached by zealous neighbouring Bishops who should expostulate with him and thus leave him without excuse. And if within six months of such admonition he has not—provided the decree has been promulgated in his Province—taken any steps to bring them back to Catholic Unity, then

V—ST. AUGUSTINE'S LETTERS, A.D. 393–402: HIS ATTITUDE ON REPRESSION

We have now arrived at the close of the year 401, and once more we must go back a little and examine some of St. Augustine's letters which had, prior to that date, dealt with the Donatists and the problem of civil intervention.

In his very first letter [1] on the subject, written in A.D. 393 to Maximinus, the Donatist occupant of the See of Sinitum in the district of Hippo, he invites him to a conference on the points in dispute. 'But this,' he says, 'I will not do in the presence of the military, lest any of you should fancy that I want to conduct this meeting in a hectoring fashion little besuiting a peaceful discussion. Let us meet, then, when the military are no longer on the spot so that all who listen may be convinced that I have no desire that men should be compelled to embrace any communion against their will.' [2] Later on Maximinus did embrace the Catholic faith and now remained on in his See of Sinitum as its Catholic Bishop.[3] The Catholics held him in high esteem, so much so that the Council of Carthage sent him, in A.D. 406, as a delegate to the Imperial Court of Ravenna; he also took part in the Conference of A.D. 411.[4]

The remark about not conferring while the military are on the spot shows that Augustine considered the Roman authorities as quite capable of enforcing compliance, but he was determined not to create the impression that he was relying on these latter to secure such a result.[5] The next three letters dealing with

no communication is to be held with him until he does take such steps. If the person charged with promulgating the decree has not reached that Bishop's district, the neglect must not be charged to the Bishop.'

Canon cxxiv. runs: 'If it can be shown that the Bishop lied when he maintained that he had got into communication with the heretics, whereas he patently had not done so, then he must resign his Bishopric,' Mansi, *Concilia*, iii. 822. These two Canons emanated from the Second Council of Milevis, held A.D. 416, Cap. xxv.; Mansi, iv. 333.

[1] *Ep.* xxiii.

[2] *Ibid.*, No. 7.

[3] *De Civitate Dei*, XXII. viii. 6.

[4] See *Collatio*, iii. 124–128, 141, 170–173; *P.L.* xi; *cf. Ep.* cv. 2, 4, 17.

[5] That the civil authorities are bound in duty to support religion, even to make legal enactments regarding its observance, was a principle with St. Augustine, see *Epp.* lxvi. 1, lxxxv. 7, lxxxviii. 7, lxxxix. 2, 7, cv. 5–6, cxli. 8, clxxxv. 8, 18–19, 25, etc. *De Unitate*, 55.

the Donatist difficulty contain no allusion to the civil authorities, for there was no occasion to speak of them.[1] But in another letter of the same year, 396, he remarks quite incidentally that the ordinary laws against criminals are not being enforced as they should be,[2] a complaint which had to be reiterated not only by the Ecclesiastical authorities but by the Emperors themselves.[3] The next letter is of peculiar interest as it shows clearly what was Augustine's whole attitude on the question. His Donatist *vis-à-vis* in the See of Hippo was a certain Proculeianus who, I am afraid, must be described as a shuffler. For when Valerius, Bishop of Hippo, summoned him by an appeal to the local municipality to give an account of some of his more flagrant misdeeds, Proculeianus evaded the enquiry on the plea of advanced years [4]; he similarly evaded the question of his complicity with the nefarious doings of the Circumcellions [5]; and when Augustine tried to induce him to meet him in a conference on the facts, rights and wrongs of the schism, he once more pleaded his years 'se tot annorum episcopum dicit.' [6] He was probably that Donatist Bishop who offered the quaint and exceedingly naïve explanation of the fact that the Ark was covered with pitch inside as well as out, an explanation which so tickled Augustine.[7] Among his other crimes Proculeianus had repeatedly been guilty of re-baptizing disaffected Catholics who, disliking strict discipline, had thought well to go over to the rival Bishop. Augustine had written to him to protest more than once, but getting no reply, felt driven to appeal to Eusebius, apparently the local magistrate, and, to judge by the terms Augustine uses in addressing him, a Catholic. Eusebius has up till now declined to take part in a dispute 'between Bishops,' 'but,' says Augustine, 'If he still refuses to take action, no one can blame me if I try to bring the facts home to him by publishing them officially;

[1] *Ep.* xxix. 11–12, A.D. 395, when Augustine was still only a Priest; *Epp.* xxxii.–xxxiii., A.D. 396, the first year of his Episcopate.
[2] *Ep.* xxxiv. 2: 'Cum etiam severitas legum sceleratissimis parcit.'
[3] See *Codex Theos.*, XVI. v. 40.
[4] *Epp.* lxxxviii. 6–7, cv. 3; *Contra Cresconium*, iii. 53.
[5] *Ibid.*
[6] *Ep.* xxxiv. 6.
[7] *De Unitate*, 9.

nor do I think that in a Roman city I shall be refused leave to take that course.' [1]

Appeal to the civil authorities, then, was, to Augustine's thinking, practical politics. For here were repeated instances of breaches of the Imperial law against re-Baptism, a practice explicitly condemned, A.D. 373, [2] and again in 377, [3] precisely as it had been condemned by Constantine at the outset,[4] and was later to be condemned over and over again by Honorius.[5] But, as always, Augustine had no wish to tamper with Proculeianus' conscience. We say 'as always,' for when the daughter of a certain Catholic unfortunately apostatized, became a Donatist, and even took the veil as a nun among them, and her father took strong measures to bring her to her senses, Augustine objected 'Ego feminam nisi volentem, et libero arbitrio meliora deligentem, suscipi noluissem.' [6]

Three of the most important letters date from A.D. 397–398.[7] In the former, *Ep.* xliii., Augustine enters into a detailed analysis of the history of the schism, pointing out, *inter alia*, that from its very inception the Donatists had made a practice of appealing to the civil authorities [8]; a practice in which he sees nothing blameworthy, though he deprecates the way in which they did it. What he does condemn, however, is that, despite their lamentable past history and the repeated condemnations of their schism by the Imperial authorities, 'they still continue to baptize outside the Church; so much so that they would, if they could, re-baptize the Church herself!' 'Nor,' he continues, 'are they disposed to be corrected by the

[1] 'Per codices publicos fecero,' *Ep.* xxxv. 3, A.D. 396.

[2] Ad Julianum Proc. Africae: Antistitem qui sanctitatem baptismi inlicita usurpatione geminaverit et contra instituta omnium eam gratiam iterando contaminarent, sacerdotio indignum censemus. February 20, 373; *Codex Theodosianus*, XVI. vi. 1, ed. Mommsen, i. 880, given in *P.L.* xi. 1180, xliii. 805; *cf. Ep.* cv. 9.

[3] October 17, 377, *Codex Theod.*, XVI. vi. 2.

[4] When he denounced the notion that Baptism depended for its validity on the merits of the minister conferring it, *Cod. Theodos.* XVI. vi. 2; *cf.* Augustine, *Ep.* cv. 12;

[5] February 12, 405, on the same date as the Decree of Unity, *Cod. Theod.*, XVI. vi. 5. Arcadius, Honorius and Theodosius. Edictum. February 12, 405, *Cod. Theodos.* XVI. vi. 2; also the Edict of Union of the same date, *ibid*, vi. 4; *cf. P.L.* xi. 1204, 1205, 1208.

[6] *Ep.* xxxv. 4, A.D. 396.

[7] *Epp.* xliii.–xliv. and liii.

[8] *Ep.* xliii. 4, A.D. 397–398.

temporal punishments inflicted by the regular human authorities with a view to their preservation from the eternal penalties due to such sacrileges.' [1] In these last words we have the true Augustinian mind on the subject: the 'City of God' is the only real goal of the City of this world; the authorities of the latter are only endowed with power in order that they may win for us their subjects security in our attainment of the former.

In A.D. 397–398 Augustine paid a chance visit to Fortunius, the Donatist Bishop of Tubursicum, when a pacific discussion of the state of affairs between the Catholics and the schismatics took place. Towards the close Fortunius and his entourage remarked that 'we were still ready to persecute them, and added that they would like to see how we should behave if such a persecution arose, whether we should consent to such cruelty or not. We replied that God sees our hearts—a thing they could not do—and said that it was ridiculous for them to fear anything of that sort; but that were such persecution to arise, that would be simply due to wicked people who by doing so would only become worse, and we added that even such persecution by bad Catholics would not afford us just cause for quitting the Catholic fold if it were done contrary to our wish.' [2]

On this Le Clerc calmly remarks that 'that there is good reason for doubting whether Augustine really meant what he said; he was probably speaking in oratorical fashion, for he was perfectly well aware of' the Theodosian penal laws against heretics! [3]

The next letter dealing with the Donatists, A.D. 398, does not touch on the question of the civil authorities.[4] But the series following coincides with the period of the Bishop's greatest literary activity against the schismatics; for round about A.D. 400 we have to place *Contra Epistolam Parmeniani*, *De Baptismo contra Donatistas*, as well as his first book, *Contra Litteras Petiliani*. Of *Epistles*, li.–liii., lvi.–lviii. and lxi., which fall within the years 399–401, only *Ep*. li. 3 contains any allusion to the civil authorities:

[1] *Ibid*., 21.
[2] *Ep*. xliv. 11.
[3] *Animadversione in Epistolas Sti. Augustini*, *P.L.* xlvii. 247. See R. Jenkin, *Defensio Sancti Augustini adversus J. Pherepone* (nom de plume used by Joannes Clercius) *in ejus opera Animadversiones*, 1728.
[4] *Ep*. xlix., A.D. 398.

You are always insisting that we persecute you through the civil authorities. Well, I am not now concerned with what you have deservedly brought on yourselves through your appalling sacrilege (*viz.* the schism), nor will I harp on the Christian moderation we ourselves have exhibited in your regard ; I will only ask you this : how—if persecution is a sin, as you say—do you explain the fact that you yourselves so cruelly persecuted the Maximianists,[1] actually invoking against them assistance from the magistrates sent you by those very Emperors whom our Communion begot in the Gospel ? [2]

Here, again, Augustine's mind is clear ; the civil authorities have an absolute right to intervene ; the only thing he blames is the inconsistency of the Donatists in appealing to them on their own behalf while resenting it when the same authorities are invoked against themselves.

The only reference to the civil authorities in the next series of letters [3] is the remark that the action of Crispinus, the Donatist Bishop of Calama who had re-baptized a number of people, was contrary to the 'jussio regalis,' [4] and that the Catholics could, in accordance with that decree, have taken action to make him pay the fine of £10 in gold which he had thereby incurred.[5]

The case of Crispinus was notorious, indeed characteristic of the Donatist when at bay. Augustine had written to him about the year 400 suggesting a meeting and a discussion. Crispinus seemed at first to take the suggestion to heart and to have agreed to meet Augustine [6] ; but soon afterwards he changed his mind and refused to attend the meeting which was, apparently, to be an official and public affair ; for, instead

[1] A body of Donatists who, under Maximianus, seceded from the parent-stock in A.D. 393 when in Councils held at Carthage and Cabarsussis they denounced Primianus the then Donatist Archbishop of Carthage, and even declared him deposed. The latter retorted by holding a Council of one hundred and ten Bishops at the Donatist stronghold of Bagai and condemning Maximianus as well as his twelve consecrators. When these latter still held to their Episcopal Sees and their property, the Donatist body did not hesitate to invoke the aid of the secular arm against them, appealing 'to two, and if I mistake not, three Proconsuls,' *Contra Gaudentium*, i. 54 ; see *Contra Litt. Petiliani*, i. 20, ii. 35, 45, 132 ; *Contra Cresconium*, iv. 5, 46–47 ; *De Gestis cum Emerito*, 9 ; *Epp*. xliv. 7, lxxxviii. 11, etc.

[2] *Ep*. li. 3.

[3] *Epp*. lxvi., lxix., lxx., referred to A.D. 402.

[4] *Ep*. lxvi. i.

[5] *Ibid*., 2.

[6] *Ep*. li. 1, A.D. 399–400.

of writing to Augustine to explain why he had elected to stay away, he wrote to the local magistrate in terms most insulting to the Catholic Bishop, even inserting in the municipal records a selection of Biblical texts expressive of his contempt for him.[1] This, however, only brought Crispinus into derision; all saw that he was afraid to meet Augustine.[2] A few days later, as Possidius, the Catholic occupant of the See of Calama and afterwards Augustine's biographer, was on a journey, he was brutally attacked by another Crispinus, a Donatist priest who is said to have been a relative of the Bishop Crispinus. Everybody naturally expected that Crispinus the Bishop would rebuke Crispinus the priest; in fact the municipal authorities took action against the Bishop in spite of the fact that 'the laws, though in existence, were not appealed to by us.'[3] 'This action of the municipality,' remarks Augustine, 'served rather to prove our meekness than a punishment for the Donatists' audacity.'[4] For when Crispinus was summoned before the Proconsul and, though he protested against the epithet, was proved to be a heretic and accordingly fined £10 in gold as Theodosius the Elder had enacted, through the intercession of his victim, Possidius, he was not compelled to pay the fine. Yet, despite this generosity Crispinus—to the disgust of many of his fellow-Donatists—appealed to the sons of Theodosius against the sentence, with the inevitable result, of course, that 'the party of Donatus' was officially told once more 'that they, in common with other heretics, were liable to the said penalty in gold.'[5] When on another occasion Crispinus actually went so far as forcibly to re-baptize some eighty country-folk whom he found on a property he had secured near Hippo,[6] Augustine, with extraordinary moderation, was content to say: 'If these people freely passed over to your communion, then let them hear both sides; let us have the arguments on

[1] *Contra Cresconium*, iii. 30.
[2] *Ibid.*
[3] *Ibid.*, 51, 'in manibus nostris quiescebant'; *cf. Vita*, 12.
[4] *Ibid.*
[5] *Contra Cresconium*, iii. 51. Even after his second condemnation and fine of £10 the Catholics secured the remission of his punishment; *cf. Contra Litt. Petiliani*, ii. 184; *Contra Cresconium*, iii. 50–51; *Vita*, auctore Possidio, xii.; *De Unitate*, 55; *Epp.* lxxxvii. 7, clxxxv. 25.
[6] *Contra Litt. Petiliani*, ii. 18, 228; *Ep.* lxvi. 1.

either side put into writing, signed by both of us, and then translated into Punic for them so that they may quite freely choose which side they will.' [1]

VI—CONCILIAR ACTION, A.D. 403–404

We referred above to the conversion of Maximinus, the Donatist Bishop of Sinitum. About the same time Maximianus, the Catholic Bishop of Bagai,[2] resigned his See 'in the interests of peace,' for which he received high commendation from St. Augustine. The details of the case are unknown to us, but it is probable that he was the same Maximianus of Bagai who was treated with such incredible brutality by the Donatists that Imperial Rome was roused, with the result that fresh endeavours were made to suppress them.[3] In fact their behaviour was so atrocious that Augustine, in words often repeated, felt compelled to speak of the schismatics as men 'who live like robbers, die like Circumcellions, yet are honoured as martyrs—though we nowhere read of robbers that they blind their victims.'[4]

Yet despite all these brutalities, when the African Bishops met in Council in the August of 403 and decided to appeal to the Proconsul, Septiminus, they did not—as they state plainly—ask for legislation against them, but only for the Proconsul's assistance in securing conferences between themselves and the schismatics :

We appeal to your benevolence, Septiminus, V.C., greatest of Proconsuls : The Catholic Church is suffering at the hands of the Donatists many things contrary to both Divine and human law. Were we, for the prohibition or suppression of such doings, to appeal to old or even to recent Imperial legislation on the subject, the said 'party' would have no reason to complain. For they well know that, though having no similar law to appeal to, they have themselves striven to secure from

[1] *Ep.* lxvi. 2, A.D. 402.

[2] 'Vagai,' *Ep.* lxix. 1, perhaps a misreading for Bagai ; see the somewhat amusing confusion between the two names at the Conference of A.D. 411, *Collatio*, i. 179–180.

[3] *Contra Cresconium*, iii. 47, where the whole story is told, not without a quaint touch.

[4] *Epp.* lxxxviii. 8, xciii. 48, cv. 5 ; *Contra Epistolam Petiliani*, ii. 184.

the local magistrates the ejection of the Maximianists from their property and their Sees because these same Maximianists had seceded from their main body. But we, for the sake of that charity whereby we are Christians, and with a view to their salvation and our own reputation, would, rather than take a similar line of action, prefer gently to admonish them so that they may upon reflection come to a sense of their error. If, however, they fancy truth is on their side, then let them uphold it, not by employing the crazy violence of the Circumcellions—with resulting destruction of public tranquillity—but rather by peaceful and rational discussion.

Since, then, we are anxious to admonish them on this point through the medium of the city magistrates and those in adjacent districts, we beg Your Excellency bid these latter provide us with copies of the local records and also arrange that the Donatists may be duly summoned to a conference such as we suggest. If you grant this request we shall owe Your Excellency a debt of gratitude before God. Given by all the Bishops of the Catholic Faith at the Council assembled at Carthage in the Consulships of Theodosius PP. Aug., and Rumoridus V.C. at Carthage, the Ides of September.[1]

To this appeal Septiminus, V.C. Proconsul, on September 13, 403, replied: For the sake of the peace of the Empire permission is granted to the Bishops of the venerable law (the Catholic religion) in all districts to collect the records; but they must pay the expenses of such magistrates as in out of the way places justly ask for it. May the result of thus bringing things out into the open be the due preservation of the law and the destruction of superstition.

Returning to the Council, for we have anticipated, Bishop Aurelius then said:

I think the decision we have come to in this discussion should be ratified by insertion in the Ecclesiastical Records. Now you decided unanimously that each of us in his own city, either independently or in conjunction with the neighbouring Bishop, should, by approaching the magistrates or representative men, invite the chief Donatists to a conference. That, I think, should be published.

[1] August 23, 403; *P.L.* xliii. 811.

To this all the Bishops answered :

We agree ; we have all subscribed to that. And we ask your Reverence to sign in the name of us all the letters to be sent from the Council to the magistrates.

Aurelius replied :

If you all agree, then let the formula for thus inviting the Donatists be read out so that we may all adhere to the same form of procedure. To this all agreed, and Laetus the notary read out the following formula :

The Bishop of the Catholic Church (Aurelius) said :

We beg your Worship [1] to have this Commission which we have obtained from the authority of this great See [2] read out, inserted in the Records, and put into execution by Your Worship. When it has been thus read and incorporated in the Records, let the Bishop of (the local) Catholic Church then say (to the magistrate of the locality) : ' Kindly agree to listen to this injunction which is to be brought by Your Worship to the attention of the Donatists, have it inserted in your Records, draw the attention of the Donatists to it, and enter the reply to it in your Records.' Then follows the formula of invitation to the Donatists to a conference with the Catholics :
As delegates authorized by our Catholic Council, and anxious for your conversion, we invite you to a conference; for we cannot but remember the charity of Christ, who said : ' Blessed are the peace-makers, for they shall be called the children of God,' who also by His Prophet admonished us that even to such as decline to be termed our Brethren we ought to say ' Ye are our Brethren.' Do not, then, despise this kindly invitation of ours, for it springs from charity. If you feel that the truth does in any sense lie with you, then do not hesitate

[1] ' Gravitas,' it is a question of the local magistrate to whom the Bishop of the place is to address himself.

[2] ' De auctoritate illius amplissimae sedis,' not the Roman See as Baronius thought (*ad* ann. 403) but the seat of the Proconsul in Africa, Septiminus, to whom the Council of Carthage had addressed its petition for permission to apply to the local magistrates who were to draw up the *Acta* of the contemplated proceedings in the various districts. The term ' illustrissima sedes ' is used of the Proconsular residence in the Conference of A.D. 411, ' eorum gestorum, id est proconsularium et illustrissimae sedis,' *Collatio*, III. 167, or ' gesta in sede illustrium,' *ibid*., 170.

to say so ; but summon a meeting and entrust your case to delegates chosen from amongst yourselves. We will do the same and will choose delegates to meet yours at some convenient time and place for the peaceful discussion of the points that divide our respective Communions. Thus in time this long-standing dispute (error) may by the blessing of God be closed and thus weak souls and ignorant men will not, through men's enmity, perish in sacrilegious schism.

If you will receive this offer in a fraternal spirit the light of truth will speedily dawn : but if you refuse, then your distrust of your own cause will be patent.[1]

This courteous invitation to a conference on the real grounds of the separation marked a distinct step in the negotiations. To secure such a meeting had been Augustine's aim from the outset. Had the Donatists met him half-way on this point a solution should—but for the vagaries of human nature—have easily been found. But the schismatics simply disregarded the invitation, and another eight years were to elapse before the contending parties met ; even then the Donatists only came because they were compelled to do so by an Imperial Rescript. Nor can we read the decisions of the Council given above without being conscious of the spirit of true charity which characterized all these proceedings. There is no suggestion of force ; no question of an appeal for civil intervention, but just the contrary. And the irony of it is that the dominating mind throughout all these Conciliar meetings is that of Augustine of Hippo—the so-called arch-persecutor !

Yet what a problem he had to face ! Unquestionably the most influential citizen in Hippo, he exercised a paramount authority, and all manner of cases were brought before his episcopal court.[2] But it was a delicate matter for him, or any other Bishop, to appeal to the secular arm for help against the criminal propensities of the schismatics. Though perfectly justified in doing so had he been a layman, could he do so as a Bishop ? Moreover, it was by no means easy to establish the guilt of the Donatist leaders. For, when taxed with the

[1] The Council of Carthage, August 25, 403 ; Canon 59 ; in the collection of African Synods, Canon xcii. ; Mansi, *Concilia*, iii. 792 ; given in *P.L.* xliii. 810–811.

[2] *Vita*, 19 ; *Retract*. ii. 21, 37 ; *Sermon* cccii. 17.

horrors perpetrated by the Circumcellions, they simply shrugged their shoulders and denied all responsibility, though everybody was well aware of their complicity in these outrages.[1] Then, again, it was not, at first sight, so easy to bring the Donatists as such under any Imperial law. Technically schismatics, was it feasible to bring them under the law which condemned heretics ? Could it be argued that no one could long remain in schism without thereby becoming *ipso facto* a heretic ? [2]

Augustine has no doubt whatever about the right of the State to intervene in the organization of religious affairs.[3] According to Roman notions Church and State were always regarded as one ; the conversion of Constantine had only meant a change from one religion to another.[4] The Donatists themselves, as Augustine keeps reminding them,[5] had not only been the first to appeal to the State authorities when at the outset of the schism they appealed to Constantine against Caecilian,[6] but they had done so all through their history, notoriously so in their appeal to the apostate Julian [7] ; even more illogically when asking the civil authorities to support them in their endeavours to evict from their Sees the Maximianists who had seceded from their own ' party.' [8]

Over and over again during the Conference of A.D. 411 did Augustine acknowledge that the Catholics had asked for that meeting, also that they had asked for the intervention of the civil authorities.[9] For he had always felt that there were but two alternative methods for ending the schism : (*a*) preaching the truth of the Catholic claims, and, when possible, holding conferences between the Catholics and the schismatics, or (*b*) appealing to the secular authorities. But the Donatists persistently evaded all attempts at getting them to a meeting,[10]

[1] *Contra Litt. Petiliani*, ii. 110 ; *Contra Epistolam Parmeniani*, i. 17 ; *Ep*. xliii. 24.

[2] *Epp*. lxi. 1, lxxxvii. 4, clxxxv. 25 ; *Retract*. ii. 5.

[3] *Contra Epistolam Parmeniani*, i. 13–16 ; *Contra Litt. Petiliani*, ii. 203.

[4] See P. Monceaux, *Histoire littéraire de L'Afrique*, vii. 217.

[5] *Contra Epistolam Parmeniani*, i. 15.

[6] *Breviculus Collationis*, iii. 14 ; *Ep*. xliii. 19, etc.

[7] *Contra Litt. Petiliani*, ii. 203, etc.

[8] *Contra Epistolam Parmeniani*, i. 16 ; *Ep*. clxxxv. 6.

[9] *Collatio*, i. 4, iii. 52, 90, 160 ; *Breviculus Collationis*, iii. 23 ; *Ep*. xciii. 17.

[10] *Post Collationem*, 1 ; *Breviculus*, *Prol*., and i. 11.

and had instead rendered themselves obnoxious to the civil authorities by their repeated atrocities. It was this last-named factor in the case which, in Augustine's eyes, alone justified the Catholics in appealing to the Imperial court for help. Had the Donatists not been criminals, in many instances even murderers, he would have continued to appeal to their better sense by the methods he had employed for so many years.[1] Though slow, that method was sure and had already produced immense results. Unfortunately, the schismatics had, by their continued violence, rendered such pacific methods insufficient.

These constantly recurring scenes of violence, arson, rapine, even murder, were the dominating fact which the African Bishops had perforce to envisage when they met in the next Council, June, 404. For the outrages then perpetrated by the Donatists had now reached such a pitch that the Fathers felt bound to appeal to the Imperial authorities for help, but they are careful to explain in detail what kind of assistance they need. Their endeavour to secure a conference with the schismatic leaders has met with contemptuous refusals and renewed acts of violence, and only the civil authorities can, they say, protect the Church from this. But on no account would they have military assistance. All they would ask is that Donatists convicted of such enormities be precluded from making or profiting by testamentary dispositions. Finally, they decide to send two representatives to state their case before the Imperial Court.

Augustine, so far as we are aware, made no demur to this Conciliar decision to apply to the Donatists the Imperial legislation debarring them from making or profiting by wills. He seems to have felt that it was not for him to go against his colleagues on this point.[2] Yet this was a terribly severe enactment and we cannot wonder that the schismatics did all they could to evade it: 'How many lawyers have you not consulted, what frauds have you not contemplated in order to get your wills validated despite the Imperial decree denying their validity!'[3]

Definite steps, however, had to be taken. So:

[1] *Ep.* xciii. 17, clxxxv. 16.
[2] *Ep.* xciii. 18.
[3] *Sermon* xlvii. 22.

" In the reign of the glorious Honorius, Aug. Consul VI, the XVIth Kal. of June, at Carthage, in the Basilica of the Second Region. In this Council Theasius and Evodius undertook an embassy against the Donatists : the following Instructions furnished them were inserted in the *Acts* :

Instructions given to the Brethren, Theasius and Evodius, legates sent by the Council of Carthage to the glorious and God-fearing Princes :

When they shall, with the Lord's assistance, have entered the Imperial Presence they shall explain that in accordance with the Council held in the previous year the Donatists had been summoned by a municipal procedure wherein it was explained to them that if they had any real confidence in their claims they would choose suitable delegates from their own body and hold a peaceful conference with us and that they need not hesitate to set forth in the spirit of Christian meekness the truth they held to. By such a conference, moreover, the sincerity of the Catholics, so conspicuous in the past, would be made clear even to people who only opposed them through ignorance or obstinacy.

But, unnerved by lack of confidence in their own case, the Donatists hardly dared make any reply. Since, then, we Bishops have done our part in peaceful fashion, and since the Donatists, unable to contradict the truth, have resorted to atrocious deeds of violence, laying ambushes for many of the Bishops and Clergy, not to speak of the laity, sacking some churches and trying to do the same with others, it is for the Imperial clemency to discover how the Catholic Church, which bore them in Christ and fed them with her solid faith, is to be protected from their assaults. For these headstrong people may, by the terror they inspire in these times of religious war, prevail over people whom they were unable to corrupt by more seductive methods. For the hateful hordes of Circumcellions are notorious ; and the Donatists make use of them, despite laws against them such as have been repeatedly promulgated by former religious-minded Princes. We could—and that with the support of the Bible—demand military protection against them as St. Paul did against the criminals conspiring against him, see the faithful narrative in the *Acts of the Apostles*. But all we ask is that some adequate protection be afforded to the officials of the Catholic churches in the various cities, also to the landed proprietors round about. The legates should also ask that the law emanating from Theodosius of glorious memory, the father of the present illustrious Princes, the law imposing a fine of £10 on heretics conferring or receiving Orders,[1] as well as on proprietors permitting them to hold their meetings on their premises,[2] should now be put in force against people whose machinations have driven the Catholics to lay this information. The thought of eternal punishment has not hitherto made them give up their schismatical or heretical perversity, but the fear of the penalties suggested may perhaps lead them to do so.

The delegates should further ask that the law prohibiting heretics from making or profiting by donations or wills [3] may be renewed so as to prevent people who blindly persist in the errors of the Donatists from inheriting as well as from making wills. At the same time such as, from a desire for unity and peace, are willing to put themselves right, should, despite this law, be able to inherit anything that may have come to them in this way while yet in a state of heresy. This latter concession, however, should not apply to people who make up their minds to pass over to the Catholics merely through dread of this law; for it is to be feared that such will be joining Catholic Unity not so much out of dread of God's judgment as for the sake of worldly convenience. And beyond all this we need the protection of the officials in every Province.

Finally, our delegates have full authority to make what arrangements they shall deem expedient for the good of the Church, and we all agreed that letters should be sent by us to the Emperors and the chief officials to testify that the said delegates have gone to the Court with our full consent. As it would be a protracted business for each of us to sign this letter with our separate signatures we ask you, Aurelius, to sign for us all. When this was agreed on, Aurelius, Bishop of Carthage, said: 'I, Aurelius, Bishop of Carthage, agreed to this decision and signed it.' The rest of the Bishops, too, agreed. Letters are also to be sent to the local magistrates asking that until the Lord grant a safe return to our delegates they would arrange for the governors of cities and the landed proprietors to protect the Catholic Church."[4]

[1] A.D. 392 and 394; *cf. Cod. Theodos.* XVI. v. 6 and 25, ed. Mommsen.
[2] A.D. 392 and 395; *Cod. Theodos.* XVI. v. 6 and 26.
[3] See *Sermon* xlvii. 22; *Ep.* xciii. 19.
[4] Council of Carthage, June 26, 404, given in *P.L.* xliii. 811–813.

VII—THE EDICT OF UNITY, A.D. 405; EPP. LXXXVI. AND LXXXIX., A.D. 405–406

These acts of successive African Councils produced their effect, for in A.D. 405 came what might almost be described as a hurricane of decrees from the Imperial court. The first of these, commonly known as the Edict of Union,[1] is dated February 12, 405:

Arcadius, Honorius et Theodosius. Edictum.

Nemo Manichaeum, nemo Donatistam, qui praecipue, ut comperimus, furere non desistunt, in memoriam revocat. Una sit catholica veneratio, una salus sit, trinitatis par sibique congruens sanctitas expetatur. Quod si quis audeat interdictis sese inlicitisque miscere, et praeteritorum innumerabilium constitutorum et legis nuper a mansuetudine nostrae prolatae laqueos non evadat et si turbae forte convenerint, seditionis concitatos aculeos acrioris commotionis non dubitet exserendos.

Dat. prid. Id. Feb. Ravennae. Stilichone ii et Anthemio conss. (Feb. 12, 405.)[2]

'Let no one so much as name a Manichaean nor a Donatist; these latter, so we learn, do not cease to rave. Catholic worship must be one, Catholic salvation one. Let due reverence be shown to the Holy Trinity. If, however, anyone shall dare to mix himself up with these forbidden and unlawful things he must not be allowed to escape the force of the innumerable previous Edicts on this point nor the law recently enacted by our clemency; and if perchance mobs should gather, let them be in no doubt but that the thorns of sedition will be rooted up by still more severe measures. Given the day before the Ides of February at Ravenna, Stilicho for the second time and Anthemius, Consuls (Feb. 12, A.D. 405).'[2]

There followed a Decree complementary to the Edict of Union of February 12, 405; in this it is laid down that the

[1] It is so termed in the Council of Carthage, June 13, 407: 'legem Imperatorum de Unitate latam,' see below, p. 340. P. Monceaux, *Histoire Littéraire de l'Afrique*, p. 124, speaks of a previous Edict of Union in A.D. 347, but this seems to be a misunderstanding; at the Council held in 348 the then Archbishop, Gratus, merely talks of the Imperial good wishes; *cf.* the same author's *Histoire de la littérature chrétienne de l'Afrique du nord*, iv. 35.

[2] *Cod. Theodos.* XVI. v. 38, ed. Mommsen and Meyer, i. 867; *P.L.* xi. 1204, xliii. 445–446. For this Edict of Union see *Epp.* lxxxvii. 7–8, lxxxviii. 5–10, lxxxix. 1, xciii. 1, xcvii. 2–4, c. 1–2, cv. 2–3, cviii. 14, clxxxv. 26; *Contra Cresconium*, iii. 45, iv. 55.

penalties against heretics are to apply to the Donatists ' since they incur it by the mere fact of belonging to the party of Donatus.' [1]

Monceaux says that the Council of June, 404, asked the Emperor to say that the Donatists were heretics and that the Edict of Union agreed to this on the ground that re-Baptism was heretical.[1] But this is hardly correct, for the Council only asked that the fine imposed on heretics should apply to the Donatists,[2] and the above Decree expressly says that the Donatists are ' heretics ' ' owing to the mere fact that they belong to the party of Donatus.' Monceaux further says that Augustine himself was not satisfied that re-Baptism was really a heresy—though it would be hard to find any justification for this statement—and he adds that Augustine ' extricated himself from the dilemma " par cette ingénieuse definition," namely that heresy is a schism grown old.' [3] But we fear it is Monceaux who is ' ingenious,' for though *Contra Cresconium*—in which this definition is fully discussed—only dates from A.D. 406, the year after the Edict of Union, yet the idea involved in the above definition was no new one, it can be traced in the discussions which were held during St. Cyprian's Council at Carthage, A.D. 256.[4]

On the same date, February 12, 405, there appeared a stern Decree against the practice of re-baptizing :

The Emperors Arcadius, Honorius and Theodosius AAA to Hadrian the Praetorian Prefect :

It is our aim to extirpate by this authoritative decree the adversaries of the Catholic faith. Hence we have thought it well to single out for destruction by this present Constitution that sect which, to escape being called a heresy, prefers the appellation of a schism. For those who are known as Donatists have gone so far in crime as to trample under foot the Sacred Mysteries by a rank and guilty repetition of Baptism ; they are reported, that is, to have defiled by a profane repetition of it, people who have already once been cleansed by God's gift.

[1] *Histoire littéraire de l'Afrique du nord*, vii. 221 ff.

[2] See above, p. 328.

[3] *Ibid.*, and *cf. Ep.* lxxxvii. 3 ; *Contra Cresconium*, ii. 9 ; *De Haeresibus*, 69, and above, pp. 285 (on Schism).

[4] *De Baptismo contra Donatistas*, vi. 22 ; *cp.* i. 19 ; see p. 284 above.

Thus from a schism has been begotten a heresy. For it is easy to persuade sinners that the pardon once received can be repeated: though we ourselves fail to see why, if repeated once, it cannot be repeated twice. These men, then, by a sacrilegious repetition of Baptism, defile free men as well as their own slaves.

By this present law, then, we enact that anyone who is in future found guilty of repeating Baptism is to be brought before the judge presiding in the district and to be fined by the sale of all his property, thus incurring the penalty of reduction to perpetual want. Their children, however, must not be deprived of their paternal inheritance if they have not concurred in their parents' guilt; moreover, if perchance they have been involved in it, opportunity for recovering their inheritance must be left open to them on condition that they show that they are now prepared to return to their Catholic allegiance. Further, such estates or properties as shall appear to have been the scene of the secret practice of such gross sacrileges must be confiscated for the benefit of the Treasury, providing, of course, that the owners of such properties, whether men or women, were present on the occasion of such practices or can be shown to have agreed to such doings on their property; they must bear the brand of the infamy due to such a condemnation. If, however, it can be shown that such doings by people who rented it or procured the use of it, were unknown to the owners of their property, then there should be no incriminating sale of their property, but the guilty authors must be scourged and sent into perpetual exile. . . .

Let those again who are not afraid to see Baptism repeated by the above-mentioned people, or who by their consent to it—shown by the fact that they continue to belong to this body—have failed to condemn their crime, know that they not only lose thereby, and for good and all, their right to make any testamentary dispositions, but also their right to profit by donations or to make any contracts unless they, on better thoughts, repudiate their errors and return to the true faith. The same penalties will be incurred by such as connive at the above-mentioned forbidden gatherings or services; hence any rulers of districts who treat this law with contempt, and think fit to sanction such proceedings, will be fined £20 in gold; their staffs, too, will incur the same penalty. Superintendents as well as the garrisons of cities who fail to carry out these commands, or who are present while violence is being done to the Catholic Church, will be subject to the same fine. Given at Ravenna, Feb. 12, 405, Stilichone ii and Anthemio conss.[1]

Another Edict to the same effect appeared on the same date: Arcadius, Honorius et Theodosius AAA. Edictum. Rebaptizantium non patimur devios errores et caetera. Dat. prid. Id. Feb. Ravennae, Stilichone ii et Anthemio coss[2]; and still another, in which the Donatists are explicitly named:

Lest the grace of God should be defiled by a repetition of Baptism in the secret services of the Donatists, we wish by the present stringent law to remove all occasion for evasion, decreeing that the penalties already laid down shall be inflicted on such people, and that those who assail the Catholic religion by their perverse tenets shall experience the full vengeance of the law. We therefore lay down that if anyone shall after this be found guilty of re-baptizing he is to be brought before the Judge at that time in the district and shall, by the confiscation of all his property, pay the penalty of falling into poverty. Given at Ravenna the day before the Ides of February, Stilicho for the second time and Anthemius, Consuls (Feb. 12, A.D. 404.)[3]

The Donatists were overwhelmed by this sheaf of condemnations and the penalties involved, and they complained bitterly that the Catholics had no right to carry an ecclesiastical matter before the civil tribunals. But Augustine reminded them of

[1] Adversarios Catholicae fidei extirpare hujus decreti auctoritate prospeximus. Ideoque intercidendam specialiter eam sectam nova constitutione censuimus, quae, ne haeresis vocaretur, appelationem schismatis praeferebat. In tantum enim sceleris progressi dicuntur hi, quos Donatistas vocant, ut baptisma sacrosanctum mysteriis recalcatis temeritate noxia iterarint et homines semel, ut traditum est, munere divinitatis ablutos contagione profanae repetitionis infecerint. Ita contingit, ut haeresis ex schismate nasceretur. . . .

There then follow the penalties: they can make no wills, receive no gifts nor inheritance; the same to apply to those who connive at their doings, *Cod. Theodos.* XVI. vi. 4; Mommsen, i. 881–882; *P.L.* xliii. 813–814.

[2] *Cod. Theodos.* XVI. vi. 3, Mommsen i. 881 (February 12, 405).

[3] *Cod. Theodos.* XVI. vi. 5; ed. Mommsen and Meyer, i. 882–883; *P.L.* xliii. 446: 'Ne divinam gratiam sub repetito baptismate polluta Donatistarum vel Montanistarum secta violaret, fallendi occasionem severitate hujus praeceptionis abolemus statuentes, ut certa hujusmodi homines poena sequatur legisque censuram experiantur ultricem, qui in Catholicam religionem perverso dogmate commisissent. Jubemus igitur, ut, si quis post haec fuerit rebaptisasse detectus, judici qui provinciae praesidet offeratur, ut facultatum omnium publicatione multatus inopiae poenam expendat, etc.'

their own past behaviour: 'we have only done what you yourselves did before and to a much greater extent'; he goes on to point out that 'previous to these fresh laws of which you complain so much you laid ambushes in the roads to ensnare our Bishops, you beat our clergy horribly and wounded some of our laity grievously, besides setting churches on fire'; he concludes with the story of their brutal treatment of a Donatist priest who had become a Catholic.[1] Rumours of the Donatist complaints would seem to have reached the Imperial court, for in the March following the publication of the Edict of Union appeared a further pronouncement directed to the Proconsul in Africa:

Under the Emperors Arcadius, Honorius and Theodosius to Diotimus, Proconsul of Africa: the Edict for Unity sent by our clemency to the districts of Africa is to be promulgated in various places so that all may know of it: that the one true Catholic faith of Almighty God which true belief professes, is to be held. Given at Ravenna the third day of the Nones of March, Stilicho for the second time and Anthemius, Consuls (March 5, A.D. 405.)[2]

A Council was held at Carthage in the August of the year in which the Edict of Union was published, and the Fathers agreed that:

Since it is only at Carthage that Unity prevails, letters should be sent to magistrates in other Provinces and cities urging them to work for the same Unity. When the delegate Bishops present their letters at the Roman Court they should express the gratitude of the Carthaginian Church—speaking in the name of the whole of Africa—for the exclusion of the Donatists.[3]

In what sense there was 'Unity' at Carthage does not appear. At any rate Primianus continued to occupy the Donatist Archiepiscopal See till after A.D. 411. The complaint about

[1] *Ep.* cviii. 5–6.
[2] *Cod. Theodos.* XVI. xi. 2, ed. Mommsen and Meyer, i. 905; *P.L.* xliii. 446; 'Edictum quod de unitate per Africanas regiones clementia nostra direxit, per diversa proponi volumus, ut omnibus innotescat dei omnipotentis unam et veram fidem Catholicam quam recta credulitas confitetur, esse retinendam.'
[3] *P.L.* xliii. 614.

other districts shows that the action of the Council held in the previous year and insisting on conferences with the local Donatists had not had much effect. Nor did the Donatists pay the fines for non-compliance with the Edict of Union, as a yet further Imperial intimation to the Proconsul shows :

Arcadius Honorius Theodosius Diotimo suo salutem.
Donatistae superstitionis haereticos quoscunque loci vel fatentes vel convictos legis tenore servato poenam debitam absque dilatione persolvere decernimus.
Dat. VI. Id. Dec. Ravennae. Stilichone ii et Anthemio conss.[1] (Dec. 8, 405.)

But the Council of Carthage in June, 407, indicates that many Donatists were making their submission ; for it was then agreed that :

Any flock converted from Donatism and having a Bishop of its own can undoubtedly retain him without consulting this Council. If, however, on the death of their own Bishop they have no wish to have a Bishop of their own but prefer to be incorporated in some other Bishop's diocese, their request should not be refused. It is further suggested that Bishops who converted their flocks previous to the Imperial Law of Unity ought to be allowed to keep them ; but if they converted them subsequent to the passing of that Law, then it is only fitting that the Catholic Bishops to whom districts now in the hands of heretics belonged—as did also the heretics themselves, whether converted to the Catholic Church or not—should lay claim to all those churches and dioceses as well as to any church property to which they have a right. If such property has been seized subsequent to the passing of this Law, those who have done so must be called to account and made to disgorge.[2]

It was perhaps in the year 405, the year in which the Edict of Unity had appeared, that Augustine wrote to Caecilianus, whom he addresses as 'Praeses,' congratulating him on the effective work he, a Catholic, has done in the cause of Unity in other parts of Africa, but regretting that he has not taken

[1] *Cod. Theodos.* XVI. v. 39, ed. Mommsen, i. 867.
[2] Mansi, *Concilia*, iii. 803 ; *Codex canonum Ecclesiae Africanae*, Can. xcix.

the same effective steps in Hippo. He adds that his fellow-Bishops, or perhaps the priest who is presenting this letter, can give him detailed information about the doings of the Donatists. 'You will doubtless see to it,' he concludes, 'that this swelling tumour of a deceptive sacrilege may rather be healed by instilling a wholesome fear than forcibly removed by vengeful proceedings.' [1]

In A.D. 406 St. Augustine addressed himself to a certain Festus, urging him to investigate on the spot the behaviour of the Donatists at Hippo. 'Your men in this district,' he says, 'are still Donatists and your letters to them have had no effect.' [2] Festus clearly held some official position though no indication of its nature is forthcoming. In this letter Augustine points out that while the schismatics could have been punished by fines or by exile, 'there is no comparison between the exceedingly merciful treatment meted out to them and the things they do in their mad folly.' [3] 'But, even so,' adds Augustine, 'either by renewed atrocities or by indifference, they resist all efforts to make them amend their ways.' 'Mad men,' he continues, 'do not like being tied up, nor do lethargic folk like being stirred up. Yet true charity keeps on with all diligence : it corrects the madman, stirs up the sluggard ; but continues to love both of them.' [4]

VIII—DECREES ISSUED, A.D. 407

The year 407 proved prolific in Decrees and pronouncements :

Arcadius et Honoris AA. Senatori Pr. Urbi : Quid de Donatistis sentiremus, nuper ostendimus. They then refer 'praecipue' to the 'Manichaeos, Frygas seu Priscillianistas' who are not to have power to make wills ; magistrates negligent in this respect are to be fined £20. February 22, 497.[5] The

[1] *Ep.* lxxxvi. The Vicar in Africa in A.D. 404 was named Caecilianus, but Pallu de Lessert, *Vicaires et Comtes de l'Afrique*, i., p. 172, holds that the present letter was not written to him but to another Caecilian ; *cf. Ep.* cli., A.D. 413.

[2] *Ep.* lxxxix. 8.

[3] *Ibid.*, 2. 'Misericordissima disciplina.'

[4] *Ibid.*, 6. 'Aut saeviendo aut pigrescendo.'

[5] *Codex Theodos.* XVI. v. 40.

adherents of Gildo are proscribed, November 11.[1] On November 15 appeared an interesting pronouncement according full absolution from penalties for Donatists returning in good faith. The terms used are worth noting :

> Although punishment is generally reserved for crimes, yet we are anxious to correct men's evil inclinations by warning them of the need of repentance. Whosoever, then, among the heretics, whether Donatists, Manichaeans or people adhering to the profane rites of any other false opinion or sect, shall by a straightforward profession of faith embrace the Catholic faith and its rites—which we desire to see all men follow. . . .[2]

But that many were still obstinate is evident from a Decree of ten days later in which the Emperors say :

> We hereby declare that all the Decrees emanating from our general laws against the Donatists—called Montenses—the Manichaeans, Priscillianists, and the heathen, do not merely remain in full force but are to be put into serious effect, and the buildings of these people are to be handed over to the churches. Moreover, the penalties laid down shall apply to

[1] Count Gildo was in command of the Roman forces A.D. 386–397, but in that year he rebelled against Honorius ; he was, however, defeated by his own brother Mascezel in 398 ; *cf.* St. Jerome, *Epp.* lxxix. and cxxiii. The Donatists, especially Optatus, the Donatist Bishop of Thamugadi, who earned thereby the soubriquet of 'Statelles Gildonis,' *cf. Contra Litt. Petiliani*, ii. 209 ; *Contra Cresconium*, iv. 31–32, supported Gildo.

[2] Licet crimina solet poena purgare, nos tamen pravas hominum voluntates admonitione poenitentiae volumus emendare. Quicunque igitur haereticorum sive Donatistae sint sive Manichaei vel cujuscunque alterius pravae opinionis ac sectae profanis ritibus aggregati, Catholicam fidem et ritum, quem per omnes homines cupimus observari, simplici confessione susceperint, licet adeo inveteratum malum longa ac diuturna meditatione nutriverint, ut etiam legibus ante latis videantur obnoxii, tamen hos, statim ut fuerint deum simplici religione confessi, ab omni noxa absolvendos esse censemus, ut ad omnem reatum, seu ante contractum est seu postea quod nolumus contrahitur, etiamsi reos poena videatur urgere, sufficiat ad abolitionem errorem proprio damnavisse judicio et dei omnipotentis nomen, inter ipsa quoque pericula, requisitum, fuisse complexum, quia nusquam debet in miseriis invocatum religionis deesse subsidium. Ut igitur priores quas statuimus leges in excidium sacrilegarum mentium omni executionis urgueri (*sic*) jubemus effectu, ita hos, qui simplicis fidem religionis licet sera confessione maluerint, censemus datis legibus non teneri. Quae ideo sanximus, quo universi cognoscant nec profanis hominum studiis deesse vindictam et ad rectum redundare cultum legum quoque adesse suffragium. November 15, 407. *Cod. Theodos.*, XVI. v. 41 ; Mommsen i, 868–869 ; *P.L.* xi. 1216.

such as declare themselves Donatists or who decline to join the Catholic body under pretext of some wicked form of religion—even though they may pretend to be Catholics.

There then follow regulations about the temple revenues, the statues and buildings for public use, while a fine of £10 in gold—' a fine inflicted some time ago '—is to be exacted of those who negligently fail to carry out these prescriptions.[1]

IX—CONCILIAR ACTION, A.D. 408 ; EP. XCIII

When the Council met at Carthage on June 16, 408, Fortunatianus undertook to go a second time to the Imperial Court and plead against the pagans and heretics. And when they met again in September, Restitutus and Florentius went on a similar embassy owing to the murder of Severus and Macarius by the Donatists who showed their resentment of the embassy by scourging Evodius, Theasius and Victor. Later they murdered Stilicho who was succeeded in his position as Magister Officiorum in Africa by Olympius. To him Augustine wrote towards the close of the same year, 408 :

Owing to the grievously disturbed state of the Church many of my brethren and colleagues have set out—practically as fugitives—for the Imperial Court. You may meet them, or if they have the chance they may write to you. But I beg you to push on as fast as possible the task committed to you and so make the enemies of the Church realize that those laws promulgated in Africa in Stilicho's lifetime about breaking up the idolatrous statues and suppressing heretics emanated directly from the Emperor himself. The heretics here, however, are trying to pretend that these Laws were made without his knowledge, even against his desire. Hence less cautious folk are much excited and attack us very violently. What I would suggest, then, to Your Excellency—and I am sure all my

[1] The opening words deserve notice : ' . . . Compulsi igitur Donatistarum pertinacia, furore gentilium, quae quidem mala desidia judicum, conniventia officiorum, ordinum contemptus accendit, necessarium putamus iterare quae jussimus. Quapropter omnia quae in Donatistas qui et Montenses vocantur, Manichaeos sive Priscillianistos vel in Gentiles a nobis generalium legum auctoritate decreta sunt, non solum manere decernimus, verum in executionem plenissimam effectumque deduci. . . .' *Cod. Theodos.*, XVI. v. 43 ; ed. Mommsen, i. 869 ; *P.L.* xi. 1217, xliii. 815.

colleagues here in Africa would agree with me—is that the very first opportunity should be seized to make these empty-headed people, whose salvation we are seeking—despite their opposition to us—realize that the said Laws, promulgated in favour of the Church of Christ, were due rather to Theodosius' son than to Stilicho.[1]

Augustine ends on a note of joy, for the laws in question had produced many conversions.

From A.D. 400 onwards Augustine was occupied with his great anti-Donatist Treatises: against Parmenian, Petilian, Cresconius, etc., besides preaching many sermons on the subject. This explains why the Letters written during the next eight years are practically silent about the schism. Moreover, the frequent Conciliar meetings on the question must have made very considerable demands on his time; he was, too, busy with several of his more famous works, *e.g.*, *De Trinitate*, *De Genesi ad Litteram*, *De Consensu Evangelistarum*, etc.

But somewhere about A.D. 408 he wrote a very lengthy letter to a certain Vincent whom he had known at Carthage,[2] but who had joined a sect which, headed by a certain Rogatus, had broken off from the main body 'pars Rogati, brevissimum frustum de frusto majori praecisum'[3]; of this sect Vincent was now head.[4] Augustine's letter might well be given in full, did space permit; we can, however, only note some salient points regarding the Imperial laws and their effects. First of all he tells Vincent of the many converts owing to the promulgation of these laws:

We rejoice in the conversion of so many who now hold fast to Catholic Unity and defend it, who are so filled with joy at their liberation from their former errors that we can but look at them with wonderment and deep thanksgiving. Yet they, through the mysterious influence of custom, would never have dreamed of changing had it not been that, stricken with fear,

[1] *Ep.* xcvii. 2, c. 2, cv. 6.
[2] *Ep.* xciii. 1.
[3] *Ibid.*, 24.
[4] *Ibid.*, 1.

they began to look more closely and anxiously into the truth of the matter.[1]

And again :

Oh, if only I could show you the number, even out of the Circumcellions, who are now openly Catholics and loud in condemnation of their former lives and of the wretched mistake they made in thinking that they were doing for God's own Church the mad things they used to do. Yet these men would never have been brought to this healthy frame of mind had they not been tied up, as madmen are tied up, by those very laws which make you so angry.[2] Further, had these people merely been terrorized, and not instructed, that would have been unwarrantable bullying. But conversely : had they been only instructed and not made to feel afraid, the force of long-standing custom would have made it hard for them to take any but tardy steps along the road that led to salvation. For many people well known to us have, when they have had to acknowledge the force and truth of the Scripture testimonies, told us that they really had wanted to become Catholics but dreaded the violence of these abandoned men (the Donatist leaders and hired bands).[3]

Augustine then faces the real issue between himself and Vincent :

Can you really maintain that no one should be compelled to be good when you read the words of the householder (in the Gospel), 'Whomsoever you shall find, compel them to come in,'[4] or when you read how Saul, afterwards Paul, was compelled by the exceeding violence of Christ who compelled him ?[5] Is there a single member of our communion or of yours who fails to commend the laws enacted by the Emperors against the sacrifices offered by the Pagans ?[6] It is no question, then, whether a person is compelled or not, but rather whence he is expelled, from something good or from something

[1] *Ibid.*, 1.
[2] *Ibid.*, 2.
[3] *Ibid.*, 3.
[4] Luke xiv. 23, where Augustine read 'coge' for the 'compelle' of the Vulgate.
[5] Acts ix. 3–7.
[6] *Ep.* xciii. 10.

bad. . . . For we have ourselves witnessed not merely individuals, but many cities which—formerly Donatist—became Catholic, people now filled with hatred of their diabolical state of schism and with an ardent love for Unity. Now these cities became Catholic simply owing to what distresses you so much, the dread aroused by the Imperial legislation from Constantine onwards.[1]

Augustine then refers to the discussions which had taken place in Councils held at Carthage [2]:

I gave in, then, after listening to these instances brought forward by my fellow-Bishops. For my feeling had originally been that no one was to be forced into the Unity of Christ; that we had to work with words (not deeds), to fight by discussions, to convince by arguments, lest otherwise we should merely be producing fictitious Catholics, men whom we should feel were really heretics all the time. But this idea of mine was negatived by demonstrable facts rather than by verbal arguments. Indeed the first fact which weighed with me was the state of my own city of Hippo. For whereas it had hitherto been wholly in the hands of the Donatist sect, it has now been converted to Catholic Unity through dread of the Imperial laws. . . . How many people there were there who to my certain knowledge had long wanted to be Catholics, convinced by the patent truth, yet who through fear of persecution at the hands of their own people, put it off from day to day! How many there are, too, who thought the sect of Donatus was really the true Church because sheer heedlessness made them too sluggish, disdainful and lazy to recognize Catholic Truth! How many, again, who thought it did not matter to what sect a Christian belonged, and who stayed among the Donatists simply because they were born among them and because no one compelled them to quit it and pass over to the Catholic Church!

Now dread of these laws,[3] by the promulgation of which 'kings serve the Lord with trembling,' was of great assistance to all these folk, so much so that some of them say now: 'We

[1] *Ep.* clxxxv. 18, 25–26.
[2] *Ibid.*, 16. See above, p. 310 ff.
[3] 'Fear,' he says repeatedly, 'will make people think,' *Epp.* lxxxvi. 2, lxxxix. 2, clxxxv. 21, 26; *Contra Litteras Petiliani*, ii. 186; *Contra Cresconium*, iv. 61.

have always wanted it! Thanks be to God who has at long last given us the opportunity of taking the step and has removed all reason for needless delay!' Others say: 'We had known all along where the truth lay, but we were kept back by some sort of traditional custom.' Others again: 'We had no idea of the truth, nor had we any wish to discover it; but fear made us eager to find out; for we dreaded lest, in addition to losing all eternal reward we should also lose our temporal well-being.' And yet others: 'We were terrified of entering amongst you owing to lying accounts of you; nor should we ever have known how untrue these rumours were if we had not gone over to you; indeed, had we not been driven to it we would never have gone over to you. Thanks be to God for having driven out our fears by His scourge and for having helped us to learn by experience how empty and idle were the lies circulated about His Church. This has helped us to believe, too, that the accusations bruited abroad by the originators of this heresy were lies, realizing, as we do now, what perjured liars their present descendants are.' Lastly, there were others who said: 'We thought it mattered little in what sect we held Christ's faith; but thanks be to God who has garnered us in out of schism and shown that it is but fitting that the One God should be served in Unity!' [1]

This lengthy letter ends with words which should—even if they stood alone—show Augustine's true mind on the subject of persecution: 'Anyone who takes advantage of this Imperial law to pursue you out of hatred and not from a desire for your correction, is no friend of mine.' [2]

Le Clerc remarks on this Epistle that Augustine 'endeavours herein to argue at great length that persecution of people whom we fancy to be in error is lawful in order to bring them to the truth.' He therefore undertakes to show that 'on this point Augustine fell into a grave error.' For the Bishop had compared the schismatics to madmen who have to be treated as such; but—argues Le Clerc—the analogy is false, for whereas madmen are undoubtedly such, those who differ from us on religious questions may be as sane as ourselves, and they have just as much right to regard us as mad as we have to regard

[1] *Ep.* xciii. 17–18.
[2] *Ibid.*, 50.

them as such; Le Clerc then tries to turn the tables on Augustine by asking what he would have said had he lived to witness the persecution of the Catholics by the Arian Vandals who deemed the Catholics mad.

But Le Clerc has missed the point. Augustine did not call the Donatists 'madmen' because they were schismatics or heretics but because of their frenzied violence towards the Catholics and their crazy cult of suicide. As for Augustine's statement about the Circumcellions who were converted, Le Clerc declines to believe in the genuineness of their conversion! And when Augustine goes on to interpret the 'Compelle intrare' of the parable (Luke xiv. 23) he sneers at his exegesis and insists that 'compelle' here merely means 'persuasion,' instancing such passages as Gen. xix. 3, Matt. xiv. 22, Luke xxiv. 29, Gal. ii. 24.[1]

But these moderate views Augustine had held consistently throughout his life. For example, he says of his treatise *Contra Partem Donati*:

> In the first Book I said that it was not at all my idea that schismatics should be violently brought back to unity by force of the secular arm. And certainly at that time it was not to my thinking; for I had not then realized either what harm would result from their impunity, nor, on the other hand, how much such careful disciplinary action would avail for their amendment.[2]

The same uncompromising attitude towards compulsion appears in his answer to Petilian who had protested that his people would never under any circumstances 'compel' anybody to embrace their tenets. To that Augustine replied:

> No person is to be compelled against his will to embrace the faith; yet unfaith is, in God's mercy, often severely

[1] Joannes Clericus (Le Clerc) or 'Pherepon,' *Animadversiones in Epistolas Sti. Augustini*, *P.L.* xlvii. 252–254.

[2] Now lost; *Retract.* ii. 5; *cp. Ep.* xciii. 1, 17, 19, xliv. 11, A.D. 397–398. He assigns this work to a place immediately after the *De Doctrina Christiana*, begun A.D. 397, though not completed till 426. No one was to be forced, but to be changed by arguments and facts, so Tillement, *Memoires à servir à l'histoire ecclésiastique*, XIII. cli. 403, ed. 1732. Augustine himself says that he will never on any account stir up persecution, *De Unitate*, 55. That he protested against the infliction of the death penalty is abundantly clear; *cf. Epp.* c. 1, cxxxiii. 1, cxxxiv. 2, cxxxix. 2, clxxxv. 26–28, cciv. 3.

chastised by the scourges of tribulation. Does it follow that because sound morals are to be chosen freely, bad morals are not to be punished by the law? At the same time corrective treatment of a disorderly life is out of place until a man has shown contempt for all attempts at teaching him how to live aright. When, then, laws are promulgated against you, they are not meant to compel you to be good but to prevent you from being bad. No one can do well unless he chooses, unless he loves what is in the power of his free will. The fear of punishment, on the contrary, even though not yet accompanied by the delight of a good conscience, at least serves as a mental check to evil desires.

He goes on to point out once more that the Donatists had brought these laws upon themselves and that they had been the first to exercise compulsion when they had the upper hand.[1]

X—IMPERIAL DECREES, A.D. 408–409; EP. C., A.D. 408–409

On August 22, 408, the Proconsul Stilicho was murdered.[2] He had applied the recent anti-Donatist legislation with effect, and many had in consequence become Catholics.[3] The Donatists, however, maintained that the laws he administered were of his own making and not Imperial in origin, and that they therefore lapsed with his death,[4] 'a lie with which you suddenly filled the whole of Africa.'[5] This led to a further denunciation of the Donatists by Honorius and Theodosius:

[1] *Contra Litt. Petiliani*, ii. 184. It is not easy to understand M. Monceaux' comment on this passage written A.D. 401: 'Chose curieuse, comme s'il était hanté par le souvenir de ses idées premières, il cherchait parfois à démontrer que l'application de ces lois ne portait nullement atteinte à la liberté de conscience.' *Histoire littéraire de l'Afrique*, vii. 224. We have to keep reminding ourselves that the method of 'peaceful penetration'—to use a modern expression—had proved ineffective, and that everyone in Africa was well aware that repressive measures were alone proving efficacious. We have to bear in mind, too, that suppression by the civil authorities had never been a principle with Augustine. When, however, these authorities took the initiative on their own responsibility, he seized the opportunity thus offered to secure all the good results which it undoubtedly offered; *cf. Contra Epistolam Parmeniani*, i. 13; *Contra Litt. Petiliani*, ii. 203; *Contra Cresconium*, ii. 4, iii. 51; *Ep.* xciii. 16; *Contra Julianum Pelagianum*, iii. 5. Such appeals to the civil authorities might be opportune, but Augustine would not have them erected into a principle.

[2] See *Epp.* xcvi. and xcvii.

[3] *Ep.* xcvii. 4, close of A.D. 408.

[4] *Ibid.*, 2; c. 2.

[5] *Ep.* cv. 6.

Have Donate, Karissime nobis. Donatistarum haereticorum Judaeorum nova atque inusitata detexit audacia, quod Catholicae fidei velint sacramenta turbare. Quae pestis cave [1] contagione latius emanat ac profluit. In eos igitur, qui aliquid, quod sit Catholicae sectae contrarium adversumque, temptaverint, supplicium justae animadversionis expromi praecipimus. Nov. 24, 408.

Hail, Donatus, our dear friend: the audacity of the Donatist heretics and the Jews [2] has taken a new and unwonted line—they try to upset the mysteries of the Catholic Faith. And this plague by a subtle (?) contagion spreads far and wide. We ordain, then, that people who attempt to do anything opposed to the Catholic body are to be subjected to just punishment.[3]

A further Decree appeared on January 15, 409, in which the same Emperors complained of gross neglect on the part of magistrates in Africa who connived at the doings of the heretics and schismatics. The lengthy document closes with the words:

Ne Donatistae vel ceterorum vanitas haereticorum aliorumque eorum, quibus Catholicae communionis cultus non potest persuaderi, Judaei atque Gentiles, quos vulgo paganos appellant, arbitrentur legum ante adversum se datarum constituta tepuisse, noverint judices universi praeceptis eorum fideli devotione parendum et inter praecipua curarum quidquid adversus eos decrevimus non ambigant exequendium. Dat. XVIII. Kal. Feb. Ra(vennae). (Jan. 15, 409.)

Lest the folly of the Donatists or of any other heretics, or of the Jews, or of the Gentiles—commonly termed 'Pagans'—people who cannot be persuaded (of the truth) of the Catholic religion, should lead them to imagine that the legal enactments against them are no longer in force, all magistrates are hereby given to understand that these orders have to be faithfully observed and must make it their care not to delay in putting into force all our Decrees against them. [4]

[1] The text is corrupt; see Haenel's ed. of the *Cod. Theodos.*, 1837, p. 1551.

[2] There is some doubt about the text.

[3] *Cod Theodos.*, XVI. v. 44, ed. Mommsen, i. 870; given in *P.L.* xi. 1218, xliii. 815.

[4] *Cod. Theodos.* XVI. v. 46, ed. Mommsen, i. 870; given in *P.L.* xi. 1220, xliii. 815.

Still another Decree, much to the same effect, appeared, June 26, 409:

Si quis contra ea, quae multipliciter pro salute communi, hoc est pro utilitatibus Catholicae Sacrosanctae Ecclesiae, adversus haereticos et diversi dogmatis sectatores constituta sunt, etiam cum adnotationis nostrae beneficio venire temptaverit, careat impetratis. June 26, 409. Dat. VI. Kal. Jul. Ravennae. Honorio VIII et The(dosio) III. Conss.

If anyone—even under pretext of a Rescript from Us—should attempt anything contrary to those many enactments which we have made for the common good—that is to say for the good of the Holy Catholic Church—against heretics and people who adhere to divergent doctrines, he must not be granted his petition.[1]

The attitude of the Imperial authorities towards people who offered violence to the established form of religion was a natural one. If such people were banded into societies, then such societies must be suppressed; this could be effected by a system of fines, by refusing to allow their members to make or profit by wills, also by deportation, and in the last resort by death. St. Augustine, on the other hand, while fully conceding the right of the State to punish violators of the established form of religion, maintained that this should only be done in the last resort, that no compulsion [2] was to be used in order to make a man change his religious beliefs, that persuasion by teaching, conferences and writings was far more effective in the long run,[3] that care must be taken to secure adequate instruction for such as embraced the Catholic Faith whether fear was the initial motive with them or not.

It must always be borne in mind that far the greater part of the Imperial legislation on the subject was already traditional by the time Augustine came on the scene, and—most important of all—that none of this legislation was initiated at the request of the Church, though where it did exist the Church authorities urged that it should be applied, and that solely to put an end

[1] *Cod. Theodos.*, XVI. v. 47.
[2] *Ep.* xxxiv. 1; *Contra Litteras Petiliani*, ii. 184.
[3] *Contra Litteras Petiliani*, ii. 184; *Contra Cresconium*, iii. 51.

to a reign of mob violence.[1] To the very end Augustine regretted the action taken by the civil authorities, though he was compelled to acknowledge that it had succeeded where all other measures had failed. He repeatedly urged that the law should be executed far less rigorously than its bare letter allowed,[2] and rejoiced to find that the penalties inflicted were 'mitissimae.'[3] Against the infliction of the death penalty he vehemently protested over and over again.[4]

At this stage in the proceedings, when, that is, the civil authorities had taken the matter seriously in hand and made up their minds to put a stop to the anarchy prevailing in Africa owing to the frenzied behaviour of the Donatists, St. Augustine addressed a letter to Donatus, the Proconsul in Africa, which is of such importance for the light it throws on the Saint's attitude with regard to the action of the Government, that we must quote from it largely. The letter is dated approximately 408–409, for Donatus was Proconsul from about the close of A.D. 408 to the middle of 410. He had, apparently, been too severe in his application of the Edict of Union of February 12, 405, and of the many subsequent Imperial pronouncements. Augustine therefore urged on him a due moderation :

We do not seek for revenge on our enemies in this world, nor have we any wish to see them reduced to the same anguish of soul as we suffer ; we are not unmindful of the precept given by Him for whose truth and Name we suffer : for we do love our enemies and we do pray for them. For that reason, owing to the opportunity which these terrible judges and their terrible laws present, we are desirous that our enemies should be set right, not put to death, and may thus escape the punishments of the Eternal Judge. And while we have no wish that the corrective laws enacted against them should be winked at, yet neither do we desire to see them suffer the penalties they have so richly deserved. Try, then, so to deal with their offences that they may repent of having offended. We beg you, therefore, forget, when you are trying cases affecting the Church—no matter

[1] *Ep.* clxxxv. 21.
[2] *Ep.* lxxxix. 2, 7, xci. 9, cxxxiii. 4, cxxxix. 2 ; *Contra Cresconium*, iii. 51.
[3] *Epp.* lxxxviii. 6, xciii. 34, c. 2, civ. 16–17—where he deprecates torture, cviii. 7.
[4] *Epp.* c. 1, cciv. 3.

how grievous you may find the injuries which She has suffered —forget, I say, that you have the power of inflicting capital punishment, but do not forget this request of ours. . . . And in your prudence you will, perhaps, reflect that none but ecclesiastical people can bring ecclesiastical cases before you. The consequence will be that if you should decide that these people are to be put to death for their crimes you will thereby deter us from being the means whereby such cases may be brought to your notice. And the moment that fact is realized, these people will be all the more bold in their attacks upon us ; with the further consequence that we shall find ourselves unavoidably compelled to prefer death at their hands than to be ourselves the cause of their deaths by bringing them before your court. . . . Meanwhile let the heretical Donatists realize by an Edict emanating from Your Excellency that the laws enacted against them still hold good despite their fanciful boasting that these same laws are now of no effect ; once they realize that, they may perhaps spare us somewhat. You will be effectively helping to render our toils and dangers really fruitful if, while, in accordance with the Imperial laws, you try to suppress this sect—empty-headed, yet swollen with pride—you at the same time avoid giving them ground for the notion that they are enduring trials and afflictions for the truth or for righteousness' sake ; more especially will you help us if you allow them to be instructed and convinced by letting them see the documents in the case which set forth the patent truth in clear fashion ; these documents are to be found among the Records of Your Excellency's court or in the courts of the lesser magistrates. It may then come to pass that people attainted at your bidding may change their obstinate minds for the better, and may be induced to read these documents to their profit.[1]

At first sight it is hard to see how the schismatics contrived to hold out so long in face of such stringent laws. But, as Bouvet has pointed out : the law and its application were two very distinct things. For laws were primarily prohibitions, and the penal laws were hardly ever applied. The State hit out as it were by sudden blows, at intervals. The pagans and sectarians were thus able to hold out for a long time, though in the end they were gradually eliminated.[2]

[1] *Ep.* c., A.D. 408–409. See above, p. 300, for H. C. Lea's version of this.
[2] *S. Augustin et la Repression de l'erreur religieuse*, 1918.

XI—THE EDICT OF TOLERANCE, A.D. 409; ITS WITHDRAWAL; THE CONFERENCE OF A.D. 411; EP. CXXXIV

These various pronouncements ratifying the laws previously passed and giving the lie to the absurd contention that they lapsed with the death of Stilicho should have cleared the situation. But then there came a 'bolt from the blue' in the shape of what is commonly known as the Edict of Toleration. Very little is known of this Edict—so far as we can discover; the sole reference to it appears to be the words of the Council of Carthage, June, 410; 'ut libera voluntate quis cultum Christianitatis acciperet.'[1] It has been suggested that this 'toleration' was due to a fear lest the Donatists should join hands with the forces of Alaric who was then proceeding to the siege of Rome[2]; St. Augustine perhaps alludes to it when, in a letter to Macrobius the then Donatist Bishop of Hippo, he says: 'ante istam legem qua gaudetis vobis redditam libertatem,'[3] also when he speaks of 'the many converts from Donatism who declined to return to you when that soul-destroying liberty was conceded to you.'[4]

The effects of such an apparent reversal of all previous legislation were at once seen in the renewed violence of the Donatists; and the African Bishops felt bound to protest to the Roman court. Unfortunately the only account of their proceedings in the Council held at Carthage in the June of that same year, 410, is tantalisingly brief:

> After the Consulates of the glorious Emperors Honorius for the eighth time and Theodosius for the fourth time (in the Council held) at Carthage on the xviiith. Kalends of June in the basilica of the second region: Florentius, Possidius, Praesidius and Benenatus, bishops, accepted the legation against the Donatists at the time when the law was made that anyone could freely embrace Christianity.[5]

[1] See below.
[2] So Binius in his notes, Labbe, *Concilia*, i. 1334.
[3] *Ep.* cviii. 18.
[4] *Contra Gaudentium*, i. 27, A.D. 420.
[5] Mansi, *Concilia*, iii. 810; *P.L.* xliii. 815; Hefele-Leclercq, *Histoire des Conciles*, ii. 159; Morcelli, *Ecclesia Africana*, iii. 43.

The petition of the Council and of the four delegates had an immediate effect ; for Honorius, despite the fact that Alaric was now at the gates of Rome—in fact he took the city just a fortnight later, September 10, 410—acted promptly by at once withdrawing the obnoxious decree : he and Theodosius wrote to the Count of Africa, Heraclianus :

Oraculo penitus remoto, quo ad ritus suos haereticae superstitionis obrepserant, sciant omnes sanctae legis inimici plectendos se poena et proscribtionis et sanguinis, si ultra convenire per publicum execranda sceleris sive temeritate temptaverint ; Datum viii. J. Kal. Sept., Varane, V.C. Cons. Aug. 25, 410.

Let all enemies of the law understand by this absolute withdrawal of a Decree—by relying on which they have insidiously crept back to the practice of their heretical rites—that if they in future criminally and audaciously endeavour to hold public meetings they will be punished by proscription and even by death.[1]

But Honorius did not stop at Decrees and fulminations. On October 14, 410, he published an ' Imperial Precept,' ordering the Donatists to meet the Catholics in a formal Conference over which Marcellinus the Tribune was to preside. This famous meeting which—for reasons best known to himself—Harnack styles ' a tragi-comedy,' [2] was held on June 1, 2 and 8, 411. Into the fascinating story of those days we cannot now enter. The rout of the Donatists was complete and Marcellinus passed sentence against them, though, if anything, he might almost be accused of having favoured their side during the discussions [3] ; he had shown himself ' magnum jurisprudentiae decus,' as Francis Baldwin remarks,[4] and a model of patience throughout all those long and wearisome discussions.[5] He reaped his eternal reward, for he was unjustly

[1] *Cod. Theodos.*, XVI. v. 51 ; Mommsen, i. 872. A similar decree is dated January 30, 412, *ibid.* 52.

[2] *History of Dogma*, i., p. 68 ; *cf.* W. J. Sparrow-Simpson, *St. Augustine and African Church Divisions*, 1910, p. 105, where he says that this meeting can ' only in irony be called a Conference '—one wonders why !

[3] *Collatio*, i. Nos. 51–54, 56, 144–146, ii. 3–7, 57, iii. 51 ff., 250–257 ; *cf. Breviculus Collationis*, iii. 4.

[4] *Historia Donatistarum*, *P.L.* xi. 1441.

[5] *De Gestis Pelagii*, 25.

put to death A.D. 413 owing, it is to be feared, to the intrigues of the Donatists.[1] His name appears in the Roman Martyrology under April 6.

Almost immediately after the Conference Augustine wrote to Marcellinus saying:

> I have heard that some Circumcellions as well as Donatist clergy have been brought before you and have pleaded guilty to the murder of a Catholic priest named Restitutus, also of having flogged another priest by name Innocentius, dug out one of his eyes and cut off one of his fingers. Hence I am much worried; for I wonder whether you may not perhaps feel that these men ought to be punished with such legal severity that they may be made to suffer what they have made others suffer.

This he begs Marcellinus not to do.[2]

At the same date and to the same effect Augustine wrote to Marcellinus' brother, Apringius, who was then Proconsul in Africa.[3]

XII—FURTHER DECREES, A.D. 412–415; EP. CXXXIX

It was not until seven months had elapsed since Marcellinus had given his decision as the result of the Conference that Honorius and Theodosius published their formal Decree on the subject. It is certainly a terrific denunciation and the penalties enacted are very severe. Yet we have to remember that many of the Donatists had committed murder,[4] and had, in addition, kept Africa in a state of turmoil for many years, also, that they had persistently defied a whole series of Imperial laws and had resisted every effort to bring about a peaceful discussion of the questions at issue.

We give Honorius' Decree in full:

[1] See *Ep.* cli. 1–3; St. Jerome, *Dial. adv. Pelagianos*, iii. 19; Orosius, *Historia*, vii. 42.

[2] *Ep.* cxxxiii., about the beginning of A.D. 412.

[3] *Ep.* cxxxiv.; *cf. Ep.* cxxxiii. 3, where Augustine tells Marcellinus that he had felt it well to write to the Proconsul as well as to himself.

[4] *Ep.* l., *c.* A.D. 399; it is not certain whether the atrocities there referred to were committed by the Donatists; *Ep.* clxxxv. 25–27; *Contra Cresconium*, iii. 51, etc.

We cassate all those concessions which their advocates have been able to secure, even those given under our own seal, and we declare that those decrees still hold good which were long since enacted on this subject, and to the non-observance of which our predecessors attached certain penalties. Consequently from the date of promulgation of this edict we declare that all Donatists, priests, clerics and laity, who shall not have returned to the Catholic Church from which they have sacrilegiously separated, shall be compelled to pay to our treasury: the 'illustres' fifty pieces of gold, the 'spectabiles' forty pieces, senators thirty pieces, 'clarissimi' twenty pieces, those of priestly rank thirty pieces, the 'principales' twenty pieces, 'decuriones' (town councillors) five pieces, tradespeople five pieces, the common people five pieces, the Circumcellions two pieces. Unless the Circumcellions are brought before the executor of this edict whose business it is to exact it by the contractors or procurators under whom they act, these latter shall be bound to pay this fine themselves; for we do not intend men, even of our own household, to be immune. Wives, too, as well as their husbands, are equally bound by this law. Confiscation of all their property will follow in the case of such as are not deterred by these fines.

Slaves should be chastised by their masters and the tillers of the soil punished by frequent floggings: thus will they be deterred from following a false religion; unless of course their masters—even Catholic masters—prefer to incur the above-mentioned penalties themselves. But clerics and their ministers, as well as their pestilent priests, are to be removed from African soil which they have defiled by their sacrilegious rites; they are to be sent man by man into exile to different provinces under suitable escort. Moreover, their Churches and meeting-places, as well as any landed property which the generosity of some of the heretics may have conferred on their Churches, are all—as we laid down long ago [1]—to become the property of the Catholic Church.

Given at Ravenna, iii. Kal. Feb. (Jan. 30, 412).

Honor. ix. et Theod. v. A.A. coss.[2]

[1] A.D. 409, see above, p. 331 ff.

[2] *Codex Theodos.* XVI. v. 52, ed. Mommsen, i. 872; *P.L.* xi. 1420; St. Augustine, *Ep.* clxxxv.; Victor of Vita, *De Persecutione Vandalica*, iii. On these Edicts and Decrees of A.D. 411–412, see *Epp.* clv. 17, clxxiii., clxxv., cciv.; *De Gestis cum Emerito*, 2; *Ad Donatistas post Collationem*, 1, 17, 21–23; *Contra Gaudentium*, i. 20, 21, 27; *Retractationes*, ii. 39, 40, 46, 48, 51, 59.

In May of the same year, 412, Augustine wrote again to Marcellinus:

As for the punishment to be inflicted on the Donatists who plead guilty to very grave crimes, I beg that it may stop short of the death penalty; and this I ask for our own conscience' sake, also in the interests of Catholic long-suffering. For we owe this resulting confession of theirs to the very fact that the Catholic Church exhibits such leniency to her most bitter enemies. Though in face of their savage cruelty any penalty short of death would seem to be leniency, and it is true that some of our own people, deeply stirred by their cruel doings, are tempted to think such leniency unfitting, if not a sign of negligent weakness; yet when the present feelings of uneasiness, naturally more vehemently aroused when events are fresh in the mind, has died down, such leniency will be seen to have been real goodness.[1]

One marvels at the obstinacy of the Donatists who should, one would have thought, have been utterly crushed by such a series of enactments. But their leaders still continued to oppose the Catholics, and seem, for the most part, to have refused to quit their Sees. In truth they had some excuse. For while the laity of the sect lost nothing now by becoming Catholics save in districts where the Circumcellions were still able to carry on their work of ravaging Catholic—and especially convert—homesteads, the Bishops had everything to lose: their flocks, their churches, their immense ill-gotten possessions, and their prestige. In many cases, too, the laity would support their pastors in their resistance to what they felt to be an invasion by an alien body of rights which, to a generation knowing nothing of the origin of the schism, seemed time-honoured. We have a notable instance of this attitude in the case of Gaudentius of Thamugadi.[2]

Still, there could be but one result of such opposition. Edicts and Decrees came from the Emperors in quick succession. In June, 414, for instance, Honorius and Theodosius

[1] *Ep.* cxxxix., May, 412.
[2] See above, pp. 273, 282, 287–8, and p. 360, below.

wrote to the then Proconsul in Africa, Julian, practically repeating the Decree *Cassatis* of January, 412 [1]:

> Donatistas atque haereticos, quos patientia clementiae nostrae huc usque servavit, competenti constituimus auctoritate percelli, quatenus evidenti praeceptione se agnoscant et intestabiles et nullam potestatem alicujus ineundi habere contractus, sed perpetuo inustos infamia a coetibus honestis. . . . Ea vero loca, in quibus dira superstitio nunc usque servata est, Catholicae venerabili ecclesiae socientur. . . . Senator. . . . inventus in grege Donatistarum centum libras solvat argenti. . . .
>
> We have decided that the Donatists and heretics with whom we have patiently borne up to now must be dealt with sternly. First of all they have to realize that by Imperial edict they are declared incapable of making a will or of entering upon any office, but are branded for ever as people of no credit who are to be rigidly excluded from all honourable assemblies and public meetings. Secondly, the places where their abominable superstition still survives are to be handed over to the venerable Catholic Church. Thirdly, their bishops, priests, presiding officers and officials are to be deprived of all their property and exiled to various islands and districts. . . .

There follows a long list of penalties much as in the former Decree.[2]

On June 14, 412, Augustine sent an open letter from the African Bishops assembled at Zerta to the Donatist body. Though written in the names of 'Silvanus, Valentinus, Aurelius—the Archbishop, Maximinus,[3] Optatus, Augustinus, Donatus et caeteri Episcopi de Concilio Zertensi,' it was, as Augustine himself tells us,[4] written by himself: 'But since all of us who were present at the Council of Numidia agreed that this should be done, it does not appear amongst my letters.'[5] The letter—which is really a compendious form of *Ad Donatistas post Collationem*, commonly known as *De Unitate*—sets out for the benefit of the laity of the sect the true account

[1] See pp. 350–351 above.
[2] *Cod. Theodos.* XVI. vi. 54, ed. Mommsen, i. 873–874.
[3] Or Maximianus, the converted Donatist Bishop of Bagai, see above, p. 116.
[4] *Retract.*, ii. 40.
[5] But now ranking as *Ep.* cxli.

of what took place at the Conference—as an antidote to the lying statements which their Bishops were publishing about the events of that meeting. The only passage which concerns us here deals with their complaints about the Imperial laws :

Whatever you have had to endure so far, as the result of those laws, has not been because of your righteousness but because of your wickedness ; nor should you say that it is we who have been lacking in fairness to you, arguing that you ought not to have been so dealt with and that the Emperor had no right to try and restrain you from your violent doings. For your own Bishops acknowledge that their predecessors dealt precisely in the same way with Caecilian as you protest that you ought not now to be treated.[1]

Once more, on August 13, 414, Honorius and Arcadius wrote to Julian, upholding the authority and permanent character of the action of Marcellinus at the Conference of A.D. 411 :

Notione et sollicitudine Marcellini spectabilis memoriae viri contra Donatistas gesta sunt ea, quae translata in publica monumenta, habere volumus perpetuam firmitatem. Neque enim morte cognitoris perire debet publica fides.

Under the careful investigation of Marcellinus, of notable memory, were carried out those dealings with the Donatists which, now enshrined in the Public Records, are by Our desire to abide in full force. For the public credit ought not to lapse with the death of him who presided over the enquiry.[2]

Once more, on August 25, 415, there appeared an Edict from Honorius addressed to Heraclianus, Count of Africa, and couched in almost precisely the same terms as the famous Decree *Oraculo penitus remoto*,[3] whereby the Emperor, writing to the same Heraclianus, had withdrawn the Edict of Toleration :

Let all who—enemies of the sacred law—have crept back to the practice of their heretical religion understand that if in future they have the audacity to assemble for the exercises of

[1] *Ep*. cxli. 8.
[2] *Cod. Theodos*. XVI. vi. 55 ; *P.L*. xi. 1128 ; xliii. 842.
[3] See above, p. 349.

their criminal rites they thereby lay themselves open to the penalties of proscription and death.[1]

XIII—EP. CLXXXV., A.D. 417

We come now to what is perhaps the most important of all St. Augustine's letters on the subject of the Donatists, more important even than *Ep.* xciii. to Vincent the Rogatist.[2] Somewhere about A.D. 416 Boniface, then Tribune, but later on Count of Africa, wrote to St. Augustine to ask for information about the Donatists. He was a curiously unstable man who was devoted to St. Augustine, had a desire to be a monk,[3] took a vow of chastity but married an Arian wife, then took a mistress,[4] then repented; finally, after fighting against the Vandals in Spain he actually invited them into Africa, 'barbari contra barbaros,'[5] and was himself slain by Aetius.[6] Augustine answered this letter at great length, so much so that it goes by the name of *De Correctione Donatistarum Liber*, is indeed called so by Augustine himself.[7] Its value lies not so much in the information it affords on the character of the schism as in the fact that it was written A.D. 417, when the great controversy had been settled, and it was possible to see the case as a whole; it is, as we shall see, peculiarly valuable for the clear statements it contains on what we may term 'quasi-coercion' to the faith.

After explaining that the Donatists were not—as Boniface seems to have imagined—Arians,[8] and after briefly stating the case of Caecilian and the origin of the schism,[9] Augustine comes at once to the question of the Imperial laws:

Just as Daniel's accusers were thrown to the lions they had prepared for him, so did the Donatists find that those civil authorities whom they had so constantly invoked for help had

1 *Cod. Theodos.* XVI. v. 56.
2 See above, p. 197.
3 *Ep.* ccxx. 3.
4 *Ibid.*, 4.
5 *Ibid.*
6 Pallu de Lessert, *Vicaires et Comtes de l'Afrique*, ii. 290.
7 *Retract.*, ii. 48.
8 *Ep.* clxxxv. 1.
9 *Ibid.*, 4–6.

now turned on them. But the result of these laws was a crowd of genuine converts.[1] The Apostle has told us to 'work good to all men' (Gal. vi. 10); let those, then, who can, do so by their sermons as Catholic preachers; others, through the laws of these Catholic rulers. Then, partly through people obeying God's admonitions, partly owing to others obeying the Imperial commands, all will be called to salvation, all will be recalled from destruction. . . . Anyone refusing to obey Imperial laws enacted for God's Truth deserves severe punishment.[2] He then deals with the preposterous claim of the Donatists that when put to death for not obeying these laws, they had won the crown of martyrdom, and points out that if the Donatists quoted in support of their contention the words: Blessed are they that suffer persecution, they must not omit the words 'for justice' sake,' adding that with the blood of so many on their hands they will find it difficult to substantiate their claim to 'justice.' If, however, we are prepared to tell or to acknowledge the truth, then there is such a thing as an unjust persecution, when, for instance, wicked men persecute the Church of Christ; and there is a just persecution, when, that is, the Church of Christ persecutes wicked men. . . . She persecutes them out of love, they out of hatred; She to correct them, they to overturn Her; She to reclaim them from error, they to drive men into error; finally, She pursues Her enemies and catches them till they quit their folly and make progress in the truth; while they, repaying good with evil, try to rob us of even this temporal life because we admonish them about the life that is eternal. So infatuated are they with murder that they even murder themselves when they can find no one else to murder.

People unfamiliar with their ways fancy that it is only now that they have taken to committing suicide, now, when such multitudes are, through these laws enacted for the procuring of Unity, being delivered from their frenzied domination. But those of us who knew what they were in the habit of doing long before these laws came into existence do not marvel at their deaths so much as recall their evil ways.[3] Augustine then gives details of the mad way in which these fanatics courted death; they insulted the Pagans when the altars of these latter were being broken down by order of the Emperors,

[1] *Ibid.*, 7.
[2] *Ibid.*, 8.
[3] 'Non eorum mirantur mortes sed recordantur mores,' *ibid.*, 12.

in the hope that they would turn on them and kill them, so that they could then claim ' perhaps a sort of shadow of martyrdom ' ; but they were conveniently forgetful of the fact that their slayers dedicated their victims to those very idols.[1]

A great mercy, then, is done them when, even by occasion of these Imperial laws, such people are snatched—at first all unwilling—from a sect wherein they have, through the teachings of lying devils, learned such evil practices, so that afterwards they may through sweet custom be healed in the Catholic Church by good precepts and sound morals. . . .The Catholic Church, indeed, earnestly desires that all may live ; but still more earnestly does She toil lest all should perish. Thanks be to God that amongst us, not indeed everywhere but still in many places, and in other parts, too, of Africa, Catholic peace has, without any of these madmen being put to death, run and still runs, ' Pax Catholica cucurrit, et currit.' [2]

As a matter of fact, previous to the coming of those laws into Africa, it seemed to some of our Brethren—and to myself among them—that though the Donatists were everywhere savagely attacking us it would be preferable not to petition the Emperor to suppress that heresy altogether by enacting penalties for all such as preferred to remain in it, but rather to ask him to make some decree which would free preachers of Catholic truth from having to suffer violence at the hands of the Donatists. This could, we thought, be secured if the Imperial authorities would make expressly applicable to the Donatists—who deny that they are heretics—the law of Theodosius which he promulgated against all heretics in general : ' Any Bishop or cleric of theirs, wheresoever found, to pay a fine of £10 in gold.' [3] Yet at the same time—so that they might not all have to pay this fine—asking him to make it applicable only in those districts where the Catholic Church has to put up with violence at the hands either of their clergy, or of the Circumcellions, or of the populace.[4] When, in such districts, Catholics have had to put up with violent attacks, they could make full statement

[1] *Ibid.*, 11–12.

[2] *Ibid.*, 14.

[3] ' It was the enormities perpetrated by Optatus, Donatist Bishop of Thamugadi, that compelled Seranus the Vicar to apply to you the law exacting a penalty of £10 in gold, a fine which none of you pay—and yet you accuse us of cruelty ! ' *Contra Litt. Petiliani*, ii. 184. For this law, as enacted in A.D. 405, see *Cod. Theodos*. XVI. vi. 4 ; for that of June 30, 412, see *ibid*. XVI. v. 52 ; for that of June 22, 414, *ibid*. XVI. v. 54.

[4] See *Ep*. lxxxviii. 7.

of the case, and then it would be the business of the local officials to see that the Donatist Bishops or other ministers were made to pay the fine. For we felt that when frightened in this manner and therefore no longer daring to do as they had been wont, it would be possible to have Catholic truth freely taught and embraced; no one would be compelled to embrace it, but those who wished to do so could do so without fear; for we have no wish to have false and pretended Catholics.

And despite the opposition of some of the Brethren, men advanced in years and who had before their eyes the spectacle of various cities and places where one could see the Catholic Church well and truly established owing to previous Imperial laws which had compelled people to embrace it, our opinion prevailed [1] and it was agreed to petition the Emperor in the sense suggested above, and an embassy was therefore despatched to the Court. But our representatives were unable to get what they wanted. For very serious complaints by some Bishops of other districts who had had to endure great hardships at the hands of the Donatists and had even been turned out of their Sees, had reached the Court before them. Peculiarly horrible was the unbelievable attack on Maximianus, the Catholic Bishop of Bagai, and it made our embassy useless. For a law had already been promulgated which pronounced that the Donatist heresy was of such an atrocious type that to spare it would have been an even greater cruelty than the enormities they themselves had perpetuated, and that this sect was not merely an unruly mob, but one which could not be allowed to go unpunished. Yet it was not to be punished by death—for Christian moderation was to be observed even towards people who were undeserving of it—but only by fines, and in the case of their Bishops, by exile.[2]

Augustine then gives in detail the horrible treatment meted out to the above-mentioned Maximianus who felt bound to appeal to the Emperor in person when he was able to get to Rome. 'Had he not done so,' remarks Augustine, 'his patience would not have been praiseworthy but his negligence blameworthy.' The result of this appeal was the Edict of

[1] Many Bishops wanted sterner measures to be taken against the Donatists owing to their violence; *cf. Epp.* cxxxix. 2, clxxxv. 25–26, cciv. 3. Dom Ceillier says, 'he asked for the laws because it was salutary for the many thus to be forced,' *Histoire Générale*, IX. i. 25, ed. Vives, 1863.

[2] *Ep.* clxxxv. 25–26.

Union, February 12, 405 [1] ; 'and as soon as these laws were promulgated in Africa, the converts flowed in.' [2]

The idea of compulsion to the Faith is in many minds so associated with St. Augustine, and the words of the Householder in the Gospel, 'Compel them to come in,' have been so identified with him that one would almost fancy that they were constantly on his lips or flowing from his pen. The idea, of course, occurs again and again, for the whole question at issue was whether people were to be driven into the fold by coercive laws. Yet—so far as we are aware—only in *Epp.* xciii. 5 and 16 and clxxxv. 24, does Augustine actually make use of the words, though he deals expressly with the problem in some twenty-three Letters and Treatises.

The modern view of the doctrine—if so it can be termed—is thus expressed by P. Monceaux :

> Telle est l'origine de la doctrine du *Compelle intrare :* la coercition pour le salut, la persécution dans l'interêt des persécutés, le Paradis forcé. Doctrine trop clairement inacceptable pour la raison, mais inquiétante pour l'Eglise elle-même, et, pour tous, dangereuse dans l'application, terrible pour les consequences. Doctrine que réprouve avec horreur la conscience du monde moderne, mais qui, au début du cinquième siècle, s'accordait trop bien avec les conceptions politiques et la législation du temps.[3]

But one may question whether he does real justice to the Saint. Many will, we fancy, prefer the more balanced statements of M. Bouvet and M. Pichon :

> Après 404, S. Augustin consent à ce que les lois coercitives soient partout en vigueur, et qu'elles obligent à rentrer dans le giron de l'Eglise du Christ. Voila le point précis du changement. S. Augustin ne dira plus qu'il recuse la contrainte, qu'il veut simplement punir les attentats contre les Catholiques. Il continuera néanmoins à affirmer que la cause initiale des lois est la fureur des Circoncellions.[4]

[1] See pp. 261, 309, 329 above.

[2] *Ep.* clxxxv. 29.

[3] *Histoire littéraire de l'Afrique du nord*, vii., p. 228.

[4] Bouvet, *S. Augustin et la répression de l'erreur religieuse*, 1918, p. 56 ; *cf. Epp.* lxxxviii. 6–7, lxxxix. 2, clxxxv. 18 ; *Contra Cresconium*, iii. 47–48, iv. 62 ; *Contra Julianum*, i. 10.

And M. Pichon : La lutte contre les Donatistes à première vue, ne semble guère comporter de discussions philosophiques, le donatisme étant moins une hérésie qu'une schisme. Mais au cours de la controverse, il suscite une question nouvelle : jusqu'à quel point l'unité de croyances peut-elle etre imposée par la force ? Il se prononce pour l'emploi de l'autorité séculière en matière ecclésiastique, et trace la théorie de la religion d'État. Tout ce qu'on a pu dire depuis, en faveur de l'intervention gouvernementale dans les querelles religieuses et contre la liberté de conscience, est résumé dans les lettres à Vincentius et à Boniface. Il démontre que la répression légale de l'hérésie est un droit et même un devoir. C'est une théorie fort discutable ; du moins, S. Augustin la formule nettement et essaie de la justifier. En pratique d'ailleurs avec une loyauté parfaite, il proteste contre les excès de l'autorité.[1]

The last phase in this long-drawn-out dispute belongs to the year 420, when, nine years after the Conference, the Tribune Dulcitius, brother of that Laurentius to whom Augustine addressed his *Enchiridion* or Manual on Faith, Hope and Charity about a year later, seems to have threatened with death some recalcitrant Donatists who were brought before him, though he explained that he had not really meant that. St. Augustine, however, felt it necessary to point out that ' you have no power of the sword conferred on you by any law ; nowhere in the Imperial Constitutions of which you are the executor is it anywhere laid down that they are to be put to death.' [2]

To the same year belongs the tragi-comical discussion between Augustine and his old antagonist at the Conference, Gaudentius, the Donatist Bishop of Thamugadi. The latter wrote that he and his flock were collected in their church and were prepared to set fire to it and perish in the flames rather than obey the Imperial Decree and surrender it to the Catholics. In his letter he harped, of course, on the ' persecution ' they were meeting with, and Augustine could only reply by reiterating the points on which he had so often insisted : when you say that you do not think that people should be compelled to

[1] Réné Pichon, *Histoire de la littérature latine,* 2nd ed., p. 864, 1898.
[2] *Ep.* cciv. 3, A.D. 420.

embrace the truth against their will 'you do greatly err, knowing neither the Scriptures nor the power of God'; for when they are driven in, unwilling, God makes them willing. Would you say that the Ninivites repented unwillingly because they only did so at the bidding of their king? What need was there of that royal command humbly to petition God—who looks not at men's lips but at their hearts—save that there were amongst them some who would have taken no interest in, and certainly would not have believed, the Divine warning, unless they had first been terror-stricken by an earthly ruler. In the same way, owing to this royal command—in opposition to which you are voluntarily courting death—an opportunity is being offered to many of securing the salvation which is in Christ. And even if such people are being brought by force to this Great Householder's Supper they find when they do come in abundant cause for rejoicing that they did come in.' [1]

[1] *Contra Gaudentium*, i. 28, A.D. 420.

IX

THE WRITINGS OF ST. AUGUSTINE

I. A Table of the Main Historical Events, A.D. 350–430—II. A List of St. Augustine's Writings : (*a*) Introductory Remarks ; (*b*) The Writings he Enumerates in the *Retractations ;* (*c*) Those not named in the *Retractations*—III. Chronological Tables of the Writings—IV. Printed Editions of St. Augustine's Works ; also some Translations.

I—THE MAIN HISTORICAL EVENTS, A.D. 350–430

	EMPERORS	POPES	FATHERS OF THE CHURCH
A.D. 350. Augustine, *b.* 354.	Constantine II, *d.* 351. Constans, *d.* 353.	Liberius, 352–366.	
A.D. 360.	Constantius, *d.* 361. Julian the Apostate, 361–363. Jovian, 364. Valentinian I, 364–375. Valens, 364–378.		
St. Optatus, *De Schismate Donatistarum*, 366.		Damasus, 366–384.	St. Hilary of Poitiers, *d.* 366.
A.D. 370. Augustine at Carthage, a Manichee, from his 19th to his 29th year.			St. Athanasius, *d.* 373. St. Epiphanius, *d.* 373.
	Valentinian II, 375–392. Gratian, 375–383. Theodosius the Great, 379–395.		St. Basil, *d.* 379.
A.D. 380. Augustine goes to Rome, (?) 383.		Council of Constantinople, 381. Siricius, 384–398.	
			St. Cyril of Jerusalem, *d.* 386.

	EMPERORS	POPES	FATHERS OF THE CHURCH
Augustine at Milan, 384–385. Conversion, Sept., 386.			
Baptized, May, 387.			
St. Monica, *d.* 387/8.			
Augustine returns to Africa, Sept., 388.			
A.D. 390.			
Augustine ordained, 391/2.			St. Gregory Nazianzen, *d.* 390.
Aurelius, Archbishop of Carthage, 391.	Honorius, 395–423.		
Council of Hippo, 393.			
A.D. 393.—*c.* 420.			
Manichaean and Donatist Controversy.			
Augustine consecrated Bishop of Hippo, 395/6.			St. Gregory of Nyssa, *d.* 395.
Council of Carthage, 397.			
			St. Ambrose, *d.* 397.
		Anastasius, 398–401/2.	
A.D. 400.			
A.D. 401. Councils of Carthage, V–VI.		Innocent I, 402–417.	
A.D. 403. ... VIII.			St. Epiphanius, *d.* 403.
A.D. 404. ... IX.			
A.D. 405. ... X.			
A.D. 407. ... XI.			
A.D. 408. ... XII–XIII.			
Decree of Union, against Donatists, Feb. 12, 405.			
A.D. 409. Council of Carthage, XIV.			St. Chrysostom, *d.* 407.
		Sack of Rome.	Rufinus, *d.* 410.
A.D. 410. ... XV.			
A.D. 411. Conference between Catholics and Donatists.			
A.D. 412–430. Anti-Pelagian controversy.			
A.D. 416. Council of Carthage, XVI, against Pelagianism. Also at Milevis.			

	EMPERORS	POPES	FATHERS OF THE CHURCH
A.D. 417–418. Council of Carthage, XVII.		Zosimus, 417–418.	
A.D. 418. Condemnation of Pelagianism.			
A.D. 418. Augustine goes to Caesarea of Mauretania.		Boniface, 418–423.	
A.D. 419. Council of Carthage, XVIII.			
A.D. 420.			St. Jerome, *d.* 420.
A.D. 421. Council of Carthage, XIX.			
	Valentinian III, 423–455.	Celestine, 423–432.	
A.D. 424. Council of Carthage, XX.			
			Theodore of Mopsuestia, *d.* 428.
A.D. 429. Aurelius, *d.* Vandal invasion.			
A.D. 430. Augustine *d.*			

II—A LIST OF ST. AUGUSTINE'S WRITINGS

(*a*) *Introductory Remarks*

The following catalogue of Augustine's writings follows the order he himself gives in his *Retractations*, the dates assigned being those given by the Maurist editors. The notes show when and why it has seemed necessary at times to dissent from their chronology, while the tables at the end give in parallel columns the Maurist chronology and that which we would suggest. Possidius' *Indiculus* is unfortunately not in chronological order but is divided up according to subject-matter.

As early as A.D. 413 Augustine wrote to Marcellinus saying that he hoped God would permit him to carry out a design he had formed, that, namely, 'of collecting together and setting down clearly all the things in all my books with which I am dissatisfied. . . .'[1] But he had to wait some fourteen years

[1] *Ep.* cxliii. 2.

for the opportunity of doing this. Four years before his death he wrote to Quodvultdeus, who had asked him to draw up a treatise on *Heresies*, saying that he was intensely busy refuting Julian the Pelagian and that therefore,

so as to fail in neither task I devote the day-time to one, the night-time to another.

What this second task was he explains :

I am busy over a very urgent matter : I am passing in review (retractabam) all my writings and am trying to show, either by correcting it or by defending it, what should be and can be read, where, that is, anything I have written displeases me or might give offence to others. I have already finished two volumes in thus rehandling (retractatis) all my books ; of their number I was unaware ; I now find they come to two hundred and thirty-two. There yet remain my Letters, also tractates delivered to the people, what the Greeks term 'Homilies.' I had already re-read some of my Letters but had dictated nothing regarding them when Julian's last volumes began to take up my time. . . . I have then to work at both tasks at once, namely, answer Julian and pass my books in review, devoting the day to one, the night to the other.[1]

In the *Prologue* to these *Retractations* he says :

I have for long been thinking over and planning a task which, with God's help, I am now undertaking because I feel it should no longer be delayed, namely, that of reconsidering (recenseam) my writings, whether Books, Letters or Tractates and censoring them with a certain judicial severity, indicating with a censor's blue pencil (censorio stylo) whatever displeases me. . . . I am glad of the opportunity of doing this so that I may put it into people's hands, for I cannot now withdraw from the public for the purpose of correction writings long ago published by me. Nor do I pass over things I wrote when only a catechumen, for they too have got into circulation and people copy them and read them. Let not those, then, who read these works imitate me in my errors but in the progress they find me making. For perchance whoso reads my writings in the

[1] *Ep*. ccxxiv. 2, *c*. 427–428 ; *P.L*. xxxiv. 1002–1003, xlii. 19.

order in which they were written will find that I did make progress as I wrote. For this reason, then, I shall take care that, so far as possible, that same order may be discoverable in this work of mine.[1]

Certain points should be noted : (*a*) Augustine intended to draw up a third volume but was prevented from doing so, partly by excessive preoccupation with his answers to Julian, partly by the threatening Vandal invasion, and to a great extent perhaps by his own advancing years ; (*b*) his writings are set down (*quantum potero*) in chronological order precisely in order that readers may be able to see for themselves how Augustine has developed in thought and accuracy of expression. It would seem, then, to be a first principle in discussing the chronology of Augustine's writings to accept the order he himself gives. The Maurist editors, however, have felt obliged at times to disregard Augustine's order, with resulting confusion. One reason for what seem at first sight to be departures by Augustine from this chronological order may be that he does not always make it clear whether he is referring to the time when he began the work in question or to the time when he completed it.[2] Moreover, he was, as we shall see, often occupied with more than one ' magnum opus ' at the same time. But we may say at once that wherever it is possible to test his order by evidence extrinsic to the *Retractations*, that order is confirmed. For instance, we know that *De Fide et Symbolo* was preached by him at the Council of Hippo in 393 ; when, then, he deals with his *Acta contra Fortunatum* immediately before that sermon we can assign that discussion to the time when he had left Tagaste for Hippo.[3]

It must not be forgotten that Augustine was a meticulously careful writer ; we have only to study his controversial writings to see this. Read, for example, *Epp*. xliii.–xliv., A.D. 397–398,

[1] *Praef*. in *Retractationes*, *P.L.* xxxii. 583–586, ed. P. Knoll, *C.S.E.L.* xxxvi. : see A. Harnack, *Die Retractationen Augustins* in *Sitzungsberichte der königlichen Akademie*, liii. 1905 ; especially J. de Ghellinck, *Les Rétractations de S. Augustin. Examen de conscience de l'écrivain*, in *Nouvelle Revue Théologique*, lvii. 1930, pp. 481–500 ; M. J. Lagrange, O.P., *Les Rétractations exégètiques de saint Augustin*, in *Miscellanea Agostiniana*, ii. 373–395, 1931.

[2] See S. M. Zarb in *Angelicum*, 1933, pp. 372 ff.

[3] *Retract*. i, 16–17.

Ep. li., A.D. 399–400, and then *Epp.* lxxxvii.–lxxxviii., written after the *Decree of Union*, February 12, 405, and it will be evident what pains he has taken to be exact in his facts and orderly in his marshalling of them;[1] see, too, how he corrects mistakes into which he had unwittingly fallen, *De Unico Baptismo*, 28, *cp. Retract.* ii. 27 and 34. In the *Retractations*, too, he is most careful in his indications of the time and place of writing, using different expressions quite consistently, for example: 'Eodem tempore,'[2] 'Tunc,'[3] 'Inter haec,'[4] 'Deinde,'[5] 'Post,'[6] 'Per idem tempus,'[7] 'Romae,'[8] 'Milano,'[9] 'Africa,'[10] 'Hippo.'[11] At other times he gives no precise indication, either because it is clear that the work in question follows immediately upon the preceding, or because he has several works on hand at the same time. For example, he says: 'De Trinitate scripsi per aliquot annos,'[12] and then on the *De Consensu* 'Per eosdem annos quibus paulatim libros *de Trinitate* dictabam scripsi et alios labore continuo.'[13] Then come three anti-Donatist works, two of them, *Contra Epistolam Parmeniani* and *De Baptismo contra Donatistas*,[14] of considerable length. There follows the lengthy letter to Januarius,[15] then, at the behest of Aurelius, *De Opere Monachorum*,[16] then *De Bono conjugali* which, as he says, necessitated its counterpart *De Sancta Virginitate*.[17] Then: 'Per idem tempus' *de Genesi ad Litteram*, of which he says 'posterius coepi sed prius terminavi quam *de Trinitate*: ideo eos nunc ordine quo coepi recolui.'[18] Then,

[1] *Cf. Contra Epistolam Parmeniani*, i. 1, *Contra Litt. Petiliani*, i. 2–3, ii. 1–2; see, too, *Sermons*, ii.–iii. *on* Ps. xxxvi.
[2] i. 16, 22; ii. 34, 36, 48, 55, 56.
[3] i. 13; ii. 42, 60.
[4] Or 'interea' i. 4, 5, 15, 24; ii. 11, 31, 38, 43, 44, 52, 58, 62.
[5] i. 11.
[6] i. 5, 15, 24; ii. 27, 46, 51.
[7] i. 3, 6, 12, 17, 19; ii. 24, 30, 47, 59; *cp.* 'per eosdem annos,' ii. 16.
[8] i. 7, 8, 9.
[9] i. 5, 6.
[10] i. 10.
[11] i. 14.
[12] ii. 15.
[13] ii. 16.
[14] ii. 17–19.
[15] ii. 20.
[16] ii. 21.
[17] ii. 22–23.
[18] ii. 24.

to our astonishment, 'Antequam finirem libros *de Trinitate* et libros *de Genesi ad Litteram* irruit causa respondendi Litteris Petiliani,' [1] and there follow three more anti-Donatist works.[2]

(*b*) *The Writings enumerated in the 'Retractations,' as well as those omitted*

Chronological Tables of St. Augustine's Works [3]

1. *Contra Academicos*, previous to his baptism, *Retract*. i. 1, at Cassiciacum, 386. *P.L.* xxxiii. 905–958 ; *C.S.E.L.* lxiii. 1922.
2. *De Beata Vita*, between *Contra Academicos* 8 and iii., at Cassiciacum, 386. *P.L.* xxxiii. 959–976 ; *Retract*. i. 2 ; *C.S.E.L.* lxiii. 1922. This Dialogue was begun on Augustine's birthday, the Ides of November, 386/7, see *Beata Vita*, 6. His earlier *De Pulchro et Apto*, written when he was between twenty-six and twenty-seven years old, *Confess*. iv. 20 and 27, has not survived.
3. *De Ordine*, at Cassiciacum, 386, *Retract*. i. 3 ; *P.L.* xxxiii. 977–1020 ; *C.S.E.L.* lxiii. 1922.[4]
4. *Soliloquia*, at Cassiciacum, 386, unfinished ?, *Retract*. i. 4 and 5 ; *P.L.* xxxiii. 869–904. A spurious *Soliloquiorum animae ad Deum Liber* will be found in *P.L.* xl. 863–898. Augustine added his *De Immortalitate Animae* to complete his *Soliloquia* 'quae imperfecta remanserant,' *Retract*. I. v. 1. Of his *De Immortalitate* he says : 'How it got into circulation contrary to my wish, and how it came to be classed among my writings, I do not know. For to begin with the argument is so tortuous and so condensed that it baffles even me when I read it, I can hardly understand it myself.' *Retract*. I. v. 1. See a treatise *De Grammatica* of doubtful authenticity, *P.L.* xxxii. 1385–1408 ; *The Soliloquies of St. Augustine : A Manual of Contemplative Prayer*, translated by L. M. F. G., 1912.
5. *De Immortalitate animae*, at Milan, 387, *Retract*. I. v. 1–3 ; *P.L.* xxxiii. 1021–1034 ; see No. 4.
6. *Disciplinarum libri*, on the eve of his baptism ; these included :
   (*a*) *De Grammatica*, this he lost, it was stolen 'ex armario,' *Retract*. i. 11.
   (*b*) *De Musica*, begun at Milan, 387, finished in Africa, 389, *Retract*. i. 11 ; *P.L.* xxx. 1081–1194.
   (*c*) *De Dialectica*, *De Rhetorica*, *De Geometria*, *De Arithmetica*, *De Philosophia* ; all these he lost, 'but I think some people have copies of them,' *Retract*. i. 6.[5]
7. *De Moribus Ecclesiae Catholicae et De Moribus Manichaeorum*, at Rome, A.D. 388/9, after his baptism, *Retract*. i. 7 ; *P.L.* xxxii. 1309–1378.

[1] ii. 25.

[2] ii. 26–29.

[3] A *Chronologia Operum S. Augustini*, by J. M. Suarez, appeared as early as 1670 ; Dom A. Wilmart, *Operum Sti. Augustini Elenchus*, *Miscellanea Agostiniana*, ii. 149–233 ; *La Tradition des grands ouvrages de S. Augustin*, Dom A. Wilmart, *ibid*., ii. 257 ff.

[4] A. Dyroff, *Ueber Form und Begriffsgehalt der Augustinischen Schrift De Ordine*, 1930.

[5] See D. Ohlmann, *De S. Augustini dialogis in Cassiciaco scriptis*, 1897 ; also E. Fischer, *De Augustini disciplinarum libro qui est 'De Dialectica,'* Jena, 1912.

8. *De Quantitate Animae*, at Rome, early in 388, *Retract.* i. 8; *P.L.* xxxiii. 1035–1080. Augustine reminds Evodius of his share in this dialogue, *Ep.* clxii. 2, *c.* A.D. 415.
9. *De Libero arbitrio*, begun at Rome, 388, finished between 391 and 395, in Africa, *P.L.* xxxiii. 1221–1310; *Retract.* i. 9. Augustine sent a copy to St. Paulinus at Nola, *Ep.* xxxi. 7, A.D. 396, and in 405 he tells Secundinus the Manichee that he 'can find a copy at Nola in Campania in the hands of God's servant Paulinus,' *Contra Secundinum*, xi.
10. *De Genesi adversus Manichaeos*, *c.* 389, *Retract.* i. 10, *P.L.* xxxiv. 173–220.
11. *De Magistro*, in the middle of 389, *Retract.* i. 12, *P.L.* xxxiii. 1195–1220.
12. *De Vera Religione*, *c.* 390, *Retract.* i. 13, *P.L.* xxxiv. 121–172; *cf.* *Ep.* clxii. 2, Evodius has a copy. The following were written at Hippo before his elevation to the Episcopate:
13. *De Utilitate credendi*, 391; *P.L.* xlii. 63–92; *Retract.* I. xiv. 1-6; ed. C. Marriott, 1869 and 1885; translated by H. de Romestin, 1885; see a study of this treatise by Mgr. Batiffol, *Rev. Biblique*, January, 1917, pp. 9 ff. If the Honoratus to whom the long *Ep.* cxl., *P.L.* xxxiii. 538–577, *De Gratia Novi Testamenti*, was addressed *c.* A.D. 412, is the person to whom *De Utilitate Credendi* was written, we may presume that Augustine's labour was not wasted and that Honoratus became a Christian.
14. *De duabus animabus contra Manichaeos*, 391; *Retract.* I. xv. 1–8; *P.L.* xlii. 93–112.
15. *Contra Fortunatum Manichaeum*, 392; *Retract.* I. xvi. 1–2; *P.L.* xlii. 111–130. Even the Donatists begged Augustine to come over to Carthage and rout Fortunatus; the latter, however, knowing that Augustine himself had once been tainted with the same errors, shrank from the discussion. But there was no escape, and he was so completely defeated that, saying he would refer the knotty question to his superiors, he fled the city, never to return, Possidius, *Vita*, vi.
16. *De Fide et Symbolo* 'coram episcopis hoc mihi jubentibus qui plenarium totius Africae concilium Hippone-regio habebant,' 393, *Retract.* I. xvii., *P.L.* xl. 181–196, *C.S.E.L.* xli.
17. *De Genesi ad litteram, Imperfectus Liber*, *c.* 393; his previous treatise had been an allegorical exposition, now Augustine attempted a literal commentary; 'But I was but a novice in expounding Holy Scripture and I collapsed beneath a load which proved too heavy,' *Retract.* I. xviii., *P.L.* xxxiv. 220–246. For the long delays in publishing this work, *cf.* *Epp.* cxliii. 4, clix. 2, clxii. 2.
18. *De Sermone Domini in monte*, 393–394; *Retract.* I. xviii. 1–9, *P.L.* xxxiv. 1250–1308. See D. Bassi, *Le Beatitudini nella Struttura del 'De Sermone Domini in Monte' di. Sant' Agostino*, in *Miscellanea Agostiniana*, ii. pp. 915–931; R. C. Trench, *An Exposition of the Sermon on the Mount, drawn from the Writings of St. Augustine*, 1844; *The Sermon on the Mount* and *The Harmony of the Gospels*, in the translation edited by M. Dods, vol. viii.
19. *Psalmus contra partem Donati*, the end of 393. This was the first-fruits of the campaign he now began against the schism which was ruining the African Church; *Retract.* I. xx., *P.L.* xliii. 23–32, *C.S.E.L.* li. An alphabetical Psalm or 'abecedarius' as Augustine terms it; for the construction see his remarks at the end of *Enarr.* xxxii. 8 *on* Ps. cxviii. For a study of it see *Journal of Theol. Studies*, July, 1927; also H. Vroom, *Le Psaume abécédaire de S. Augustin et la poésie latine rhythmique*, 1933; F. Ermini, *Il 'Psalmus contra Partem*

Donati,' Miscellanea Agostiniana, ii. 341–352; H. J. Rose, *St. Augustine as a forerunner of Mediaeval Hymnology, J. T. S.*, July, 1927, pp. 383–392.

20. *Contra Epistolam Donati haeretici*, 'qui secundus post Majorinum episcopus apud Carthaginem fuit,' 394. This, the only treatise directly levelled against the man who gave his name to the sect though he was not its originator, is unfortunately lost; *Retract.* I. xxi. 1–3.
21. *Contra Adimantum Manichaei discipulum*, 394; *Retract.* I. xxii. 1–4; *P.L.* xlii. 129–172. Adimantus was held in high esteem by the Manichees: Faustus says: 'After our blessed Father, Manichaeus, Adimantus is the only person for us (Manichees) to study,' *Contra Faustum*, I. ii.
22. *Expositio quarundam propositionum ex Epistola Apostoli ad Romanos*, 394; *Retract.* I. xxiii. 1–4; *P.L.* xxxv. 2063–2088.
23. *Expositio Epistolae ad Galatas*, 394; *Retract.* I. xxiv. 1–2; *P.L.* xxxv. 2105–2148.
24. *Epistolae ad Romanos inchoata Expositio*, 394. This Augustine found too much for him: 'operis magnitudine ac labore deterritus et in alia faciliora deflexus sum,' *Retract.* I. xxv.; *P.L.* 2087–2108.
25. *De diversis Quaestionibus octoginta tribus*. Begun in Africa shortly after his conversion, the scattered sheets were collected by Augustine perhaps shortly before his consecration; *cf. Retract.* I. xxvi.; *P.L.* vi. 11–100.
26. *De mendacio*, 395, a work Augustine would have gladly withdrawn from circulation 'quia obscurus et anfractuosus et omnino molestus mihi videbatur'; he felt this the more strongly because he was satisfied with his later work, *Contra mendacium*, see below; *Retract.* I. xxvii., *P.L.* vi. 487–518, *C.S.E.L.* xli., ed. Zycha. This 'obscurity' abundantly appears, for example, in No. 16, *P.L.* xl. col. 500.
27. *Ad Simplicianum, c.* 397. This, Augustine's first work as a Bishop, was addressed to that Simplicianus whom he later immortalized in his *Confessions*, for it was to him he went for help in his perplexities. St. Ambrose died in A.D. 397 and Simplicianus succeeded him in the See of Milan, *Retract.* II. i. 1–2, *P.L.* xl. 101–148. The Maurists suppose that Simplicianus was already a Bishop and had succeeded St. Ambrose, who died April 4, 397. But if so, this treatise cannot be earlier than that date, and as Augustine puts *Contra Epistolam Manichaei*, *De Agone*, *De Doctrina Christiana*, *Contra Partem Donati* and the *Confessions*, *Retract.* II. 2-6, after *Ad Simplicianum*, it seems impossible to refer all the above writings to A.D. 396–398, as do the Maurists. As a matter of fact there is no suggestion in *Ad Simplicianum* that the latter was a Bishop.
28. *Contra epistolam* (Manichaei) *quam vocant fundamenti, c.* 397; *Retract.* II. ii., *P.L.* xlii. 173–206. 'This Epistle "of the Foundation" is usually most familiar to those among you who are known as the "Illuminati,"' *ibid.* 28, *P.L.* xlii. 192: 'that Epistle,' declared Felix the Manichee in his disputation with Augustine, 'is the beginning, middle and end,' *Acta cum Felice*, ii. 1, *P.L.* xlii. 536.
29. *De Agone Christiano* 'fratribus in eloquio Latino ineruditis,' 396, 'aut paulo post,' *Retract.* II. iii., *P.L.* xl. 289–310, *C.S.E.L.* xli., ed. Zycha.
30. *De Doctrina Christiana*, Bks. i.–iii. 36 were written *c.* 397, and Augustine completed the work only in 426; *Retract.* II. iv. 1–2; *P.L.* xxxiv. 15–122. St. Augustine says he 'found the work incomplete' presumably at the time of drawing up these *Retractations*, viz. A.D. 426. This is more precisely stated in *De Doctrina*, iv. 55, where he refers to his visit to Caesarea in Mauretania as being

' ferme octo vel amplius anni ' previously. But he was sent thither by Pope Zosimus, 417–418 ; *cf. Ep.* cxc. 1, cxciii. 1, Possidius, *Vita*, 14, and this visit is again precisely dated ' Honorio duodecimum et Theodosio octavum consulibus, duodecimo calendis Octobris,' viz. September 20, 418 ; the *De Doctrina Christiana*, then, will in its completed state date from A.D. 426/427. This does not mean that there were, as Dom De Bruyne at one time held, two editions of the *De Doctrina Christiana ;* Augustine's words are clear : ' I found the Books of the *De Doctrina Christiana* incomplete and I thought it better to complete them rather than to leave them as they were and pass on to the reconsideration (retractanda) of my other works,' *Retract.* II. iv. 1. Dom De Bruyne, after noting that such authorities as Bardenhewer, Cavallera and d'Alès had endorsed his notion that there were two editions, says, ' the edition of 397 never existed save in my imagination,' *Rev. d'Hist. Ecclésiastique*, 1927, p. 783, quoted by Zarb, *Angelicum*, 1933, p. 481, note. As Augustine himself quotes *De Doctrina Christiana*, ii. 60, on the spoliation of the Egyptians, in his *Contra Faustum*, XXII. xci., A.D. 400, we have a confirmation of the date suggested by the position given to it in the *Retractations*.

The *De Doctrina Christiana, Bk. iv., a Commentary and a Revised Text*, by Theresa Sullivan, Washington University, 1930 ; the whole ed. by H. J. Vogels, Bonn, 1930 ; Francey, *Les Ideés littéraires de S. Augustin dans le De Doctrina Christiana*, Fribourg, 1920. *The Christian Doctrine*, in the translation edited by M. Dods, vol. ix.

31. *Contra partem Donati*, *c.* 397 ; another anti-Donatist work which has not survived, *Retract.* II. v.

32. *Confessionum libri tredecim*, *c.* 400, *Retract.* II. vi. 1–2 ; *P.L.* xxxiii. 659–868. The ' Confessions ' seem to end naturally with Bk. ix ; Bks. x.–xiii. are simply an allegorical explanation of *Genesis*, due perhaps to the fact that he was already working on his *De Genesi ad litteram* where, II. ix. 22, he refers to ' my allegorical views on this point which will be found,' he says, ' in Bk. xiii. of my *Confessions* ' ; as he began Bk. xii. of *De Genesi ad Litt.* in A.D. 401, it is clear that the last four Bks. of the *Confessions* had been added at the latest by 401. That the earlier Bks. of the *Confessions* date from the beginning of 397 seems to follow from the way in which, *Confess.* viii. 3, he speaks of St. Ambrose as a Bishop at the time he is writing—and Ambrose died April 4, 397, while Simplicianus, referred to in the same passage, is not styled a Bishop.

Of the numerous editions of the *Confessions* we need only mention :

Sti. Augustini Confessiones, ex recensione P. Knoll, 1926.

Confessionum libri tredecim, ed. post Knoll, M. Skutella, 1934.

Confessions, ed. J. Gibb and W. Montgomery, 1908, 2nd ed., 1927 ; A. Harnack, *Monasticism and the Confessions of St. Augustine*, 1901.

S. Augustin : Confessions : texte établi et traduit, par P. de Labriolle, 2 vols., 1925–1926.

S. Augustini, Confessiones, ed. C. H. Bruder, 1924.

St. Augustini, Confessions, in the translation edited by M. Dods, vol. xiv.

The Confessions of St. Augustine, in the Translation of Sir Tobie Matthew, 1620 *and* 1638, *revised and amended* by Dom Roger Huddleston, O.S.B., 1923 ; see, too, *The Unmasking of a Massemonger . . . or the Vindication of St. Augustine's ' Confessions ' from the . . . Calumniations of a late noted Apostate* (Sir Tobie Matthew), 1626.

R. L. Ottley, *Studies in the ' Confessions ' of St. Augustine*, 1919.

St. Augustine's Confessions, with an English Translation, by William Watts, 1631, ed. by T. E. Page and W. H. Rouse, 1912.

H. Gros, *La Valeur documentaire des ' Confessions ' de S. Augustin*, 1927.

P. Fabo, *La Juventud de San Agustin ante la critica moderna*, 1929.

Desjardins, *Essai sur les Confessions de S. Augustin*, 1858.

33. *Contra Faustum Manichaeum.* Faustus, who came to Carthage A.D. 383, had ' blasphemed the Law and the Prophets, as well as their God and Christ's Incarnation.' Augustine, who had longed to meet him, hoping to glean from him some answer to his difficulties, *Confess.* v. 10–11, but was bitterly disappointed, wrote this ' grande opus ' in thirty-three books about A.D. 400 ; *Retract.* II. vii. 1–3 ; *P.L.* xlii. 207–518. This is not an actual dialogue but a refutation of a book by Faustus and cast in the form of a dialogue, I. i., *P.L.* xlii. 207. The same applies to *Contra Litteras Petiliani*, where Augustine's replies to Petilian's letters are, by the insertion of passages from the latter, made to read like a dialogue, *P.L.* xliii. *Contra Litt. Petiliani*, ii. 1, col. 259 ; *cf. De Unitate*, 1, *ibid.*, col. 391. For the character of Faustus, see Combès, *La Doctrine politique de S. Augustin*, 1922, p. 267. The date of the *Contra Faustum* can be approximately determined by Augustine's words to St. Jerome, *Ep.* lxxxii. 17 (*Ep.* cxvi. *inter Epp. S. Hieronymi*) : ' Long before I received your letters (*Epp.* lxxii., lxxv. and lxxxi. *inter Epp. S. Augustini*) I had, when writing against Faustus . . .,' and this *Ep.* lxxxii. almost certainly dates from A.D. 405/6 ; so, too, *De Consensu Evangelistarum*, ii. 8; he refers to what he had written against Faustus on Lia and Rachel, *Contra Faustum*, XXII. lii. Both points serve to endorse the position of the *Contra Faustum* in the *Retractations*, *c.* A.D. 400.

34. *Contra Felicem Manichaeum*, Augustine's written account of a two days' discussion in the church, December 7 and 12, 404, *Retract.* II. viii. ; *P.L.* xlii. 519–552 ; *C.S.E.L.*, ed. J. Zycha, 1892. If the unnamed Manichaean to whom Augustine addressed *Ep.* lxxix. was Felix, as the Benedictine editors suggest, then Felix would seem to have been brought forward by the Manichees in place of the discredited Fortunatus. The date usually assigned to the *Acta cum Felice*, A.D. 404, depends on the reading ' Honorio Augusto *sextum* consule,' I. i., *P.L.* xlii. 519. But if ' sextum,' or A.D. 404, is to stand, it will follow that St. Augustine did not draw up the list of his works in the *Retractations* in chronological order, for several works afterwards enumerated were unquestionably written before that date. But if, as suggested by P. Monceaux in *Comptes rendus de l'Académie*, 1908, 51–53, VI. has been written instead of IV., the date of these *Acta* would be A.D. 398, in which year fell Honorius' fourth consulate.

35. *De Natura Boni*, 404, *Retract.* II. ix. ; *P.L.* xlii. 551–572 ; *C.S.E.L.* ed. Zycha, 1892. St. Thomas I. *Sententiarum*, XIX. v. 3, *Sed contra*, quotes this work by the old title ' De vera Innocentia.' Zarb, *Angelicum*, 1933, pp. 484–485, would on the strength of their position in the *Retractations* and on the supposition that the date assigned to *Contra Felicem*, see No 34 above, refer this and the five following works to A.D. 399.

36. *Contra Secundinum Manichaeum*, *c.* 405, *Retract.* II. x. ; *P.L.* xlii. 578–602 ; *C.S.E.L.*, ed. Zycha, 1892. Secundinus, Augustine tells us, was not one of the Manichaean ' elect,' but only an ' auditor,' and, though Augustine had never seen him, wrote to him as to an old friend, *Retract.* II. x. ; for Secundinus' letter see *P.L.* xlii. 571–578.

37. *Contra Hilarum* ; Hilarus had objected to the singing of the Offertory Psalm. Augustine's reply is unfortunately lost, *Retract.* II. xi. *c.* 405.
38. *Quaestiones Evangeliorum*, only on St. Matthew and St. Luke, *c.* 400 ; *Retract.* II. xii. ; *P.L.* xxxv. 1323–1364.
39. *Annotationes in Job*, *c.* 400. As taken down by his hearers Augustine found these Notes unintelligible, all the more that the Latin text he had to use was a deplorably bad one, *Retract.* II. xiii. ; *P.L.* xxxiv. 825–886. This seems to have been a collection of notes taken by Augustine's disciples and may therefore have covered the years 395–400.
40. *De Catechizandis rudibus*, *c.* 400, *Retract.* II. xiv. ; *P.L.* xl. 309–348. Deogratias the Deacon, to whom it is addressed, may be the same as the Deogratias to whom Augustine answers questions put by a pagan, *Ep.* cii., 408–409. The treatise has often been edited : C. C. Marriott, 1878, and since ; W. Y. Fausset, 2nd ed., 1912, *De Catechizandis Rudibus, translated with Introduction and Commentary*, by J. P. Christopher, 1926 ; also A. Souter, *The Text of De Catechizandis rudibus, Miscellanea Agostiniana*, ii. 253–255.
41. *De Trinitate.* Begun *c.* A.D. 400, it was only finished in 416 ; *Retract.* II. xv. ; *P.L.* xlii. 819–1098. For fear of misunderstandings Augustine had made up his mind to publish the various Books together, but before Bk. xii. was finished he found that copies less perfect than he could have wished were already in circulation, *Retract.* II. xv. 1. Hence, though begun in A.D. 400, it was still incomplete in 412, *Ep.* cxliii. 4 to Marcellinus : 'the words of Horace haunt me : "Nescit vox missa reverti" ; hence I am keeping back the volumes on *Genesis* and the *Trinity* ; for they deal with the most searching questions' ; the same again two years later, *Ep.* clix. 2, and after yet another year, *Ep.* clxii. 2, 'quos (libros) nondum edidi,' until at last, in 416, he sends the completed work to Archbishop Aurelius : 'juvenis inchoavi, senex edidi,' *Ep.* clxxiv. From the reference in xiii. 12 to an explanation already given in *De Civitate Dei*, XII. xx.—a work only completed in 416—it may be that Augustine brought out a second edition of the *De Trinitate* ; and from the fact that in Bk. xv. 48 he quotes a long passage from *Tract.* xc. 8–9 *in Joannem* which, as we have seen above, there is good reason to think was not written till 418 at the earliest, it seems that *De Trinitate* cannot have been completed before 418–419 ; see No. 42 below. *On the Trinity*, in the translation edited by M. Dods, vol. vii.
42. *De Consensu Evangelistarum.* Augustine's opening words of *Retract.* II. xvi. are instructive as showing how he composed his works : 'During those same years in which I was by degrees dictating the Books on the Trinity I wrote others too ; the labour was unceasing, but I worked in these others while still occupied with those on the Trinity. Among them the *De Consensu Evangelistarum*,' *c.* 400. The Bishop had, then, several books on hand at the same time, a fact which explains so many being assigned to approximately the same year, *Retract.* ii. 15 ; *P.L.* xxxv. 1042–1230 ; *C.S.E.L.* xliii., ed. Weihrich. Bks. ii.–iv. give a Harmony of the Gospels, Bk. i. is directed against those who argued that Christ Himself wrote nothing and that the Evangelists lied in making Him out to be God, I. vii. (10). Augustine himself tells us of the labour involved in thus harmonizing the Gospel narratives, and he warns those sufficiently interested to study his *De Consensu Evangelistarum* that it must be done 'nec stando et audiendo, sed potius sedendo et legendo,' *Tract.* cxii. 1 and cxvii. 2 *in Joann.* When writing to

St. Jerome in 403, *Ep.* lxxi. 6 (*Ep.* civ. *inter Epp. S. Hieronymi*) St. Augustine thanks him for the work he has done on the Gospels, adding, 'for practically nowhere does it disagree with the Greek when I compared it with the Greek text.' Zarb, *Angelicum*, 1933, p. 490, suggests that since the Latin text of the Gospels used by Augustine in the *De Consensu* is that of St. Jerome's Vulgate, it would seem that the latter had been carried through before A.D. 403. The critical edition of *De Consensu* is by H. J. Vogels, Fribourg, 1908; *The Harmony of the Gospels*, in the translation edited by M. Dods, vol. viii.

43. *Contra Epistolam Parmeniani*, *c.* 400. The first important work against the Donatists that has survived, *Retract.* II. xvii.; *P.L.* xliii. 33–108; *C.E.L.S.* li. The allusions to Optatus, called the 'Gildonian' because he acted as a species of satellite to Count Gildo, as already dead—he is always spoken of in the past tense, *Contra Epistolam Parmeniani*, ii. 2, 8, 19, 34—gives a *terminus a quo*, for Optatus died in A.D. 398. Further, the reference, i. 15, to the recent enactments against pagans delimits us yet further, for those laws were enacted A.D. 399, and could hardly have been described as 'recent' after A.D. 400.

44. *De Baptismo contra Donatistas*, *c.* 400; a refutation of the Donatist claim that St. Cyprian's teaching was the same as theirs. Books vi.–vii. are peculiarly valuable in that they have preserved for us much of the *Acts* of the Council held by St. Cyprian at Carthage, 256; *Retract.* II. xviii.; *P.L.* xliii. 107–244; *C.E.L.S.* li. In *Contra Epistolam Parmeniani*, ii. 32, Augustine promised to deal more fully with the question of Baptism and the Donatists, and as he enumerates *De Baptismo contra Donatistas* immediately after *Contra Epistolam Parmeniani* in the *Retractations*, we can hardly be far wrong in referring it to A.D. 401.

45. *Contra quod attulit Centurius a Donatistis*, *c.* 400. This was an answer to a Donatist presentation of their case which Centurius, a Donatist at the time, had brought to Augustine; unhappily lost, *Retract.* II. xix. Zarb, *Angelicum*, 1933, 491 ff., would refer this and the four following works to A.D. 401.

46. *Ad Inquisitiones Januarii*, *c.* 400; given as *Epp.* liv.–lv.; *P.L.* xxxiii. 199–223; *Retract.* II. xx.

47. *De Opere monachorum*, *c.* 400, written at the wish of Aurelius the Archbishop of Carthage and intended to correct mistaken ideas on the monastic life, *Retract.* II. xxi.; *P.L.* xl. 547–582; *C.S.E.L.* xli., ed. Zycha.

48. *De Bono conjugali*, 401, against the teachings of Jovinian since it was being maintained that the only valid answer to him would involve a condemnation of marriage, *Retract.* II. xxii. 1–2; *P.L.* xl. 375–396; *C.S.E.L.* xli.

49. *De Sancta Virginitate*, as a necessary corollary to the preceding, 401, *Retract.* II. xxiii.; *P.L.* xl. 395–428; *C.S.E.L.* xli.

50. *De Genesi ad litteram*. This was begun A.D. 401, but only finished in 415, *Retract.* II. xxiv.; *P.L.* xxxiv. 245–486. Since St. Augustine explicitly says that he 'begun *De Genesi ad Litteram* before beginning *De Trinitate* but finished it before the last-named,' *Retract.* II. 24, the *De Genesi* must have been finished before A.D. 418–419, the year in which the *De Trinitate* was finished, see No. 41 above. Further, both works are mentioned as incomplete in A.D. 414, *Ep.* clxii., yet in 415 only *De Trinitate* is referred to as incomplete, *Ep.* clxix., thus leaving the completion of *De Genesi ad Litteram* to 414–415.

51 *Contra litteras Petiliani*, 1–88 iii. Book i. was written *c.* 400 in answer

to the first half of a species of Encyclical in which Petilian, Donatist Bishop of Cirta, had assailed the Catholic Church. While Augustine was answering the latter half—which he had only seen later—Petilian replied to Augustine's Bk. i., hence the latter felt compelled to write Bk. iii., *c.* 402 ; *Retract.* II. xxv. ; *P.L.* xliii. 245–388 ; *C.E.S.L.* lii., ed. Petschenig, 1908–1909. The date of the second book can be approximately fixed by the reference, ii. 118, to Pope Anastasius as then reigning, for he occupied the See of Peter A.D. 399–April 27, 402 ; *cf. Ep.* liii. 2, where the list of the Popes ends with Anastasius. *The Donatist Controversy*, in the translation edited by M. Dods, vol. iii.

52. *Ad Catholicos Epistola contra Donatistas*, or *De Unitate Ecclesiae Catholicae*. This, a species of counterblast to Petilian's Encyclical, see above, was apparently written *c.* 402 and before the publication of *Contra Litt. Petiliani*, iii. ; *P.L.* xliii. 391–446 ; *C.E.L.S.* lii. Doubts have always been thrown on the authenticity of the *De Unitate* which, it is true, is not enumerated in the *Retractations*, perhaps because Augustine regarded it as a letter. The opening formulae are not quite what we are accustomed to, nor are the Biblical quotations from the Latin text Augustine generally used. But the style is indubitably that of St. Augustine ; *cf. P.L.* xliii. 389–390.
53. *Ad Cresconium Grammaticum partis Donati*, *c.* 406. Cresconius bitterly resented Augustine's attack on Petilian, *Contra Litt. Petiliani*, i., *Retract.* II. xxvi. ; *P.L.* xliii. 445–594 ; *C.E.L.S.* lii.
54. *Probationum et Testimoniorum contra Donatistas, Liber unus*. This assemblage of documents on the story of the schism the Bishop had pinned up on the walls of the Donatist church in Hippo. It was written after the *Contra Cresconium*, *c.* 407, *Retract.* II. xxvii. It has not survived. This and the two following anti-Donatist works may well have been due to the recrudescence of violence on the part of the Donatists owing to the Imperial Decree of Union, February 12, 405.
55. *Contra Donatistam nescio quem*, *c.* 407. This, together with the preceding, was pinned up on the Donatist church. It also is lost. *Retract.* II. xxviii.
56. *Admonitio Donatistarum de Maximianistis* ; a brief summary dealing with the Maximianists who had separated off from the main Donatist body and whose treatment at the hands of the parent body afforded the best disproof of the claims of the schismatics. It, too, has failed to survive ; *c.* 407, *Retract.* II. xxix.
57. *De Divinatione Daemonum*, 'per idem tempus,' *viz. c.* 407, *Retract.* II. xxx. ; *P.L.* xl. 581–592 ; *C.S.E.L.* xli.
58. *Quaestiones expositae contra Paganos*. These were in answer to questions sent by a Carthaginian pagan whom Augustine hoped to convert ; they are given as *Ep.* cii. 2–38 ; *P.L.* xxxiii. 371–386 ; *Retract.* II. xxxi. Their position here would refer them to A.D. 408–409.
59. *Expositio Epistolae Jacobi ad duodecim tribus*. This was made on the basis of a poor Latin version, as Augustine acknowledges, *Retract.* II. xxxii. ; it is no longer extant, *c.* 408–409.
60. *De Peccatorum Meritis et Remissione, et De Baptismo Parvulorum, ad Marcellinum* ; 'Adversus novam Pelagianam haeresim,' *c.* 412, *Retract.* II. xxxiii. ; *P.L.* 109–200 ; *C.S.E.L.* 1903. 'Pelagius came to Africa and to Hippo during my absence. . . . Later on when at Carthage and much occupied with preparations for the Conference we were going to have with the Donatists, I caught sight of him once or twice so far as I can recall,' *De Gestis Pelagii*, 46. Augustine was away from Hippo during part at least of the year 410 ;

cf. Ep. cxxiv. 2, and the reference to the preparations for the Conference shows that Pelagius was in Carthage in 411. One of the first to take alarm at his doctrines was Marcellinus the Tribune who was put to death in September, 413. He wrote to Augustine on the subject and the latter replied with *De Peccatorum Meritis et Remissione* and *De Baptismo Parvulorum*, to which *De Spiritu et Littera* is a species of sequel described by Augustine as 'prolixum librum (quem) modo de hac quaestione edidi,' *De Fide et Operibus*, 21. The first two anti-Pelagian treatises, then, namely *De Peccatorum Meritis et Remissione* and *De Spiritu et Littera*, being addressed to Marcellinus, will fall between 411 and September, 413, and *De Fide et Operibus* will have been written early in 413. Towards the close of 415 Augustine writes to Evodius saying: 'I have also written a big book against the heresy of Pelagius . . . (this) you can have if you like, but send some one to copy (it) for you,' *Ep.* clxix. 13. A copy was also sent to John of Jerusalem in 416, *Ep.* clxxix., and in the same year to Pope Innocent I., *Ep.* clxxvii. 6; Julian the Pelagian took care to misrepresent its teaching on free will, *Contra Julianum, Opus imperfectum*, iv. 112.

While Donatism, then, was in its death throes owing to the Conference, Pelagianism was beginning to show its teeth. It is quite in accordance with these facts that in his *Retractations* St. Augustine gives, almost as alternating with one another, a series of works dealing now with one, now with another, of these errors.

61. *De Unico Baptismo*, 410, in answer to a treatise by Petilian bearing the same title, *Retract.* II. xxxiv.; *P.L.* xliii. 595–614. Since this answer to Petilian is deliberately placed after *De Peccatorum Meritis et Remissione* in the *Retractations* we should prefer to assign it to the close of A.D. 412. *Select Anti-Pelagian Treatises, and the Acts of the Second Council of Orange*, ed. W. Bright, 1880.
62. *De Maximianistis contra Donatistas*, 'non brevissimum sicut antea (*cf.* No. 56 above) sed grandem et multo diligentius,' *c.* 412; *Retract.* II. xxxv.; not extant.
63. *De Gratia Testamenti Novi*, answers to questions sent from Carthage by Honoratus 'eo ipso tempore quo contra Donatistas vehementer exercebamur et contra Pelagianos exerceri jam coeperamus'; given as *Ep.* cxl.; *P.L.* xxxiii. 538–577; *cf. Ep.* cxxxix. 3; *c.* 412, *Retract.* II. xxxvi.
64. *De Spiritu et Littera*, 412 at the end, to Marcellinus who was perplexed by a passage in *De Peccatorum Meritis*, *Retract.* II. xxxvii.; *P.L.* xliv. 199–246; *C.E.L.S.* 1903. *On the Spirit and the Letter*, translated by W. J. S. Simpson, 1925.
65. *De Fide et Operibus*, 'interea missa sunt . . . scripta nonnulla,' early in 413, *Retract.* II. xxxviii.; *P.L.* xl. 197–230; *C.S.E.L.* xli.
66. *Breviculus Collationis cum Donatistis*, at the close of A.D. 411, the year in which the Conference was held, *Retract.* II. xxxix.; *P.L.* xliii. 613–650. The Conference took place in the June of 411, and Augustine, writing to Marcellinus—therefore before September, 413 when he was slain—says, *Ep.* cxxxix. 3, that he has (*a*) sent him *De Baptismo Parvulorum* (see No. 60 above); (*b*) has already written the *Breviculus* and *Ad Donatistas post Collationem*, and (*c*) is now engaged on *Ep.* cxl., *De Gratia Novi Testamenti*. This would suggest A.D. 412 for the *Breviculus*, were it not for its position in the *Retractations* after *De Gratia Novi Testamenti*, *De Spiritu et Littera* and *De Fide et Operibus* which would suggest that the *Breviculus* was at any rate not completed till after those treatises and may therefore date from the early part of 413. The same will apply to *Ad Donatistas post Collationem*.

67. *Post Collationem, ad Donatistas,* 412; at the same time Augustine wrote—for the Bishops of Numidia assembled at Zerta, June 14, 412, an appeal to the Donatists, *Ep.* cxli. among his Epistles, *P.L.* xxxiii. 577–583; *Retract.* II. xl.; *P.L.* xliii. 651–690.
68. *De videndo Deo, ad Paulinam, Ep.* cxlvii.; *P.L.* xxxiii. 596–622, *cf. Ep.* cxlviii, *ibid.* 622–630; *Retract.* II. xli, 413(?). *S. Augustini Liber de Videndo Deo, seu Epistula cxlvii.*, ed. M. Schmaus, Bonn, *Florilegium Patristicum,* 1930.
69. *De Natura et Gratia,* 'Venit etiam tunc . . . quidam Pelagii liber,' 415; *Retract.* II. xlii.; *P.L.* xliv. 247–290; *C.E.L.S.* 1903.
70. *De Perfectione Justitiae,* the end of 415, *P.L.* xliv. 291–318; *C.S.E.L.* xlii., ed. Urba and Zycha.
71. *De Civitate Dei,* begun in 413, finished 426, *Retract.* II. xliii.; *P.L.* xli.; *C.S.E.L.* xl. Dedicated to Marcellinus, this work, which owed its inception to the sack of Rome by Alaric in 410 and the consequent assertion by the pagans that this disaster was due to the advance of Christianity, must therefore have been begun before September, 413, the date of Marcellinus' death; throughout *Epp.* cxxxvi.–cxxxviii. we can see how the problems which he faces in the *De Civitate Dei* occupy his mind and how he is reading assiduously among the profane authors, yet *Ep.* cxxxviii. 20—to Marcellinus, and almost certainly dating from A.D. 412—ends with the words: 'Try and discover what arguments people are using and write and tell me, so that I may with God's help, try, whether by letters or in books, to answer all that they have to say,' words which at least suggest that Augustine had not yet begun the *De Civitate Dei.* This becomes clearer from his words to Evodius towards the end of A.D. 415 in *Ep.* clxix. 1—that treasure-house of information on the Bishop's literary labours—'Many tasks are now completed which I began during Lent this year before Easter,' and he goes on to say that he has now written Bks. i.–v. of the *De Civitate Dei.* Further, Orosius, in his *Preface* to his *Historia* which he began in A.D. 417, knows only of Bk. xi.; we have no means of knowing by what stages the other books were added till it was completed in 426. In Bk. xviii. liv. 2, St. Augustine says: 'In the famous and glorious city of Carthage Gaudentius and Jovius, Counts of the Emperor Honorius, overthrew, on the XIV. Kal. of April, the temples of the false gods and smashed their images. Who has failed to notice how from that date until the present time—practically thirty years—the worship of Christ's Name has grown?' Since that destruction of the heathen shrines took place in A.D. 399 it really seems necessary to place the completion of the *De Civitate Dei* in 428–429, and we can hardly read into Augustine's 'ferme' 'practically' 'round numbers with a difference of three or four years' as do the Maurist editors, see note, *P.L.* xli. 620. Nor does the statement, XXII. viii. 20, that 'it is not yet two years since the establishment at Hippo of a "memoria" to St. Stephen' disprove this; the Maurists themselves say: 'hence we gather that this Book was written towards the close of the year 426, "*aut non multum serius,*"' *ibid. col.* 768. If, however, this is felt to be an impossibly late date for the *De Civitate Dei* it might be legitimate to see in the former passage, XVIII. liv. 2, a species of colophon added by Augustine when revising his work. Ludovicus Vives dedicated his Comments on the *De Civitate Dei* 'Inclyto Principe Henrico VIII. Angliae Regi, Hiberniae Domino, etc.' *P.L.* xlvii. 435–506.

The bibliography on the *De Civitate Dei* is immense:

S. Angus, *The Sources of Augustine's 'De Civitate Dei,'* Bks. i.–x., 1906.

F. Cayre, *Le Cité de Dieu*, in *Rev. Thomiste*, 1930, pp. 487 ff.
De Civitate Dei libri XXII., ex recensione B. Dombart, quartum recognovit A. Kalb, 1928–1929.
J. N. Figgis, *The Political Aspects of St. Augustine's 'City of God,'* 1921.
The City of God, in the translation edited by M. Dods, vols. i.–ii.
The City of God by St. Augustine. Translated by John Healey, with an Introduction by Ernest Barker, 1931.
O. Schilling, *Die Stadslehre des hl. Augustins nach 'De Civitate Dei,'* 1930.
E. Stegemann, *Augustins Gottestaat*, 1928.
H. Vogels, *De Civitate Dei*, a critical edition, Bonn, 1930.
For fuller bibliography, see Labriolle, *Latin Christianity*, English translation, p. 412, note.

72. *De Bono Viduitatis*, 414 ; *P.L.* xl. 429–450 ; *C.S.E.L.* xli.
73. *Ad Orosium contra Priscillianistas*, 'Inter haec,' viz. *De Civitate Dei*, *c.* 415 ; *Retract.* II. xliv. ; *P.L.* xlii. 669–678 ; for Orosius' letter, *ibid.* 665–670. See J. A. Davids, *De Orosio et S. Augustino Priscillianistarum Adversariis*, 1930.
74. *Ad Hieronymum . . . De Origine animae et de Sententia Jacobi*, or *Epp.* clxvi.–vii. ; early in 418 ; *Retract.* II. xlv. ; *C.E.L.S.*, 1903. From the same letter to Evodius, *Ep.* clxix. 13, A.D. 415, we learn that in addition to *De Civitate Dei* i.–v. and an *Exposition* of Pss. lxii., lxxi. and lxxvii., *ibid.* 1, 'I have also written to Jerome on the *Origin of the Soul*,' that is 'during Lent'; *cf. ibid.* 1, of 415. But in contradistinction to his principles when compiling the *Retractations*, Augustine is referring to the date of completion of the specified writings, not to the time when he began them.
75. *Tractatus cxxiv in Joannis Evangelium*, 416 ; *P.L.* xxxv. 1379–1976. The *Tractatus in Joannem* with the *Ten Tractatus in 1m. Epistolam Joannis* have, ever since the days of the Maurist editors, been assigned to A.D. 416, see their arguments, *P.L.* xxxv. 1375–1378. But there are exceedingly strong reasons for questioning this date and it seems certain that the *Tractatus in Joannem* fall into two distinct sets : (*a*) i.–liv. preached A.D. 413 ; (*b*) lv.–cxxiv. completed in 418 but never delivered. Certain important consequences follow. For in *De Trinitate* xv. 47, St. Augustine quotes one of these latter *Tractatus*, viz. xcix., and in *De Trinitate* xiii. 12, he quotes *De Civitate Dei*, XII. xx. But Augustine's disciple Orosius, in the Preface to his *Historia adversus Paganos* written in 417, mentions the fact that so far only Bks. i.–xi. of the *De Civitate Dei* have appeared ; whence it follows that neither the *De Civitate Dei* nor the *De Trinitate* can have been published before 418 ; and as during part at least of that year Augustine was on a special embassy to Caesarea of Mauretania at the behest of Pope Zosimus, only returning thence in the October of 418, it seems more probable that these two great works were published at least three to four years later than has generally been thought.

Nor is this all. For the dates assigned by the Maurists to several *Epistles* depend entirely on the dates they assigned to the *Tractatus in Joannem*, and by consequence to the *Civitate Dei* and the *De Trinitate*. *Ep.* clxxiv., for instance, in which Augustine presents to Aurelius his completed work on the Trinity, will have to be dated 418–419 instead of 416. See, for these points especially, S. M. Zarb, O.P., *Chronologia Tractatuum S. Augustini in Evangelium Primamque Epistolam Joannis Apostoli*, reprinted from the *Angelicum*, X., 1933, pp. 50–110, also in the same year, *Chronologia Operum S. Augustini*, pp. 359–396, 478–512. We must confess, however, that this late date is hard to reconcile with the place given it in the *Retractations*.

See J. Deferrari, *On the Date and Order of Delivery of St. Augustine's Tractates on the Gospel and Epistle of St. John*, in *Classical Philology*, 1917; M. Comeau, *S. Augustin exégète du Quatrième Évangile*, 1930. *S. Aurelii Augustini in Joannis Evangelium, Tractatus cxxiv.*, 2 vols., ed. Hurter, 1884. Translated as *Homilies on St. John*, Oxford, 1878.

76. *Tractatus Decem in Epistolam Joannis ad Parthos*, 416; *P.L.* xxxv. 1977–2062.

77. *Ad Emeritum Donatistarum Episcopum, post Collationem* (411) 'aliquanto post eandem collationem scripsi librum satis utilem,' *c.* 413 (?); *Retract.* II. xlvi.; not extant. If the arguments given above are sound, then, considering that Augustine carefully assigns this treatise a place after the *Tractatus in Joannem*, we feel compelled to date it A.D. 416, though we confess that it is hard to see how he can speak of the five years which would then have elapsed since the Conference in 411 as 'aliquanto post eandem collationem,' see No. 75.

78. *De Gestis Pelagii*, 'Per idem tempus,' *Retract.* II. xlvii., at the beginning of A.D. 417; *P.L.* xliv. 319–360; *C.S.E.L.* xl. The above date seems confirmed by the position given here to the *De Gestis Pelagii*. For whereas the Fathers assembled at Carthage in 416 knew nothing of the *Acta* of the Synod held in December, 415, at Diospolis when the case of Pelagius was most inadequately investigated, *Ep.* clxxv. 4, and whereas Augustine, Aurelius, Alypius, Evodius and Possidius are equally ignorant of their existence when writing to the same Pontiff in the same year, 'Gesta ecclesiastica facta esse jactantur,' *Ep.* clxxvii. 2, and we find Augustine writing, again in the same year 416, to John of Jerusalem for a sight of the supposed *Acta*—yet by the middle of A.D. 417 he rejoices in their possession which enables him to arrive at a definitive judgment on the case, *Ep.* clxxxvi. 2. Since, then, he opens the *De Gestis Pelagii* by telling his Archbishop, Aurelius, that having now received the aforesaid *Acta* 'cunctatio mea terminum accepit,' that treatise must date from that same year, 417. But the above arguments would indicate the close of that year rather than its beginning, as the Maurists say, *P.L.* xliv. 319, note.

79. *De Correctione Donatistarum*, or *Ep.* clxxxv. ad Bonifacium Tribunum, *P.L.* xxxiii. 792–815; *Retract.* II. xlviii. 417.

80. *De Praesentia Dei, ad Dardanum*, *Ep.* clxxxvii., *P.L.* xxxiii. 832–848 'ubi nostra intentio contra haeresim Pelagianam maxime vigilat, non expresse nominatam,' *Retract.* II. xlix., therefore before 418, after which time Augustine names Pelagius, *cf. ibid.* xxxiii.

81. *De Patientia*, *P.L.* xl. 611–626; *C.S.E.L.* xli.; before 418, see No. 80 above; *cf. Ep.* ccxxxi. 7.

82. *Contra Pelagium et Coelestium, de Gratia Christi et de Peccato Originali*, ad Albinam, Pinianum et Melaniam, after the condemnation in A.D. 418; *Retract.* II. l.; *P.L.* xliv. 359–410; *C.S.E.L.* xl.

83. *De Gestis cum Emerito Donatista*, 418; *Retract.* II. li.; *P.L.* xliii. 697–706; *C.E.L.S.* lii.; *cf. Sermo ad Caesareensis Ecclesiae Plebem*, *ibid.* 689–698. These *Gesta* are precisely dated in the opening words: 'Honorio duodecimum et Theodosio octavum consulibus, duodecimo calendas Octobris' or September 20, 418.

84. *Contra Sermonem Arianorum*: 'Inter haec venit in manus . . .' therefore *c.* 418–419; for the *Sermo Arianorum* see *P.L.* xlii. 678–684, and for Augustine's reply, *ibid.* 683–708; *Retract.* II. lii. Allowing for the journey back to Hippo it would be safe to say that this treatise was not written before 419.

85. *De Nuptiis et Concupiscentiis*, ad Valerium Comitem, i.–ii., *c.* 419 at the beginning; Julian the Pelagian answered Bk. i. in four books, hence Augustine's reply, *de Nuptiis*, Bk. ii. 419–420; *P.L.* xliv. 413–474; *Retract.* II. liii.; *C.S.E.L.* xlii. Time must be allowed for Julian to compose his four Books, also for their condensation into one volume for Count Valerius, also for that volume to reach Augustine, and for him to write *De Nuptiis* ii.; hence we can assign *De Nuptiis* i. to 419, and ii. to 420 if not 421.

86. *Locutionum in Heptateuchum libri septem*, *c.* 419–420; *P.L.* xxxiv. 485–546; *Retract.* II. liv.

87. *Quaestionum* (de Libris eisdem) *libri septem*, 'eodem tempore,' *P.L.* xxxiv. 547–824; *Retract.* II. lv. 'Eodem tempore scripsi . . .' therefore *c.* 419–420. These two lengthy works must have demanded considerable time as well as leisure; they might seem to mark a period of comparative quiescence in the Pelagian controversy; hence we fancy that Zarb, *Angelicum*, 1933, p. 509, puts them too early, 419–420, we should prefer 422–423. See Rüting, *Untersuchungen über Augustins Quaestiones und Locutiones in Heptateuchum*, Paderborn, 1916.

88. *De Anima et ejus Origine*: 'Eodem tempore . . .' the end of A.D. 419. A certain Vincentius Victor, who had assumed the name 'Vincentius' out of devotion to Vincent the Rogatist, *cf. Ep.* xciii., finding a treatise by Augustine in which the latter hesitated to dogmatize about the origin of the soul, undertook to show Augustine's incompetence on the subject, *P.L.* xliv. 475–548; *Retract.* II. lvi. So proud was Vincent of his feat that he actually declaimed his pages to his people at Caesarea and dedicated them to a Spaniard named Peter in whose house he had come across Augustine's treatise. Augustine's answer is in four Books, but they are not all addressed to the same people. For Bk. i. is addressed to Renatus, a priest at Caesarea who when Augustine was there in 418 (see above, No. 83) had shown to the Bishop of Hippo a letter written to him by Optatus on the same subject, and this letter Augustine had answered, *Ep.* cxc. On seeing Vincentius' work Renatus at once copied it and sent it to Augustine. Bk. ii. is addressed to Peter the Spaniard to whom Vincent had sent his book, and Bks. iii.–iv. to Vincent himself. Now the foregoing details show that it was owing to the interest aroused at Caesarea by Augustine's stay there and his truly wonderful encounter with Emeritus (*cf. Sermo ad Plebem Caesariensem* and *De Gestis cum Emerito*) that Vincentius was led into his unhappy attempt to lessen the esteem in which all men were holding the Bishop of Hippo; this might seem to justify the date towards the close of 419, assigned to it by the Maurists, *P.L.* xliv. 475, were it not for the place assigned to these four Books in the *Retractations* after the two works on *Genesis* which must have demanded considerable time. Hence Zarb, *l.c.* suggests the year 420 for Bks. i.–ii. and 421 for Bks. iii.–iv. How distinct these last two were from Bks. i.–ii. appears from ii. 7, where Augustine says that he hopes to answer Vincent. We should be inclined to put them even later, perhaps 423–424.

89. *De Adulterinis conjugiis, ad Pollentium*: 'cupiens solvere difficillimam quaestionem,' *c.* 419; *P.L.* xl. 451–486; *Retract.* II. lvii; *C.S.E.L.* xli. If the above arguments hold good, it will follow that the dates assigned by the Maurists for the next nine works will have to be brought down in proportion. In fact if this is not done the remaining years of Augustine's literary life would have been singularly barren in comparison with his former prodigious output.

90. *Contra Adversarium Legis et Prophetarum*, against an unknown

heretic: 'Interea liber quidam . . . apud Carthaginem multis confluentibus et attentissime audientibus, in platea maritima legeretur,' *Retract.* II. lviii.; *P.L.* xlii. 603–666, *c.* 420.

91. *Contra Gaudentium:* 'Per idem tempus . . .' or *c.* 420: Dulcitius the Tribune had demanded of Gaudentius, the Donatist Bishop of Thamugadi or Timgad, the surrender of his church and property in accordance with the Imperial order resulting from the decision adverse to the Donatists after the Conference of A.D. 411. Gaudentius declared that he and all his flock would prefer to set their church on fire and be burned with it. He wrote two letters to this effect to the Tribune who sent them to Augustine for him to reply. Gaudentius was still unconsumed when Augustine sent him his second Book! *P.L.* xliii. 707–752; *Retract.* II. lix; *C.E.L.S.* lii. If we are correct in assigning the *De Anima et ejus Origine* to 423–424, then the works hitherto attributed to A.D. 420–422 will have to be placed correspondingly later, namely *Contra Mendacium*, *Contra duas Epistolas Pelagianorum*, *Contra Julianum libri sex*, the *Enchiridion* and *De Cura pro mortuis;* see the alternative date, 425–426 suggested for *De Octo Quaestionibus ad Dulcitium*, No. 97.

92. *Contra Mendacium*, against the Priscillianists: 'Tunc et contra mendacium . . .,' or *c.* 420; *P.L.* xl. 517–548; *cf.* No. 26 above; *Retract.* II. lx.; *C.S.E.L.* xli. In the *De Mendacio* Augustine does not, curiously enough, examine the case of Jacob's claim to be Esau; but in *Contra Mendacium* 24 he does so, and we have the familiar 'non est mendacium sed mysterium,' *cf. Sermon* iv. 23, *Enchiridion*, 22, *Epp.* lxxxii. 21, clxxx. 3. See E. Recejac, *De Mendacio, quid senserit Augustinus?* 1896.

93. *Contra duas Epistolas Pelagianorum*, or four Books in answer to Pelagian Letters addressed to Pope Boniface, 420, 'or a little later.' *Retract.* II. lxi.; *P.L.* xliv. 549–638; *C.E.L.S.* 1903. For the date of this and the three following see notes on *De Adulterinis Conjugiis* above, and on the *De Anima et ejus Origine*.

94. *Contra Julianum, libri sex.* Augustine discovered to his dismay that the excerpts from Julian's four Books against *De Nuptiis* i. had been inaccurately made; he therefore wrote these six Books against him, *c.* 421 'aut paulo post'; *Retract.* II. lxii.; *P.L.* xliv. 641–874.

95. *Ad Laurentium, de Fide, Spe, et Charitate;* 'opusculum de suis manibus non recessurum; quod genus Graeci "Enchiridion" vocant,' *c.* 421 'aut paulo post,' *Retract.* II. lxiii., hence the usual title of the work; *P.L.* xl. 231–290.
The *Enchiridion*, in the translation edited by M. Dods, vol. ix.

96. *De Cura pro mortuis gerenda*, ad Paulinum Episcopum, *P.L.* xl. 591–610; *Retract.* II. lxiv.; *C.S.E.L.* xli., *c.* 421.

97. *De Octo Dulcitii Quaestionibus*, *c.* '422 or 425,' *P.L.* xl. 147–170; *Retract.* II. lxv. In his *Preface* St. Augustine says that he received Dulcitius' letter, 'per Pascha hoc anno quo Dominicus ejus fuit *tertio* kalendas aprilis.' But only in A.D. 419 and 430 did Easter fall on the III. Kal. Aprilis. Mistakes in writing the figures for dates are frequent, and if for III. we read VII. the date would be 422; if we read XI. we should arrive at 425; if for 'Kal.' we read 'Idus,' this would agree with Easter, 426.

98. *De Gratia et Libero Arbitrio*, ad Valentinum et cum illo monachos, '426 or 427,' *P.L.* xliv. 881–912; *Retract.* II. lxvi. See *Epp.* ccxiv.–ccxv.; *P.L.* xxxiii. 968–974, xliv. 875–880; for Valentinus' letter on receipt of *De Gratia et Libero Arbitrio*, *ibid.* cols. 911–916.

99. *De Correptione et Gratia*, addressed to the same as above, No. 98, '426 or 427'; *P.L.* xliv. 915–946; *Retract.* II. lxvii.

100. *Collatio cum Maximino Arianorum Episcopo*, '427 or 428,' *P.L.* xlii. 709–742.
101. *Contra Maximinum Haereticum*, c. 428 ; *P.L.* xlii. 742–814.
102. *Speculum* 'Quis ignorat in Scripturis sanctis. . . .,' 427 ; *P.L.* xxxiv. 887–1040.
103. *De Haeresibus*, c. 428 ; *P.L.* xlii. 21–50. For the correspondence which led to the composition of this treatise, see *Epp.* ccxxi.-ccxxiv. *De Haeresibus et les sources*, by G. Bardy, *Miscellanea*, ii. 397–416.
104. *Adversus Judaeos*, *P.L.* xlii. 51–64.
105. *De Dono Perseverantiae*, *P.L.* xlv. 993–1034. Written after the *Retractationes*, therefore A.D. 428–429.
106. *Contra secundam Juliani Responsionem, imperfectum Opus*, *P.L.* xlv. 1049–1608 ; A.D. 428–429.

(c) *Those not named in the 'Retractations'*

There follow a number of Works, given in alphabetical order, which are not enumerated by St. Augustine in his *Retractations* [1] either because they were written later, or because they came under the heading of those 'popular discourses' which he had decided not to include, or because he was reserving them—like his Sermons—for the third volume which he never had time to complete. Several of the following writings are falsely or at least doubtfully attributed to him ; but since many people unconsciously quote them as though they really were St. Augustine's unquestioned work, we include them here.

1. *De Cataclysmo*,* [2] *P.L.* xl. 693–700, rejected by the Maurists, *ob.* 626.
2. *De Cantico novo*, *ib.* xl. 677–686, only hesitatingly accepted by the Maurists.
3. *De Continentia*, *P.L.* xl. 349–3732 ; *C.S.E.L.* xli. ; Augustine mentions this work, *Ep.* ccxxxi. 7.
4. *De Ecclesiasticis Dogmatibus*,* *P.L.* xlii. 1213–1222, almost certainly by Gennadius, as St. Thomas remarks, *Catena aurea* on Matt. i. ; *cf.* C. H. Turner in *J.T.S.* October, 1905, January, 1907.
5. *De Fide rerum quae non videntur*, *P.L.* xl. 171–180 ; *cf. Ep.* ccxxxi. 7.
6. *De Gratia et Libero Arbitrio ad Rufinum*,* written by Prosper of Aquitaine during Augustine's lifetime, *P.L.* xlv. 1795–1802.
7. *Adversus Judaeos*, *P.L.* xlii. 51–64.[3]
8. *Manuale*,* *P.L.* xl. 951–968, attributed to St. Anselm or to Hugh of St. Victor.
9. *Meditationes*,* *P.L.* xl. 901–942 ; constantly spoken of as the genuine

[1] In some MSS. of the *Retractations* are added 'Books which subsequent to the correction of the foregoing were written and published by Augustine : the *Speculum*, *De Praedestinatione Sanctorum*, *De Haeresibus*, *Gesta cum Maximino*, *Contra Julianum*, *Opus imperfectum*, the 7th unfinished, the 8th not begun,' *P.L.* xxxii. 656.

[2] An * signifies an unquestionably spurious work.

[3] Possidius, *Indiculus*, i., *P.L.* xlvi. 6, refers us to *Quaestio* lvi. inter *De Diversis Quaestionibus* lxxxiii., *P.L.* xl. 39, also to *Ep.* cxcvi., *P.L.* xxxiii. 891–899. He adds : 'Adversus quos supra Tractatus duo,' but only one has come down to us.

work of St. Augustine, but almost certainly to be attributed to John the Abbot, *ibid.* 898. *Les Soliloques, les Méditations et le Manuel*, traduit par M. Dubois, O.S.B.; *Meditations, Soliloquia and Manuall of the Glorious Doctour S. Augustin: newly translated into English* by Nicolas de la Coste, 1631.

10. *De Mirabilibus Sacrae Scripturae,* P.L.* xxxv. 3149–2200: St. Thomas long ago declared that it was not the work of St. Augustine, *Summa Theol.* III. xlv. 3; the author would seem to have been an Irishman, for he asks in derision, i. 7, 'who would bring wolves, deer, boars, foxes, hares, yew-trees, and "sesquivolos" (?) to Ireland?' See *Proc. of the Royal Irish Academy*, xxxv., sect. C., No. 2, 1919.
11. *De Praedestinatione Sanctorum, P.L.* xliv. 959–992, *c.* 428–429.
12. *Quaestiones XVII in Evangelium secundum Matthaeum,* P.L.* xxxv., 1365–1376; it is exceedingly doubtful whether this is a genuine work of St. Augustine, *ibid.* 1363.
13. *Quaestiones Veteris et Novi Testamenti, P.L.* xxxv. 2205–2298; *C.S.E.L.* li., ed. Souter, 1908, rejected by the Maurists; a work with the same title, *ibid.* 2385–2412, is also rejected. Souter maintains that the author was Isaac or the 'Ambrosiaster' who commented on the Pauline Epistles. This edition claims to have made some 3,000 improvements on the Benedictine text as given in Migne.
14. *De Quarta Feria,* P.L.* xl. 685–694, is of very questionable authenticity, *cf. ibid.* 626.
15. *Regula ad servos Dei, P.L.* xxxii. 1377–1384, also as *Ep.* ccxi., *P.L.* xxxiii. 958–965, where we have this 'rule' in its original form written for the community of nuns over whom 'praeposita soror mea' had ruled, *cf. Ep.* ccx. The death of Augustine's sister is generally referred to A.D. 424, so that the date, 423, of the Maurists seems hardly tenable, *cf. Vita*, Possidii, 26.
16. *De Spiritu et Anima,* P.L.* xl. 679–832. On this work St. Thomas remarked long ago: 'Non est Augustini sed dicitur cujusdam Cisterciensis fuisse; nec est multum curandum de his quae in eo dicuntur,' *De Anima* xii., *ad* 1m.
17. *De Tempore Barbarico,* P.L.* xl. 699–708, rejected by the Maurists, *ibid.* 626.
18. *De Urbis excidio, P.L.* xl. 715–724, is quoted by Ven. Bede.
19. *De Utilitate jejunii, P.L.* xl. 707–716, given by Possidius in his *Indiculus. De Octo Quaestionibus ex Veteri Testamento.* In the *Rev. Bénédictine*, 1911, pp. 1–10, Dom Morin published from two MSS. a treatise with the above title, but while holding that Questions i.–iii. were probably a genuine work of St. Augustine, and referring the remaining five to the year 418, since quoted by Augustine in his *Quaestiones in Heptateuchum*, ii. 90 (*P.L.* xxxiv. 629, note) he yet felt it difficult to regard these latter as genuine. Dom D. de Bruyne has, however, triumphantly vindicated their genuine character,[1] and Dom Morin expresses his entire agreement with his conclusions.[2]

The words with which Possidius closes his *Indiculus Opusculorum S. Augustini* will serve as a fitting close to this list:

Whence it will appear that the said Bishop Augustine, led by the Holy Spirit, composed in the Holy Catholic Church

[1] In *Miscellanea Agostiniana* ii., pp. 321–340; the actual text is given pp. 333–337.
[2] *Ibid.*, p. 340.

for the instruction of men's souls, books, treatises and letters to the number of 1,030, and this not including such as cannot be enumerated since he himself has nowhere given us their number.[1]

III—CHRONOLOGICAL TABLES OF ST. AUGUSTINE'S WRITINGS

In the tables which follow we enumerate the books, treatises, etc., which St. Augustine wrote as a Bishop ; but in the left-hand column we group them according to the years to which the Maurist editors assigned them ; the centre column shows the reference—if any—to the *Retractations* ; the right-hand column gives the dates we have suggested in the preceding notes. In their edition of the *Retractations* the Maurists give no indication of the dates to which they would refer the various writings, but in their Prefaces, and in a footnote to their edition of each work, they sometimes state positively to what year a particular work is to be referred, but more often than not they are content to say ' it seems to have been written in such and such a year ' or ' about such and such a year.'[2] But these editors were driven to the conclusion that at least in the Second Book of the *Retractations*, where Augustine deals with his writings as a Bishop, he did not adhere strictly to the chronological order. These tables, then, will serve to show to what extent the Maurists departed from the order given by Augustine himself. Feeling, as they did, that they had not sufficient grounds for positive assertions as to dates, they qualified the dates they suggested with a ' circiter ' and grouped the writings round a probable central year. To the reader who neglects the word ' circiter ' it might seem at first sight as though the Benedictine editors imagined that Augustine wrote in one year all the formidable works grouped under the date A.D. 400.

But it is matter for regret that they so far deserted Augustine's order that they assign to *c.* 404–5 the four treatises *Contra Felicem*, *De Natura Boni*, *Contra Secundinum* and *Contra Hilarum*, all of which Augustine himself enumerated immediately after the *Contra Faustum*, which dates *c.* 400.

[1] *P.L.* xlvi. 22.

[2] For a brief summary of the chronology adopted by the Maurists see *P.L.* xlvii. 24–34, also for a list of lost or spurious works, *ibid.*, 34–40.

A.D. 396–397	RETRACT II.	SUGGESTED DATES
Ad Simplicianum	1	397
Contra Epistolam Manichaei	2	397
De Agone	3	397
A.D. 397		
De Doctrina Christiana	4	397
A lost *anti-Donatist* work	5	397
A.D. 398		
No works seem to be assigned to this year.		
A.D. 399		
Ditto.		
A.D. 400		
Confessions	6	397–401
Contra Faustum	7	400
Annotations in Job	13	395–400
De Catechizandis rudibus	14	400
De Trinitate, 400–416	15	400–419
De Consensu Evangelistarum	16	400–402
Contra Epistolam Parmeniani	17	400
De Baptismo contra Donatistas	18	401
A lost *anti-Donatist* treatise	19	401
Ad Inquisitiones Januarii	20	401
De Opere Monachorum	21	401
Contra Litteras Petiliani	25	400–402
A.D. 401		
De Bono conjugali	22	401
De Sancta Virginitate	23	401
De Genesi ad Litteram	24	401–415
A.D. 402		
De Unitate. (Not given in *Retract.*)		
A.D. 403		
No works assigned to this year by the Maurists.		
A.D. 404		
Contra Felicem Manichaeum	8	398
De Natura Boni	9	399
Contra Secundinum	10	399
A.D. 405		
Contra Hilarum	11	399
A.D. 406		
Contra Cresconium	26	406
A.D. 407		
Probationum contra Donatistas (lost)	27	407
Contra Donatistam nescio quem (lost)	28	407
Admonitio Donatistarum (lost)	29	407
De Divinatione Daemonum	30	407
Quaestiones contra Paganos	31	408–409
Expositio Epistolae Jacobi	32	407

	RETRACT II.	SUGGESTED DATES
A.D. 408		
No works assigned to this year by the Maurists.		
A.D. 409		
Ditto.		
A.D. 410		
De Unico Baptismo	34	412
De Maximianistis contra Donatistas (lost)	35	412
A.D. 411		
The year of the Conference between the Catholics and the Donatists; hence the Bishop had no leisure for his literary work.		
A.D. 412		
De Gratia Novi Testamenti	36	412
De Spiritu et Littera	37	412
Breviculus Collationis, 411–412	38	413
Post Collationem ad Donatistas, 411–412	40	413
De Peccatorum Meritis et Remissione	33	412
A.D. 413		
De Fide et Operibus	38	413
De Civitate Dei	43	413–426
Ad Emeritum, post Collationem	46	416
A.D. 413–414		
De Videndo Deo	41	413–414
A.D. 414		
De Bono Viduitatis.	(Not in *Retract.*)	414?
A.D. 415		
De Natura et Gratia	42	
De Perfectione Justitiae.	(Not in *Retract.*)	
Ad Orosium, contra Priscillianistas	44	
Ad Hieronymum: De Origine animae et de Sent. Jacobi	45	415
A.D. 416		
Tract in Joannem et in Epist.	(Not in *Retract.*)	413 and 419
A.D. 417		
De Gestis Pelagii	47	
De Correctione Donatistarum	48	
De Praesentia Dei	49	
De Patientia.	(Not in *Retract.*)	
A.D. 418		
Contra Pelagium et Coelestium	50	
A.D. 418–419		
Gesta cum Emerito	51	
Contra Sermonem Arianorum	52	419

A.D. 419–420	RETRACT II.	SUGGESTED DATES
De Nuptiis et Concupiscentiis	53	419 and 422
Locutiones in Heptateuchum	54	422–423
Quaestiones in Heptateuchum	55	422–423
De Anima et ejus Origine	56	423–424
De Adulterinis Conjugiis	57	
A.D. 420		
Contra Adversarium Legis et Prophetarum	58	424–426?
Contra Gaudentium	59	424–426
Contra Mendacium	60	424–426
Contra Duas Epistolas Pelagianorum	61	424–426
A.D. 421–422		
Contra Julianum	62	424–426
Enchiridion	63	424–426
De Cura pro mortuis	64	424–426
A.D. 422		
De Octo Dulcitii Quaestionibus	65	426
A.D. 426–427		
De Gratia et Libero arbitrio	66	426–427
De Correptione et Gratia	67	426–427

IV—PRINTED EDITIONS OF ST. AUGUSTINE'S WORKS; ALSO SOME TRANSLATIONS [1]

The first seems to have been that of Amerbach, 9 vols. folio, Basle. Then came Erasmus' 10 vols., folio, 1528–1529 and 1541–1543, Basle.[2] This was followed by the edition published by the Louvain Theologians, 11 vols., folio, 1577, Louvain; to these Jerome Vignier, the Oratorian, added two more, Paris, 1654–1658. The Benedictines of the Congregation of St. Maur began to print their first volume on October 5th, 1677, and it appeared early in 1680, the tenth volume appearing in 1690. The names of these great men deserve to be remembered: F. Delfau, who inaugurated the work, T. Blampin, to whom we owe the Notes and the minor Prefaces—the General Preface being by Mabillon, P. Coustant who with Guesnié and Martene compiled the *Indices* and was himself responsible for the discriminations between the genuine and

[1] For more detailed information on these early editions see *P.L.* xlvii. 43–127.

[2] Erasmus' critical comments will be found in *P.L.* xlvii.

the spurious works of St. Augustine, H. Vaillant and du Frische who wrote the lengthy *Vita S. Augustini*. Vol. xi. appeared in 1700, but meanwhile a pirated edition had appeared in 1689 and was made to antedate the Maurist edition by being falsely dated 1679. Other editions appeared at Antwerp, 1700–1701, Venice, 1729–1735, 1765–1769—this last with Montfaucon's *Vindiciae* of 1699. Previous *Vindiciae* by O. Worst, a Capuchin, had been frequently published from 1566 onwards; another edition came from Venice, 1797–1807; also from Paris, 1833–1839; the edition by Migne, *Patrologia Latina*, appeared in 1841 and 1865. Montfaucon published his *Vindiciae* or *Défense de l'édition de S. Augustin faite par les pp. Bénédictins* owing to the accusation of Jansenism which had been brought against the editors, see H. Didio et A. N. Ingold, *Histoire de l'édition bénédictine de S. Augustin, avec le Journal inédit de Dom Ruinart*, pp. 155–193, 1903. See, too, H. de Noris, *Vindiciae Augustinianae quibus S. Doctoris Scripta contra Pelagianos et Semi-Pelagianos a recentioribus censuris asseruntur*, *P.L.* xlvii. 571–884. See, too, *La Tradition des grands ouvrages de S. Augustin*, *Miscellanea Agostiniana*, ii. 257 ff.; also *A List of the oldest Manuscripts of St. Augustine*, by E. A. Lowe, *ibid.*, pp. 235–251.

TRANSLATIONS

In addition to those already mentioned, translations of St. Augustine's Works will be found in *Nicene and Post-Nicene Fathers*, ed. Schaff and Wace. Vols. i.–viii. give a translation of St. Augustine's Works by J. G. Pilkington and others, 1892 onwards. Also in the Oxford Library of the Fathers, where the *Seventeen Short Treatises by St. Augustine*, 1747, includes:

Concerning Faith of Things not Seen.
Of Faith and of the Creed.
Of Faith and Works.
Enchiridion to Laurentius on Faith, Hope and Charity.
On the Christian Conflict.
On the Catechising of the Unlearned.

Of Continence.
On the Good of Marriage.
Of Holy Virginity.
On the Good of Widowhood.
On Lying.
To Consentius : Against Lying.
On the Work of Monks.
On Care to be had for the Dead.
On Patience.
On the Creed : a Sermon to Catechumens.
On the Profit of Believing.

See, too, K. M. Balfe, *Thoughts of St. Augustine for Every Day*, 1926. *A Daily Thought from St. Augustine*, Anonymous, 1925. M. H. Allies, *Leaves from St. Augustine*, 1886, 1899, 1910.

INDEX

INDEX

INDEX

INDEX